Roberto Braccini

Dictionary of Musical Terms
In Four Languages

American – Italian – French – German

For il tasto vivo

SEM 8076
ISBN 978-3-7957-8076-0
© Schott Music GmbH & Co. KG, 2014
This title is a revised and enhanced edition of "Praktisches Wörterbuch der Musik"
by Roberto Braccini © 1992, 2009 Schott Music GmbH & Co. KG, Mainz
www.schott-music.com
www.schott-buch.de

Typeset by Text & Grafik Service Martin, Birstein
Printed in Germany by CPI – Clausen & Bosse, Leck
BSS 55762

I sincerely wish to thank the following highly competent people
who had the kindness to help me.

Desidero ringraziare di cuore le seguenti persone,
più che competenti, le quali hanno avuto la gentilezza di aiutarmi.

Je désire sincèrement remercier les personnes suivantes,
plus que compétentes, qui ont eu la gentilesse de m'aider.

Es ist mir ein Bedürfnis, mich bei den nachfolgend genannten
kompetenten Persönlichkeiten zu bedanken,
die die Freundlichkeit hatten, mich bei meiner Arbeit zu unterstützen.

Ellen Frau, San Francisco
Eva Schoenenberger-Groebner, Wien
Maître Michel Vigneau, Paris

6

Contents

Preface 11
Stringed instruments 14
  Component parts and accessories 16
  Playing techniques 18
Wind instruments 20
  Component parts and accessories 24
  Playing techniques 28
Percussion instruments 28
  Component parts and accessories 34
  Playing techniques 36
Keyboard instruments 36
  Component parts and accessories 38
  Playing techniques 40
Mechanical musical instruments 42
Electric/electronic musical instruments,
recording of music and playback units 42
Singers and singing 50
  Voice types and singing techniques 52
The language of the scores 58
  Velocity 58
  Dynamics and articulation 64
  Character and expression 70
  Miscellany 106
Music theory 118
  Notes 138
  Time value of notes 140
  Intervals 140
  Genres and forms 142
Every day language 158
  Verbs 158
  A small collection of words 170
  The human body 200
  The professions 204
Appendix 209
  French specialist terms 210
  German specialist terms 218
  English and American specialist terms 228
  Jazz, Rock, Pop 238
  Dances 246
  100 famous works 248
  Opera 260
Index 261

Preface

This four-language dictionary of music is intended for musicians, teachers, students and amateurs who wish to understand and use specialist foreign terms. The book is not academic in scope; it is based on practical experience, derived from the examination of directions given on a large number of orchestral scores, piano pieces and transcriptions, and instrumental parts. In order to complement and clarify this vocabulary, specialist dictionaries and reference books have been consulted. Contemporary musical terms taken, for example, from the fields of jazz, pop and electronic music, have also been included.

How to use this dictionary

The entries are arranged alphabetically within the individual sections – except for English resp. American, German and French specialist terms – on the basis of initial headwords given in Italian. The correct stress is indicated by a short line under the appropriate vowel; English, German and French translations follow. Each headword is given an entry number which applies to all four languages; the headwords are then listed alphabetically in the index, along with their assigned numbers and an initial indicating the respective language. This index allows for:

1. the translation of a foreign word into English
2. the translation of an English word into another language
3. the translation of a foreign word from one language into another.

For each of the above, proceed as follows:

If, for example, you find the word "sempre" in a score – assuming that its meaning is unknown to you – look it up in the index. There you will find an "I" (for Italian) and the entry number. Now locate the number in the first part of the book, where you will find English, German and French translations of the word.

Detailed technical terms (from p. 210) have not been included in the index but have to be looked up there and then according to the alphabetical order (of their first word).

Abbreviations:

I	Italian	F	French	*m*	masculine
E	English	L	Latin	*f*	feminine
D	German	Am.	American	*n*	neuter
				pl	plural

8

Indice

Prefazione 9

Strumenti a corda 14
  Parti componenti ed accessori 16
  Modi di suonare 18

Strumenti a fiato 20
  Parti componenti ed accessori 24
  Modi di suonare 28

Strumenti a percussione 28
  Parti componenti ed accessori 34
  Modi di suonare 36

Strumenti a tastiera 36
  Parti componenti ed accessori 38
  Modi di suonare 40

Strumenti musicali meccanici 42

Strumenti elettrici/elettronici,
registrazione e riproduzione 42

Cantanti e canto 50
  Modi di cantare e tecniche vocali 52

Il linguaggio delle partiture 58
  Velocità 58
  Dinamica e articulazione 64
  Carattere ed espressione 70
  Diversi 106

Teoria musicale 118
  Note 138
  Valori delle note 140
  Intervalli 140
  Generi e forma 142

Il linguaggio di ogni giorno 158
  Verbi 158
  Piccola raccolta di parole 170
  Il corpo umano 200
  I mestieri 204

Appendice 209
  Terminologia francese 210
  Terminologia tedesca 218
  Terminologia inglese ed americana 228
  Jazz, Rock, Pop 238
  Danze 246
  100 composizioni celebri 248
  Opera 260

Indice alfabetico 261

Prefazione

Lo scopo di questo libro, che non deve essere inteso come una enciclopedia, è di poter aiutare qualsiasi persona interessata alla musica a trovare la traduzione d'una determinata parola nelle seguenti lingue: italiano, inglese, tedesco e francese. E stato concepito sfogliando innumerevoli composizioni. Alcune parole antiquate, oppure scritte con errori sono rimaste volutamente tali. Inoltre, un gran numero di dizionari specializzati sono stati consultati per completarne il suo vocabolario. Forme musicali recenti come la musica pop, il jazz e la musica elettronica sono ugualmente incluse.

Instruzioni per l'uso di questo libro

Tutti i capitoli sono raggruppati alfabeticamente. I termini italiani sono sempre menzionati per primi ad eccezione di quelli concernenti la terminologia inglese ed americana, la terminologia francese e quella tedesca. Seguono le traduzioni in inglese, tedesco e francese. Ogni rigo ha il suo numero, identico per le quattro lingue. Una linetta sotto una sillaba italiana indica dove cade l'accento. Tutte queste parole si ritrovano nell'indice alfabetico finale. Accanto ad ognuna di esse si trova l'iniziale della lingua alla quale appartiene (per es. E per l'inglese) ed il suo numero. Questo capitolo vi offre la possibilità di:

1. Tradurre una parola straniera in italiano.
2. Tradurre una parola italiana in una lingua straniera.
3. Tradurre una parola straniera in un'altra lingua straniera.

Nei tre casi, il modo di procedere sarà lo stesso. Esempio:

In una partitura, s'incontra la parola „immer" e si desidera sapere il significato in italiano. Nell'indice alfabetico, accanto a „immer" ci sarà la lettera D (tedesco) ed un numero. Basterà cercare questo numero in uno dei capitoli precedenti. Avendolo trovato, si vedrà alla sua destra „sempre" ed il termine corrispondente in inglese, tedesco e francese.

Le frasi specifiche dei differenti idiomi non sono riprodotte nell'indice finale. Il lettore dovrà cercarle (da pag. 210) per ordine alfabetico nella lingua desiderata.

Abbreviazioni:

I	Italiano	F	Francese	m	maschile
E	Inglese	L	Latino	f	femminile
D	Tedesco	Am.	Americano	n	neutro
				pl	plurale

10

Contenu

Préface 13
Instruments à cordes 15
    Parties composantes et accessoires 17
    Façons de jouer 19
Instruments à vent 21
    Parties composantes et accessoires 25
    Façons de jouer 29
Instruments à percussion 29
    Parties composantes et accessoires 35
    Façons de jouer 37
Instruments à clavier 37
    Parties composantes et accessoires 39
    Façons de jouer 41
Instruments musicaux mécaniques 43
Instruments électriques/électroniques,
enregistrement et reproduction 43
Chanteurs et chant 51
    Façons de chanter et technique vocale 53
Le langage des partitions 59
    Vitesse 59
    Dynamique et articulation 65
    Caractère et expression 71
    Divers 107
Théorie musicale 119
    Notes 139
    Valeur des notes 141
    Intervalles 141
    Genres et formes 143
Le langage de tous les jours 159
    Verbes 159
    Petite collection de mots 171
    Le corps humain 201
    Les métiers 205
Appendice 209
    Terminologie française 210
    Terminologie allemande 218
    Terminologie anglaise et américaine 228
    Jazz, Rock, Pop 238
    Danses 246
    100 œuvres célèbres 249
    Opéra 260
Index 261

Préface

Le but de ce livre est d'aider toute personne intéressée à la musique, à trouver la traduction d'un mot déterminé dans les langues suivantes: italien, anglais, allemand et français. Ce livre ne doit pas être considéré comme une encyclopédie. C'est en parcourant d'innombrables partitions musicales qu'il a été conçu. Un grand nombre de dictionnaires musicaux spécialisés ont été consultés pour en compléter son vocabulaire. Les formes musicales récentes comme la musique pop, le jazz et la musique électronique y sont également incluses.

Instructions pour l'usage de ce livre

Tous les chapitres sont groupés alphabétiquement. Les termes italiens sont mentionnés en premier à l'exception de ceux concernant la terminologie anglaise et américaine, la terminologie française et celle allemande. Suivent les traductions en anglais, allemand et français. Chaque ligne a son propre numéro qui est le même pour les quatre langues. Un petit trait sous un mot italien signifie qu'il faut accentuer cette voyelle. On retrouve tous ces mots dans l'index alphabétique. A côté de chaque mot se trouve l'initiale de la langue en question (par exemple E pour l'anglais). Ce chapitre vous donne la possibilité de:

1. traduire un mot étranger en français
2. traduire un mot français dans une langue étrangère
3. traduire un mot étranger dans une autre langue étrangère

Dans les trois cas, on procédera de la même façon. Exemple:

Dans une partition, il y a le terme „sempre" et on désire savoir ce qu'il signifie en français. On le cherche dans l'index alphabétique. A côté de „sempre" on trouvera la lettre I (italien) ainsi qu'un numéro. On cherchera celui-ci dans un des chapitres précédents. On verra alors „sempre" et le terme correspondant en anglais, allemand et français.

Les termes techniques décrits en détail (à partir de p. 210) n'ont pas été inclus dans l'index mais doivent être cherchés par ordre alphabétique dans la langue désirée.

Abréviations:

I	Italien	F	Français	*m*	masculin
E	Anglais	L	Latin	*f*	féminin
D	Allemand	Am.	Américain	*n*	neutre
				pl	pluriel

12

Inhalt

Vorwort 7
Saiteninstrumente 15
　Bestandteile und Zubehör 17
　Spielarten 19
Blasinstrumente 21
　Bestandteile und Zubehör 25
　Spielarten 29
Schlaginstrumente 29
　Bestandteile und Zubehör 35
　Spielarten 37
Tasteninstrumente 37
　Bestandteile und Zubehör 39
　Spielarten 41
Mechanische Musikinstrumente 43
Elektrische/elektronische Musikinstrumente,
Musikaufnahme- und Wiedergabegeräte 43
Sänger und Gesang 51
　Gesangsarten und -technik 53
Die Sprache der Partituren 59
　Tempo 59
　Dynamik und Artikulation 65
　Charakter und Ausdruck 71
　Verschiedenes 107
Musiktheorie 119
　Noten 139
　Notenwerte 141
　Intervalle 141
　Gattungen und Formen 143
Die tägliche Sprache 159
　Verben 159
　Kleine Wörtersammlung 171
　Der menschliche Körper 201
　Die Berufe 205
Anhang 209
　Französische Fachausdrücke 210
　Deutsche Fachausdrücke 218
　Englische und amerikanische Fachausdrücke 228
　Jazz, Rock, Pop 238
　Tänze 246
　100 berühmte Kompositionen 249
　Oper 260
Register 261

Vorwort

Das vorliegende Fachwörterbuch der Musik in vier Sprachen wendet sich an Musiker, Lehrer, Studenten und Laien, die die Übertragung fremdsprachiger Fachwörter suchen und verwenden möchten. Das Buch erhebt keinen wissenschaftlichen Anspruch. Es ist aus der Praxis heraus entstanden, ausgehend von der Sammlung von Anweisungen in unzähligen Partituren, Klavierauszügen und Notenstimmen. Zur Vervollständigung und Abrundung des Wortschatzes wurden Fachlexika und Fachwörterbücher ausgewertet. Zeitnahe Sachgebiete, wie zum Beispiel Jazz-, Pop- und elektronische Musik, sind eingeschlossen.

Hinweise zur Benutzung dieses Buches

Die in den einzelnen Kapiteln alphabetisch zusammengestellten Stichwörter gehen – mit Ausnahme der Kapitel „Englische und amerikanische Fachausdrücke" , „Deutsche Fachausdrücke" und „Französische Fachausdrücke" – von der italienischen Sprache aus, wobei die korrekte Silbenbetonung durch Unterstreichung des betreffenden Vokals angezeigt wird. Die englische, deutsche und französische Übertragung schließen sich an. Jedes Stichwort ist mit fortlaufenden Zahlen versehen, die für alle Sprachen gelten. In einem Register erscheinen alle Stichwörter in alphabetischer Reihenfolge mit den ihnen zugeordneten Zahlen, denen die Abkürzung der zugehörigen Sprache beigefügt ist. Mit Hilfe dieses Registers kann man

1. ein fremdsprachiges Wort ins Deutsche,
2. ein deutsches Wort in eine Fremdsprache und
3. ein fremdsprachiges Wort in eine andere Fremdsprache übersetzen.

In allen Fällen geht man wie folgt vor:
Man trifft in einer Partitur beispielsweise auf das Wort „sempre". Vorausgesetzt, das Wort ist einem nicht bekannt, sucht man „sempre" im Register. Dort steht neben „sempre" ein I (für Italienisch) und eine Zahl. Nun erblättert man diese Zahl im vorderen Teil des Buches und findet dort die deutsche, englische und französische Bedeutung.
Sehr ausführlich formulierte Fachausdrücke (ab S. 210) wurden nicht ins Register aufgenommen, sondern müssen an Ort und Stelle entsprechend der alphabetischen Reihenfolge (ihres 1. Wortes) aufgesucht werden.

Abkürzungen:

I	Italienisch	F	Französisch	*m*	Maskulinum
E	Englisch	L	Latein	*f*	Femininum
D	Deutsch	Am.	Amerikanisch	*n*	Neutrum
				Pl	Plural

Strumenti a corda	Stringed instruments
1 arciliuto *m*	archlute
2 arpa *f* / arpa a pedali *f*	harp / pedal harp
3 arpa a doppio movimento *f*	double action harp
4 autoarpa *f*	autoharp
5 balalaica *f*	balalaika
6 banjo *m*	banjo
7 cetra *f*	cittern
8 cetra da tavolo *f*	zither
9 cimbalom *m*	cimbalom
10 chitarra *f*	guitar
11 chitarra battente *f* / chitarra jazz *f*	jazz guitar
12 chitarra hawaiana *f*	Hawaiian guitar
13 colascione *m*	colascione
14 contrabbasso *m*	double bass
15 contrabbasso a pizzico *m*	slap bass
16 crotta *f*	crowd
17 ghironda *f*	hurdy-gurdy
18 Hardingfele *m*	Harding / Hardanger fiddle
19 lira *f*	lyre
20 liuto *m*	lute
21 mandolino *m*	mandolin
22 pochette *f*	kit
23 salterio *m*	psaltery
24 salterio tedesco *m*	dulcimer
25 sitar *f*	sitar
26 tiorba *f*	theorbo
27 viella *f*	fiddle
28 viola *f*	viola
29 viola da gamba *f*	viola da gamba
30 violino *m*	violin
31 violino di ferro *m*	nail violin
32 violoncello *m*	violoncello

Saiteninstrumente	Instruments à cordes	
Erzlaute *f*	archiluth *m*	1
Harfe *f* / Pedalharfe *f*	harpe *f* / harpe à pédales simples *f*	2
Doppelpedalharfe *f*	harpe à double mouvement *f*	3
Akkordzither *f*	cithare d'amateur *f*	4
Balalaika *f*	balalaika *f*	5
Banjo *n*	banjo *m*	6
Cister *f*	cistre *m*	7
Zither *f*	cithare *f*	8
Zimbal *n* / Cymbal *n*	cymbalum *m*	9
Gitarre *f*	guitare *f*	10
Schlaggitarre *f* / Jazzgitarre *f*	guitare de jazz *f*	11
Hawaii-Gitarre *f*	guitare hawaïenne *f*	12
Colascione *m*	colachon *m*	13
Kontrabass *m*	contrebasse *f*	14
Schlagbass *m*	contrebasse jouée sans archet *f*	15
Chrotta *f*	chrotta *f*	16
Drehleier *f* / Radleier *f* / Leier *f*	vielle à roue *f*	17
Hardanger Fiedel *f*	violon de Hardanger *m*	18
Lyra *f*	lyre *f*	19
Laute *f*	luth *m*	20
Mandoline *f*	mandoline *f*	21
Taschengeige *f*	pochette *f*	22
Psalterium *n*	psaltérion *m*	23
Hackbrett *n*	tympanon *m*	24
Sitar *f*	sitar *m*	25
Theorbe *f*	théorbe *m*	26
Fiedel *f* / Fidel *f*	vièle *f* / vielle *f* / violon rustique *m*	27
Viola *f* / Bratsche *f*	alto *m*	28
Gambe *f*	viole de gambe *f*	29
Violine *f* / Geige *f*	violon *m*	30
Nagelgeige *f*	violon de fer *m*	31
Violoncello *n*	violoncelle *m*	32

Parti componenti ed accessori **Component parts and accessories**

33	anima *f*	sound post
34	archetto *m* / arco *m*	bow
35	astuccio *m* / custodia *f*	case
36	bischero *m* / pirolo *m* / voluta *f*	tuning peg / tuning pin
37	bottone *m*	endpin
38	cantino *m*	treble
39	capotasto *m*	capotasto / top nut
40	cassa armonica *f* / cassa di risonanza *f*	resonant body / sound-box
41	catena *f*	bass-bar / tuning bar
42	cavigliere *m*	peg box
43	colofonia *f*	rosin / resin
44	corda *f*	string
45	corda del sol *f* / quarta corda *f*	bass string
46	corda di budello *f*	gut string
47	corda d'acciaio *f*	steel string
48	corda di metallo *f*	metal string
49	corda di bordone *f*	drone string
50	corda di risonanza *f*	aliquot string
51	corda melodica *f*	treblestring / fretted string
52	corda simpatica *f*	sympathetic string
53	cordiera *f*	tailpiece / string holder
54	coro *m*	course
55	crini dell'arco *m pl*	hair of the bow
56	curva della meccanica *f*	neck / harmonic curve
57	effe *f*	sound-hole
58	fascia *f*	side / rib
59	filetto *m*	purfling
60	fondo *m*	back
61	manico *m*	neck
62	mentoniera *f*	chin-rest
63	parapenne *m*	plectrum guard
64	plettro *m*	jack / plectrum
65	ponticello *m*	bridge
66	punta *f* / nasello *m*	tip / peak / point
67	puntale *m*	tailpin / spike
68	riccio *m* / chiocciola *f*	scroll

Bestandteile und Zubehör

Parties composantes et accessoires

Stimmstock *m*	âme *f*	33
Bogen *m*	archet *m*	34
Kasten *m*	étui *m* / housse *f*	35
Wirbel *m*	cheville *f*	36
Knopf *m*	bouton *m*	37
Sangsaite *f* / Singsaite *f*	chanterelle *f*	38
Kapodaster *m* / Saitenfessel *f* / Obersattel *m*	capodaste *m* / barre *f*	39
Resonanzkörper *m* / Resonanzboden *m* / Schallkasten *m*	caisse de résonance *f*	40
Bassbalken *m* / Stimmbalken *m*	barre *f*	41
Wirbelkasten *m*	chevillier *m*	42
Kolophonium *n*	colophane *f*	43
Saite *f*	corde *f*	44
G-Saite *f*	quatrième corde *f*	45
Darmsaite *f*	corde de boyau *f*	46
Stahlsaite *f*	corde d'acier *f*	47
Metallsaite *f*	corde métallique *f*	48
Bordunsaite *f*	corde hors manche *f*	49
Aliquotsaite *f*	corde de résonance *f*	50
Melodiesaite *f*	corde mélodique *f*	51
Resonanzsaite *f*	corde sympathique *f*	52
Saitenhalter *m*	cordier *m*	53
Saitenchor *m*	jeu *m* / chœur *m*	54
Bogenhaare *n Pl*	crins de l'archet *m pl*	55
Mechanikbogen *m*	console *f*	56
F-Loch *n*	ouïe *f*	57
Zarge *f*	éclisse *f*	58
Einlage *f* / Ader *f*	filet *m*	59
Boden *m*	fond *m*	60
Hals *m*	manche *m*	61
Kinnhalter *m*	mentonnière *f*	62
Schlagbrett *n*	plaque de protection *f*	63
Spielblättchen *n* / Plektrum *n*	plectre *m*	64
Steg *m*	chevalet *m*	65
Spitze *f*	pointe *f*	66
Stachel *m*	pied *m*	67
Schnecke *f*	volute *f* / coquille *f*	68

69	rosa *f*	rose
70	ruota a sfregamento *f*	friction wheel
71	sella *f*	saddle
72	spalliera *f*	shoulder rest
73	tallone *m*	heel / frog
74	tastato	fretted
75	tastiera *f*	fingerboard / fretboard
76	tasto *m*	fret
77	tavola armonica *f*	table / belly
78	uncino *m*	fork
79	volta superiore *f* / sagoma superiore *f*	upper bout
80	volta inferiore *f* / sagoma inferiore *f*	lower bout
81	zoccolo *m*	pedestal

Modi di suonare   Playing techniques

82	alla corda	on the string
83	alla punta d'arco / colla punta d'arco, -di arco/-dell'arco	at the point / tip of the bow
84	al tallone *m*	at the heel / at the frog
85	arcata *f* / colpo d'arco *m*	bowing / stroke of the bow
86	arcata in giù *f*	down-bow
87	arcata in su *f*	up-bow
88	archeggiamento	whipped
89	balzato	bouncing / springing (bowing)
90	balzellato	bouncing / springing
91	barré	barré
92	bisbigliando (arpa)	tremolo (harp)
93	cambiamento di posizione *m*	shift
94	coll'arco *m*	with the bow
95	col legno *m* / picchettato	with the wood
96	con sordina / con sordino	muted
97	corda vuota *f*	empty string / open string
98	disperdere	to die out
99	doppia corda *f*	double stop
100	emissione *f*	speech / reponse

Rosette *f*	rose *f*	69
Streichrad *n*	roue de frottement *f*	70
Sattel *m*	sillet *m*	71
Schulterstütze *f*	coussin *m*	72
Frosch *m*	talon *m* / hausse *f*	73
mit Bünden versehen	avec sillets	74
Griffbrett *n*	touche *f*	75
Bund *m*	sillet *m*	76
Decke *f*	table d'harmonie *f*	77
Gabel *f*	fourchette *f*	78
Oberbügel *m*	courbe supérieure *f*	79
Unterbügel *m*	courbe inférieure *f*	80
Fuß *m* (Harfe)	cuvette *f* / socle *m*	81

Spielarten   ## Façons de jouer

auf der Saite / an der Saite	à la corde	82
an der Bogenspitze *f*	avec la pointe de l'archet / de/à la pointe	83
am Frosch *m*	au talon *m* / à la hausse *f*	84
Bogenführung *f* / Bogen-strich *m* / Strichart *f*	coup d'archet *m*	85
Abstrich *m*	tiré *m*	86
Aufstrich *m* / Anstrich *m*	poussé *m*	87
gepeitscht	fouetté	88
Springbogen *m* / fliegendes Staccato	bondi / staccato volant	89
gehüpft	sautillé	90
barré (Quergriff bei Gitarre / Laute)	barré	91
tremolo (Harfe)	trémolo (harpe)	92
Lagenwechsel *m*	changement de position *m*	93
mit dem Bogen	avec l'archet *m*	94
mit der Bogenstange *f*	avec le bois *m*	95
mit Dämpfer	avec sourdine / étouffé	96
leere Saite *f*	corde à vide *f*	97
ausschwingen	cesser de vibrer	98
Doppelgriff *m*	double corde *f*	99
Ansprache *f*	émission *f*	100

101	gettato	thrown
102	ondeggiando	undulating
103	piccato / picchiettato	lightly detached
104	pizzicato	plucked
105	presso la tavola	near the sounding board
106	rimbalzando	rebounding
107	saltato	jumped
108	saltellato / balzellato	bouncing / springing
109	scordatura *f*	scordatura
110	senza sordina	without mute
111	separato / staccato	detached
112	spiccato / saltato	detached staccato (bowing)
113	strappato	torn / raked
114	strisciando	touching slightly
115	sulla tastiera / flautando	on the fingerboard
116	sul ponticello	close to the bridge

Strumenti a fiato   Wind instruments

117	armonica a bocca *f*	mouth organ
118	bombarda *f*	bombarde
119	bombardino *m*	euphonium / baritone
120	bombardone *m*	bombardon
121	cennamella *f* / ciaramella *f*	shawm
122	clarinetto *m*	clarinet
123	clarinetto piccolo *m*	soprano clarinet
124	clarinetto basso *m*	bass clarinet
125	clarinetto contrabbasso *m*	double bass clarinet
126	clarinetto contralto *m*	alto clarinet
127	contrafagotto *m*	double bassoon / contrabassoon
128	cornetta *f*	cornet
129	cornetta a pistoni *f*	valve cornet
130	cornetto *m*	cornett
131	corno *m*	French horn / horn
132	corno da caccia *m*	hunting horn
133	corno delle Alpi *m*	Alphorn / Alpenhorn
134	corno di bassetto *m*	bassethorn
135	corno di postiglione *m* / cornetta di postiglione *f*	post horn

Saiteninstrumente Instruments à cordes 21

geworfen	jeté	101
wogend	ondoyant	102
gestochen	piqué	103
gezupft / gezwickt	pizzicato / pincé	104
nahe am Korpus anzupfen	près de la table	105
abprallendes Stakkato	ricochet	106
gesprungen	sauté	107
gehüpft (Bogenstrich)	sautillé	108
Skordatur *f*	scordatura *f*	109
ohne Dämpfer	sans sourdine	110
abgesetzt / getrennt	détaché	111
deutlich getrennt	très détaché / très net	112
gerissen	arraché	113
streifend	en frôlant	114
nahe am Griffbrett	sur la touche	115
am Steg	près du chevalet	116

Blasinstrumente ## Instruments à vent

Mundharmonika *f*	harmonica *f*	117
Bomhard *m* / Pommer *m*	bombarde *f*	118
Baritonhorn *n*	euphonium *m*	119
Basstuba *f* / Bombardon *n*	bombardon *m*	120
Schalmei *f* / Hirtenpfeife *f*	pipeau *m* / chalumeau *m*	121
Klarinette *f*	clarinette *f*	122
kleine Klarinette *f*	petite clarinette *f*	123
Bassklarinette *f*	clarinette basse *f*	124
Kontrabassklarinette *f*	clarinette contrebasse *f*	125
Altklarinette *f*	clarinette alto *f*	126
Kontrafagott *n*	contrebasson *m*	127
Kornett *n*	cornet *m*	128
Piston *m* / Ventilkornett *n*	cornet à pistons *m*	129
Zink *m*	cornet à bouquin *m*	130
Horn *n* / Waldhorn *n*	cor *m*	131
Jagdhorn *n* / Signalhorn *n*	cor de chasse *m* / bugle *m*	132
Alphorn *n*	cor des Alpes *m*	133
Bassetthorn *n*	cor de basset *m*	134
Posthorn *n*	cor de postillion *m* / cornet de poste *m*	135

136	corno inglese *m*	cor anglais (E) / English horn (Am.)
137	corno di toro *m*	cow horn
138	cromorno *m*	crumhorn
139	dulciana *f*	dulcian
140	elicon *m*	helicon
141	fagotto *m*	bassoon
142	fischietto *m*	whistle / fife / pipe
143	flauto *m*	flute
144	flauto a becco basso *m*	bass recorder
145	flauto a becco contralto *m*	alto recorder (Am.) / treble recorder (E)
146	flauto a becco sopranino *m*	sopranino recorder
147	flauto a becco soprano *m*	soprano recorder (Am.) / descant recorder (E)
148	flauto a becco tenore *m*	tenor recorder
149	flauto a tiro *m* / zufolo a pistone *m*	swanee whistle / piston flute
150	flauto contralto *m*	alto flute / bass flute
151	flauto di Pan *m* / siringa *f*	panpipes
152	flauto dolce *m* / flauto diritto *m*	recorder
153	flauto traverso *m*	transverse flute / German flute
154	flicorno *m*	flugelhorn / saxhorn
155	Heckelphon *m*	heckelphone
156	oboe *m*	oboe
157	oboe d'amore *m*	oboe d'amore
158	ocarina *f*	ocarina
159	oficleide *m*	ophicleide
160	ottavino *m* / flauto piccolo *m*	piccolo
161	piffero *m* / fiffero *m*	fife
162	piva *f* / cornamusa *f*	bagpipe
163	rankett *m* / rocchetta *f*	racket / rankett
164	sarrusofono *m*	sarrusophone
165	sassofono *m*	saxophone
166	sassofono baritono *m*	baritone saxophone
167	sassofono basso *m*	bass saxophone
168	sassofono contralto *m*	alto saxophone
169	sassofono soprano *m*	soprano saxophone
170	sassofono tenore *m*	tenor saxophone
171	serpentone *m*	serpent
172	sordone *m*	sordun

Englischhorn *n*	cor anglais *m*	136
Stierhorn *n*	cor de vache *m*	137
Krummhorn *n*	cromorne *m*	138
Dulzian *m*	douçaine *f*	139
Helikon *n*	hélicon *m*	140
Fagott *n*	basson *m*	141
Pfeife *f*	sifflet *m*	142
Flöte *f*	flûte *f*	143
Bassblockflöte *f*	flûte à bec basse *f*	144
Altblockflöte *f*	flûte alto / flûte à bec alto *f*	145
Sopraninoblockflöte *f*	flûte à bec sopranino *f*	146
Sopranblockflöte *f*	flûte à bec soprano *f*	147
Tenorblockflöte *f*	flûte à bec ténor *f*	148
Lotusflöte *f* / Stempelflöte *f*	flûte lotine *f* / flûte à coulisse *f*	149
Altflöte *f*	flûte alto *f* / flûte basse *f*	150
Panflöte *f*	flûte de Pan *f* / syrinx *m*	151
Blockflöte *f*	flûte douce *f* / flûte droite *f*	152
Querflöte *f*	flûte traversière *f*	153
Bügelhorn *n* / Flügelhorn *n*	flicorne *m* / bugle à pistons *m*	154
Heckelphon *n*	heckelphone *m*	155
Oboe *f*	hautbois *m*	156
Oboe d'amore *f* / Liebesoboe *f*	hautbois d'amour *m*	157
Okarina *f*	ocarina *m*	158
Ophikleide *f*	ophicléide *m*	159
Pikkolo *n* / kleine Flöte *f*	petite flûte *f* / piccolo *f*	160
Querpfeife *f*	fifre *m*	161
Dudelsack *m* / Sackpfeife *f*	cornemuse *f*	162
Rankett *n* / Stockfagott *n* / Wurstfagott *n*	racket *m* / cervelas *m*	163
Sarrusophon *n*	sarrusophone *m*	164
Saxophon *n*	saxophone *m*	165
Baritonsaxophon *n*	saxophone baryton *m*	166
Basssaxophon *n*	saxophone basse *m*	167
Altsaxophon *n*	saxophone alto *m*	168
Sopransaxophon *n*	saxophone soprano *m*	169
Tenorsaxophon *n*	saxophone ténor *m*	170
Serpent *m* / Schlangenbass *m*	serpent *m*	171
Sordun *m*	sordun *m*	172

173	sousafono *m*	sousaphone
174	tromba *f*	trumpet
175	tromba bassa *f*	bass trumpet
176	tromba da jazz *f*	jazz trumpet
177	tromba naturale *f*	natural trumpet
178	tromba a pistoni *f*	valve trumpet
179	tromba a tirarsi *f* / tromba a tiro *f*	slide trumpet
180	trombone *m*	trombone
181	trombone a cilindri *m*	valve trombone
182	trombone contrabbasso *m*	contrabass trombone / double-bass trombone
183	trombone da jazz *m*	jazz trombone
184	trombone a tiro *m*	slide trombone
185	tuba *f*	tuba
186	tuba bassa *f*	bass tuba
187	tuba contrabbasso *f*	double-bass saxhorn
188	tuba wagneriana *f*	Wagner tuba
189	zampogna *f*	bagpipe
190	zufolo *m*	whistle / tin whistle

	Parti componenti ed accessori	**Component parts and accessories**
191	ancia *f*	reed
192	ancia battente *f*	striking reed / beating reed
193	ancia doppia *f*	double reed
194	anello *m*	ring key
195	anello del pollice *m*	thumb-hold
196	apertura *f*	aperture
197	barilotto *m*	barrel socket
198	becco *m*	mouthpiece
199	bocchino *m*	mouthpiece
200	campana *f*	bell
201	camera d'aria *f*	windway / air-passage

Sousaphon *n*	sousaphone *m*	173
Trompete *f*	trompette *f*	174
Basstrompete *f*	trompette basse *f*	175
Jazztrompete *f*	trompette de jazz *f*	176
Naturtrompete *f*	trompette naturelle *f*	177
Ventiltrompete *f*	trompette à pistons *f*	178
Zugtrompete *f*	trompette à coulisse *f*	179
Posaune *f*	trombone *m*	180
Ventilposaune *f*	trombone à pistons *m*	181
Kontrabassposaune f	trombone contrebasse *m*	182
Jazzposaune *f*	trombone de jazz *m*	183
Zugposaune *f*	trombone à coulisse *m*	184
Tuba *f*	tuba *m*	185
Basstuba *f*	tuba basse *m* / contrebasse à pistons *f*	186
Kontrabasstuba *f*	contrebasse à pistons *f* / saxhorn contrebasse *m*	187
Wagner-Tuba *f* / Waldhorn-Tuba *f*	tuba Wagner *m* / tuba ténor *m*	188
Sackpfeife *f*	biniou *m*	189
Hirtenpfeife *f*	chalumeau *m* / pipeau *m*	190

Bestandteile und Zubehör	**Parties composantes et accessoires**	
Rohrblatt *n*	anche *f* / épiglotte *f*	191
aufschlagendes Rohrblatt *n* / Gegenschlagzunge *f*	anche battante f	192
Doppelrohrblatt *n* / Doppel-zunge *f*	anche double *f*	193
Brille *f*	anneau *m*	194
Daumenring *m*	anneau du pouce *m*	195
Mundspalt *m* / Aufschnitt *m*	lumière *f* / ouverture *f* / biseau *m*	196
Birne *f* / Wulst *m*	baril *m* / barillet *m*	197
Schnabel *m*	bec *m*	198
Mundstück *n*	embouchure *f*	199
Schallbecher m / Stürze *f*	pavillon *m* / bonnet *m*	200
Kernspalt *m*	canal pour l'air *m*	201

202	capsula *f* / copri-ancia *m*	windcap
203	chiave *f*	key
204	chiave dell'acqua *f*	water key
205	cilindro rotativo *m*	rotary valve
206	cuscinetto *m*	plate / cup
207	foro *m*	finger-hole / tone hole
208	imboccatura *f*	mouth-hole / embouchure
209	linguetta *f*	tongue
210	macchina *f*	valve unit
211	meccanismo delle chiavi *m*	key work
212	padiglione *m*	bell
213	padiglione piriforme *m*	pear-shaped bell
214	pezzo di mezzo *m*	middle joint
215	pezzo inferiore *m*	lower joint
216	pistone *m*	piston / valve
217	pompa mobile a coulisse *f* / pompa a tiro *f*	slide
218	portamusica *f*	music lyre
219	ritorto *m*	crook
220	rotella *f*	shank
221	sacco *m*	double joint / butt
222	sordina a cappello *f*	hat mute
223	sordina a doppio cono *f*	double mute
224	sordina di cartone *f*	cardboard mute
225	sordina di metallo *f*	metal mute
226	sordina diritta *f*	straight mute
227	sordina hush-hush *f*	hush mute
228	sordina wawa *f*	wow-wow mute
229	tazza *f*	cup
230	testata con becco *f*	head joint with beak
231	tiro *m*	slide casing / case
232	traversino *m*	cross-stay
233	tubetto *m*	tube / staple
234	tubo piccolo *m* / aletta *f*	wing / tenor joint
235	vite *f*	screw

Windkapsel *f*	bocal *m* / capsule *f*	202
Klappe *f*	clé *f*	203
Wasserklappe *f*	clé d'eau *f*	204
Drehventil *n* / Zylinderventil *n*	cylindre à rotation *m*	205
Deckel *m*	plateau *m*	206
Griffloch *n* / Fingerloch *n*	trou *m*	207
Mundloch *n* / Ansatz *m*	embouchure *f*	208
Zunge *f*	anche *f*	209
Ventilmaschine *f*	mécanisme du piston *m*	210
Klappenmechanik *f*	mécanisme des clefs *m*	211
Aufsatz *m* / Schallbecher *m* / Schallstück *n*	pavillon *m*	212
Liebesfuß *m*	pavillon piriforme *m*	213
Mittelstück *n*	second corps *m*	214
Fußstück *n* / Unterstück *n*	patte *f* / troisième corps *m*	215
Ventil *n* / Pumpventil *n*	piston *m* / cylindre *m*	216
Zug *m*	coulisse *f*	217
Notenhalter *m*	pupitre portatif *m*	218
Stimmbogen *m* / Aufsatz- bogen *m*	corps de rechange *m*	219
Walze *f*	rouleau *m*	220
Stiefel *m* / Bogen *m* / Doppel- loch *n*	culasse *f*	221
Hutdämpfer *m*	sourdine à calotte *f*	222
Doppelkegeldämpfer *m*	sourdine à double cône *f*	223
Kartondämpfer *m*	sourdine en carton *f*	224
Metalldämpfer *m*	sourdine en métal *f*	225
Spitzdämpfer *m*	sourdine droite *f*	226
Huschdämpfer *m*	sourdine à calotte *f*	227
Wau-wau-Dämpfer *m*	sourdine wa-wa *f*	228
Kessel *m*	bassin *m*	229
Kopfstück mit Schnabel *n*	corps supérieur *m* / tête avec bec *f*	230
Scheide *f*	coulisse *f*	231
Quersteg *m*	barrette *f*	232
Hülse *f* / Stift *m*	corps *m*	233
Flügelröhre *f* / Oberstück *n*	petit corps *m* / petite branche *f*	234
Schraube *f*	vis *f*	235

	Modi di suonare	**Playing techniques**
236	attacco *m*	attack
237	campane in alto / padiglioni in alto	bell up / bell in the air / raise the bell
238	chiuso / tappato	stopped
239	colpo di lingua *m*	attack with the tongue
240	colpo di lingua semplice *m*	single tonguing
241	doppio colpo di lingua *m*	double tonguing
242	forchetta *f*	fork fingering / cross-fingering
243	frullato	flutter-tonguing
244	imboccatura *f*	embouchure / lip
245	metalizzare il suono / ottavizzare / quinteggiare	brassy overblowing
246	mettere la sordina	to mute
247	posizione normale	bell down
248	togliere la sordina	mute off / to take off the mute
249	triplo colpo di lingua *m*	triple-tonguing

Strumenti a percussione   Percussion instruments

250	almgloken *f*	almglocken
251	armonica / armonica a vetro *f*	glass harmonica
252	asse per lavare *f*	washboard
253	batteria *f*	drums
254	block cinese *m* / testa di morto *f* / wood block *m*	temple block / Chinese block / wood block
255	bongo *m*	bongo
256	cabaza *f*	cabasa
257	campana *f*	bell
258	campanaccio *m*	cowbell
259	campane doriche *f pl*	Dorian bells
260	campane tubolari *f pl*	tubular bells
261	campanelli *m pl*	glockenspiel
262	campanello *m* / campanella *f*	handbell
263	campanelli della messa *m pl*	sanctus bells
264	campanelli a tastiera *m pl*	keyed glockenspiel

Spielarten	Façons de jouer	
Anstoß *m*	attaque *f*	236
Stürze hoch / Schalltrichter hoch	pavillon en l'air	237
gestopft / gedeckt	bouché / étouffé	238
Zungenstoß *m* / Zungen- schlag *m*	coup de langue *m*	239
einfacher Zungenstoß *m*	coup de langue simple *m*	240
Doppelzunge *f*	double articulation *f*	241
Gabelgriff *m*	doigté fourché *m*	242
Flatterzunge *f*	trémolo dental *m*	243
Embouchure *f* / Ansatz *m*	embouchure *f*	244
schmettern / überblasen	cuivrer / quintage / action d'octavier	245
Dämpfer auf / dämpfen	mettre la sourdine	246
natürliche Position	position naturelle	247
Dämpfer weg / Dämpfer ab	ôter la sourdine / enlever la sourdine	248
Tripelzunge *f*	triple articulation *f* / triple coup de langue *m*	249

Schlaginstrumente	Instruments à percussion	
Almglocken *f Pl*	almglocken *f*	250
Glasharmonika *f*	harmonica de verre *f*	251
Waschbrett *n*	washboard *m* / planche à laver *f*	252
Schlagzeug *n*	batterie *f*	253
Tempelblock *m* / Wood- block *m* / Holzblock *m*	templeblock *m* / wood bloc *m* / bloc de bois m	254
Bongo *n* / Bongotrommel *f*	tambour bongo *m*	255
Cabaza *f*	calebasse *f*	256
Glocke *f*	cloche *f*	257
Kuhglocke *f*	cloche de vache *f*	258
dorische Glocken *f Pl*	cloches doriennes *f pl*	259
Röhrenglocken *f Pl*	cloches tubulaires *f pl*	260
Glockenspiel *n* / Stabglocken- spiel *n*	jeu de timbres *m*	261
Handglocke *f*	clochette *f*	262
Messglöckchen *n* / Mess- klingeln *m Pl*	clochettes pour la messe *f pl*	263
Klaviaturglockenspiel *n*	timbres à clavier *m pl*	264

265	carillon *m*	carillon
266	carillon a tastiera *m*	carillon
267	cassa *f*	drum
268	cassa rullante *f* / cassa chiara *f*	tenor drum
269	castagnette *f pl* / nacchere *f pl*	castanets
270	castagnette con manico *f pl*	handle castanets
271	castagnette di metallo *f pl*	metal castanets
272	castagnette spagnole *f pl*	hand castanets
273	caccavella *f* / tamburo a frizione *m*	friction drum / string drum
274	catene *f pl*	chains
275	charleston *m*	hi-hat pedal
276	chocallo *m* / tubo sonoro *m*	chocolo / chocalho
277	cimbali *m pl*	antique cymbals
278	cimbalini *m pl*	finger-cymbals / crotales
279	claves *f pl* / bacchette *f pl* / legnetti da percuotere *m pl*	claves
280	conga *m* / rumba *m*	conga
281	corno da nebbia *m*	fog horn
282	cuculo *m*	cuckoo
283	cuica *f*	cuica
284	eolifono *m*	wind machine
285	flexaton *m*	flexatone
286	frusta *f*	whip
287	gong *m*	gong
288	gong cinesi *m pl*	tuned gong-carillon
289	grancassa *f*	bass drum / big drum
290	guiro *m*	guiro / scraper
291	incudine *f*	anvil
292	lastra *f*	steel plate
293	legno frullante *m* / tavoletta sibilante *f*	thunder stick / bull roarer
294	litofono *m*	litophone / stone discs
295	macchina per il tuono *f*	thunder machine

Turmglockenspiel *n* / Glockenspiel *n*	carillon *m*	265
Klaviaturglockenspiel *n*	carillon à clavier *m*	266
Trommel *f*	caisse *f*	267
Rührtrommel *f* / Rolltrommel *f* / Wirbeltrommel *f* / Tenortrommel *f*	caisse roulante *f*	268
Kastagnetten *f Pl*	castagnettes *f pl*	269
Stielkastagnetten *f Pl*	castagnettes à manches *f pl*	270
Metallkastagnetten *f Pl* / Gabelbecken *f Pl*	castagnettes de métal *f pl*	271
Tanzkastagnetten *f* Pl	castagnettes espagnoles *f pl*	272
Reibtrommel *f* / Brummtopf *m*	tambour à friction *m*	273
Ketten *f Pl*	chaînes *f pl*	274
Charlestonmaschine *f*	pédale hi-hat *f*	275
Chocolo *m* / Tubo *m*	chocolo *m*	276
antike Cymbeln *f Pl*	cymbales antiques *f pl*	277
Fingercymbeln *f Pl* / Crotales *f pl*	cymbales digitales *f pl* / crotales *f pl*	278
Holzstäbe *m Pl* / Klangstäbe *m Pl* / Klanghölzer *n Pl* / Rumbastäbe *m Pl* / Schlagstäbe *m Pl*	claves *f pl* / baguettes de percussion *f pl* / baguettes entrechoquées *f pl*	279
Conga *f*	conga *m*	280
Nebelhorn *n*	sirène de brume *f*	281
Kuckuckspfeife *f*	coucou *m*	282
Cuica *f*	cuica *f*	283
Windmaschine *f*	machine à vent *f*	284
Flexaton *n*	flexaton *m*	285
Peitsche *f* / Klappholz *n*	fouet *m*	286
Gong *m*	gong *m*	287
Gongspiel *n* (chromatisch)	jeu de gongs *m pl*	288
große Trommel *f*	grosse caisse *f*	289
Guiro m / Kürbisrassel *f*	guiro *m*	290
Amboss *m*	enclume *f*	291
Stahlplatte *f*	feuille d'acier *f*	292
Schwirrholz *n*	planchette ronflante *f*	293
Litophon *n* / Steinspiel *n*	litophone *m*	294
Donnermaschine *f*	machine pour le tonnerre *f*	295

296	maracas *f pl*	maracas
297	marimba *f*	marimba(phone)
298	metal block *m*	metal block
299	metalofono *m*	metalophone
300	mezza luna f / cappello cinese *m*	bell tree
301	mirliton *m*	kazoo / eunuch flute
302	naccherone *m*	nakers
303	piatti *m pl* / cinelle *f pl*	cymbals
304	piatti chiodati *m pl*	rivet cymbals / sizzle cymbals
305	piatti cinesi *m pl*	Chinese cymbals
306	piatti turchi *m pl*	Turkish cymbals
307	piatto charleston *m*	charleston cymbal
308	piatto sospeso *m*	suspended cymbal
309	raganella *f*	rattle
310	raspa *f*	raspe / scraper
311	reco-reco *m*	bamboo scraper
312	richiamo per uccelli *m*	bird pipe
313	sansa *f* / mbira *f*	sansa
314	sapo cubano *m*	sapo
315	scacciapensieri *m*	jew's harp
316	sega *f*	musical saw
317	shaker *m*	shaker
318	sirena *f*	siren
319	sistro *m*	sistrum
320	sonagliera *f*	sleigh bells
321	sonaglio *m*	rattle / clapper
322	spazzolino metallico *m*	wire / rhythm brush
323	tamburello m / tamburo a cornice *m*	frame drum
324	tamburello basco *m* / tamburo basso *m*	tambourine / timbrel
325	tamburino provenzale *m*	tabor
326	tamburino *m*	tambourine
327	tamburo *m*	drum
328	tamburo a mano *m*	hand drum
329	tamburo di legno *m*	wood drum
330	tamburo di legno a fessura *m*	slit drum

Kürbisrassel *f* / Rumba-kugeln *f Pl*	maracas *m pl*	296
Marimbaphon *n*	marimba *m*	297
Metallblock *m*	metal block *m*	298
Metallophon *n*	métalophone *m*	299
Schellenbaum *m*	pavillon *m* / chapeau chinois *m*	300
Mirliton *m* / Flatsche *f* / Zwiebelflöte *f*	mirliton *m*	301
Nacara *f* (sarazenische Hand-pauke)	nacaire *m*	302
Becken *n Pl*	cymbales *f pl*	303
Nietenbecken *n Pl*	cymbales sur tiges *f pl*	304
chinesische Becken *n Pl*	cymbales chinoises *f pl*	305
türkische Becken *n Pl*	cymbales turques *f pl*	306
Charleston-Becken *n*	cymbale charleston *f*	307
hängendes Becken *n*	cymbale suspendue *f*	308
Ratsche *f* / Knarre *f* / Schnarre *f*	crécelle *f*	309
Raspel *f*	râpeur *m*	310
Bambusraspel *f*	reco-reco *m* / râpeur en bambou *m*	311
Vogelpfeife *f*	appeau *m*	312
Sansa *f* / Zanza *f*	sansa *f*	313
Sapo *m*	sapo *m*	314
Maultrommel *f* / Brummeisen *n*	guimbarde *f*	315
singende Säge *f*	scie musicale *f*	316
Schüttelrohr *n*	batteur *m*	317
Sirene *f*	sirène *f*	318
Sistrum *n*	sistre *m*	319
Schellengeläute *n*	sonnailles *f pl*	320
Schelle *f* / Rassel *f*	crécelle *f* / hochet *m*	321
Jazzbesen *m*	brosse *f* / balai de jazz *m*	322
Rahmentrommel *f* / Hand-trommel *f*	tambour de cadre *m* / tambourin à main *m*	323
Schellentrommel *f* / Tamburin *n*	tambour de basque *m* / tambourin basque *m*	324
Provenzalische Trommel *f* / Tamburin *n*	tambour de provence *m* / tambourin provençal *m*	325
Tamburin *n*	tambourin *m*	326
Trommel *f*	tambour *m*	327
Handtrommel *f*	tambour *m*	328
Holztrommel *f*	tambour en bois *m*	329
Schlitztrommel *f*	tambour de bois *m*	330

331	tamburo di latta *m* / tamburo di ferro *m*	steel drum
332	tamburo militare *m* / cassa chiara *f*	snare drum / sidedrum
333	tavola da frizione *f*	friction board
334	tavoletta *f*	bones
335	tam-tam *m*	tam-tam
336	timpani *m pl*	timpani *pl* / kettledrums *pl*
337	timpano a macchina *m*	machine drum
338	timpano cromatico *m*	chromatic timpano
339	timpano pedale *m*	pedal drum
340	tom-tom *m* / tamburo muto *m*	tom-tom
341	triangolo *m*	triangle
342	tubo sonoro di bambù *m*	bamboo brasilene
343	vibrafono *m*	vibraphone
344	xilofono *m*	xylophone
345	xilofono a tastiera *m*	keyed xylophone
346	xilomarimba *f*	xylomarimba

Parti componenti ed accessori   **Component parts and accessories**

347	bacchetta *f*	stick / beater / striker
348	bacchetta da tamburo *f*	drum stick
349	bacchetta di cuoio *f*	leather stick
350	bacchetta di feltro *f*	felt stick
351	bacchetta di legno *f*	wooden stick
352	bacchetta di spugna *f*	sponge-headed stick
353	bacchetta imbottita *f*	padded stick
354	bacchetta per piatti *f*	cymbal stick
355	bacchetta per timpani *f*	timpani stick
356	battaglio *m* / battente *m*	clapper
357	battitoia *f*	drumhead / skin
358	bordoniera *f*	snare
359	caldaia *f*	shell
360	cerchio *m*	counter-hoop
361	fascia *f*	shell / body
362	mazza *f* / mazzuolo *m*	mallet
363	mazza del tambur maggiore *f*	drum major's baton

Steel-Drum *f* / Benzinfass *n*	steel-drum *m*	331
Militärtrommel *f* / kleine Trommel *f*	tambour militaire *m* / caisse claire *f*	332
Reibbrett *n*	planche de friction *f*	333
Brettchenklapper *f*	tablette *f*	334
Tam-tam *n*	tam-tam *m*	335
Pauken *f Pl*	timbales *f pl*	336
Maschinenpauke *f*	timbale mécanique *f*	337
chromatische Pauke *f*	timbale chromatique *f*	338
Pedalpauke *f*	timbale chromatique mécanique *f*	339
Tom-tom *n*	tom-tom *m*	340
Triangel *n*	triangle *m*	341
Bambusschüttelrohr *n*	bambou brésilien *m*	342
Vibraphon *n*	vibraphone *m*	343
Xylophon *n*	xylophone *m*	344
Klaviaturxylophon *n*	xylophone à clavier *m*	345
Xylomarimba *n*	xylomarimba *f*	346

Bestandteile und Zubehör	**Parties composantes et accessoires**	
Schlägel *m*	baguette *f*	347
Trommelschlägel *m*	baguette de tambour *f*	348
Lederschlägel *m*	baguette de cuir *f*	349
Filzschlägel *m*	baguette de feutre *f*	350
Holzschlägel *m*	baguette de bois *f*	351
Schwammschlägel *m*	baguette d'éponge *f*	352
wattierter Schlägel *m*	baguette rembourrée *f*	353
Beckenschlägel *m*	baguette de cymbales *f*	354
Paukenschlägel *m*	baguette de timbales *f*	355
Klöppel *m*	battant *m*	356
Schlagfell *n*	peau supérieure *f* / peau de batterie *f*	357
Schnarrsaite *f* / Trommelsaite *f*	timbre *m*	358
Kessel *m*	fût *m*	359
Trommelreifen *m*	cadre *m*	360
Zarge *f*	fût *m*	361
Schlägel *m*	mailloche *f*	362
Tambourstab *m*	canne de tambour major *f*	363

364	martello *m*	hammer
365	membrana *f*	drumhead / vellum
366	orlo *f*	rim / edge
367	pedale della gran cassa *m*	bass drum pedal
368	pelle *f* / membrana *f*	skin / vellum
369	risuonatore *m*	resonator
370	spazzole *f pl*	wire brushes / steel brushes
371	tiracorda *f*	strainer
372	verga *f*	twig brush

Modi di suonare   Playing techniques

373	al centro	stroked in the middle
374	colpo *m* / battito *m*	beat
375	colpo del battaglio *m*	bell stroke
376	colpo di tamburo *m*	drumbeat
377	con due bacchette	with two sticks
378	con la mano	with the hand
379	coperto / velato	muffled
380	percuotere	to strike
381	raschiare	to scrape
382	rullo di tamburo *m*	drum roll
383	rullo del timpano *m*	drum roll
384	scoperto	uncovered
385	scuotere	to shake
386	sfregare	to rub
387	sul bordo *m* / sull'orlo *m*	at the edge / on the rim
388	tendere	to tighten
389	velare / coprire	to choke / to damp / to muffle

Strumenti a tastiera   Keyboard instruments

390	armonio *m*	harmonium / reed organ
391	bandoneon *m*	bandoneon
392	celesta *f*	celesta
393	clavicembalo *m* / gravi-cembalo *m*	harpsichord
394	clavicordo *m*	clavichord

Hammer *m*	marteau *m*	364
Fell *n* / Paukenfell *n* / Trommelfell *n*	peau *f*	365
Rand *m*	bord *m*	366
Fußmaschine *f*	pédale de la grosse caisse *f*	367
Fell *n*	peau *f*	368
Resonator *m*	résonateur *m*	369
Besen *m Pl*	balais *m pl*	370
Saitenschraube *f*	pontet *m*	371
Rute *f*	verge *f*	372

Spielarten / Façons de jouer

in der Mitte geschlagen	au centre frappé	373
Schlag *m*	battement *m* / coup *m*	374
Glockenschlag *m*	coup de cloche *m*	375
Trommelschlag *m*	coup de tambour *m*	376
mit zwei Schlägeln	avec deux baguettes	377
mit der Hand	avec la main	378
bedeckt	couvert / sourd	379
schlagen	frapper	380
schrapen	râper	381
Trommelwirbel *m*	roulement de tambour *m*	382
Paukenwirbel *m*	roulement de timbales *m*	383
unbedeckt	découvert	384
schütteln	secouer	385
reiben	frotter	386
am Rand *m*	sur le bord *m*	387
spannen / schränken	tendre	388
dämpfen / abdämpfen	étouffer	389

Tasteninstrumente / Instruments à clavier

Harmonium *n*	harmonium *m*	390
Bandoneon *n*	bandonéon *m*	391
Celesta *f*	célesta *m*	392
Cembalo *n*	clavecin *m*	393
Klavichord *n*	clavicorde *m*	394

395	fisarmonica *f*	accordion
396	fisarmonica a bottoni *f* / fisarmonica bitonica *f*	button accordion
397	fisarmonica con tastiera di pianoforte *f*	piano accordion
398	organo *m*	organ
399	organo portativo *m*	portative organ
400	pianoforte *m*	piano
401	pianoforte a coda *m*	grand piano
402	pianoforte preparato *m*	prepared piano
403	pianoforte a un quarto di coda *m*	baby grand
404	pianoforte verticale *m*	upright piano
405	spinetta *f*	spinet
406	virginale *m*	virginal

Parti componenti ed accessori — Component parts and accessories

407	accoppiamento *m*	coupler
408	anima *f*	block
409	bilancia *f*	tongue
410	bottone *m*	press stud
411	bottoni dei registri *m pl*	draw-stops
412	canale *m*	groove / channel
413	canna *f*	pipe
414	canna ad ancia *f*	reed pipe
415	canna labiale *f*	labial pipe / flute pipe
416	cassa *f*	body / case
417	cassa espressiva *f*	swell-box
418	cilindro *m*	player roll
419	consolle *f*	console
420	coperchio *m*	roller / lid / fall
421	corde incrociate *f pl*	cross-strung / overstrung scale
422	cuscinetto *m*	cushion
423	doppio scappamento *m*	doublehopper / escapement
424	feltro *m*	felt
425	fori *m*	bore
426	grand'organo *m*	full organ / great organ

Handharmonika f / Akkordeon m	accordéon m	395
Knopfgriff-Akkordeon m	accordéon à boutons	396
Pianoakkordeon n / Schiffer-klavier n	accordéon à clavier m	397
Orgel f	orgue m	398
Portativ n	orgue portatif m	399
Klavier n	piano m / pianoforte m	400
Flügel m	piano à queue m	401
präpariertes Klavier n	piano préparé m	402
Stutzflügel m	crapaud m	403
Klavier n / Pianino m	piano droit m	404
Spinett n	épinette f	405
Virginal n	virginal m	406

Bestandteile und Zubehör	**Parties composantes et accessoires**	
Koppel f	accouplement m	407
Kern m	biseau m	408
Zunge f	languette f	409
Knopf m	bouton m	410
Registerzüge m Pl / Züge m Pl	boutons de registres m pl	411
Windladenraum m	gravure f	412
Pfeife f	tuyau m	413
Zungenpfeife f	tuyau à anche m	414
Labialpfeife f	tuyau à bouche m	415
Gehäuse	buffet m / caisse f	416
Schwellkasten m	boîte expressive f	417
Walze f	cylindre m / rouleau m	418
Spieltisch m	console f	419
Deckel m / Welle f / Klappe f	couvercle m / rouleau m	420
kreuzsaitig	cordes croisées f pl	421
Polster n	garniture f	422
doppelte Auslösung f	coussinet m / double échappement m	423
Filz m	feutre m	424
Bohrung f	perce f	425
Hauptwerk n	grand orgue m	426

427	manetta *f*	hard lever
428	mantice *m*	bellows
429	manuale *m*	manual
430	martello *m* / martelletto *m*	hammer
431	meccanica *f*	action
432	pedale *m*	pedal
433	pedale destro *m* / pedale di risonanza *m*	right pedal / sustaining pedal
434	pedale sinistro *m* / pedale del piano *m*	left pedal / damping pedal / soft pedal
435	pedale tonale *m*	sostenuto pedal
436	pedaliera *f*	pedal keyboard
437	perno *m*	centre pin
438	plettro *m*	plectrum / quill / jack
439	registro *m*	stop / register
440	salterello *m*	jack
441	scappamento *m*	escapement lever / hopper
442	segreta *f*	wind chest
443	sgabello *m* / panchina *f*	piano stool
444	smorzo *m*	damper
445	somiere *m*	windchest / sound-board
446	tangente *f*	tangent
447	tastiera *f*	keyboard
448	tasto *m*	key
449	tavola armonica *f*	sound board
450	telaio *m*	frame
451	trasmissione *f*	action
452	tremolo *m*	tremulant
453	tirante *m*	tracker
454	valvola *f*	pallet / valve

Modi di suonare   **Playing techniques**

455	a due manuali	double manual
456	a quattro mani	for four hands
457	arpeggiato	arpeggiated
458	a un manuale	single manual
459	con sordina	with damper

Manubrium *n*	registre *m*	427
Balg *m*	soufflet *m*	428
Manual *n*	manuel *m*	429
Hammer *m*	marteau *m*	430
Mechanik *f*	mécanique *f*	431
Pedal *n* / Pedalwerk *n*	pédale *f*	432
rechtes Pedal *n* / Fortepedal *n*	pédale droite *f* / pédale forte *f*	433
linkes Pedal *n* / Verschiebungs-pedal *n* / Dämpfer *m*	pédale gauche *f* / sourdine *f*	434
Tonhaltepedal *n*	pédale de prolongation *f*	435
Pedalklaviatur *f*	pédalier *m*	436
Achse *f*	axe *m*	437
Plektrum *n* / Kiel *m*	plectre *m* / bec *m*	438
Register *n*	registre *m* / jeux d'orgue *m pl*	439
Docke *f* / Springer *m*	sautereau *m*	440
Auslöser *m*	échappement *m*	441
Windkasten *m*	laye *f*	442
Klavierstuhl *m*	tabouret de piano *m* / banquette *f*	443
Dämpfer *m*	étouffoir *m* / sourdine *f*	444
Windlade *f*	sommier *m*	445
Tangente *f*	tangente *f*	446
Klaviatur *f*	clavier *m*	447
Taste *f*	touche *f*	448
Klangboden *m* / Resonanz-boden *m*	table d'harmonie *f*	449
Rahmen *m*	cadre *m*	450
Traktur *f*	traction *f*	451
Tremulant *m*	tremblant *m*	452
Abstrakte *f* / Zug *m*	vergette *f* / tirant *m*	453
Ventil *n*	soupape *f*	454

Spielarten   Façons de jouer

zweimanualig	à deux claviers manuels	455
vierhändig	à quatre mains	456
arpeggiert	arpégé	457
einmanualig	à un (seul) clavier manuel	458
mit Dämpfer	avec sourdine / en sourdine	459

460	disposizione *f*	specification
461	due corde	two strings
462	mani incrociate / volteggiando	crossing hands
463	martellato	hammered
464	organo pieno *m*	full organ
465	passaggio del pollice *m*	passing the thumb under
466	perlato	pearly
467	peso del braccio *m*	armweight
468	peso del corpo *m*	bodyweight
469	registrazione *f*	registration
470	sostituzione delle dita *f*	change of finger
471	tocco *m* / attacco *m*	touch / action
472	togliere il pedale sinistro	take the damper away
473	tre corde	three strings
474	una corda	one string

Strumenti musicali meccanici

Mechanical musical instruments

475	carillon *m* / scatola musicale *f*	musical box / snuff box
476	orchestrion *m*	orchestrion
477	organetto automatico *m* / orologio a soneria *m*	musical clock
478	organo di Barberia *m* / organetto *m*	barrel-organ / street organ
479	orologio a carillon *m* / cariglione *m*	musical clock / musical box
480	pianola *f*	player piano

Strumenti elettrici/ elettronici, registrazione e riproduzione

Electric/electronic musical instruments, recording of music and playback units

481	altoparlante *m*	loudspeaker
482	ampiezza *f*	amplitude
483	amplificatore *m*	amplifier
484	attrezzature ritmiche *f pl*	rhythm units

Disposition *f*	disposition *f*	460
zwei Saiten	deux cordes	461
Hände kreuzend / übergreifen	mains croisées	462
gehämmert	martelé	463
volles Werk *n*	plein jeu *m*	464
Daumenuntersatz *m*	passage du pouce *m*	465
perlend	jeu perlé / perlé	466
Armgewicht *n*	poids du bras *m*	467
Körpergewicht *n*	poids du corps *m*	468
Registrierung *f*	registration *f*	469
Fingerwechsel *m*	substitution des doigts *f*	470
Anschlag *m*	toucher *m* / attaque *f*	471
mit aufgehobener Dämpfung	enlever la pédale gauche	472
drei Saiten	trois cordes	473
eine Saite	une corde	474

Mechanische Musikinstrumente
Instruments musicaux mécaniques

Spieldose *f*	boîte à musique *f* / tabatière à musique *f*	475
Orchestrion *m*	orchestrion *m*	476
Flötenuhr *f* / Flötenwerk *n*	pendule à carillon *f*	477
Drehorgel *f* / Leierkasten *m*	orgue de Barbarie *m*	478
Spieluhr *f*	pendule à carillon *f* / pendule à musique *f*	479
Pianola *n*	piano mécanique *m*	480

Elektrische/elektronische Musikinstrumente, Musikaufnahme- und Wiedergabegeräte
Instruments électriques/ électroniques, enregistrement et reproduction

Lautsprecher *m*	hautparleur *m*	481
Amplitude *f*	amplitude *f*	482
Verstärker *m*	amplificateur *m*	483
Rhythmusmaschine *f*	machine à rythme *f*	484

485	banda di frequenza *f*	frequency band
486	batteria elettronica *f*	electronic drums
487	battimento *m*	beat
488	canale *m*	channel
489	cancellare / annullare	to erase
490	chitarra elettrica *f*	electric guitar
491	colonna sonora *f*	soundtrack
492	comando del suono *m*	sound control
493	compressore *m*	compressor
494	correttore di tonalità *m* / regolatore del suono *m*	tone control
495	cuffia *f*	headphone
496	decibel *m*	decibel
497	dente di sega *m*	saw tooth
498	diaframma *m*	cartridge / pick-up
499	digitale	digital
500	disco *m*	record
501	distorsione *f*	distortion
502	eco *m*	echo
503	effetto sonoro *m*	tonal effect / sound effect
504	elaboratore *m*	computer
505	elaboratore musicale *m*	music computer
506	elettroacustica *f*	electroacoustics
507	elettrofono *m* / strumento elettrofono *m*	electrophone / electrophonic instrument
508	elettronica musicale *f*	musical electronics
509	entrata *f*	input
510	equalizzatore *m*	equalizer
511	filtro *m*	filter
512	filtro passabanda *m*	bandpass filter
513	frequenza *f*	frequency
514	generatore *m*	generator
515	generatore di suoni sinusoidali *m*	sine-wave generator
516	giradischi *m*	record player
517	grammofono *m*	gramophone (Engl.) / phonograph (Am.)
518	impulso *m*	impulse
519	larghezza di banda *f*	bandwidth
520	limitatore *m*	limiter

Frequenzband n	bande de fréquences f	485
elektronisches Schlagzeug n	instrument de percussion électronique m	486
Schwebung f	battement m	487
Kanal m	chaîne f	488
löschen	effacer / annuler	489
Elektrogitarre f / E-Gitarre f	guitare électrique f	490
Tonspur f	colonne sonore f	491
Klangsteuerung f	commande du son f	492
Kompressor m	compresseur m	493
Klangregler m	régleur de tonalité m	494
Kopfhörer m	casque d'écoute m	495
Dezibel n	décibel m	496
Sägezahn m	dent de scie f	497
Schalldose f	diaphragme m	498
digital	numérique	499
Schallplatte f	disque m	500
Verzerrung f	distorsion f	501
Echo n / Nachhall m	écho m	502
Klangeffekt m	effet sonore m	503
Computer m / Rechner m	calculateur m	504
Musikcomputer m	ordinateur musical m	505
Elektroakustik f	électro-acoustique f	506
Elektrophon n	électrophone m	507
Musikelektronik f	électronique musicale f	508
Eingang m	entrée f	509
Entzerrer m	égalisateur m	510
Filter m/n	filtre m	511
Bandpassfilter m	filtre passe-bande m	512
Frequenz f	fréquence f	513
Generator m	générateur m	514
Sinustongenerator m	générateur de sons sinussoidaux m	515
Plattenspieler m	tourne-disques m	516
Grammophon n	gramophone m	517
Impuls m	impulsion f	518
Bandbreite f	largeur de bande f	519
Begrenzer m	limiteur m	520

521	lineare	linear
522	livello *m*	level
523	lunghezza d'onda *f*	wave-length
524	mellotron *m*	mellotron
525	memorizzazione *f*	storage
526	memorizzazione del suono *f*	sound storage
527	mescolatore di suono *m* / tavolo di missaggio *m*	sound mixer / mixing board
528	microfono *m*	microphone
529	microfono a condensatore *m*	condenser microphone
530	microfono a contatto *m*	contact microphone
531	microfono elettrodinamico *m*	electrodynamic microphone
532	microfono elettromagnetico *m*	electromagnetic microphone
533	microsolco *m*	long-playing record / LP
534	miscelare	to mix
535	mistura *f*	tone mixture / sound mixture
536	musica informatica *f*	computer music
537	nastro magnetico *m*	magnetic tape
538	onda *f*	wave
539	organo elettronico *m*	electronic organ
540	organo Hammond *m*	Hammond organ
541	oscillatore *m*	oscillator
542	oscillazione *f*	oscillation / beat
543	parametro *m*	parameter
544	playback *m*	playback
545	potenziometro *m*	potentiometer
546	produzione del suono *f*	sound production
547	puntina *f*	needle
548	quadrifonia *f*	quadrophony
549	quadro di distribuzione *m*	switchboard
550	reazione *f*	feed back
551	regia *f*	studio (transmitting station)
552	registratore *m*	tape-recorder
553	registratori a cassetta *m pl*	cassette recorder
554	registrazione *f*	recording
555	registrazione a più piste *f*	multitrack recording
556	registrazione dal vero *f*	live recording

linear	linéaire	521
Pegel *m*	niveau *m*	522
Wellenlänge *f*	longueur d'onde *f*	523
Mellotron *n*	mélotron *m*	524
Speicherung *f*	mémorisation *f*	525
Klangspeicherung *f*	mémorisation du son *f*	526
Tonmischpult *n* / Mischpult *n*	mélangeur de son *m*	527
Mikrophon *n*	microphone *m*	528
Kondensatormikrophon *n*	microphone à condensateur *m*	529
Kontaktmikrophon *n*	microphone à contact *m*	530
elektrodynamisches Mikrophon *n*	microphone électrodynamique *m*	531
elektromagnetisches Mikrophon *n*	microphone électromagnétique *m*	532
Langspielplatte *f* / LP *f*	microsillon *m*	533
abmischen	mélanger / mixer	534
Tongemisch *n* / Klanggemisch *n*	mixage *m*	535
Computermusik *f*	musique par ordinateur *f*	536
Tonband *n* / Magnetband *n*	bande magnétique *f*	537
Welle *f*	onde *f*	538
elektronische Orgel *f*	orgue électronique *m*	539
Hammondorgel *f*	orgue Hammond *m*	540
Oszillator *m* / Schwingungserzeuger *m*	oscillateur *m*	541
Schwingung *f* / Schwebung *f*	oscillation *f* / battement *m*	542
Parameter *m*	paramètre *m*	543
Playback *n*	playback *m* / réenregistrement *m*	544
Potentiometer *n*	potentiomètre *m*	545
Klangerzeugung *f*	production du son *f*	546
Nadel *f* (Grammophon)	aiguille *f* (phono)	547
Quadrophonie *f*	quadrophonie *f*	548
Schalttafel *f*	tableau de distribution *m*	549
Rückkoppelung *f*	réaction *f*	550
Aufnahmestudio *n*	studio *m* / atelier *m*	551
Magnetbandgerät *n* / Tonbandgerät *n*	magnétophone *m*	552
Kassettenrekorder *m*	cassettophone *m*	553
Aufzeichnung *f* / Aufnahme *f*	enregistrement *m*	554
Mehrspurverfahren *n*	enregistrement à pistes multiples *m*	555
Mitschnitt *m* / Live-Aufnahme *f*	enregistrement original *m*	556

557	registrazione di dimostrazione *f*	demo tape
558	registrazione radiofonica *f*	radio recording
559	registrazione televisiva *f*	television recording
560	rettangolo *m*	rectangle
561	riduttore di rumore *m*	noise reduction / noise supression
562	riproduzione *f*	reproduction
563	risonanza *f*	resonance
564	rivelatore *m*	pick-up
565	riverbo *m*	reverb
566	rumore *m*	noise
567	scatola dell'altoparlante *f*	speaker cabinet
568	scurire	to cover
569	sequencer *m*	sequencer
570	sfiorare	to scan
571	sincronizzazione *f*	synchronization
572	sintetizzatore *m*	synthesizer / moog
573	sintesi del suono *f*	tone synthesis
574	sound sampler *m* (memorizzazione del suono)	sound sampler
575	spettro *m*	spectrum
576	stereofonia *f*	stereophony / stereo
577	strumenti a tastiera elettronica *m pl*	keyboards / electronic keyboards
578	strumenti generatori di effetti *m pl*	special effects equipment
579	suono sinusoidale *m*	sine tone
580	suono trasduttore *m*	sound transducer
581	supporti a lettura ottica *m pl*	compact disc / CD
582	taglio *m*	cut
583	tecnica digitale *f*	digital techniques
584	telecomando *m*	remote control
585	testina magnetica *f*	magnetic head
586	trasformatore *m*	transformer
587	trasformazione del suono *f*	sound modulation / sound shaping
588	trasmissione radiofonica *f*	radio transmission
589	trasmissione televisiva *f*	television transmission
590	transistor *m*	transistor

Demo-Aufnahme *f* / Demo-Band *n*	enregistrement de démonstration *m*	557
Rundfunkaufnahme *f*	enregistrement radiophonique *m*	558
Fernsehaufnahme	enregistrement télévisé *m*	559
Rechteck *n*	rectangle *m*	560
Rauschunterdrückung *f*	suppression du bruit *f* / amortissement du bruit *m*	561
Wiedergabe *f*	reproduction *f*	562
Resonanz *f* / Nachklang *m*	résonance *f*	563
Tonabnehmer *m*	pick-up *m*	564
Hall *m*	révérbération	565
Rauschen *n* / Geräusch *n* / Lärm *m*	bruit *m*	566
Lautsprecherbox *f*	haut-parleur en coffret *m*	567
decken	couvrir	568
Sequencer *m*	sequencer *m*	569
abtasten	lire / explorer	570
Synchronisation *f*	synchronisation *f*	571
Synthesizer *m*	synthétiseur *m*	572
Klangsynthese *f*	synthèse électronique *f*	573
Sound Sampler *m* / Naturklangspeicher *m*	soundsampler / enregistrement du son *m*	574
Spektrum *n*	spectre *m*	575
Stereophonie *f* / Raumklang *m*	stéréophonie *f*	576
elektronische Tasteninstrumente *n Pl*	claviers éléctroniques *m pl*	577
Effektgerät *n*	appareils générateurs d'effets *m pl*	578
Sinuston *m*	son sinussoidale *m*	579
Schallwandler *m*	transducteur acoustique *m* / transducteur de son *m*	580
CD *f* (Abk. für Compact Disc)	disque compact *m*	581
Schnitt *m*	coupure *f*	582
Digitaltechnik *f*	technique numérique *f*	583
Fernbedienung *f*	télécommande *f*	584
Magnetkopf *m* / Tonkopf *m*	tête magnétique *f*	585
Wandler *m*	transformateur *m*	586
Klangumwandlung *f*	transformation du son *f*	587
Rundfunkübertragung *f*	diffusion radiophonique *f*	588
Fernsehübertragung *f*	diffusion télévisée *f*	589
Transistor *m*	transistor *m*	590

591	trasmissione dal vivo *f*	live broadcast / live transmission
592	triangolo *m*	triangle / triangle-wave (oscillation)
593	uscita *f*	output
594	variazione del suono *f*	sound moderation
595	velocità del nastro *f*	tape speed
596	vibrazione *f*	vibration / sound wave
597	voltaggio *m*	voltage
598	volume sonoro *m*	loudness / intensity

Cantanti e canto   Singers and singing

599	baritono *m*	baritone
600	basso *m*	bass
601	basso buffo *m*	basso buffo
602	contralto *m*	contralto / alto
603	contraltista *m* / falsettista *m*	countertenor
604	educazione della voce *f* / formazione della voce *f*	vocal training / voice training
605	esercizio vocale *m*	vocal exercise
606	estensione vocale *f* / tessitura *f*	range
607	filar la voce	to spin the voice
608	fioritura *f* / gorgia *f*	florid ornaments
609	gorgheggio *m*	warble
610	gutturale	guttural
611	inflessione *f*	inflection
612	innalzare la voce	to raise the voice
613	messa di (in) voce *f* / impostazione *f*	placing of the voice
614	mezza voce	with half voice
615	mezzosoprano *m*	mezzo soprano
616	muta *f* / cambio della voce *m*	mutation
617	nasale	nasal
618	partitura vocale *f*	vocal score
619	portamento	carrying the voice
620	prima donna *f*	leading soprano
621	pronuncia *f*	pronunciation
622	rauco / roco	hoarse / raucous
623	registro *m*	register
624	respiro *m*	breathing pause

Live-Sendung *f*	émission originale *f*	591
Dreieck *n* (besser: Dreieck-schwingung)	triangle *m* / oscillation triangulaire *f*	592
Ausgang *m*	sortie *f*	593
Klangänderung *f*	modification du son *f*	594
Bandgeschwindigkeit *f*	vitesse de la bande *f*	595
Schwingung *f*	vibration *f*	596
Spannung *f*	voltage *m*	597
Schallstärke *f* / Lautstärke *f*	intensité du son *f* / volume *m*	598

Sänger und Gesang

Chanteurs et chant

Bariton *m*	baryton *m*	599
Bass *m*	basse *f*	600
Bass-Buffo *m*	basse bouffe *f*	601
Alt *m* / Altistin *f*	alto *m*	602
Kontratenor *m*	haute-contre *f*	603
Stimmbildung *f*	éducation de la voix *f*	604
Gesangsübung *f*	exercice vocal *m*	605
Stimmumfang *m*	registre *m* / tessiture *f*	606
den Ton ausspinnen	filer le son	607
Verzierung *f*	fioriture *f*	608
Gurgeltriller *m*	roulade *f*	609
kehlig	guttural	610
Tonfall *m* / Stimmfall *m*	inflexion *f*	611
die Stimme heben	lever la voix	612
Führung der Stimme *f* / Ansatz der Stimme *m*	pose de la voix *f*	613
mit halber Stimme	à mi-voix	614
Mezzosopran *m*	mezzo-soprano *m*	615
Mutation *f* / Stimmbruch *m*	mue *f*	616
nasal	nasal	617
Gesangspartitur *f*	partition vocale *f*	618
Tragen der Stimme *n*	porter la voix	619
erste Sängerin *f*	première chanteuse *f*	620
Aussprache *f*	prononciation *f*	621
heiser / rau	rauque / enroué / éraillé	622
Register *m* / Stimmlage *f*	registre *m*	623
Luftpause *f* / Atempause *f*	respiration *f* / soupir *m*	624

625	ribattuta di gola *f*	ribattuta
626	schiarirsi la voce	to clear one's voice
627	soprano *m*	soprano
628	soprano drammatico *m*	dramatic soprano / high dramatic soprano
629	soprano leggero *m*	coloratura soprano
630	soprano lirico *m*	lyric soprano
631	soprano lirico spinto *m*	young dramatic soprano
632	tenore *m*	tenor
633	tenore drammatico *m* / tenore eroico *m* / tenore di forza *m*	heroic tenor
634	tenore lirico *m*	lyrical tenor
635	a bassa voce / sommesso	to speak in a low voice / with a damped voice
636	a bocca chiusa	humming / with mouth closed
637	a mezza voce	with half voice

Modi di cantare e tecniche vocali

Voice types and singing techniques

638	afono	voiceless
639	appoggiare	to support
640	appoggio (sulla maschera) *m*	voice / breath support
641	arte del canto *f*	art of singing / vocal art
642	associazione corale *f* / società di canto *f*	choral society
643	atono	toneless
644	attacco dolce *m*	soft attack
645	attacco duro *m*	glottal attack
646	attacco sul fiato *m*	aspirated attack
647	a voce piena / spiegata	with full voice
648	bel canto *m*	beautiful singing
649	bisbigliare / sussurrare	to whisper
650	calare	to sing flat
651	canoro	for singing
652	cantare a prima vista	to sight-sing
653	cantare giusto	to sing in tune
654	canticchiare	to hum
655	canto parlato *m*	speech song

Zurückschlag *m* (Verzierung)	ribattuta *f*	625
sich räuspern	s'éclaircir la voix	626
Sopran *m* / Sopranistin *f*	soprano *m*	627
dramatischer Sopran *m* / hoch-dramatischer Sopran *m*	soprano dramatique *m*	628
Koloratursopran *m*	soprano léger *m*	629
lyrischer Sopran *m*	soprano lyrique *m*	630
jugendlich-dramatischer Sopran *m*	soprano dramatique lyrique d'agilité *m*	631
Tenor *m*	ténor *m*	632
Heldentenor *m*	ténor dramatique *m* / ténor héroïque *m*	633
lyrischer Tenor *m*	ténor lyrique *m*	634
mit leiser Stimme / mit gedämpfter Stimme	à voix basse	635
summen / mit geschlossenem Mund	à bouche fermée	636
mit halber Stimme	à mi-voix	637

Gesangsarten und -technik **Façons de chanter et technique vocale**

stimmlos	aphone	638
stützen	appuyer	639
Atemstütze *f*	appui du souffle *m*	640
Gesangskunst *f*	art vocal *m* / art du chant *m*	641
Gesangverein *m*	société chorale *f*	642
tonlos	atone	643
weicher Einsatz *m*	entrée douce *f*	644
harter Einsatz *m* / Glottis-schlag *m*	attaque dure *f* / coup de glotte *m*	645
gehauchter Einsatz *m*	attaque murmurée *f*	646
mit voller Stimme	à pleine voix	647
schöner Gesang *m*	beau chant *m*	648
flüstern / lispeln	chuchoter / susurrer	649
zu tief singen	chanter trop bas	650
für Gesang	pour le chant	651
vom Blatt singen	chanter à vue	652
rein singen	chanter juste	653
trällern	chantonner	654
Sprechgesang *m*	chant parlé *m*	655

656	castrato *m* / evirato *m*	castrato
657	catena di trilli *f*	chain of trills
658	cerone *m*	grease point
659	classi vocali *f pl*	voice type
660	coro *m*	choir / chorus
661	coro della radio *m*	radio choir / radio chorus
662	coro di chiesa *m*	church choir
663	coro di fanciulli *m*	boys' choir / children's choir
664	coro d'opera *m*	opera chorus
665	coro femminile *m*	women's choir / women's chorus
666	coro maschile *m*	men's choir / men's chorus
667	coro misto *m*	mixed chorus / choir
668	coro parlato *m*	choral speaking
669	coloratura *f*	coloratura
670	corde vocali *f pl*	vocal cords
671	crescere	to sing sharp
672	crudele	cruel
673	declamazione *f*	declamation
674	direttore del coro *m*	choral conductor / choirmaster
675	dizione *f*	diction
676	falsetto *f*	falsetto
677	fato *m* / destino *m*	destiny
678	libretto *m*	libretto
679	lirica *f*	lyric
680	morire	to die
681	pietà *f*	pity / mercy
682	ridente / rioso	laughing
683	sbadigliare	to yawn
684	schiarirsi la gola	to clear one's throat
685	simulare / fingere	to feign / to sham
686	singhiozzando	sobbing
687	sorridendo	smiling
688	sospiro *m*	sigh
689	sostenere	to support
690	soubrette *f*	soubrette
691	spinto	pushed
692	stonare	to sing out of tune
693	tecnica della respirazione *f*	breath control

Kastrat *m*	castrat *m*	656
Trillerkette *f*	série de trilles *f*	657
(Theater-)Schminke *f*	fard *m* (pour la scène)	658
Stimmgattung *f*	catégories de voix *f pl*	659
Chor *m*	chœur *m*	660
Rundfunkchor *m*	chœur de radio *m*	661
Kirchenchor *m*	chœur d'église *m*	662
Knabenchor *m* / Kinderchor *m*	chœur de garçons *m* / chœur d'enfants *m*	663
Opernchor *m*	chœur d'opéra *m*	664
Frauenchor *m*	chœur de femmes *m*	665
Männerchor *m*	chœur d'hommes *m*	666
gemischter Chor *m*	chœur mixte *m*	667
Sprechchor *m*	chœur parlé *m*	668
Koloratur *f*	coloratura *f*	669
Stimmbänder *n Pl*	cordes vocales *f pl*	670
zu hoch singen	chanter trop haut	671
grausam	cruel	672
Deklamation *f*	déclamation *f*	673
Chordirigent *m*	chef de chœur *m*	674
Diktion *f* / Vortrag *m*	diction *f*	675
Falsett *n* / Fistelstimme *f*	fausset *f*	676
Schicksal *n*	destin *m* / sort *m*	677
Operntextbuch *n* / Textbuch *n*	livret d'opéra *m* / livret *m*	678
Lyrik *f*	lyrique *f*	679
sterben	mourir	680
Erbarmen *n* / Mitleid *n*	pitié *f*	681
lachend	en riant / rieur	682
gähnen	baîller	683
(sich) räuspern	s'éclaircir la voix	684
heucheln / vorgeben	simuler / feindre	685
schluchzend	en sanglotant	686
lächelnd	en souriant	687
Seufzer *m*	soupir *m*	688
stützen	soutenir	689
Soubrette *f*	soubrette *f*	690
gestoßen	poussé	691
detonieren / falsch singen	détonner	692
Atemtechnik *f* / Atembehandlung *f*	contrôle du souffle *m*	693

694	tecnica vocale *f*	vocal techniques
695	tossire	to cough
696	tremolando	tremolando
697	tremolare	to wobble
698	tremolo *m*	tremolo
699	usignolo *m*	nightingale
700	velato / fioco	veiled / husky
701	vendetta *f*	vengeance
702	vincere	to win
703	vocale	vocal
704	vocalizzo *m*	vocalise
705	voce *f*	voice
706	voce aspra *f*	harsh voice
707	voce chiara *f*	clear voice
708	voce cupa *f*	deep voice
709	voce di gola *f*	throat voice
710	voce di petto *f*	chest voice
711	voce di testa *f*	head voice
712	voce femminile *f*	female voice
713	voce granita *f*	solid voice
714	voce infantile *f*	child's voice
715	voce maschile *f*	male voice
716	voci miste *f pl*	mixed voices
717	zufolando / fischiettando	whistling

Gesangstechnik *f* / Stimm-technik *f*	technique vocale *f*	694
husten	tousser	695
bebend / tremolierend	en tremblottant / en chevrottant	696
tremolieren / wackeln	chevroter	697
Tremolo *n*	trémolo *m*	698
Nachtigall *f*	rossignol *m*	699
verschleiert	voilé	700
Rache *f*	vengeance *f*	701
siegen	vaincre / gagner	702
vokal / sanglich	vocal	703
Vokalise *f*	vocalise *f*	704
Stimme *f*	voix *f*	705
barsche Stimme *f*	voix âpre *f*	706
helle/klare Stimme *f*	voix claire *f*	707
dunkle Stimme *f*	voix grave *f*	708
Kehlstimme *f*	voix de gorge *f*	709
Bruststimme *f*	voix de poitrine *f*	710
Kopfstimme *f*	voix de tête *f*	711
Frauenstimme *f*	voix féminine *f*	712
volle, kräftige Stimme *f*	voix pleine *f*	713
Kinderstimme *f*	voix enfantine *f*	714
Männerstimme *f*	voix masculine *f*	715
gemischte Stimmen *f Pl*	voix mixtes *f pl*	716
pfeifend	en sifflotant	717

Il linguaggio delle partiture

The language of the scores

Velocità

Le parole con * possono significare al tempo stesso più presto e più forte oppure più lento e più piano.

Velocity

The words marked by * can indicate faster and louder as well as slower and softer.

718	a beneplacito	as you like
719	a piacere / a volontà	at one's pleasure
720	a tempo / in tempo / a battuta / a misura / in misura	in time
721	adagietto / adagino	somewhat faster and lighter than adagio
722	adagio	slow
723	adagissimo / lentissimo	extremely slow
724	ad libitum (L)	at one's pleasure
725	affrettato	hurried
726	allegretto	not as fast as allegro
727	allegrissimo / allegro assai	very fast / very lively
728	allegro	lively / cheerful
729	andante	walking pace
730	andantino	somewhat quicker or slower than andante
731	animato	animated
732	celeramente / celere	swiftly / swift
733	circolando	circulating
734	con celerità	with celerity
735	con fretta / in fretta	with haste / in haste
736	con lentezza	with slowness
737	con molta libertà	with much freedom
738	con moto / con movimento	with movement
739	con precipitazione	with precipitation
740	con qualche licenza	somewhat freely
741	con rapidità / con prestezza	with rapidity / with speed
742	con rigore	with rigour
743	con speditezza / con prontezza	with quickness
744	con velocità	with velocity
745	corrente / correndo	running
746	esitando / esitante	hesitating
747	frettoloso	in a hurry / hasty

Die Sprache der Partituren

Le langage des partitions

Tempo

Vitesse

Die mit * gekennzeichneten Wörter können gleichzeitig schneller und lauter oder langsamer und leiser bedeuten.	Les mots marqués avec * peuvent signifier en même temps plus vite et plus fort ou plus lent et plus doucement.	
nach Belieben	à votre gré	718
nach Belieben	librement	719
im Takt / im Zeitmaß	en mesure / au mouvement / bien en mesure	720
ziemlich langsam / kürzer und schneller als Adagio	plus court et plus rapide que adagio	721
langsam	lent / adage	722
sehr langsam	très lent / extrêmement lent	723
nach Belieben	à volonté	724
eilig / übereilt	hâté	725
weniger bewegt als Allegro	moins rapide que allegro	726
sehr lebhaft / sehr schnell	très rapide / très vif	727
lebhaft / heiter	allègre	728
gehend / mäßig bewegt	en allant	729
schneller oder langsamer als Andante	plus lent ou plus rapide que andante	730
belebt	animé	731
rasch	rapidement / rapide	732
kreisend	en circulant	733
schnell	avec célérité	734
eilig / hastig	avec hâte	735
mit Langsamkeit	avec lenteur	736
mit großer Freiheit	avec beaucoup de liberté	737
bewegt	avec mouvement / avec allant	738
überstürzt	avec précipitation	739
mit einiger Freiheit	avec quelques licences	740
mit Schnelligkeit	avec rapidité	741
mit Strenge / streng im Takt	avec rigueur	742
mit Geläufigkeit	avec promptitude	743
mit Geschwindigkeit	avec vélocité	744
laufend / rennend	courant / en courant	745
zögernd / stockend	en hésitant / hésitant	746
hastig / hektisch	pressé	747

748	grave	very slow
749	incalzante	pressing on
750	larghetto	somewhat quicker and lighter than largo
751	largo	broad
752	largo assai	very slow
753	lentamente	slowly
754	lento / tardo	slow
755	libero	free
756	l'istesso tempo / lo stesso tempo / medesimo tempo	the same speed / the same pace
757	moderatamente	moderately
758	moderato	moderate
759	mosso	with movement
760	non presto	not fast
761	precipitato / precipitoso	precipitate / tumbling
762	prestissimo	extremely fast
763	presto	fast
764	prontamente / pronto	promptly
765	rapidamente / prestamente	rapidly
766	rapido	rapid
767	riprendendo / rimettendo	picking up again speed / picking up again volume
768	rubato / rubando	"robbed" / with some freedom
769	senza fretta	without haste
770	senza misura	without measure
771	senza strascicare / senza trascicare	without dragging
772	sollecito	prompt
773	sostenuto	sustained
774	spedito	quick
775	svelto	speedy
776	tempo anteriore	former speed / previous tempo
777	tempo giusto	appropriate speed
778	tempo primo / tempo ordinario	original speed
779	tornando al tempo	returning to the original speed
780	tostamente / tosto	fleetly / fleet
781	velocemente / veloce	quickly / quick

sehr langsam	très lent	748
drängend	talonnant	749
kürzer und schneller als Largo	plus court et plus rapide que largo	750
breit	large	751
sehr langsam	extrêmement lent	752
langsam	lentement	753
langsam	lent	754
frei	libre	755
im gleichen Tempo / dasselbe Zeitmaß	le même mouvement / au même mouvement	756
in mäßiger Weise	modérément	757
gemäßigt / mäßig	modéré	758
bewegt	mû	759
nicht schnell	pas vite	760
überstürzt / überhetzt	précipité / bousculé	761
sehr schnell	très vite	762
schnell / mit großer Geschwindigkeit	vite	763
prompt	promptement / prompt	764
schnell / in schneller Weise	rapidement	765
schnell / zügig	rapide	766
wieder aufnehmend / zurücksetzend	en reprenant / en remettant	767
„geraubt" / ein wenig frei	volé / dérobé / en dérobant	768
ohne Eile	sans se presser	769
ohne bestimmtes Zeitmaß	sans mesure	770
ohne zu schleppen	sans traîner	771
schleunig	empressé	772
verhalten / getragen	soutenu	773
geläufig	expédié	774
geschwind	svelte	775
voriges Zeitmaß	au tempo précédent / au mouvement antérieur	776
richtiges Zeitmaß / angemessenes Zeitmaß	temps juste	777
erstes Zeitmaß / Anfangstempo	temps premier / mouvement initial	778
zum Zeitmaß zurückkehrend	en revenant au mouvement	779
hurtig	vite	780
rasch	rapidement / rapide	781

782	vivace	vivacious
783	vivacissimo	most vivacious
784	vivamente	lively

SINONIMI   SYNONYMS

Più presto   Faster

785	accelerando / sollecitando	getting faster / urging
786	accelerato	accelerated
787	affrettando / frettando	hastening / hurrying
788	andando / procedendo	going on / to proceed
789	animando*	becoming more animated
790	avanti / avanzando	forward / moving forward
791	avvivando*	enlivening
792	camminando	walking
793	doppio movimento	double the speed
794	incalzando*	in a hectic pace
795	movendo / muovendo	moving
796	più tosto	swifter
797	più veloce	quicker
798	precipitando	precipitately / rushing
799	pressando / pressante	pressing
800	ravvivando*	reviving
801	ravvivato*	revived
802	rianimando*	reanimating
803	riscaldando*	warming up
804	ristringendo	restricting / drawing together again
805	sempre più animato	always more animated
806	serrato	tightly
807	spedendo	promptly
808	spingendo	pushing / pressing forward
809	stretto / ristretto	drawn together / tight
810	stringendo / serrando	drawing together / tightening
811	urgente	urgent

lebhaft	vivace	782
sehr lebhaft	très vif	783
auf lebhafte Weise	vivement	784

SYNONYME

SYNONIMES

Schneller

Plus vite

beschleunigend	en accélerant	785
beschleunigt	accéléré	786
eilend	en pressant	787
vorwärts gehend / fortschreitend	en allant / en procédant	788
belebend / lebhafter werdend	en animant	789
vorwärts / vorantreibend	en avant / en avançant	790
neu belebend	en ranimant	791
gehend / vorangehend / vorwärts gehend	en marchant	792
doppelt so schnell	en doublant le mouvement	793
drängend	en talonnant	794
bewegend	mouvant	795
eiliger	plus vite	796
mit höherem Tempo	plus rapide	797
sich überstürzend / gehetzt	en précipitant	798
bedrängend	en pressant / pressez	799
wiederbelebend	en ravivant	800
wieder belebt	ravivé	801
wieder lebhafter	en ranimant	802
erwärmend	en réchauffant	803
enger werdend	en resserrant	804

immer belebter	de plus en plus animé	805
gedrängt	serré	806
beeilend	en se hâtant	807
stoßend / treibend	en poussant	808
eng	serré / étroit	809
zusammendrängend / allmählich schneller werdend	en serrant	810
dringend	urgent	811

Il linguaggio delle partiture:
The language of the scores:
64   Velocità
Velocity

Più lento

Slower

	Italian	English
812	allargando / slargando	broadening
813	allentando / slentando	loosening
814	allungando / dilungando	stretching out
815	calmando*	calming
816	calmandosi*	calming down
817	estendendo / espandendosi	extending
818	estenuandosi*	getting exhausted
819	frenando / raffrenando	braking
820	indugiando	delaying
821	largando	widening
822	mancando*	lacking
823	moderando	moderating
824	morendo*	dying away
825	prolungando	prolonging
826	rallentando / lentando	getting slower / slowing down
827	rallentato	slower
828	rilasciando / rilassando	releasing
829	ritardando / tardando	retarding
830	ritardato	delayed
831	ritenuto / trattenuto	held back
832	spirando / espirando*	fading away / dying out
833	stentando / penando	toiling / struggling
834	stiracchiando	tugging
835	stirando	stretching
836	strascinando / trascinando / trascicando / trainando	dragging
837	svanendo*	vanishing
838	tirando	drawing / pulling
839	trattenendo / rattenendo / ritenendo	holding back
840	tratto	dragged

Dinamica e articulazione

Dynamics and articulation

	Italian	English
841	accentuato	accentuated
842	appoggiando	leaning
843	appoggiato / poggiato	leaned

Langsamer   Plus lent

breiter werdend	en élargissant	812
lockernd	en relâchant	813
verlängernd	en allongeant	814
beruhigend	en calmant	815
sich besänftigend	en se calmant	816
ausdehnend	en s'étandant	817
sich erschöpfend	en s'exténuant	818
bremsend	en freinant	819
zögernd	en s'attardant	820
verbreiternd	en élargissant	821
entschwindend / ausklingen lassend	en défaillant	822
mäßigend	en modérant	823
sterbend / ersterbend	en mourant	824
verlängernd	en prolongeant	825
langsamer werdend	en ralentissant	826
verlangsamt	ralenti	827
nachlassend	en relâchant	828
verzögernd	en retardant	829
verzögert	retardé	830
zurückgehalten	retenu	831
hinsterbend / ausatmend	en expirant	832
angestrengt	en peinant	833
zerrend	en tiraillant	834
dehnend	en s'étendant	835
schleppend / verschleppend	en traînant	836
entschwindend	en s'estompant / en s'effaçant	837
ziehend	en tirant	838
zurückhaltend	en retenant	839
geschleppt	traîné	840

Dynamik und Artikulation   Dynamique et articulation

betont	accentué / ponctué	841
stützend / betonend	en appuyant	842
gestützt	appuyé	843

844	articolando	articulating
845	articolato	articulated
846	ben ritmato	well rhythmed
847	con tutta la forza	with full force
848	estinto / spento	extinguished
849	forte	strong / loud
850	fortissimo	very loud
851	forzando	forcing
852	forzato	forced
853	glissando	sliding
854	legato / ligado	bound / tied
855	lontano	far away
856	marcando	marking
857	marcato	marked
858	martellando	hammering
859	mezzoforte	half loud
860	mezzopiano	half soft
861	molto accentuato	very accentuated
862	percosso	struck
863	pianissimo	extremely soft
864	piano	soft / low
865	più forte possibile	as loud as possible
866	più piano possibile	as soft as possible
867	portando	carrying over
868	portato	carried over
869	quasi niente	almost nothing
870	risaltato	emphasized
871	ritmico / ritmato	rhythmical / rhythmic
872	sferzando	whipping
873	sforzato / sforzando	forced / forcing
874	slegato / non legato	not slurred
875	smorzato	subdued
876	sottovoce	"under the voice" / in an undertone
877	staccato	detached
878	tremolando	trembling / tremolo
879	vibrato	vibrato / "vibrated"

artikulierend	en articulant	844
artikuliert	articulé	845
sehr rhythmisch	bien rythmé	846
mit voller Kraft / mit größter Kraft	de toutes ses forces	847
erlöscht / ausgelöscht	éteint	848
kräftig / stark / laut	fort	849
sehr laut	très fort	850
forcierend / stark betonend	en contraignant	851
forciert / stark betont	contraint	852
gleitend	en glissant / glisser	853
gebunden	lié	854
fern / weit / entfernt	lointain	855
markierend	en marquant	856
markiert	marqué	857
hämmernd	en martelant	858
halblaut / mittelstark	mi-fort	859
halbleise / mittelleise	mi-doux	860
sehr betont	très accentué	861
geschlagen	percuté	862
sehr leise	très doucement	863
leise	doucement	864
so laut wie möglich	le plus fort possible	865
so leise wie möglich	le plus doucement possible	866
tragend	en portant	867
getragen	porté	868
fast nichts	presque rien	869
hervorgehoben	mis en relief	870
rhythmisch	rythmique / rythmé	871
peitschend	en cinglant	872
stark hervorgehoben	forcé / en forçant	873
ungebunden	non lié	874
gedämpft	amorti	875
„unter der Stimme" / mit leiser Stimme	à voix basse	876
abgestoßen	détaché / piqué	877
tremolierend / bebend	trembloté / trémolo	878
vibriert / Bebung *f*	vibré	879

SINONIMI

Più forte

SYNONYMS

Louder

880	accrescendo	augmenting
881	alzando	rising
882	ampliando	amplifying
883	aumentando	increasing
884	calcando / premendo	compressing
885	crescendo	growing louder
886	rafforzando / rinforzando	strengthening
887	rinforzato	strengthened
888	risvegliando* / risvegliato	re-awakening
889	spiegando	unfolding
890	svegliando*	wakening

Più piano

Softer

891	abbassando	lowering
892	acchetandosi* / acquietandosi	becoming calmer
893	addolcendo	softening
894	affievolendo / indebolendo	weakening
895	allontanandosi / allontanando	receding / moving away
896	assottigliando	dwindling
897	attenuando	lessing
898	calando* / calante	waning / lowering
899	cedendo*	yielding
900	decrescendo	decreasing
901	diluendo	thinning out / weakening
902	diminuendo / sminuendo	diminishing
903	estinguendosi / estinguendo	extinguishing
904	evaporandosi	evaporating
905	perdendosi*	decreasing to nothing
906	placando / mitigando	appeasing
907	raddolcendo / raddolcente	sweetening
908	scemando / deficiendo	getting less
909	smorzando	subduing

SYNONYME SYNONIMES

Lauter Plus fort

vermehrend / zunehmend	en accroissant	880
erhebend	en élevant	881
erweiternd	en agrandissant	882
steigernd / vermehrend / zunehmend	en augmentant	883
betonend / drängend	en comprimant	884
anwachsend / anschwellend	en croissant	885
verstärkend	en renforçant	886
verstärkt	renforcé	887
wieder erweckend	en réveillant / réveillé	888
entfaltend	en déployant	889
erweckend	en réveillant	890

Leiser Plus doucement

absinkend	en abaissant	891
sich beruhigend	en s'apaisant	892
sanft werdend / abmildernd	en adoucissant	893
abschwächend / schwächer werdend	en affaiblissant	894
sich entfernend / entfernend	en s'éloignant	895
verringernd	en amenuisant	896
dämpfend	en attenuant	897
absinkend	en faisant descendre / en descendant	898
nachgebend	en cédant	899
abnehmend	en décroissant	900
auflösend / verdünnend	en diluant	901
vermindernd	en diminuant	902
verlöschend	en s'éteignant	903
verdunstend	en s'évaporant	904
sich verlierend / verebbend	en se perdant	905
besänftigend	en apaisant	906
sanfter werdend	en adoucissant	907
abnehmend	en amoindrissant	908
dämpfend / abschwächend	en amortissant	909

910	spegnendo*	extinguishing
911	stinto / spento	extinguished
912	temperando	moderating
913	togliendo*	taking away

Carattere ed espressione   Character and expression

914	a ballata	in a ballad style
915	abbandonandosi	abandoning oneself
916	abbandonatamente / abbandono (con)	with abandonment
917	a capriccio	capricious
918	accarezzando / accarezze-volmente / accarezzevole / carezzevole	caressing / cuddle
919	accoramento (con) / afflizione (con)	with grief
920	accoratamente / accorato	sorrowful / grieved
921	accuratamente / accurato	carefully / careful
922	accuratezza (con) / cura (con)	with care
923	adiratamente	wrathful
924	adirato / stizzito	angry
925	adorazione (con)	adoringly (with adoration)
926	adornando / ornando	adorning
927	adornato / ornato	adorned
928	aereo / arioso	airy
929	affabile / cortesemente	affable / courteous
930	affannato	breathless
931	affanno (con) / angustia (con) / affannosamente / affannoso	with anxiety / anxious
932	affettato / manierato	affected
933	affetto (con)	with affection
934	affettuosamente	affectionately
935	affettuoso	lovingly
936	agevole	at ease
937	agevolezza (con) / facilità (con)	with ease
938	aggiustamente	very measured
939	agiatamente	comfortable
940	agile / agilmente	agile / nimble
941	agilità (con)	with agility

auslöschend	en éteignant	910
erloschen / erlöscht	éteint	911
mäßigend	en modérant	912
wegnehmend	en ôtant	913

Charakter und Ausdruck Caractère et expression

wie eine Ballade	comme une ballade	914
sich hingebend	en s'abandonnant	915
mit Hingabe	avec abandon	916
launenhaft / kapriziös	capricieusement	917
liebkosend	en caressant / câlin	918
mit Betrübnis / trübselig	attristé	919
betrübt	chagriné	920
sorgfältig	soigneusement / soigné	921
mit Sorgfalt	avec soin	922
zornig / aufgebracht	coléreusement	923
erzürnt	en colère	924
mit Anbetung	avec adoration	925
zierend / schmückend	en ornant	926
verziert	orné	927
luftig	aéré	928
leutselig / mit Höflichkeit	affable / courtois	929
atemlos	essouflé	930
bangend	tourmenté / anxieusement	931
geziert / affektiert	affecté / maniéré	932
mit Zuneigung / liebevoll	avec affection	933
in herzlicher Weise	affectueusement	934
gemütsbewegend	affectueux	935
bequem	aisé	936
mit Leichtigkeit	avec aisance	937
genau im Takt	très en mesure	938
gemächlich / gemütlich	aisément	939
behände	agile / agilement	940
mit Behändigkeit	avec agilité	941

942	agitato / concitato / agitazione (con) / concitazione (con)	agitated / with agitation
943	agreste / campestre	rural
944	all'antica	in old style
945	alla contadina	like a peasant dance
946	alla maniera di / a la maniera	in the manner of
947	alla marcia	like a march
948	alla militare / militarmente	militarily
949	alla tedesca	in the style of German dance
950	alla turca	in Turkish style
951	alla zingara	in gipsy style
952	alla zoppa / zoppo	limping / lame
953	allarmato	alarmed
954	allegramente	briskly
955	allegrezza (con) / allegria (con)	cheerfully
956	all'ungherese / all'ongarese	in Hungarian style
957	altero / superbo	haughty
958	amabilità (con) / garbo (con)	with amiability
959	amabile / garbato	amiable
960	amaramente	bitterly
961	amareggiato	embittered
962	amarezza (con)	with bitterness
963	amaro	bitter
964	amore (con)	with love
965	amorevole / amoroso	tenderly
966	amorevolmente / amorosamente	lovingly
967	ampiezza (con)	with breadth
968	ampio / vasto	vast / spreading
969	ampolloso	inflated / bombastic
970	anelante / ansante	gasping / panting
971	angelico	angelic
972	angoscia (con)	with anguish
973	angoscioso / angosciosamente	anguished
974	anima (con)	with soul / with feeling
975	animo (con) / coraggio (con)	with courage
976	animoso / coraggioso	brave / courageous
977	ansia (con) / ansietà (con)	with anxiety
978	ansiosamente	anxiously
979	ansioso / trepidante	anxious
980	apatico	apathetic

erregt / unruhig	agité / avec agitation	942
ländlich	champêtre	943
im alten Stil	dans le style ancien	944
wie ein Bauerntanz / bäurisch	comme une danse paysanne	945
nach Art der/des/von	à la manière de	946
wie ein Marsch	dans le caractère d'une marche	947
militärisch	militairement	948
nach deutscher Tanzart	à l'allemande	949
nach türkischer Art (im Stil der Janitscharen-Musik)	à la turque	950
nach Art der Zigeuner	à la tzigane	951
hinkend	boiteux	952
beunruhigt	alarmé	953
fröhlich / flott	allégrement	954
mit Fröhlichkeit	avec allégresse	955
nach ungarischer Art	à la hongroise	956
hochmütig	hautain	957
mit Liebenswürdigkeit	avec amabilité	958
liebenswürdig	aimable	959
in bitterer Weise	amèrement	960
verbittert / erbittert	aigri	961
mit Bitterkeit	avec amertume	962
bitter	amer	963
mit Liebe	avec amour	964
liebevoll	doux / tendre	965
in liebevoller Weise	tendrement	966
mit Weite / mit Ausdehnung	avec ampleur	967
weit / ausgedehnt / ausladend	ample / vaste	968
schwülstig	enflé / ampoulé	969
keuchend	haletant	970
engelhaft	angélique	971
mit Seelenqual	avec angoisse	972
angstvoll	angoissant	973
mit Seele / gemütvoll	avec âme	974
mit Mut	avec courage	975
beherzt / mutig	hardi / courageux	976
mit Bangen	avec anxiété	977
bangend	anxieusement	978
bange	anxieux	979
apathisch	apathique	980

981	appassionatamente / sviscerato / appassionato / passionato	passionately / passionate
982	appenato	distressed
983	arcigno / scontroso	surly
984	ardente / rovente / fiammante	ardent
985	ardentemente	ardently
986	arditamente	boldly
987	arditezza (con)	with boldness
988	ardito / temerario	daring
989	ardore (con) / lena (con)	with ardour
990	armoniosamente / armonioso	harmoniously / harmonious
991	arrabbiato / rabbioso	angry
992	arroganza (con) / superbia (con)	with arrogance
993	artificiale / artificioso	artificial
994	arzillo	cheerily
995	asprezza (con)	with harshness
996	aspro	harsh
997	audace / franco	audacious
998	audacemente	audaciously
999	audacia (con)	with audacity
1000	autoritario	authoritarian
1001	balbettando / tartagliando	stammering
1002	baldanza (con) / baldanzoso	with boldness / bold
1003	barbaro	barbarous
1004	barcollando / vacillando	staggering / tottering
1005	beato	blissful
1006	beffardo / derisione (con)	mocking
1007	bellicoso / aggressivo / grintoso	bellicose / aggressive
1008	bilanciato / equilibrato	balanced / well balanced
1009	bizzarro / eccentrico	bizarre / eccentric
1010	bramosia (con)	with hankering
1011	bramoso / avido / famelico	greedy / craving
1012	bravura (con)	with skill
1013	brillante / lucente / luccicante	brilliant / shining / shimmering
1014	brio (con)	full of live
1015	brioso	full of pep / snappy
1016	brontolando / borbottando	grumbling
1017	brusco / bruscamente	brusque

leidenschaftlich	passionnément / passionné	981
bekümmert	peiné	982
mürrisch	hargneux / revêche	983
glühend / feurig	ardent / brûlant	984
brennend / heiß	ardemment	985
in kühner Weise	hardiment	986
mit Kühnheit / mit Verwegenheit	avec hardiesse	987
kühn / tollkühn	hardi / téméraire	988
voller Glut	avec ardeur	989
wohlklingend	harmonieusement / harmonieux	990
wütend / aufgebracht	enragé / rageur	991
anmaßend / mit Hochmut	avec arrogance	992
künstlich / gekünstelt	artificiel	993
munter / quietschfidel	guilleret	994
mit Schärfe	avec âpreté	995
harsch	âpre	996
kühn / verwegen	audacieux	997
in kühner Weise	audacieusement	998
mit Kühnheit	avec audace	999
autoritär	autoritaire	1000
stammelnd	en balbutiant	1001
mit Keckheit	avec assurance / crânement	1002
barbarisch	barbare	1003
wankend / schwankend	en chancelant / en vacillant	1004
glückselig	bienheureux	1005
spöttisch / höhnisch	railleur	1006
angreifend / aggressiv	belliqueux / agressif	1007
ausgewogen	balancé / équilibré	1008
sonderbar / wunderlich	bizarre / excentrique	1009
mit Begierde	avec convoitise	1010
begierig / gierig	désireux / avide	1011
mit Bravour	avec bravoure	1012
glänzend / schimmernd	brillant / luisant / miroitant	1013
voll Lebhaftigkeit / schwungvoll	avec verve / enlevé	1014
pfiffig / voll Leben / spritzig	plein d'allant / entraînant	1015
brummend	grognon	1016
brüsk / barsch	brusque / brusquement	1017

1018	brutale	brutal
1019	burlando / motteggiando	joking
1020	burlescamente / burlesco	mockingly
1021	caldamente	warmly
1022	caldo	warm
1023	calma (con) / calmamente	calmly
1024	calmo / quieto	calm / quiet
1025	calore (con)	with warmth
1026	calorosamente / caloroso	heartily
1027	candido / candidamente	candid / candidly
1028	candore (con)	with candour
1029	cantabile	in a singing style
1030	cantando	singing
1031	canzonando / deridendo	making fun / mocking
1032	caparbio / testardo	stubborn
1033	capricciosamente / capriccioso	capricious / whimsically
1034	carattere (con) / grinta (con)	with character
1035	caricato	charged
1036	carino / leggiadro	nice / lovely / charming
1037	casto / illibato	chaste
1038	cavalleresco	chivalrous
1039	celeste / celestiale	heavenly
1040	chiamando / invocando	calling / invocating
1041	chiaramente	clearly / distinctly
1042	chiarezza (con)	with clarity
1043	chiaro / limpido / nitido	clear / limpid
1044	cinetico / motore	kinetic / motor
1045	civettando	coquettish
1046	civetteria (con) / civettuolo	coquettishly
1047	collera (con) / incollerito	with anger / with wrath
1048	colorato	coloured
1049	comico / buffo	comical
1050	commosso	moved
1051	commovente	moving / touching
1052	comodamente	comfortably
1053	comodo / commodo	feeling comfortable / cosy
1054	concentrato	concentrated
1055	consolante / confortante	consoling
1056	con somma bravura	with the highest virtuosity
1057	contemplativo	contemplative

brutal / roh	brutal	1018
scherzend / spaßhaft	moquant	1019
scherzhaft / possenhaft	de façon burlesque	1020
in warmherziger Weise	chaleureusement	1021
warm	chaud	1022
mit Ruhe	avec calme	1023
ruhig	calme / calmement	1024
mit Wärme / seelenvoll	avec chaleur	1025
herzlich / warmherzig	chaleureusement / chaleureux	1026
treuherzig	candide / candidement	1027
einfältig	avec candeur	1028
gesanglich / gesangvoll	chantant	1029
singend	en chantant	1030
spottend / auslachend	moqueusement / avec dérision	1031
trotzig / eigensinnig / störrisch	têtu / entêté	1032
in launenhafter Weise / launisch	capricieusement / capricieux	1033
mit Charakter	avec caractère	1034
überladen	chargé	1035
reizend	mignon / charmant	1036
keusch / tugendhaft	chaste	1037
ritterlich	chevaleresque	1038
himmlisch	céleste	1039
rufend / anrufend	en appelant / en invoquant	1040
in klarer Weise	clairement	1041
mit Klarheit / mit Deutlichkeit	avec clarté	1042
klar / hell	clair / limpide	1043
motorisch	cinétique / moteur	1044
kokettierend / kokett	en coquettant / coquet	1045
mit Koketterie	avec coquetterie	1046
mit Zorn / mit Entrüstung	avec colère	1047
farbig	coloré / plein de couleur	1048
komisch / ulkig	comique / drôle	1049
gerührt / bewegt	ému	1050
rührend	émouvant / touchant	1051
in bequemer Weise / behaglich	commodément	1052
sich wohl fühlend / bequem	à l'aise	1053
konzentriert	concentré	1054
tröstend	consolant / reconfortant	1055
mit höchster Virtuosität	avec la plus haute virtuosité	1056
beschaulich	contemplatif	1057

1058	convinzione (con)	with conviction
1059	convulso	convulsive
1060	coscienzoso	conscientious
1061	costante / stabile	steady / stable
1062	cristallino	crystalline
1063	cristiano	christian
1064	cullando	rocking
1065	cuore (con)	with heart
1066	cupo / fosco	gloomy / dusky
1067	curioso	curious
1068	danzante / ballabile	in a dance style
1069	debile / debole / fievole	weak / faint
1070	debolezza (con)	with weakness
1071	debolmente	weakly
1072	decisione (con)	decisively
1073	deciso / risoluto	decided / resolute
1074	declamando	declaiming
1075	declamato	declaimed
1076	degno	worthy / dignified
1077	deliberatamente	deliberately
1078	delicatamente	delicately
1079	delicatezza (con)	with delicacy
1080	delicato	delicate / dainty
1081	delirando / vaneggiando	raving
1082	delirante / deliroso	delirious
1083	delirio (con)	with frenzy
1084	delizia (con) / diletto (con)	with delight
1085	deliziosamente	delightfully
1086	demoniaco	demonic
1087	denso / compatto	dense / compact
1088	descrittivo	descriptive
1089	desiderio (con) / vagheggiando	with desire
1090	desolato / sconsolato	desolate / disconsolate
1091	desto / sveglio	awake
1092	destrezza (con) / abilità (con)	with dexterity
1093	determinato	determined
1094	determinazione (con)	with determination
1095	devoto / divoto	devout
1096	dignità (con)	with dignity
1097	diligenza (con)	with diligence

mit Überzeugung	avec conviction / pénétré	1058
zuckend	convulsé	1059
gewissenhaft	concencieux	1060
beständig / stetig	constant / stable	1061
kristallklar	cristallin	1062
christlich	chrétien	1063
wiegend	en berçant	1064
mit Herz	avec cœur	1065
düster / dumpf	sombre / morne	1066
neugierig	curieux	1067
tanzend / tänzerisch	dansant	1068
schwächlich / schwach	faible	1069
mit Schwäche	avec faiblesse	1070
in schwacher Weise	faiblement	1071
mit Entschlossenheit	avec décision	1072
entschlossen / entschieden	décidé	1073
deklamierend	en déclamant	1074
deklamiert	déclamé	1075
würdig / würdevoll	digne / plein de dignité	1076
in entschlossener Weise	délibérément	1077
in zarter Weise	délicatement	1078
mit Zartheit	avec délicatesse	1079
zartfühlend	délicat / mignon	1080
irreredend	en délirant	1081
geistesverwirrt	délirant	1082
im Delirium / in Raserei	avec délire	1083
mit Wonne / mit Ergötzen	avec délice	1084
in entzückender Weise	délicieusement	1085
dämonisch	démoniaque	1086
dicht	dense / compact	1087
beschreibend	descriptif	1088
erwünscht / ersehnt	avec désir	1089
trostlos	désolé	1090
wach / aufgeweckt	éveillé	1091
mit Geschicklichkeit / mit Fertigkeit	avec adresse / avec dextérité	1092
bestimmt	déterminé	1093
mit Bestimmtheit	avec détermination	1094
andächtig	dévot	1095
mit Würde	avec dignité	1096
mit Fleiß	avec diligence	1097

1098	dinamico	dynamic
1099	discrezione (con)	with discretion
1100	disinvolto	unconstrained
1101	disinvoltura (con)	with unconstraint
1102	disordinato / confuso	untidy
1103	disperatamente	desperately
1104	disperato	desperate
1105	disperazione (con)	with despair
1106	disprezzo (con)	with scorn
1107	distante / in lontananza	distant / far away
1108	distinto / distintamente	distinct / distinctly
1109	divagando	wandering
1110	divertimento (con) / piacere (con)	with amusement / with pleasure
1111	doglia (con) / patimento (con)	with pain
1112	dolce	sweet / soft
1113	dolcemente	gently
1114	dolcezza (con)	with softness
1115	dolcissimo	very soft
1116	dolendo / soffrendo	suffering
1117	dolente / doglioso	in pain
1118	dolore (con) / duolo (con)	with pain
1119	doloroso / addolorato	painful / grieved
1120	dondolando	swinging
1121	drammatico	dramatic
1122	durezza (con)	with hardness
1123	duro	hard
1124	ebbrezza (con) / inebriante	with rapture
1125	eccitato / eccitante	excited / exciting
1126	elegantemente	elegantly
1127	eleganza (con)	with elegance
1128	elegiaco	elegiac
1129	elevamento (con) / elevatezza (con) / elevato	with loftiness / elevated
1130	emozione (con)	with emotion
1131	energia (con)	with energy
1132	energico	energetic / forceful
1133	enfasi (con)	with emphasis
1134	enfatico	emphatic

dynamisch	dynamique	1098
mit Diskretion	avec discrétion	1099
unbefangen	désinvolte / d'aplomb	1100
mit Unbefangenheit	avec désinvolture	1101
unordentlich	désordonné	1102
verzweiflungsvoll	désespérément	1103
verzweifelt	désespéré	1104
mit Verzweiflung	avec désespoir	1105
mit Verachtung	avec mépris	1106
entfernt	distant / éloigné	1107
deutlich / in deutlicher Weise	distinct / distinctement	1108
abschweifend	en divaguant	1109
mit Vergnügen	avec amusement / avec plaisir	1110
mit Schmerz	avec douleur	1111
sanft / weich	doux	1112
in sanfter Weise	doucement	1113
mit Sanftheit / mit Sanftmut	avec douceur	1114
sehr sanft	très doux	1115
leidend	en souffrant	1116
schmerzend / peinvoll	douloureusement	1117
mit Schmerz	avec douleur	1118
schmerzlich / schmerzhaft	douloureux	1119
schaukelnd	en balançant	1120
dramatisch	dramatique	1121
mit Härte	avec dureté	1122
hart	dur	1123
berauschend / wie im Rausch	avec ivresse	1124
aufgeregt / aufregend / spannend	excité / exitant	1125
in eleganter Weise	élégamment	1126
mit Eleganz	avec élégance	1127
elegisch	élégiaque	1128
mit Erhabenheit / erhaben	avec élévation / élevé	1129
mit Erregung / mit Gemüts-bewegung	avec émotion	1130
mit Energie / mit Nachdruck	avec énergie	1131
energisch / nachdrücklich / markig	énergique	1132
mit Emphase	avec emphase	1133
emphatisch	emphatique	1134

1135	enigmatico	puzzling
1136	entusiasmo (con) / trasporto (con)	with enthusiasm
1137	epico	epic
1138	eroico / glorioso	heroic / glorious
1139	erotico	erotic
1140	esagerato	exaggerated
1141	esaltante	exalting
1142	esaltato	exalted
1143	esaltazione (con)	with exaltation
1144	esasperato	exasperated
1145	esattezza (con)	with exactitude
1146	esatto / giusto	exact / right
1147	esile / sottile / tenue / fioco	slender
1148	espansione (con)	with expansion
1149	espressione (con)	with expression
1150	espressivo	expressive
1151	estasi (con)	with ecstasy
1152	estatico	ecstatic
1153	estro (con)	with brightness
1154	estroso / ghiribizzoso	whimsical
1155	esultante / giubilante	exultant / jubilant
1156	esultanza (con) / esultazione (con)	with exultation
1157	etereo	ethereal
1158	facezia (con) / celia (con)	with jest
1159	facilmente	easily
1160	falso / traditore / perfido	false / treacherous
1161	fanatico	fanatic
1162	fantasia (con)	with fantasy
1163	fantasioso	fanciful
1164	fantastico	fantastic
1165	farsesco	farcical
1166	fascino (con)	with charm
1167	fastoso	sumptuous / costly
1168	fatica (con) / faticoso	with effort / tiring
1169	febbrile	feverish
1170	fermamente	firmly
1171	fermezza (con)	with firmness
1172	fermo	firm

rätselhaft	énigmatique	1135
mit Begeisterung / mit Überschwang	avec enthousiasme / avec transport	1136
episch	épique	1137
heroisch / glorreich	héroïque / glorieux	1138
erotisch	érotique	1139
übertrieben	exagéré	1140
schwärmerisch	exaltant	1141
überschwänglich / überspannt	exalté	1142
mit Überschwänglichkeit	avec exaltation	1143
aufgebracht	exaspéré	1144
mit Genauigkeit	avec exactitude	1145
genau / richtig	exact / juste	1146
schmächtig	grêle / mince / fluet / effilé	1147
mit Ausdehnung	avec expansion	1148
mit Ausdruck	avec expression	1149
ausdrucksvoll	expressif	1150
mit Verzückung / mit Ekstase	avec extase	1151
ekstatisch	extatique	1152
einer Eingebung folgend	avec inspiration	1153
schrullig / wunderlich	fantasque	1154
frohlockend	en exultant	1155
mit Jubel / mit Frohlocken	en jubilant	1156
ätherisch	éthéré	1157
mit Spaß	avec facétie	1158
in leichter Weise	facilement	1159
verräterisch / falsch / heimtückisch	faux / traître / perfide	1160
fanatisch	fanatique	1161
mit Phantasie	avec fantaisie	1162
schwärmerisch	fantasque	1163
phantastisch	fantastique	1164
possenhaft	farceur	1165
mit Zauber	avec charme	1166
prächtig / prachtvoll	fastueux / somptueux	1167
mit Mühe / mühsam	avec peine / avec fatigue	1168
fieberhaft	fébrile	1169
entschieden	fermement	1170
mit Festigkeit	avec fermeté	1171
standhaft	ferme	1172

1173	feroce	ferocious / fierce
1174	ferocia (con)	with ferocity
1175	fervido	fervid
1176	fervore (con)	with fervour
1177	festeggiante	rejoicing
1178	festivo / festoso	festive
1179	fiducia (con) / fede (con)	with confidence / with trust
1180	fieramente	proudly
1181	fierezza (con)	with pride
1182	filando	spinning
1183	fine / fino	fine
1184	finezza (con)	with fineness
1185	fioreggiando / fiorettando	embellishing / decorating
1186	flebile	plaintive
1187	flessibilità (con)	with flexibility
1188	fluidezza (con) / fluidità	with fluency
1189	fluido / fluente	fluent
1190	focoso / fuocoso	fiery
1191	folleggiando	frolicsome
1192	follemente / folle / insano	madly / mad / foolish
1193	forza (con)	with force
1194	fragile	fragile
1195	fragoroso / strepitoso	roaring
1196	francamente	frankly
1197	franchezza (con)	with frankness
1198	freddamente	coldly
1199	freddezza (con)	with coldness
1200	freddo	cold
1201	fremebondo / fremente	quivering
1202	fremito (con)	with thrill
1203	frenetico / frenesia (con)	frantic / frenzied
1204	freschezza (con)	with freshness
1205	fresco	fresh
1206	frivolo / futile	frivolous / trifling
1207	frizzante / spumeggiante	sparkling
1208	frusciando	rustling
1209	frustato	whipped
1210	fugace / sfuggevole	fleeting
1211	fulgido / splendido	resplendent / splendid
1212	fulminante / folgorante	fulminating

wild	féroce	1173
mit Wildheit	avec férocité	1174
inbrünstig	fervent	1175
mit Inbrunst	avec ferveur	1176
feiernd	joyeusement	1177
festlich	air de fête	1178
mit Vertrauen	avec confiance	1179
in stolzer Weise	fièrement	1180
mit Stolz	avec fierté / avec panache	1181
spinnend	en filant	1182
fein	fin	1183
mit Feinheit	avec finesse	1184
verzierend	en fleurissant	1185
kläglich / wehmütig	plaintif	1186
mit Flexibilität	avec flexibilité	1187
in fließender Weise	avec fluidité	1188
fließend	fluide	1189
feurig	fougeux	1190
in närrischer Weise	en folâtrant	1191
närrisch / wahnsinnig	follement / fou	1192
mit Kraft	avec force	1193
zerbrechlich	fragile	1194
tosend / polternd	retentissant / éclatant	1195
freimütig	franchement	1196
mit Freimut	avec franchise	1197
kühl	froidement	1198
mit Kälte	avec froideur	1199
kalt	froid	1200
bebend / schnaubend	frémissant	1201
mit Beben / mit Schaudern	avec frémissements	1202
tobend / mit Raserei	frénétique / avec frénésie	1203
mit Frische	avec fraîcheur	1204
frisch	frais	1205
leichtfertig / nichtig	frivole	1206
prickelnd / schäumend	pétillant	1207
raschelnd	en froufroutant	1208
gepeitscht	fouetté	1209
flüchtig	fugace / fuyant	1210
glänzend	resplendissant / splendide	1211
blitzend	fulminant / fulgurant	1212

1213	funebre / funereo	mournful / funereal
1214	fuoco (con)	with fire
1215	furbescamente / furbo	cunning / artful
1216	furente / furioso / furibondo	furious
1217	furia (con) / furore (con)	with fury
1218	fuso / omogeneo	melted / homogeneous
1219	gagliardo	vigorous
1220	gaiamente	gaily
1221	gaiezza (con)	with gaiety
1222	gaio	gay
1223	galante	gallant
1224	galanteria (con)	with gallantry
1225	galleggiante	floating
1226	gaudio (con) / godimento (con)	with happiness
1227	gelido	icy / freezing
1228	gemebondo / gemendo	moaning
1229	generoso	generous
1230	gentilezza (con) / compiacenza (con)	with kindness
1231	gentilmente / compiacente / compiacevole	kindly
1232	gigantesco / colossale	gigantic
1233	giocondo	playful / jolly
1234	giocoso	playful
1235	gioia (con) / letizia (con)	with joy
1236	gioioso	joyful
1237	gioviale	jovial
1238	giubilo (con) / giubilante	with jubilation / jubilant
1239	goffo / maldestro / impacciato	awkward / clumsy
1240	gracile	frail
1241	gradevole / gradito / aggradevole	agreeable
1242	grandezza (con)	with grandeur
1243	grandioso	grandiose
1244	gravità (con)	with gravity
1245	grazia (con) / vaghezza (con) / grazioso	with grace / graceful
1246	grossolano / rozzo	coarse
1247	grottesco	grotesque
1248	guerresco / guerriero	warlike
1249	gusto (con)	with taste

trauervoll	funèbre	1213
mit Feuer	avec feu	1214
schlau / schalkhaft	avec fourberie / rusé / malin	1215
rasend	furieux / furibond	1216
tobsüchtig	avec fureur / avec emportement	1217
verschmolzen / gleichartig	fondu / homogène	1218
stramm	gaillard	1219
in heiterer Weise	gaîment	1220
mit Heiterkeit	avec gaîté	1221
lustig	gai	1222
galant	galant / galamment	1223
mit Galanterie	avec galanterie	1224
schwimmend	flottant	1225
mit Genuss / mit Hochgenuss	avec bonheur	1226
eisig	glacial / glacé	1227
stöhnend	gémissant	1228
großmütig / großzügig	généreux	1229
mit Liebenswürdigkeit / mit Gefälligkeit	avec gentillesse	1230
gefällig	gentiment / complaisant	1231
riesig / riesenhaft	gigantesque	1232
fröhlich	gai	1233
spielerisch	enjoué	1234
mit Freude / mit Glückseligkeit	avec joie	1235
freudig	joyeux	1236
jovial	jovial	1237
jauchzend / jubelnd	jubilant	1238
plump / linkisch / tölpelhaft	pataud / maladroit	1239
schmächtig	frêle	1240
angenehm	agréable	1241
mit Größe	avec grandeur	1242
großartig	grandiose	1243
mit Ernsthaftigkeit	avec gravité	1244
anmutig / graziös	avec grâce / gracieux / gracieusement	1245
grob / derb	grossier	1246
grotesk	grotesque	1247
kriegerisch	guerrier	1248
mit Geschmack	avec goût	1249

1250	idilliaco	idyllic
1251	immaginazione (con)	with imagination
1252	impaziente	impatient
1253	impazienza (con)	with impatience
1254	imperioso	imperious
1255	impeto (con) / foga (con)	vehemently / with impulsion
1256	impetuoso / tumultuoso	impetuous / tumultuous
1257	implacabile	implacable
1258	implorante	imploring
1259	imponente	impressive
1260	improvvisando	improvising
1261	inafferando / incomprensibile	elusive
1262	incantato	charmed / enchanted
1263	incantevole / incanto (con)	charming / with enchantment
1264	incisivo	incisive
1265	indeciso	undecided
1266	indifferenza (con) / indifferente	with indifference / indifferent
1267	indignato	indignantly
1268	indistinto / indistinguibile	indistinctly
1269	indolenza (con) / indolente	with indolence / indolent
1270	indomito / indomabile / indocile	indomitable
1271	indulgente / clemente	lenient
1272	infantile	childish
1273	infernale / diabolico	infernal / diabolical
1274	infiammato / acceso	inflamed
1275	infocato	burning
1276	infuriato	enraged
1277	ingegnoso	ingenious
1278	ingenuo	ingenuous
1279	innocenza (con)	with innocence
1280	inquietante	disquieting
1281	inquieto / irrequieto	restless
1282	insensibile	insensible
1283	insensibilmente	insensitively
1284	insinuante / subdolo	ingratiating / stealthily
1285	insistenza (con)	with insistence
1286	insolenza (con) / insolente	with insolence
1287	in stile recitativo	recitative-like
1288	intensivo / intenso	intense

idyllisch	idyllique	1250
mit Vorstellungskraft	avec imagination	1251
ungeduldig	impatient	1252
mit Ungeduld	avec impatience	1253
gebieterisch	impérieux / impérieusement	1254
mit Ungestüm / mit Wucht	avec impétuosité / avec fougue	1255
ungestüm / wuchtig	impétueux / emporté / tumultueux	1256
unerbittlich	implacable	1257
erflehend	implorant	1258
eindrucksvoll	imposant	1259
improvisierend	en improvisant	1260
unfassbar / unverständlich	sans comprendre / insaisissable	1261
bezaubert	charmé	1262
zauberhaft / betörend	enchanteur / incantatoire	1263
einschneidend	incisif	1264
unentschlossen / unentschieden	indécis	1265
mit Gleichgültigkeit / gleichgültig	avec indifférence / indifférent	1266
entrüstet	indigné	1267
verschwommen / undeutlich	flou	1268
mit Trägheit / lässig	avec indolence / indolent	1269
zügellos / ungebändigt	indomptable	1270
nachsichtig / gütig	indulgent / clément	1271
kindlich	infantile / enfantin	1272
höllisch / teuflisch	infernal / diabolique	1273
entzündet	enflammé / allumé	1274
glühend / mit Liebesglut	embrasé	1275
rasend	furieux	1276
erfinderisch	ingénieux	1277
naiv / einfältig	ingénu / naïvement / naïf	1278
mit Unschuld	avec innocence	1279
beunruhigend	inquiétant	1280
beunruhigt / mit Unruhe	inquiet / avec inquiétude	1281
empfindungslos	insensible	1282
gefühllos / gemütlos	insensiblement	1283
einschmeichelnd	insinuant / sournois	1284
mit Beharrlichkeit	avec insistance	1285
mit Frechheit	avec insolence	1286
rezitativisch	en style récitatif	1287
intensiv	intensif / intense	1288

1289	intimo / interno	intimate / inward
1290	intrepido / impavido	intrepid
1291	invettivando / insultando	abusive
1292	iracondo / irascibile	irascible
1293	irato / iroso	irritated
1294	ironia (con)	with irony
1295	ironico	ironical
1296	irresoluto / titubante	irresolute
1297	irritante	irritating
1298	irritato	irritated
1299	lacero / squarciato	lacerated / torn
1300	lacrimoso / lagrimoso	tearful
1301	lamentoso / lagnoso	lamenting
1302	languendo / languidamente / languidezza (con)	languishing
1303	languido / illanguidendosi	languid
1304	largamente	broadly
1305	lasso / fiacco	tired / weary
1306	leggerezza (con) / leggermente	lightly / with lightness
1307	leggero / leggiero / lieve	light
1308	lesto / solerte	swift
1309	leziosamente / svenevole	affected
1310	liberamente / licenza (con)	freely
1311	lieto / ilare / giulivo	cheerful / joyous / glad
1312	liquido	liquid
1313	liricamente / lirico	in a lyrical way
1314	liscio / piatto	smooth / even
1315	lucido / lucidamente	lucid
1316	lugubre / tetro / sinistro	gloomy / sinister
1317	luminoso / lucente	bright
1318	lusingando / allettando	alluring
1319	lusingato	flattered
1320	lustro (con)	with lustre
1321	luttuosamente / funesto	mournful
1322	maestoso	majestic
1323	maestria (con)	with skill / mastery
1324	magico	magic
1325	malinconia (con)	with melancholy
1326	malinconico / melanconico	melancholic
1327	malizioso / maligno	malicious
1328	marziale	martial

innerst / innig / innerlich	intime / intérieur	1289
furchtlos	intrépide	1290
schmähend / beleidigend	invectivant / en insultant	1291
jähzornig	coléreux / irascible	1292
zornig	en colère	1293
mit Ironie	avec ironie	1294
ironisch	ironique	1295
unentschlossen / zaudernd	irrésolu / en titubant	1296
aufreizend	irritant	1297
gereizt	irrité	1298
zerrissen	déchiré	1299
tränenvoll	larmoyant	1300
klagend / wehklagend	plaintif / en gémissant	1301
schmachtend / mit Schmelz	languissamment / avec langueur	1302
schmachtend	languissant / languide	1303
ausgedehnt	largement	1304
ermattet / ermüdet	las / lassé	1305
mit Leichtigkeit	avec légèreté / légèrement	1306
leicht / duftig	léger	1307
flink	leste	1308
geziert	avec affectation	1309
in freier Weise / frei im Vortrag	dégagé / librement	1310
fröhlich / vergnügt	joyeux	1311
flüssig	liquide	1312
lyrisch	d'une façon lyrique	1313
glatt / schlicht	lisse / plat	1314
klar	lucide	1315
unheimlich / bedrohlich	lugubre / sinistre	1316
leuchtend / hell	lumineux	1317
schmeichelnd / verlockend	flatteur	1318
geschmeichelt	flatté	1319
mit Glanz	avec lustre	1320
trauernd	douloureusement / funeste	1321
majestätisch	majestueux	1322
mit Meisterschaft	avec maîtrise	1323
magisch	magique	1324
mit Schwermut	avec mélancolie	1325
schwermütig	mélancolique	1326
boshaft / verschmitzt	malicieux / espiègle	1327
kriegerisch	martial	1328

1329	maschio / virile	manly / virile
1330	meccanicamente	mechanically
1331	meditando / meditativo	meditating
1332	melodico	melodic
1333	melodioso	melodious
1334	mestamente	mournfully
1335	mesto / afflitto	afflicted
1336	minacciosamente / minaccioso	threatening / menacing
1337	misteriosamente / misterioso	mysterious
1338	mistico	mystic
1339	mobile / incostante	changeable / movable
1340	moderazione (con) / castigato	with moderation
1341	molle / floscio / mollezza (con)	flabby / with flabbiness
1342	monotono / tedioso	monotonous
1343	morbidezza (con)	limply
1344	mordace / mordente	biting
1345	mormorando / mormorato	murmuring
1346	narrante / narrando	narrating
1347	naturalezza (con)	naturally
1348	nebbioso	foggy / misty
1349	nebuloso	nebulous
1350	negligentemente	negligently
1351	nervosamente	nervously
1352	nettamente	clearly
1353	nobilmente	nobly
1354	nobiltà (con)	with nobility
1355	noncuranza (con)	carelessly
1356	nostalgico	nostalgic / longing
1357	nutrito	nourished
1358	nuziale	nuptial
1359	offeso	offended
1360	ondeggiante / ondulante	undulating / rolling
1361	opaco	opaque / dull
1362	oppresso	oppressed
1363	orgoglioso / fiero	proud
1364	orrendo / orrido / spaventoso	horrifying
1365	osservanza (con) / rispetto (con)	with respect
1366	ostinatezza (con) / ostinazione (con)	obstinately

männlich	viril	1329
mechanisch	mécaniquement	1330
sinnend / nachdenkend	en méditant / méditatif	1331
melodisch	mélodieux	1332
melodiös	mélodieusement	1333
auf betrübte Weise	tristement	1334
niedergeschlagen	affligé / triste / chagrin	1335
drohend	menaçant	1336
geheimnisvoll	mystérieusement / mystérieux	1337
mystisch	mystique	1338
beweglich / unbeständig / wankelmütig	mobile	1339
mit Mäßigung	avec modération	1340
schlaff	mou / flasque / avec mollesse	1341
eintönig / monoton	monotone	1342
weichlich	avec douceur	1343
bissig / spitzig	mordant	1344
murmelnd / gemurmelt / rauschend	en murmurant / en gazouillant	1345
erzählend	en narrant	1346
mit Natürlichkeit	naturellement	1347
neblig / vernebelt	brumeux	1348
nebelhaft / unklar	nébuleux	1349
nachlässig / sorglos	négligemment	1350
nervös / nervig	nerveusement	1351
in klarer Weise	nettement	1352
edel	noblement	1353
mit Adel	avec noblesse	1354
mit Sorglosigkeit	avec nonchalance	1355
nostalgisch	nostalgique	1356
voll / gesättigt	plein / nourri	1357
hochzeitlich	nuptial	1358
beleidigt	offensé	1359
wogend / wallend	en ondoyant / onduleux	1360
undurchsichtig / matt / trüb	opaque	1361
unterdrückt	opprimé / oppressé	1362
stolz	orgueilleux / fier	1363
fürchterlich / entsetzlich	horrible / affreux	1364
mit Hochachtung	avec respect	1365
mit Hartnäckigkeit	avec obstination	1366

1367	ostinato / persistente	obstinate / persistent
1368	pacatamente	peaceably / peaceful
1369	pacato / pacifico	peaceable
1370	pace (con)	with peace
1371	paradisiaco	paradisiac
1372	parlando / dicendo	speaking / saying
1373	passione (con)	with passion
1374	pastorale / bucolico	pastoral
1375	pastoso	mellow
1376	patetico	pathetic
1377	paura (con)	with fear
1378	pauroso / paventato	fearful / timorous
1379	pazzamente / pazzescamente	madly / wantonly
1380	penetrante	penetrating / percing
1381	penoso	painful
1382	pensando	thinking
1383	pensieroso / pensoso	pensive
1384	pensosamente	thoughtful
1385	perseveranza (con) / costanza (con)	with perseverance / with steadfastness
1386	pesante	heavy
1387	pesato / ponderato	weighted
1388	piacevole / ameno / piacevolezza (con)	pleasant / pleasing
1389	piangendo / lacrimando	crying
1390	piangevole / piangente	weeping / weepy
1391	piccante / pungente	sharp / spiky / prikly
1392	pietoso / toccante	pitying / merciful
1393	pigro	lazy
1394	pio	pious
1395	pittoresco	picturesque
1396	placido / mite / mansueto	placid / mild / meek
1397	poetico	poetic
1398	pompa (con)	with pomp
1399	ponderoso	ponderous
1400	portamento (con)	with dignity / bearing
1401	posatamente / posato	calm / sedate / sedately
1402	possente / potente / poderoso	powerful
1403	precisione (con)	with precision
1404	preciso	precise
1405	pregando / invocando	praying / invoking

hartnäckig / eigensinnig	obstiné / persistant	1367
in ruhiger Weise	paisiblement	1368
ruhig / friedlich	paisible	1369
mit Frieden / mit Seelenfrieden	avec paix	1370
paradiesisch	paradisiaque	1371
sprechend / redend	en parlant / en disant	1372
mit Leidenschaft	avec passion	1373
nach Art der Hirten	pastoral	1374
geschmeidig	moelleux	1375
pathetisch	pathétique	1376
angstvoll	avec effroi	1377
ängstlich / furchtsam	peureux / craintif	1378
wahnsinnig / verrückt	follement	1379
durchdringend	pénétrant / perçant	1380
mühselig	pénible	1381
denkend	en réfléchissant	1382
gedankenvoll	pensif	1383
nachdenklich	gravement	1384
mit Ausdauer / mit Beständigkeit	avec persévérance / avec constance	1385
schwer / schwerfällig	pesant / lourd	1386
wohl erwogen / bedächtig	pesé / réfléchi	1387
angenehm / erfreulich	plaisant / avec agrément	1388
weinend	en pleurs	1389
weinerlich	larmoyant	1390
scharf / stechend	piquant / pointu	1391
mitleidig / barmherzig	charitable	1392
träge / behäbig / faul	paresseux	1393
fromm / ergeben	pieux	1394
malerisch	pittoresque	1395
friedlich / sanftmütig / gutmütig	débonnairement / placide	1396
dichterisch	poétique	1397
mit Feierlichkeit / mit Prunk	avec pompe	1398
gewichtig	pondéré	1399
mit Haltung	avec maintien	1400
gesetzt / bedächtig	posément / posé	1401
mächtig / gewaltig	puissant	1402
mit Präzision	avec précision	1403
präzis	précis	1404
betend / anrufend	en priant / en invoquant	1405

1406	profondo	profound / deep
1407	pronunciato / pronunziato	pronounced
1408	provocante	provocative
1409	prudente / cauto	prudent
1410	prudenza (con)	with prudence
1411	purezza (con) / purità (con)	with purity
1412	puritano	puritan
1413	puro / schietto / mero	pure
1414	quasi una fantasia	almost like a fantasy
1415	rabbia (con) / ira (con)	with rage / with wrath
1416	raccapriccio (con) / orrore (con)	with horror
1417	raccoglimento (con)	with devotion
1418	raccolto	thoughtful
1419	raccontando	narrating
1420	radioso / raggiante	radiant / beaming
1421	raffinatezza (con)	with refinement
1422	rallegrato / contento	pleased / delighted
1423	rassegnato	resigned
1424	rassegnazione (con)	with resignation
1425	recitando	reciting
1426	religioso	religious
1427	respirando / aspiratamente	breathing
1428	ribrezzo (con) / disgusto (con)	with disgust
1429	ricercatezza (con)	with refinement
1430	ricercato	exquisite / precious
1431	ricco	rich / wealthy
1432	ricordando / reminiscendo	reminiscing
1433	ridicolo / ridicolosamente	ridiculous
1434	rigidezza (con)	with rigidity
1435	rigido	rigid
1436	rigoglioso / florido	luxuriant / flourishing
1437	rigoroso	rigorous
1438	rilassato	relaxed
1439	rimbombante / rintronante	bombastic / roaring
1440	rimpianto (con)	with regret
1441	risentimento (con) / risentito	with resentment / resentful
1442	risolutezza (con) / risoluzione (con)	with resolution
1443	risonante / echeggiante	resonant / resoundig
1444	rispetto (con) / deferente	with respect / respectful

tief / tiefgründig	profond	1406
deutlich ausgesprochen	prononcé	1407
herausfordernd	provocant	1408
vorsichtig	prudent	1409
mit Vorsicht	avec prudence	1410
mit Reinheit	avec pureté	1411
puritanisch	puritain	1412
rein / echt	pur	1413
fast wie eine Fantasie	presque comme une fantaisie	1414
mit Wut	avec rage	1415
mit Schaudern	avec horreur	1416
mit Andacht	avec recueillement	1417
gesammelt / andächtig	recueilli	1418
erzählend	en racontant	1419
strahlend	radieux	1420
mit Raffinesse	avec raffinement	1421
erfreut	réjoui	1422
resigniert	résigné	1423
mit Ergebung	avec résignation	1424
rezitierend / vortragend	en récitant / en récit	1425
religiös	religieux	1426
atmend	en respirant	1427
mit Abscheu	avec dégoût	1428
mit Geziertheit	avec recherche / avec préciosité	1429
gesucht	recherché	1430
reich	riche	1431
sich erinnernd	en se souvenant	1432
lächerlich	ridicule	1433
mit Steifheit / mit Strenge	avec raideur	1434
steif / starr	raide / rigide	1435
üppig / blühend	exubérant / florissant	1436
streng	rigoureux	1437
entspannt / gelassen	détendu / décontracté	1438
dröhnend	retentissant / résonnant	1439
mit Bedauern	avec regret	1440
mit Groll	avec rancune / avec ressentiment	1441
mit Entschlossenheit	avec résolution	1442
schallend / widerhallend	résonnant	1443
mit Respekt / ehrerbietig	avec respect / avec déférence	1444

1445	riverente	reverent
1446	romantico	romantic
1447	rotondo / tondo	round
1448	rumoroso / rumorosamente	noisy / noisily
1449	rusticano / rustico / villanesco	rustic
1450	ruvido / rude / grezzo	rough
1451	saggiamente	wisely / sagely
1452	salmeggiando	psalmodic
1453	saltellando	hopping
1454	sarcastico	sarcastic
1455	scatenato	unrestrained
1456	scattante	darting
1457	scherno (con)	with mockery
1458	scherzando / scherzoso	jesting
1459	sciolto	free and easy
1460	scoppiante / crepitante	bursting / crackling
1461	scoramento (con) / avvilito	with discouragement
1462	scorrevole / scorrendo	flowing
1463	scrupoloso / minuzioso / meticoloso	scrupulous / meticulous / painstaking
1464	sdegno (con) / sdegnoso / disdegnoso	with disdain / disdainful
1465	secco	dry
1466	seducente	seductive
1467	selvaggio	wild
1468	semplice / scarno	simple
1469	semplicemente	simply
1470	semplicità (con)	with simplicity
1471	sensibilità (con)	with sensitivity
1472	sensibilmente	sensitively
1473	sensuale	sensual
1474	sentimentale	sentimental
1475	sentimento (con)	with feeling
1476	sentito	heart-felt
1477	senza colore / stinto	without colour
1478	senza sforzo	effortless
1479	serafico	seraphic
1480	serenità (con)	with serenity
1481	sereno	serene
1482	serietà (con)	with seriousness
1483	serio / grave / serioso	serious

ehrfurchtsvoll	révérenciel	1445
romantisch	romantique	1446
rund / voll	rond	1447
lärmend / geräuschvoll	bruyant / bruyamment	1448
ländlich	rustique	1449
grob / rau	rugueux / rude	1450
in besonnener Weise	sagement	1451
psalmodierend	en psalmodiant	1452
hüpfend	en sautillant	1453
sarkastisch	sarcastique	1454
entfesselt	déchaîné	1455
losschnellend	bondissant	1456
mit Hohn	avec moquerie	1457
scherzend / neckisch	en badinant / en plaisantant	1458
ungebunden	délié	1459
berstend	éclatant / crépitant	1460
mit Niedergeschlagenheit	avec accablement	1461
dahinfließend	coulant / coulamment	1462
peinlich genau / minuziös	scrupuleux / méticuleux	1463
verächtlich / mit Gering-schätzung	avec dédain / dédaigneux	1464
trocken	sec	1465
verführerisch	séduisant	1466
wild	sauvage	1467
einfach	simple / dépouillé	1468
in einfacher Weise	simplement	1469
mit Einfachheit	avec simplicité	1470
mit Empfindsamkeit	avec sensibilité	1471
empfindlich	sensiblement	1472
sinnlich	sensuel	1473
sentimental	sentimental	1474
mit Empfindung / mit Gefühl	avec sentiment	1475
tief empfunden	ressenti	1476
farblos	sans couleur	1477
ohne Anstrengung	sans effort	1478
engelhaft	séraphique	1479
mit heiterer Gelassenheit	avec sérénité	1480
heiter	serein	1481
mit Ernsthaftigkeit	avec gravité	1482
ernst / würdevoll	sérieux / grave	1483

1484	severità (con)	with severity
1485	severo	severe
1486	sfacciato	cheeky
1487	sfarzo (con)	with splendor
1488	sfarzoso / pomposo	pompous
1489	sfavillante / scintillante	sparkling / scintilleting
1490	sfidando	defiant
1491	sfoggiando / ostentativo	showing off
1492	sfolgorante / splendente	resplendent
1493	sfrenato	unbridled / wantonly
1494	sfrontato / impertinente	impertinent / impudent
1495	sfumato / sfumando	shaded
1496	sgomento (con)	with dismay
1497	sibillino / enigmatico	mysterious
1498	sicurezza (con)	with selfconfidence
1499	silenzioso	silent
1500	sincero	sincere
1501	slancio (con)	with verve / with dash
1502	smania (con)	with restlessness
1503	smanioso	restless
1504	soave	suave
1505	sobrietà (con)	with sobriety
1506	sobrio / castigato	sober
1507	sognante / trasognato	dreaming
1508	solenne	solemn
1509	solennità (con)	with solemnity
1510	sommesso / sottomesso	submissive
1511	sonoro	sonorous
1512	sorvolando	flying above
1513	sospirando	sighing
1514	spassionato	dispassionate
1515	spazioso / ampio	spacious
1516	spensierato	without sorrow
1517	spettrale	ghastly / ghostly
1518	spianato	smooth / even
1519	spiccatamente	standing out
1520	spiegato	spread out
1521	spigliatezza (con)	with ease
1522	spigliato / disinvolto	free and easy / confident
1523	spirito (con)	with spirit

mit Strenge	avec sévérité	1484
streng	sévère	1485
frech / unverschämt	effronté	1486
mit Prunk	avec faste	1487
prunkvoll	fastueux / pompeux	1488
funkelnd / glitzernd	étincelant	1489
herausfordernd	avec défi	1490
prahlerisch	ostentatoire	1491
blendend	éblouissant	1492
zügellos / unbändig	effréné	1493
dreist / vorlaut	impertinent / impudent	1494
schattiert / verhaucht	estompé / en estompant	1495
bestürzt	avec désarroi	1496
geheimnisvoll / rätselhaft	sybillin	1497
mit Sicherheit	avec sûreté	1498
still	silencieux	1499
aufrichtig	sincère	1500
mit Schwung / mit Aufschwung	avec élan / envolé / avec essor	1501
mit Rastlosigkeit	avec frénésie	1502
rastlos	agité	1503
lieblich	suave	1504
mit Zurückhaltung	avec sobriété	1505
enthaltsam	sobre	1506
träumend / träumerisch / verträumt	en rêvant / rêveur	1507
feierlich	solennel	1508
mit Feierlichkeit	avec solennité	1509
unterwürfig	soumis	1510
klangvoll	sonore	1511
überfliegend	en survolant	1512
seufzend	en soupirant	1513
leidenschaftslos	sans passion	1514
geräumig	spacieux	1515
leichtsinnig / unbekümmert	sans soucis	1516
gespenstisch / geisterhaft	spectral	1517
geebnet / ungekünstelt	aplani	1518
in hervorstechender Weise	de façon saillante	1519
entfaltet	déployé	1520
mit Ungezwungenheit	avec aisance	1521
ungezwungen / keck	alerte / dégagé	1522
geistreich	avec esprit	1523

1524	spiritoso / spirituoso	spirited / witty
1525	spirituale	spiritual
1526	spontaneo	spontaneous
1527	squillante / argentino	ringing / piercing
1528	stanchezza (con) / stanco	with weariness / tired
1529	stentato / penosamente	arduous
1530	steso / disteso / esteso	stretched
1531	strano / strambo	odd / strange
1532	stravagante	extravagant
1533	straziante / lancinante	heart-breaking
1534	strepito (con)	with noise / with din
1535	stridente	screaching
1536	stridulo	shrill
1537	stupore (con) / meraviglia (con)	with amazement
1538	sublime	sublime
1539	sufficienza (con) / sussiego (con)	with conceit
1540	supplicando / implorando	pleadingly / imploring
1541	tempestosamente / tempestoso	tempestuous
1542	temporalesco / burrascoso	thundery / stormy
1543	tenace	tenacious
1544	tenebroso / scuro / oscuro	dark
1545	teneramente	tenderly
1546	tenerezza (con)	with tenderness
1547	tenero / morbido	tender / silky
1548	tepido / tiepido	tepid / lukewarm
1549	terribile / atroce	terrible / dreadful
1550	teso	tense
1551	tiepidamente	tepidly / lukewarmly
1552	tiepidezza (con) / distacco (con)	with tepidness / with detachment
1553	timidamente	timidly
1554	timidezza (con)	with timidity
1555	timore (con)	with dread
1556	timorosamente	timorously
1557	tintinnando	tinkling
1558	tonando / tuonando / tonante	thundering
1559	tormentato	tormented
1560	tormentoso	tormenting
1561	torvo / bieco / losco	grim / shifty
1562	tragico	tragic

geistreich / geistvoll / witzig	spirituel	1524
geistlich	spirituel	1525
spontan	spontané	1526
schallend / durchdringend	retentissant / comme une sonnerie	1527
mit Müdigkeit / müde	avec lassitude / fatigué	1528
mühevoll	laborieux / péniblement	1529
ausgedehnt / gedehnt	étendu	1530
seltsam	étrange	1531
extravagant	extravagant	1532
herzzerreißend / ergreifend	déchirant / poignant	1533
mit Lärm	avec fracas	1534
kreischend	strident	1535
schrill	perçant	1536
mit Staunen	avec stupeur	1537
erhaben	sublime	1538
mit Selbstgefälligkeit	avec suffisance	1539
flehend / anflehend	en suppliant / suppliant	1540
stürmisch	orageusement	1541
gewitterhaft	orageux / tempétueux	1542
hartnäckig / zäh	tenace	1543
finster / dunkel	ténébreux / obscur	1544
zärtlich	tendrement	1545
mit Zärtlichkeit	avec tendresse	1546
zart	tendre / soyeux	1547
lau	tiède	1548
schrecklich / entsetzlich	terrible / épouvantable	1549
straff / gespannt	tendu	1550
lau / leidenschaftslos	tièdement	1551
mit Leidenschaftslosigkeit / mit Lauheit	avec tièdeur / détaché	1552
schüchtern	timidement	1553
mit Schüchternheit	avec timidité	1554
mit Furcht	avec crainte	1555
furchtsam	craintivement	1556
klingelnd	en tintinnabulant	1557
donnernd / dröhnend	en tonnant / tonnant	1558
gequält	tourmenté	1559
qualvoll	torturant	1560
grimmig / verdächtig	torve / louche	1561
tragisch	tragique	1562

1563	tragicomico	tragi-comic
1564	tranquillità (con)	with calmness
1565	tranquillamente / tranquillo	quietly
1566	trasfigurato / trasmutato	transfigured
1567	trasparente / diafano	transparent
1568	tramando	conspiring
1569	tremando	trembling
1570	tremendo	tremendous
1571	trionfante	triumphant
1572	triste / contristato	sad
1573	tristemente	sadly
1574	tristezza (con) / mestizia (con)	with sadness
1575	turbato	disturbed / distracted
1576	umile / modestamente	humble / modest
1577	umore (con)	with humour
1578	umoristico	humorous
1579	uniforme	uniform / equable
1580	urlando / gridando	shouting / screaming
1581	vagamente / vago	vague
1582	valore (con)	with valour
1583	valoroso / valente	valorous
1584	vaporoso / evanescente	vaporous
1585	veemente / irruente	vehement
1586	veemenza (con)	with vehemence
1587	vellutato	velvety
1588	venerazione (con)	with veneration
1589	venusto / vezzoso	pretty
1590	vezzeggiando	fondling
1591	vibrando / vibrante	vibrant
1592	vigore (con)	with vigour
1593	vigoroso / robusto	vigorous
1594	violento / prepotente	violent / overbearing
1595	violenza (con)	with violence
1596	virtuosità (con) / virtuoso	with virtuosity / virtuoso
1597	vispo	brisk
1598	vistoso / sgargiante	showy
1599	vittorioso / vincitore	victorious
1600	vivacità (con) / vivezza (con)	with liveliness / with animation
1601	vivido / esuberante	vivid
1602	vivo / vivente	alive / lively

tragikomisch	tragi-comique	1563
mit Ruhe	avec tranquillité	1564
ruhig / ruhevoll	tranquillement / tranquille	1565
verändert / verklärt	transfiguré	1566
durchsichtig	transparent	1567
verschwörerisch	en conspirant	1568
zitternd	tremblant	1569
furchtbar	effrayant	1570
triumphierend	triomphal	1571
traurig	triste	1572
in trauriger Weise	tristement	1573
mit Traurigkeit	avec tristesse	1574
verstört / verwirrt	troublé	1575
demütig / dürftig / bescheiden	humble / modestement	1576
mit Humor	avec humour	1577
humoristisch	humoristique	1578
gleichmäßig / einheitlich	uniforme	1579
schreiend / aufschreiend	en hurlant / en criant	1580
unbestimmt	vaguement / vague	1581
mit Tapferkeit / mit Bedeutung	avec vaillance	1582
tapfer	vaillant / valeureux	1583
dunstig	vaporeux	1584
heftig	véhément / emporté	1585
mit Heftigkeit / mit Vehemenz	avec véhémence	1586
samtartig	velouté	1587
mit Verehrung	avec vénération	1588
reizvoll / hübsch / hold	joli	1589
hätschelnd	en cajolant	1590
vibrierend	en vibrant / vibrant	1591
mit Lebenskraft	avec vigueur	1592
kräftig / kraftvoll	vigoureux / robuste	1593
gewaltsam / anmaßend	violent	1594
mit Gewalt	avec violence	1595
mit Virtuosität / virtuos	avec virtuosité / virtuose	1596
voll Lebendigkeit	plein de vivacité	1597
auffallend	voyant	1598
siegreich	victorieux	1599
mit Lebhaftigkeit	avec vivacité / avec entrain	1600
sehr lebhaft / überschwänglich	exubérant	1601
lebendig	vif / vivant	1602

1603	voglia (con) / desio (con)	with desire / wishful
1604	volando / volante / volteggiando	flying / flying away
1605	volontà (con) / volenteroso	with will / willing
1606	volubile / incostante	fickle
1607	volubilità (con)	with fickleness
1608	voluttuoso	voluptuous
1609	zelo (con) / zelante	with zeal / zealous

Diversi	**Miscellany**

1610	abbastanza / assai	enough / quite
1611	ab initio (L) / ab inizio	from the beginning
1612	a cappella	unaccompanied vocal music
1613	accanto	beside
1614	accompagnando	accompanying
1615	acuto	shrill
1616	a due	in two
1617	a due volte / due volte	twice
1618	a fior di labbro	on the tip of the tongue
1619	al fine	to the end
1620	all'improvvista	improvised
1621	all'ottava	at the octave
1622	alla breve	minim beat
1623	alla coda	to the coda / to the final part
1624	alla meglio	as well as possible
1625	alquanto	some / rather
1626	al rigore di tempo	strictly in time
1627	al segno	to the sign
1628	al suo posto	on his place
1629	al tempo precedente	at the preceding pace
1630	allargato	broadened
1631	alternando	alternating / alternatively
1632	alternato	alternate
1633	altrimenti	otherwise
1634	altro	other
1635	anche	too / also

mit Lust / wünschend	avec envie / avec désir	1603
fliegend	en volant / volant	1604
mit Willen / willig	avec volonté / de bonne volonté	1605
unbeständig / flatterhaft	volage	1606
mit Unbeständigkeit	avec volubilité	1607
wollüstig	voluptueux	1608
mit Eifer / eifrig	avec zèle / zélé	1609

Verschiedenes   **Divers**

genug / genügend / ziemlich	assez / suffisamment	1610
von Anfang an	du début	1611
ohne Instrumente	sans instruments / style de chapelle	1612
neben	à côté	1613
begleitend	en accompagnant	1614
scharf	aigu	1615
in zwei Zählzeiten / zu zweit	à deux	1616
zweimal	deux fois	1617
fast unvernehmlich	du bout des lèvres	1618
bis zum Ende	à la fin	1619
unvorbereitet / improvisiert	improvisé	1620
in der Oktave	à l'octave	1621
in halben Noten	à la blanche	1622
zum Anhang / bis zum Schluss-teil	à la partie finale	1623
so gut es geht	le mieux possible	1624
etwas / ziemlich	quelque peu	1625
streng im Takt	rigoureusement en mesure	1626
bis zum Zeichen	au signe	1627
an seiner Stelle	à sa place	1628
ins vorige Zeitmaß zurück-kehrend	au mouvement précédent	1629
verbreitert	élargi	1630
abwechselnd / alternierend	en alternant	1631
abgewechselt	alterné	1632
sonst / anderenfalls	autrement	1633
anderer	autre	1634
auch	aussi	1635

1636	ancora	still / again
1637	ancora una volta	once again
1638	aperto / sfogato	open
1639	appena	scarcely
1640	approssimativo	approximately
1641	appuntino	done neatly
1642	assolutamente	absolutely / continuously
1643	assoluto	absolute
1644	assordante	ear-deafening
1645	attacca	"attack!" / begin / go on
1646	attacca subito	immediate attack
1647	bastante / sufficiente	sufficient
1648	ben / bene	well
1649	bicordo	bichord
1650	breve / corto	short / brief
1651	cadenzale / cadenzante	cadential / cadencing
1652	cambiando / cangiando / mutando	changing
1653	che	that / who / which / what
1654	circa	about
1655	coda f	"tail" / final part
1656	coinvolto	involved
1657	colla voce / con la voce	with the voice
1658	colpo m	stroke
1659	come	as / how / like
1660	come al principio	as the beginning
1661	come prima / di sopra	as before
1662	come sopra	as above
1663	come stà	as it is
1664	come una cadenza	like a cadenza
1665	cominciando	beginning
1666	con / col / colla / coi / colle	with / with the
1667	con un dito	with one finger
1668	concertante	concertante
1669	conciso / stringato	concise
1670	contano	count
1671	continua	go on
1672	continuo / continuamente	continuous

noch / wieder	encore	1636
noch einmal	encore une fois	1637
offen	ouvert	1638
kaum / knapp	à peine	1639
annähernd	approximatif	1640
ganz richtig / genau	bien comme il faut	1641
durchaus / unbedingt	absolument	1642
absolut	absolu	1643
ohrenbetäubend	assourdissant	1644
„falle ein" / beginne	attaque / commence	1645
anknüpfen / unmittelbar anschließen	enchaîner	1646
genügend	suffisant	1647
gut	bien	1648
Doppelgriff	à doubles cordes	1649
kurz	bref / court	1650
kadenzierend	cadentiel	1651
wechselnd	en changeant	1652
welcher / welche / welches	que	1653
ungefähr	environ	1654
„Schwanz" *m* / Anhang *m* / Schlussteil *m*	„queue" *f* / partie finale *f*	1655
einbezogen / verwickelt in etwas	engagé	1656
mit der Stimme	avec la voix	1657
Schlag *m* / Stoß *m*	coup *m*	1658
wie / wie bei	comme	1659
wie anfangs / wie beim Eingang	comme au début	1660
wie vorher / wie früher	comme avant	1661
wie oben	comme plus haut	1662
wie es dasteht	tel quel	1663
wie eine Kadenz	comme une cadence	1664
anfangend	en commençant	1665
mit / mit dem / - der / - den	avec / avec le / - la / - les	1666
mit einem Finger	avec un doigt	1667
konzertierend / konzertant	concertant	1668
bündig / knapp	concis	1669
zählen Sie (bei Pausen)	comptez	1670
setzen Sie fort	continuez	1671
ununterbrochen / durchgehend	continu / continuellement	1672

1673	contro	against
1674	da	from
1675	da capo / daccapo / dal principio	from the beginning
1676	da capo al fine	from the beginning to the end
1677	da capo al segno	from the beginning to the sign
1678	dal principio alla fine	throughout
1679	dal segno	from the sign
1680	dal segno al fine	from the sign to the end
1681	dappertutto	everywhere
1682	da qui	from here
1683	davanti	in front
1684	dietro / indietro	back / backwards
1685	di colpo / repente	sudden
1686	di nuovo	once more / again
1687	diritto / retto	right / straight
1688	diverso	different
1689	divisi / diviso	divided
1690	dopo / poi	after / afterwards
1691	doppio	double
1692	durante	during
1693	eccessivamente	excessively
1694	eccetto	except
1695	eccezione *f*	exception
1696	enormemente	enormously
1697	equabilmente	equitably
1698	estremamente	extremely
1699	facoltativo	optional
1700	fate vibrare / lasciate vibrare	make vibrate
1701	fine *f*	end
1702	finito	finished
1703	fino al / sino al	up to / to the / until
1704	fino al segno	up to the sign
1705	già	already
1706	giustamente	suitably
1707	gli altri	the others
1708	gli stessi	the same
1709	gradatamente / gradualmente	gradually
1710	gran / grande	great / much / big

gegen	contre	1673
von	depuis	1674
von vorne / von Anfang an	du début	1675
wieder von Anfang an bis zum Schluss	du début à la fin	1676
wieder von Anfang an bis zum Zeichen	du début au signe	1677
durchweg	du début à la fin	1678
vom Zeichen	du signe	1679
vom Zeichen bis zum Schluss	du signe à la fin	1680
überall	partout	1681
von hier ab	depuis ici	1682
vorne / davor	devant	1683
hinten / zurück / rückwärts	derrière / en arrière	1684
plötzlich	tout à coup	1685
nochmals / von neuem	à nouveau	1686
gerade	droit	1687
verschieden	différent	1688
geteilt	divisé	1689
dann / anschließend / nach	après / ensuite	1690
doppelt	double	1691
während	durant / pendant	1692
übermäßig	excessivement	1693
ausgenommen	excepté	1694
Ausnahme f	exception f	1695
in enormer Weise	énormément	1696
in gleichförmiger Weise / auf dieselbe Art	équitablement	1697
äußerst	extrèmement	1698
wahlfrei / beliebig	facultatif	1699
vibrieren lassen / klingen lassen	laissez vibrer	1700
Schluss m	fin f	1701
beendet	terminé	1702
bis zu / bis zum	jusqu'au	1703
bis zum Zeichen	jusqu'au signe	1704
schon / bereits	déjà	1705
angemessen	justement	1706
die Übrigen	les autres	1707
dieselben	les mêmes	1708
stufenweise	graduellement	1709
groß / viel	grand	1710

1711	il più …	the most …
1712	il più possibile	as much as possible
1713	imitando	imitating
1714	immutato / inalterato	unchanged
1715	improvvisamente / improvviso	suddenly
1716	in fuori / in evidenza	bring out / bring forward
1717	in giù / giù	below
1718	in luogo di	in place of
1719	in mancanza di	in the absence of
1720	in maniera / in modo	in a … way / in a … manner
1721	in nessun caso	in no case
1722	in primo piano	in the foreground
1723	in rilievo / prominente	pointed out
1724	in risalto	to emphasize
1725	insieme / assieme	together
1726	in su	above
1727	lasciar vibrare	let sound / let vibrate
1728	levate i sordini	remove the mutes
1729	loco (L) / al luogo	sounding as written
1730	lungo / a lungo	long
1731	luogo *m* / posto *m*	place
1732	ma	but
1733	ma non tanto / ma non troppo	but not too much
1734	massimo	greatest
1735	medesimo / stesso / istesso	same / the same
1736	meno	less
1737	metà *f*	half
1738	mezzo / mezza	half
1739	mezza forza	half strength
1740	minimo	minimum
1741	misto	mixed
1742	misurato	measured
1743	moltissimo	very much
1744	molto / di molto / assai	much / very
1745	moto *m* / movimento *m*	motion
1746	multiplo	multiple
1747	muta / cambia	change
1748	nascosto	hidden
1749	nel / nella	in the

das meiste / äußerst …	le plus …	1711
so viel wie möglich	le plus possible	1712
nachahmend	en imitant	1713
unverändert	inchangé	1714
plötzlich	soudain	1715
außerhalb / hervortretend / hervor	en dehors / en évidence	1716
nach unten / abwärts / unten	en bas	1717
an Stelle von	au lieu de	1718
in Ermangelung von	à défaut de	1719
in … Weise	de façon / de manière	1720
keinesfalls / in keinem Fall	en aucun cas	1721
im Vordergrund	au premier plan	1722
hervorgehoben	en valeur / relevé / en relief	1723
hervorbringen / hervorstechend	mettre en valeur	1724
zusammen	ensemble	1725
aufwärts / nach oben / oben	en haut	1726
klingen lassen	laisser vibrer / résonner	1727
Dämpfer abnehmen	enlever la sourdine	1728
an seinem Platz (Oktavierung aufgehoben)	à sa place	1729
lang / in langer Weise	long / longuement	1730
Stelle f / Ort m	endroit m / lieu m	1731
aber / jedoch	mais	1732
aber nicht zu sehr	mais pas trop	1733
(der) größte	maximum	1734
derselbe / dieselbe / dasselbe	la même chose / même (le)	1735
weniger	moins	1736
Hälfte f	moitié f	1737
halb	demi / demie	1738
halbe Kraft	demi force	1739
(der) kleinste	minimum	1740
gemischt	mélangé / mixte	1741
gemessen	mesuré	1742
sehr viel	énormément	1743
viel / sehr / gar	très / beaucoup	1744
Bewegung f	mouvement m	1745
vielfach	multiple	1746
verändere	change	1747
verborgen / versteckt	caché	1748
im / in	dans le / dans la	1749

1750	nello (allo) stesso modo	in the same way
1751	nessuno	no one / nobody
1752	niente / nulla	nothing / not at all
1753	non	not
1754	non molto	not much / not very
1755	non tanto	not very / not so
1756	non tenuto	not held
1757	non troppo	not too much
1758	obbligato / obbligatorio	obligatory / compulsory
1759	ogni / ciascuno	every / each
1760	ogni volta	every time
1761	omesso	omitted
1762	ordinario / usuale	ordinary
1763	ossia / oppure / ovvero	otherwise / or / else
1764	per	for / to
1765	per finire	to end / in order to finish
1766	per l'ultima volta	for the last time
1767	per tutta la durata	for the whole length
1768	però	however
1769	pieno	full
1770	più / di più	more
1771	più che / più del	more then
1772	piuttosto	rather
1773	poco / scarso / piccolo	little / few / small
1774	poco a poco	little by little
1775	poco a poco meno	gradually less
1776	poco a poco più	gradually more
1777	poco meno	a little less
1778	poco più	a little more
1779	poi segue	then follows
1780	possibile	(as) possible
1781	possibilmente	if possible
1782	precedente / anteriore	preceding
1783	prima	before
1784	prima che / prima di	before
1785	prossimo	next
1786	qua / qui	here
1787	qualche / alcune	some
1788	quanto	as much as
1789	quasi	almost /nearly / as if

auf dieselbe Art	de la même façon	1750
niemand / kein	personne / aucun	1751
nichts / gar nichts	rien / du tout	1752
nicht	ne....pas	1753
nicht viel / nicht sehr	pas beaucoup	1754
nicht zu sehr	pas trop	1755
nicht gehalten	non tenu	1756
nicht zu viel	pas trop	1757
obligat / verpflichtend / bindend	obligé / obligatoire	1758
jede / jeder / jedes	chaque / chacun	1759
jedes Mal	chaque fois	1760
unterlassen	omis	1761
gewöhnlich / üblich	habituel	1762
oder / oder auch	ou bien	1763
für / durch	pour	1764
zum Schluss	pour finir	1765
zum letzten Mal	pour la dernière fois	1766
für die ganze Dauer	pendant toute la durée	1767
dennoch / jedoch	pourtant	1768
mit vollem Ton / voll	plein	1769
mehr	plus / davantage	1770
mehr als	plus que / plus du	1771
eher / lieber	plutôt	1772
wenig / knapp / klein	peu / petit	1773
allmählich	peu à peu	1774
allmählich weniger	de moins en moins	1775
allmählich mehr	de plus en plus	1776
etwas weniger	un peu moins	1777
etwas mehr	un peu plus	1778
sodann folgt	puis poursuit	1779
möglich	possible	1780
möglichst	si cela est possible	1781
vorhergehend / im Vorigen	précédent / antérieur	1782
früher / vorher / zuvor	avant	1783
bevor	avant que / avant de	1784
nächste / nächstfolgend	prochain	1785
hier	ici	1786
einige	quelque (s)	1787
so viel wie	autant que	1788
fast / beinahe / wie / als ob	presque	1789

1790	rigorosamente	rigorously
1791	rispettare il testo	respect the text
1792	ritornando / tornando	returning
1793	se	if
1794	se bisogna	if necessary
1795	segno *m*	sign / mark
1796	segue	it follows
1797	seguite	follow
1798	sempre / costantemente	always
1799	sempre lo stesso	always the same
1800	senza	without
1801	senza cambiare	without changing
1802	senza correre	without hurrying
1803	senza fermarsi / senza interruzioni	without interruptions
1804	senza replica	without repetition
1805	senza strumenti	without instruments
1806	separato	separated
1807	si leva / si toglie	take away
1808	simile / lo stesso	similar
1809	sin / sino	until
1810	solito	usual
1811	solo / soli / assolo	alone
1812	soltanto	only / just
1813	sommo	highest
1814	sopra	on / upon
1815	soprattutto	mainly / above all
1816	sordina *f* / sordino *m*	mute / damper / muffle
1817	sotto	under
1818	sovente / spesso	often
1819	spostamento *m*	shift
1820	strettamente	strictly
1821	su / sul / sulla	on / on the
1822	subito / immediatamente	at once / immediately
1823	tace / tacesi / taci	remain silent / be quiet
1824	tacet (L)	silent
1825	tale	such
1826	tantino	a little bit

in strenger Weise	rigoureusement	1790
den Text respektieren	respecter le texte	1791
zurückkommend / zurückkehrend	en revenant	1792
wenn / falls / sofern	si	1793
wenn nötig	si nécessaire	1794
Zeichen *n*	signe *m*	1795
es folgt	ça suit	1796
folgen Sie	suivez	1797
immer / stets / ständig	toujours / constamment	1798
stets das Gleiche	toujours le (la) même	1799
ohne	sans	1800
ohne zu wechseln	sans changer	1801
ohne davonzurennen	sans courir	1802
durchgehend / ohne Unterbrechung	sans s'arrêter / sans interruptions	1803
ohne Wiederholung	sans reprise	1804
ohne Instrumente	sans instruments	1805
getrennt	séparé	1806
man nehme weg	on enlève	1807
gleich	semblable / pareil	1808
bis / zu	jusque	1809
gewohnt / auf gewohnte Weise	habituel	1810
allein	seul	1811
nur	seulement	1812
höchst	suprême	1813
auf / über / oben	dessus	1814
vor allem / überhaupt	surtout	1815
Dämpfer *m*	sourdine *f*	1816
unter	dessous / sous	1817
oft / oftmals / häufig	souvent	1818
Verschiebung *f*	déplacement *m*	1819
sehr genau	strictement	1820
auf / auf der / auf die / auf das	sur / sur le / sur la	1821
sofort / unmittelbar / sogleich	immédiatement / tout de suite	1822
schweige / nicht mitwirken / pausiere	tais-toi	1823
schweigen / nicht mitwirken / pausieren	se taire	1824
solch	tel	1825
ein bißchen	un tantinet	1826

1827	tanto	so / so much / many
1828	tempo precedente	preceding tempo
1829	tenendo	holding
1830	tenete / mantenete	keep on
1831	tenuto	held
1832	trillato	shaken
1833	triplo	triple
1834	troppo	too much
1835	troppo poco	not enough
1836	tutta	all
1837	tutta la forza	all the force
1838	tutte / tutti	everybody
1839	tutto	all
1840	udibile	audible
1841	uguale / eguale	equal
1842	ultima volta	last time
1843	ultimo / ultima	last
1844	un'altra volta	another time
1845	una volta	once
1846	unico	unique / sole
1847	unito / unitamente / nello stesso tempo	together / at the same time
1848	un pochettino / un pochino	a very little
1849	un poco	a little / somewhat
1850	un poco più	a little more
1851	variabile / variante	variable / varying
1852	variato	varied
1853	vicendevole	alternate
1854	vide (L)	see
1855	…volta	…times
1856	volta subito	turn the page immediately
1857	volti	turn
1858	vuoto	empty

Teoria musicale   Music theory

| 1859 | a due voci | two voices |
| 1860 | a forma aperta | through composed |

so viel / so sehr	tant / autant	1827
voriges Zeitmaß	tempo précédent	1828
haltend	en tenant	1829
halten Sie	tenez / gardez / maintenez	1830
gehalten / ausgehalten	tenu / lourré	1831
getrillert	trillé	1832
dreifach	triple	1833
zu viel	trop	1834
nicht genug	trop peu	1835
die ganze	toute	1836
die ganze Kraft	de toutes ses forces	1837
alle	toutes / tous	1838
all / alles / ganz	tout	1839
hörbar	audible	1840
gleich / gleichmäßig	égal	1841
letztes Mal	dernière fois	1842
letzter / letzte	dernier / dernière	1843
ein anderes Mal	une autre fois	1844
einmal	une fois	1845
einzig	unique	1846
gleichzeitig / zusammen	uni / en même temps	1847
ein klein wenig	un petit peu	1848
ein wenig / etwas	un peu	1849
ein wenig mehr	un peu plus	1850
veränderlich	variable	1851
variiert / verändert	varié	1852
abwechselnd	alternativement	1853
siehe	vois	1854
…fach / …mal	…fois	1855
sofort umblättern	tournez aussitôt	1856
blättere um	tournez	1857
leer	vide	1858

## Musiktheorie	## Théorie musicale

| zweistimmig | à deux voix | 1859 |
| durchkomponiert | de forme ouverte | 1860 |

1861	a più voci / a molte parti	in many parts
1862	a quattro voci	four voices
1863	a tre voci	three voices
1864	abbellimento *m*	embellishment
1865	abbellito	embellished
1866	abbreviatura *f* / abbreviazione *f*	abbreviation
1867	accento *m*	stress / accent
1868	accento principale	main accent
1869	accento secondario	secondary accent
1870	acciaccatura *f*	crushed note / short appoggiatura
1871	acciaccatura doppia *f*	slide
1872	accidente *m* / alterazione *f*	accidental / alteration
1873	accollatura *f*	brace / bracket
1874	accordo *m*	chord
1875	accordo di passaggio *m*	passing chord
1876	accordo di settima di dominante *m*	dominant seventh chord
1877	accordo perfetto *m*	common chord
1878	accordo spezzato *m*	broken chord
1879	agogica *f*	agogic
1880	alterato	altered
1881	altezza del suono *f*	pitch / pitch level
1882	anacrusi *f*	anacrusis
1883	analisi *f*	analysis
1884	andamento *m*	fugal episode
1885	antecedente *m*	antecedent
1886	anticipazione *f*	anticipation
1887	appoggiatura *f*	grace-note
1888	appoggiatura doppia *f*	double appoggiatura
1889	armatura di chiave *f*	key signature
1890	armonia *f*	harmony
1891	armonico	harmonic
1892	arpeggio *m*	arpeggio / battery
1893	arsi *f*	arsis
1894	ascendente	ascending
1895	atonale	atonal

mehrstimmig	à plusieurs voix / à plusieurs parties	1861
vierstimmig	à quatre voix	1862
dreistimmig	à trois voix	1863
Verzierung *f*	agrément *m* / broderie *f*	1864
verziert	ornementé	1865
Kürzung *f* / Verkürzung *f*	abréviation *f*	1866
Akzent *m* / Betonung *f* / Schwerpunkt *m*	accent *m*	1867
Hauptbetonung *f*	accent principal *m*	1868
Nebenbetonung *f*	accent secondaire *m*	1869
kurzer Vorschlag *m* / Quetschung *f*	appogiature brève *f* / pincé étouffé *m*	1870
Schleifer *m*	coulé *m*	1871
Versetzungszeichen *n* / Vorzeichen *n* / Alteration *f*	altération *f* / accident *m*	1872
Klammer *f*	accolade *f*	1873
Akkord *m*	accord *m*	1874
Durchgangsakkord *m*	accord de passage *m*	1875
Dominantseptakkord *m*	accord de séptième de dominante *m*	1876
Dreiklang *m*	accord parfait *m*	1877
gebrochener Akkord *m*	accord brisé *m*	1878
Agogik *f*	agogique *f*	1879
verändert / alteriert	altéré	1880
Tonhöhe *f*	hauteur du son *f*	1881
Anakrusis *f* / Auftakt *m*	anacrouse *f*	1882
Analyse *f*	analyse *f*	1883
Fugen-Zwischenspiel *n* / längeres Fugenthema *n*	divertissement *m*	1884
Dux *m* / Führer *m*	antécédent *m*	1885
Antizipation *f* / Vorausnahme *f*	anticipation *f*	1886
Vorschlag *m*	appoggiature *f*	1887
Doppelvorschlag *m*	appoggiature double *f*	1888
Tonartvorzeichnung *f* / Vorzeichen *n*	armure de la clé *f* / armature *f*	1889
Harmonie *f*	harmonie *f*	1890
harmonisch	harmonique	1891
Arpeggio *n*	arpège *m*	1892
Arsis *f* / Hebung *f*	arsis *f*	1893
aufsteigend	ascendant	1894
atonal	atonal	1895

1896	aumentato / eccedente	raised / augmented
1897	aumentazione *f* / aggrava-mento *m*	augmentation
1898	autentico	authentic
1899	basso cifrato m / basso numerato *m*	figured bass
1900	basso continuo	through-bass
1901	basso ostinato *m*	ground bass
1902	battuta *f*	beat / bar
1903	battuta composta *f*	compound time
1904	battuta semplice *f*	simple time
1905	bemolle *m*	flat
1906	bequadro *m*	natural
1907	binario	binary
1908	bitonalità *f*	bitonality
1909	bordone *m*	bourdon
1910	cadenza *f*	cadenza / cadence
1911	cadenza evitata *f* / cadenza d'inganno *f*	delusive cadence / deceptive cadence (Am.)
1912	cadenza finale *f*	final cadenza
1913	cadenza imperfetta *f*	imperfect cadence / half-close
1914	cadenza perfetta *f*	perfect cadence / authentic cadence
1915	cadenza plagale *f*	plagal cadence
1916	cadenza sospesa *f*	delayed cadence
1917	cambiamento di tempo *m* / cambio di misura *m*	change of time / change of meter
1918	cambio di tonalità *m*	key change
1919	canto fermo *m*	cantus firmus
1920	cesura *f*	caesura
1921	chiave *f*	clef
1922	chiave di baritono *f*	baritone clef
1923	chiave di basso *f*	bass clef
1924	chiave di contralto *f*	alto clef
1925	chiave di do *f*	C clef
1926	chiave di mezzosoprano *f*	mezzo-soprano clef
1927	chiave di soprano *f*	soprano clef

übermäßig / hochalteriert	augmenté	1896
Vergrößerung *f* (der Zeitwerte)	augmentation *f*	1897
authentisch	authentique	1898
bezifferter Bass *m* / General-bass *m*	basse chiffrée f	1899
Generalbass *m*	basse continue *f*	1900
Basso ostinato *m* / Ostinato *m*	basse obstinée *f* / basse contrainte *f*	1901
Schlag *m* / Takt *m* / Takt-schlag *m*	mesure *f*	1902
zusammengesetzter Takt *m*	mesure composée *f*	1903
einfacher Takt	mesure simple *f*	1904
B *n* / Erniedrigungszeichen *n*	bémol *m*	1905
Auflösungszeichen *n*	bécarre *m*	1906
zweiteilig	binaire	1907
Bitonalität *f*	bitonalité *f*	1908
Bordun *m*	bourdon *m*	1909
Kadenz *f*	cadence *f*	1910
Trugschluss *m*	cadence rompue *f*	1911
Schlusskadenz *f*	cadence finale *f*	1912
Halbschluss *m*	cadence suspendue *f* / demi-cadence *f*	1913
authentische Kadenz *f* / voll-kommene Kadenz *f* / Ganz-schluss *m*	cadence parfaite *f*	1914
plagale Kadenz *f*	cadence plagale *f*	1915
unvollkommene Kadenz *f* / Halbkadenz *f*	cadence suspendue *f* / cadence interrompue *f*	1916
Taktwechsel *m*	changement de mesure *m* / changement de temps *m*	1917
Tonartwechsel *m*	changement de tonalité *m*	1918
Cantus firmus *m*	cantus firmus *m*	1919
Zäsur *f*	césure *f*	1920
Schlüssel *m*	clé *f* / clef *f*	1921
Baritonschlüssel *m*	clé de fa troisième ligne *f*	1922
Bassschlüssel *m*	clé de fa quatrième ligne *f*	1923
Altschlüssel *m*	clé d'ut troisième ligne *f*	1924
C-Schlüssel *m*	clé d'ut *f*	1925
Mezzosopranschlüssel *m*	clé d'ut seconde ligne *f*	1926
Sopranschlüssel *m*	clé d'ut première ligne *f*	1927

1928	chiave di tenore *f*	tenor clef
1929	chiave di violino *f*	treble clef
1930	chiusa del trillo *f*	termination of trill
1931	cifrare	to figure
1932	cifratura *f*	figuring / figuration
1933	circolo delle quinte *m*	circle of fifths
1934	codetta *f*	tail / flag
1935	comma *m*	comma
1936	conclusione *f*	conclusion
1937	condotta delle parti *f*	linear construction
1938	condotta delle voci *f*	part-writing / voice-leading
1939	congiunto	by step / conjunct
1940	consonanza *f*	consonance
1941	contrappunto *m*	counterpoint
1942	contrappunto fiorito *m* / contrappunto florido *m*	florid counterpoint
1943	controsoggetto *m*	counter subject
1944	contrattempo *m*	syncopation
1945	controcanto m / controtema *m*	counter voice / counter part / counter melody
1946	corona *f*	pause / fermata
1947	cromatico	chromatic
1948	cromatismo *m*	chromaticism
1949	dattilo *m*	dactyl
1950	dettato *m*	dictation
1951	dettato musicale *m*	music dictation
1952	diatonico	diatonic
1953	diatonismo *m*	diatonicism
1954	diesis *m*	sharp
1955	diminuito	diminished
1956	diminuzione *f*	diminution
1957	discendente	descending
1958	dissonanza *f*	dissonance
1959	dodecafonia *f*	twelve-tone music
1960	dominante *f*	dominant
1961	dominante di passaggio *f* / dominante secondaria *f*	secondary dominant
1962	doppia stanghetta *f*	double bar

Tenorschlüssel *m*	clé d'ut quatrième ligne *f*	1928
Violinschlüssel *m*	clé de sol *f*	1929
Nachschlag *m*	gruppetto final *m* / terminaison *f*	1930
beziffern	chiffrer	1931
Bezifferung *f*	chiffrage *f*	1932
Quintenzirkel *m*	cycle des quintes *m*	1933
Notenfahne *f* / Fähnchen *n*	crochet *m*	1934
Komma *n*	comma *m*	1935
Schlusssatz *m* / Abschluss *m* / Beschluss *m*	conclusion *f*	1936
Linienführung *f*	construction linéaire *f*	1937
Stimmführung *f*	conduite des voix *f*	1938
schrittweise / stufenweise	conjoint	1939
Konsonanz *f*	consonance *f*	1940
Kontrapunkt *m*	contrepoint *m*	1941
„blühender" Kontrapunkt *m*	contrepoint fleuri *m*	1942
Kontrasubjekt *n* / Gegen-thema *n* / Gegensatz *m*	contresujet *m*	1943
Gegenzeit *f* (Betonung auf dem schlechten Taktteil)	contre-temps *m*	1944
Gegenstimme *f*	contre-chant *m*	1945
Fermate *f*	point d'arrêt *m* / point d'orgue *m*	1946
chromatisch	chromatique	1947
Chromatik *f*	chromatisme *m*	1948
Daktylos *m*	dactyle *m*	1949
Diktat *n*	dictée *f*	1950
Musikdiktat *n*	dictée musicale *f*	1951
diatonisch	diatonique	1952
Diatonik *f*	diatonisme *m*	1953
Kreuz *n* / Erhöhungszeichen *n*	dièse *m*	1954
vermindert	diminué	1955
Verkleinerung *f* (der Noten-werte)	diminution *f*	1956
absteigend	descendant	1957
Dissonanz *f*	dissonance *f*	1958
Zwölftontechnik *f*	dodécaphonisme *m*	1959
Dominante *f*	dominante *f*	1960
Zwischendominante *f*	dominante de passage *f*	1961
Doppelstrich *m*	double barre *f*	1962

1963	doppio bemolle *m*	double flat
1964	doppio diesis *m*	double sharp
1965	dorico	dorian
1966	duina *f*	duplet
1967	durata del suono *f*	sound duration
1968	enarmonico	enharmonic
1969	entrata *f*	entry
1970	eolio	aeolian
1971	episodio *m*	episode
1972	esacordo *m*	hexachord
1973	esposizione *f*	exposition
1974	falsa relazione *f*	false relation
1975	falso bordone *m*	faburden / fauxbourdon
1976	figura *f*	figure
1977	figurato	figured
1978	fioritura *f*	embellishment
1979	fondamentale	fundamental
1980	forma *f*	form
1981	forma binaria *f*	binary form
1982	forma ciclica *f*	cyclic form
1983	forma ternaria *f*	ternary form
1984	frase *f*	phrase
1985	fraseggio *m*	phrasing
1986	frigio	phrygian
1987	fugato	in fugal style
1988	funzione *f*	function
1989	gambo *m*	stem
1990	giambo *m*	iamb
1991	giusto	perfect
1992	grado *m*	degree
1993	gruppetto m / groppo *m*	turn
1994	gruppo di suoni m / gruppo di note *m*	note cluster / tone cluster
1995	hemiolia *f*	hemiola
1996	imitazione *f*	imitation
1997	imperfetto	imperfect
1998	in battere	downbeat
1999	in levare / levata *f*	up beat
2000	intavolatura *f*	tablature
2001	intervallo *m*	interval

Doppel-B *n*	double bémol *m*	1963
Doppelkreuz *n*	double dièse *m*	1964
dorisch	dorien	1965
Duole *f*	duolet *m*	1966
Tonlänge *f* / Tondauer *f*	durée du son *f*	1967
enharmonisch	enharmonique	1968
Einsatz *m*	entrée *f*	1969
äolisch	éolien	1970
Episode *f* / Zwischensatz *m*	épisode *m*	1971
Hexachord *n*	hexacorde *m*	1972
Exposition *f*	exposition *f*	1973
Querstand *m*	fausse relation *f*	1974
Fauxbourdon *m*	faux-bourdon *m*	1975
Figur *f*	figure *f*	1976
figuriert	figuré	1977
Blume *f* (Verzierung)	fioriture *f*	1978
wesentlich	fondamental	1979
Form *f* / Gestalt *f*	forme *f*	1980
zweiteilige Form *f*	forme binaire *f*	1981
zyklische Form *f*	forme cyclique *f*	1982
dreiteilige Form *f*	forme ternaire *f*	1983
Phrase *f*	phrase *f*	1984
Phrasierung *f*	phrasé	1985
phrygisch	phrygien	1986
fugenartig	fugué	1987
Funktion *f*	fonction *f*	1988
Notenhals *m*	hampe *f* / queue de la note *f*	1989
Jambus *m*	jambus *m*	1990
richtig	juste	1991
Stufe *f* / Schritt *m*	degré *m*	1992
Doppelschlag *m*	doublé *m* / double cadence *f*	1993
Tontraube *f* / Tonballung *f*	groupe de sons *m* / groupe de notes *m*	1994
Hemiole *f*	hemiolios *m*	1995
Imitation *f* / Nachahmung *f*	imitation *f*	1996
unvollkommen	imparfait	1997
abtaktig	frappé	1998
Aufschlag *m* / Auftakt *m*	sur la levée / levée *f*	1999
Tabulatur *f*	tablature *f*	2000
Intervall *n* / Abstand *m*	intervalle *m*	2001

2002	intonazione *f*	intonation / pitch
2003	ionico	ionian
2004	legatura *f*	slur
2005	legatura di fraseggio *f*	phrase mark
2006	legatura di valore *f*	tie
2007	lidio	lydian
2008	maggiore	major
2009	mano guidoniana *f*	guidonian hand
2010	mediante *f*	mediant
2011	melodia *f*	melody / tune
2012	melodico	melodic
2013	metrico	metric(al)
2014	metro *m*	metre
2015	mettere il punto di valore	to dot
2016	minore	minor
2017	misolidio	mixolydian
2018	misura *f*	bar / measure / mensuration
2019	modale	modal
2020	modalità *f*	modality
2021	modo *m*	mode / modus
2022	modo ecclesiastico *m*	church mode
2023	modulare	to modulate
2024	modulazione *f*	modulation
2025	modulazione di transizione *f*	temporary modulation
2026	monodia *f* / monofonia *f*	monody / monophony
2027	mordente *m*	mordent / shake
2028	mordente inferiore *m*	mordent
2029	mordente superiore *m*	inverted mordent / mordent with note above
2030	motivo *m*	motif
2031	motivo conduttore *m* / motivo ricorrente *m*	leading motif
2032	moto contrario *m*	contrary motion
2033	moto obliquo *m*	oblique motion
2034	moto retto *m*	parallel motion
2035	movimento *m* / tempo *m*	movement
2036	movimento parallelo *m*	parallel movement
2037	neuma *m*	neuma / neume
2038	nota *f*	note
2039	nota ausiliare *f*	auxiliary note

Intonation *f* / Stimmung *f* / Ton-gebung *f*	intonation *f*	2002
ionisch	ionien	2003
Bindebogen *m*	liaison *f*	2004
Phrasierungsbogen *m*	signe de liaison du phrasé *m*	2005
Haltebogen *m*	signe de tenue *m*	2006
lydisch	lydien	2007
Dur	majeur	2008
Guidonische Hand *f*	main guidonienne *f*	2009
Mediante *f*	médiante *f*	2010
Melodie *f*	mélodie *f*	2011
melodisch	mélodique	2012
metrisch	métrique	2013
Metrum *n*	mètre *m*	2014
punktieren	pointer	2015
Moll / klein (Intervall)	mineur	2016
mixolydisch	mixo-lydien	2017
Takt *m* / Mensur *f* / Metrum *n*	mesure *f*	2018
modal	modal	2019
Modalität *f*	modalité *f*	2020
Tongeschlecht *n* / Modus *m*	mode *m*	2021
Kirchentonart *f*	mode ecclésiastique *m*	2022
modulieren	moduler	2023
Modulation *f*	modulation *f*	2024
Ausweichung *f*	modulation passagère *f*	2025
Monodie *f* / Einstimmigkeit *f*	monodie *f*	2026
Mordent *m*	mordant *m* / battement *m*	2027
Mordent *m*	mordant *m* / pincé *m*	2028
Pralltriller *m* / Schneller *m* / Praller *m*	mordant supérieur *m*	2029
Motiv *n*	motif *m*	2030
Leitmotiv *n*	motif conducteur *m* / idée fixe *f*	2031
Gegenbewegung *f*	mouvement contraire *m*	2032
Seitenbewegung *f*	mouvement oblique *m*	2033
Parallelbewegung *f*	mouvement parallèle *m*	2034
Satz *m*	mouvement *m*	2035
Parallelführung *f*	mouvement parallèle *m*	2036
Neumen *f pl*	neume *f*	2037
Note *f*	note *f*	2038
Nebennote *f*	note secondaire *f*	2039

2040	nota cambiata *f*	changing note
2041	nota di passaggio *f*	passing note
2042	nota principale *f*	essential note
2043	nota puntata *f*	dotted note
2044	notazione *f*	notation
2045	notina *f*	cue note
2046	numero di battute *m*	bar number / measure number
2047	obbligato	obbligato
2048	omofonia *f*	homophony
2049	orchestrazione *f*	orchestration
2050	orizzontale	horizontal
2051	ornamento *m* / adornamento *m*	ornament
2052	parallele nascoste *f pl*	hidden consecutives
2053	parallelo	parallel
2054	parte estrema *f* / voce estrema *f*	outer part
2055	parte inferiore *f* / voce inferiore	lower part / lowest part
2056	parte intermedia *f* / voce intermedia *f*	middle part / inner part
2057	parte melodica *f*	melody part
2058	parte superiore *f* / voce superiore *f*	upper part / top part
2059	passaggio *m*	passage / transition
2060	pausa *f* / silenzio *m*	rest
2061	pausa generale *f* / vuoto *m*	general pause
2062	pedale d'armonia *m*	pedal point
2063	pentagramma *m*	staves / system
2064	pèntatonico	pentatonic
2065	periodo *m*	period
2066	plagale	plagal
2067	policoralità *f* / polifonia policorale *f*	polychoral music
2068	polifonia *f*	polyphony
2069	polimetria *f*	polymetre
2070	poliritmica *f*	polyrhythm
2071	politonalità *f*	polytonality

Wechselnote *f* / Wechselton *m*	cambiata *f* / note changée *f*	2040
Durchgangsnote *f* / Durchgangston *m*	note de passage *f*	2041
Hauptnote *f*	note principale *f*	2042
punktierte Note *f*	note pointée *f*	2043
Notation *f* / Notenschrift *f*	notation *f*	2044
Stichnote *f*	petite note *f*	2045
Taktzahl *f*	nombre de mesures *m*	2046
obligat	obligé	2047
Homophonie *f*	homophonie *f*	2048
Orchestration *f* / Orchestrierung *f*	orchestration *f*	2049
waagrecht / horizontal	horizontal	2050
Verzierung *f* / Ornament *n*	ornement *m* / broderie *f*	2051
verdeckte Parallelen *f Pl*	parallèles cachées *f pl*	2052
parallel	parallèle	2053
Außenstimme *f*	voix extrême *f* / partie extrême *f*	2054
Unterstimme *f*	voix inférieure *f* / partie inférieure *f*	2055
Mittelstimme *f* / Innenstimme *f*	voix intermédiaire *f* / voix intérieure *f*	2056
Melodiestimme *f*	partie mélodique *f*	2057
Oberstimme *f*	voix supérieure *f* / partie supérieure *f* / partie de dessus *f*	2058
Passage *f* / Durchgang *m* / Überleitung *f*	passage *m* / transition *f*	2059
Pause *f*	pause *f* / silence *m*	2060
Generalpause *f*	pause générale *f*	2061
Orgelpunkt *m*	pédale inférieure *f*	2062
Liniensystem *n* / Fünfliniensystem *n*	portée *f*	2063
pentatonisch	pentatonique	2064
Periode *f*	période *f*	2065
plagal	plagal	2066
Mehrchörigkeit *f*	pluralité des chœurs *f*	2067
Polyphonie *f* / Mehrstimmigkeit *f*	polyphonie *f*	2068
Polymetrik *f*	polymétrie *f*	2069
Polyrhythmik *f*	polyrythmie *f*	2070
Polytonalität *f*	polytonalité *f*	2071

2072	ponte *m*	bridge
2073	posizione fondamentale *f*	fondamental position
2074	posizione lata *f*	open / extended position
2075	posizione stretta *f*	close position
2076	preparazione *f*	preparation
2077	prima frase *f*	first phrase
2078	primo tema *m* / tema principale *m*	main theme
2079	primo tempo *m*	first movement
2080	principale	main
2081	progressione *f*	progression
2082	proposta *f*	antecedent
2083	puntato	dotted
2084	punto di valore *m*	dot
2085	punto doppio *m*	double dot
2086	quartina *f*	quadruplet
2087	quarto tempo *m*	fourth movement
2088	quintina *f*	quintuplet
2089	quinto tempo *m*	fifth movement
2090	raddoppio *m*	doubling
2091	realizzazione *f*	realization
2092	relativo / affine	relative
2093	relazione *f* / affinità *f*	relationship
2094	retrogrado	retrograde
2095	rigo *m* / linea *f*	line
2096	ripetizione *f* / ripresa *f*	repetition / repeat
2097	ripresa *f* / riesposizione *f*	repeat / recapitulation / return
2098	risoluzione *f*	resolution
2099	risposta *f* / conseguente *m*	answer / consequent
2100	risposta reale *f*	real answer
2101	risposta tonale *f*	tonal answer
2102	ritardo *m*	suspension / retardation
2103	ritmo *m*	rhythm
2104	ritmo lombardo *m*	scotch snap
2105	ritornello *m*	refrain
2106	riverso	backwards
2107	rivolto *m* / rovescio *m*	inversion
2108	salmodia *f*	psalmody
2109	scala *f*	scale

Überleitung *f*	transition *f* / pont *m*	2072
Grundstellung *f*	position fondamentale *f*	2073
weite Lage *f*	position large *f*	2074
enge Lage *f*	position serrée *f*	2075
Vorbereitung *f*	préparation *f*	2076
Vordersatz *m*	proposition *f*	2077
Hauptthema *n*	thème principal *m*	2078
erster Satz *m* / Kopfsatz *m*	premier mouvement *m*	2079
Haupt-...	principal	2080
Fortschreitung *f*	progression *f*	2081
Proposta *f*	proposition *f* / antécédent *m*	2082
punktiert	pointé	2083
Punkt *m*	point *m*	2084
Doppelpunkt *m*	double point *m*	2085
Quartole *f*	quartolet *m*	2086
vierter Satz *m*	quatrième mouvement *m*	2087
Quintole *f*	quintolet *m*	2088
fünfter Satz *m*	cinquième mouvement *m*	2089
Verdopplung *f*	redoublement *m*	2090
Aussetzung *f* (eines bezifferten Basses)	réalisation *f*	2091
verwandt / bezüglich (Parallel-tonart)	relatif	2092
Verwandtschaft *f*	relation *f*	2093
krebsgängig / rückwärtsgehend	rétrograde	2094
Linie *f*	ligne *f*	2095
Wiederholung *f*	répétition *f* / reprise *f*	2096
Reprise *f* / Wiederkehr *f*	reprise *f* / réexposition *f*	2097
Auflösung *f* (einer Dissonanz)	résolution *f*	2098
Antwort *f* / Comes *m*	réponse *f* / conséquent *m*	2099
reale Antwort *f*	réponse réelle *f*	2100
tonale Antwort *f*	réponse tonale *f*	2101
Verzögerung *f* / Vorhalt *m*	retard *m*	2102
Rhythmus *m*	rythme *m*	2103
lombardischer Rhythmus *m*	rythme lombard *m*	2104
Refrain *m* / Kehrreim *m*	refrain *m*	2105
von rückwärts	à la renverse	2106
Umkehrung *f*	inversion *f*	2107
Psalmodie *f*	psalmodie *f*	2108
Tonleiter *f*	gamme *f*	2109

2110	scala esatonale *f*	whole-tone scale
2111	secondario	secondary
2112	secondo tema *m* / tema secondario *m*	second theme / secondary subject
2113	secondo tempo *m*	second movement
2114	segno d'espressione *m*	expression mark
2115	segno dinamico *m*	dynamic sign / dynamic mark
2116	segno di ripetizione *m* / segno di ritornello *m*	repeat sign
2117	semitono *m*	semitone
2118	sensibile *f*	leading note / leading tone
2119	sequenza *f*	sequence
2120	serie *f*	series / row
2121	sesta napolitana *f*	neapolitan sixth
2122	sestina *f*	sextuplet
2123	settima di dominante *f*	dominant seventh
2124	settimina *f*	septuplet
2125	sincope *f*	syncopation
2126	sistema tonale *m*	tonal system / tone system
2127	soggetto *m*	subject
2128	solfeggio *m*	tonic sol-fa
2129	solmisazione *f*	solmization
2130	sostituzione enarmonica *f*	enharmonic change
2131	sottodominante *f*	subdominant
2132	sovrapposizione *f*	superimposition
2133	spazio *m*	space
2134	stanghetta *f* / barra *f*	beam / bar-line / ligature
2135	stretta *f*	stretto
2136	stretto *m*	stretto
2137	strofa *f*	verse
2138	strumentazione *f*	instrumentation
2139	struttura *f* / costruzione *f*	structure / construction
2140	successione *f*	succession
2141	successioni parallele *f pl*	consecutives
2142	suono *m*	sound
2143	suono fondamentale *m*	fundamental / tonic
2144	suono simpatico *m*	sympathetic tone
2145	suoni armonici *m pl* / flautato	harmonics

Ganztonleiter *f*	gamme par tons *f*	2110
neben	secondaire	2111
Seitenthema *n*	second thème *m* / thème secondaire *m*	2112
zweiter Satz *n*	deuxième mouvement *m*	2113
Vortragsbezeichnung *f* / Ausdrucksbezeichnung *f*	signe d'interprétation *m* / signe d'expression *m*	2114
dynamisches Zeichen *n*	signe dynamique *m*	2115
Wiederholungszeichen n	signe de répétition *m*	2116
Halbton *m*	demi-ton *m*	2117
Leitton *m*	sensible *f*	2118
Sequenz *f*	sequence *f*	2119
Reihe *f* / Tonreihe *f*	série *f*	2120
neapolitanische Sexte *f*	sixte napolitaine *f*	2121
Sextole *f*	sextolet *m*	2122
Dominantseptime *f*	septième de dominante *f*	2123
Septole *f*	septolet *m*	2124
Synkope *f*	syncope *f*	2125
Tonsystem *n*	système tonal *m*	2126
Subjekt *n* / Dux *m*	sujet *m*	2127
Solfeggio *n*	solfège *m*	2128
Solmisation *f*	solmisation *f*	2129
enharmonische Verwechslung *f*	substitution enharmonique *f*	2130
Subdominante *f*	sous-dominante *f*	2131
Schichtung *f*	superposition *f*	2132
Zwischenraum *m*	interligne *m*	2133
Notenbalken *m* / Taktstrich *m*	barre de mesure *f*	2134
schneller Schlussteil *m*	strette *f*	2135
Engführung *f*	strette *f*	2136
Strophe *f*	strophe *f* / couplet *m*	2137
Instrumentierung *f*	instrumentation *f*	2138
Aufbau *m* / Struktur *f*	construction *f* / structure *f*	2139
Folge *f*	succession *f*	2140
Parallelen *f Pl*	successions parallèles *f pl*	2141
Klang *m* / Schall *m*	son *m*	2142
Grundton *m* / Tonika *f*	son fondamental *m*	2143
Eigenton *m*	vibration sympathique *f*	2144
Obertöne *m Pl* / Flageolett-Töne *m pl*	sons harmoniques *m pl*	2145

2146	suoni naturali *m pl*	natural notes / natural tones
2147	suoni parziali *m pl*	partials
2148	sviluppo *m* / svolgimento *m*	development
2149	taglio addizionale *m* / righetta *f*	leger line
2150	tema *m*	theme
2151	temperamento *m*	equal temperament
2152	tempo *m*	speed / time / pace / metre
2153	tempo *m*	time signature
2154	tempo binario *m* / tempo pari *m*	duple time
2155	tempo debole *m*	off-beat / weak beat
2156	tempo forte *m*	strong beat / accentuated beat
2157	tempo ternario *m* / tempo dispari *m*	triple time
2158	ternario	ternary
2159	terza picarda *f*	picardy third
2160	terzina *f*	triplet
2161	terzo tempo *m*	third movement
2162	tesi *f*	thesis
2163	tetracordo *m*	tetrachord
2164	tonale	tonal
2165	tonalità *f*	tonality
2166	tonalità affine *f*	related key
2167	tonalità relativa *f*	related key
2168	tonica *f*	tonic / key-note
2169	tono *m*	tone / key
2170	tono intero *m*	whole tone
2171	tono naturale *m*	pure tone
2172	tono secondario *m*	neighbour note
2173	transizione *f*	transition
2174	trasporto *m*	transposition
2175	trattato d'armonia *m*	theory of harmony
2176	tratto d'unione *m*	cross / beam
2177	triade *f*	triad
2178	trillo *m*	trill / shake
2179	tritono *m*	tritone
2180	ultimo tempo *m* / ultimo movimento *m*	last movement

Naturtöne *m Pl*	sons ouverts *m pl* / sons naturels *m pl*	2146
Teiltöne *m Pl*	sons partiels *m pl*	2147
Entwicklung *f* / Durchführung *f*	développement *m*	2148
Hilfslinie *f*	ligne supplémentaire *f*	2149
Thema *n*	thème *m*	2150
Temperatur *f* / temperierte Stimmung *f*	tempérament *m*	2151
Zeitmaß *n* / Zählzeit *f*	temps *m* / mesure *f*	2152
Taktart *f*	indication de la mesure *f*	2153
gerader Takt *m*	mesure binaire *f*	2154
schwacher Taktteil *m* / schlechter Taktteil *m*	temps faible *m*	2155
starker Taktteil *m* / schwerer Taktteil *m*	temps fort *m*	2156
ungerader Takt *m*	mesure ternaire *f*	2157
dreiteilig	ternaire	2158
picardische Terz *f*	tierce picarde *f*	2159
Triole *f*	triolet *m*	2160
dritter Satz *m*	troisième mouvement *m*	2161
Thesis *f* / Senkung *f*	thésis *f*	2162
Tetrachord *m*	tétracorde *m*	2163
tonal	tonal	2164
Tonalität *f* / Tonart *f*	tonalité *f*	2165
verwandte Tonart *f*	tonalité voisine *f*	2166
Paralleltonart *f*	tonalité relative *f*	2167
Tonika *f* / Grundton *m*	tonique *f*	2168
Ton *m* / Tonart *f*	ton *m* / tonalité *f*	2169
Ganzton *m*	ton entier *m*	2170
reiner Ton *m*	ton naturel *m*	2171
Nebenton *m*	ton concomittant *m*	2172
Übergang *m* / Durchgang *m*	transition *f*	2173
Transposition *f* / Transponierung *f*	transposition *f*	2174
Harmonielehre *f*	traité d'harmonie *m*	2175
Notenbalken *m* / Querbalken *m*	barre transversale *f*	2176
Dreiklang *m*	triade *f*	2177
Triller *m*	trille *m* / tremblement *m*	2178
Tritonus *m*	triton *m*	2179
Schlusssatz *m*	dernier mouvement *m*	2180

2181	unisono (all') *m*	in unison
2182	valore *m*	value
2183	valore della nota *m*	note value
2184	valore della pausa *m*	rest value
2185	veloce passaggio di note *m*	run / quick passage
2186	verticale	vertical
2187	voce di ripieno *f* / parte di ripieno *f*	filling-in part
2188	voce principale *f*	principal part / principal voice

Note   Notes

2189	Do *m*	C
2190	Do diesis *m*	C sharp
2191	Do bemolle *m*	C flat
2192	Do doppio diesis *m*	C double sharp
2193	Do doppio bemolle *m*	C double flat
2194	Re *m*	D
2195	Re diesis *m*	D sharp
2196	Re bemolle *m*	D flat
2197	Re doppio diesis *m*	D double sharp
2198	Re doppio bemolle *m*	D double flat
2199	Mi *m*	E
2200	Mi diesis *m*	E sharp
2201	Mi bemolle *m*	E flat
2202	Mi doppio diesis *m*	E double sharp
2203	Mi doppio bemolle *m*	E double flat
2204	Fa *m*	F
2205	Fa diesis *m*	F sharp
2206	Fa bemolle *m*	F flat
2207	Fa doppio diesis *m*	F double sharp
2208	Fa doppio bemolle *m*	F double flat
2209	Sol *m*	G
2210	Sol diesis *m*	G sharp
2211	Sol bemolle *m*	G flat
2212	Sol doppio diesis *m*	G double sharp
2213	Sol doppio bemolle *m*	G double flat
2214	La *m*	A
2215	La diesis *m*	A sharp

im Einklang *m*	à l'unisson *m*	2181
Wert *m*	valeur *f*	2182
Notenwert *m*	valeur de la note *f*	2183
Pausenwert *m*	valeur de la pause *f*	2184
Lauf *m*	passage rapide de notes *m*	2185
senkrecht / vertikal	vertical	2186
Füllstimme *f*	voix de remplissage *f* / parties de remplissage *f pl*	2187
Hauptstimme *f*	partie principale *f* / voix principale *f*	2188

Noten   Notes

C *n*	Do / Ut *m*	2189
Cis *n*	Do dièse *m*	2190
Ces *n*	Do bémol *m*	2191
Cisis *n*	Do double dièse *m*	2192
Ceses *n*	Do double bémol *m*	2193
D *n*	Ré *m*	2194
Dis *n*	Ré dièse *m*	2195
Des *n*	Ré bémol *m*	2196
Disis *n*	Ré double dièse *m*	2197
Deses *n*	Ré double bémol *m*	2198
E *n*	Mi *m*	2199
Eis *n*	Mi dièse *m*	2200
Es *n*	Mi bémol *m*	2201
Eisis *n*	Mi double dièse *m*	2202
Eses *n*	Mi double bémol *m*	2203
F *n*	Fa *m*	2204
Fis *n*	Fa dièse *m*	2205
Fes *n*	Fa bémol *m*	2206
Fisis *n*	Fa double dièse *m*	2207
Feses *n*	Fa double bémol *m*	2208
G *n*	Sol *m*	2209
Gis *n*	Sol dièse *m*	2210
Ges *n*	Sol bémol *m*	2211
Gisis *n*	Sol double dièse *m*	2212
Geses *n*	Sol double bémol *m*	2213
A *n*	La *m*	2214
Ais *n*	La dièse *m*	2215

2216	La bemolle *m*	A flat
2217	La doppio diesis *m*	A double sharp
2218	La doppio bemolle *m*	A double flat
2219	Si *m*	B
2220	Si diesis *m*	B sharp
2221	Si bemolle *m*	B flat
2222	Si doppio diesis *m*	B double sharp
2223	Si doppio bemolle *m*	B double flat

Valori delle note   Time value of notes

2224	intero *m* / semibreve *f*	semibreve (E) / whole note (Am.)
2225	metà *f* / minima *f*	minim (E) / half note (Am.)
2226	quarto *m* / semiminima *f*	crotchet (E) / quarter note (Am.)
2227	ottavo *m* / croma *f*	quaver (E) / eighth note (Am.)
2228	sedicesimo *m* / semicroma *f*	semiquaver (E) / sixteenth note (Am.)
2229	trentaduesimo *m* / biscroma *f*	demisemiquaver (E) / thirty-second note (Am.)
2230	sessantaquattresimo *m* / semibiscroma *f*	hemidemisemiquaver (E) / sixty-fourth note (Am.)
2231	pausa di semibreve *f*	semibreve rest (E) / whole note rest (Am.)
2232	pausa di minima *f*	minim rest (E) / half note rest (Am.)
2233	pausa di semiminima *f*	crotchet rest (E) / quarter note rest (Am.)
2234	pausa di croma *f*	quaver rest (E) / eighth note rest (Am.)
2235	pausa di semicroma *f*	semiquaver rest (E) / sixteenth note rest (Am.)
2236	pausa di biscroma *f*	demisemiquaver rest (E) / thirty-second note rest (Am.)
2237	pausa di semibiscroma *f*	hemidemisemiquaver rest (E) / sixty-fourth note rest (Am.)

As *n*	La bémol *m*	2216
Aisis *n*	La double dièse *m*	2217
Ases *n*	La double bémol *m*	2218
H *n*	Si *m*	2219
His *n*	Si dièse *m*	2220
B *n*	Si bémol *m*	2221
Hisis *n*	Si double dièse *m*	2222
Heses *n*	Si double bémol *m*	2223

Notenwerte   Valeur des notes

Ganze *f*	ronde *f*	2224
Halbe *f*	blanche *f*	2225
Viertel *f*	noire *f*	2226
Achtel *f*	croche *f*	2227
Sechzehntel *f*	double croche *f*	2228
Zweiunddreißigstel *f*	triple croche *f*	2229
Vierundsechzigstel *f*	quadruple croche *f*	2230
ganze Pause *f*	pause *f*	2231
halbe Pause *f*	demi-pause *f*	2232
Viertelpause *f*	soupir *m*	2233
Achtelpause *f*	demi-soupir *m*	2234
Sechzehntelpause *f*	quart de soupir *m*	2235
Zweiunddreißigstelpause *f*	huitième de soupir *m*	2236
Vierundsechzigstelpause *f*	seizième de soupir *m*	2237

	Intervalli	**Intervals**
2238	unisono *m*	unison (E) / prime (Am.)
2239	seconda *f*	second
2240	terza *f*	third
2241	quarta *f*	fourth
2242	quinta *f*	fifth
2243	sesta *f*	sixth
2244	settima *f*	seventh
2245	ottava *f*	octave
2246	nona *f*	ninth
2247	decima *f*	tenth

	Generi e forma	**Genres and forms**
2248	alba *f*	aubade (song at dawn)
2249	allemanda *f*	allemande / almand
2250	antifona *f*	antiphon
2251	arabesca *f*	arabesque
2252	aria *f*	air / aria
2253	aria concertante *f*	concert aria
2254	aria d'opera *f*	operatic aria
2255	aria di bravura *f*	bravura aria
2256	aria di coloratura *f*	coloratura aria
2257	aria di corte *f*	court song
2258	arietta *f*	short aria
2259	arioso *m*	aria-like
2260	baccanale *f*	bacchanal
2261	bagatella *f*	bagatelle
2262	ballata *f*	ballad
2263	balletto *m*	ballet
2264	balletto di corte *m*	court dance
2265	ballo tedesco *m* / danza tedesca *f*	German dance
2266	barcarola *f*	barcarole
2267	bassa danza *f*	basse danse
2268	battaglia *f*	battle
2269	bergamasca *f*	bergamask
2270	bourrée *f*	bourée / buree / borry
2271	brando *m*	branle

Intervalle

Intervalles

Prime *f*	unisson *m*	2238
Sekunde *f*	seconde *f*	2239
Terz *f*	tierce *f*	2240
Quarte *f*	quarte *f*	2241
Quinte *f*	quinte *f*	2242
Sexte *f*	sixte *f*	2243
Septime *f*	septième *f*	2244
Oktave *f*	octave *f*	2245
None *f*	none *f*	2246
Dezime *f*	dixième *f*	2247

Gattungen und Formen

Genres et formes

Tagelied *n*	aube *f* / aubade *f*	2248
Allemande *f*	allemande *f*	2249
Antiphon *f*	antienne *f*	2250
Arabeske *f*	arabesque *f*	2251
Arie *f*	air *m*	2252
Konzertarie *f*	air de concert *m*	2253
Opernarie *f*	air d'opéra *m*	2254
Bravourarie *f*	air de bravoure *m*	2255
Koloraturarie *f*	air avec colorature *m* / air à vocalises *m*	2256
höfisches Lied *n*	air de cour *m*	2257
kleine Arie *f*	ariette *f*	2258
wie eine Arie	comme une aria	2259
Bacchanal *n*	bacchanale *f*	2260
Bagatelle *f*	bagatelle *f*	2261
Ballade *f*	ballade *f*	2262
Ballett *n*	ballet *m*	2263
höfischer Tanz *m*	ballet de cour *m*	2264
Deutscher Tanz *m*	danse allemande *f*	2265
Barkarole *f*	barcarolle *f*	2266
Basse danse *f*	basse danse *f*	2267
Schlacht *f*	bataille *f*	2268
Bergamasker Tanz *m*	bergamasque *f*	2269
Bourrée *f*	bourrée *f*	2270
Branle *m*	branle m / bransle *m*	2271

2272	brindisi *m* / ditirambo *m*	drinking song
2273	bolero *m*	bolero
2274	burlesca *f*	burlesque
2275	burletta *f*	little jest
2276	cabaletta *f*	cabaletta
2277	caccia *f*	hunt
2278	canaria *f*	canary
2279	canone *m*	canon
2280	cantata *f*	cantata
2281	cantata da camera *f*	chamber cantata
2282	cantata da chiesa *f*	church cantata
2283	cantata profana *f*	secular cantata
2284	cantata su un corale *f*	choral cantata
2285	cantico *m*	canticle
2286	cantilena *f*	cantilena
2287	canto carnascialesco *m*	carnival song
2288	canto di lavoro *m*	work song
2289	canto di Natale *m*	Christmas song
2290	canto funebre *m*	dirge
2291	canto gitano *m*	gipsy song
2292	canto goliardico *m*	student song
2293	canto gregoriano *m*	plainsong (Gregorian chant)
2294	canto nuziale *m*	bridal song (wedding song)
2295	canzone *f*	song
2296	canzone della sera *f*	evening song
2297	canzone infantile *f*	nursery song
2298	canzone moderna *f* / canzonetta *f*	song / pop song
2299	canzone popolare *f*	folk song
2300	canzonetta *f*	canzonet
2301	capriccio *m*	capriccio
2302	carmagnola *f*	carmagnole
2303	carola *f*	carol
2304	cassazione *f*	cassation
2305	cavatina *f*	cavatina
2306	ciaccona *f*	chaconne
2307	commedia musicale *f*	musical
2308	commedia per musica *f*	musical comedy

Trinklied *n*	chanson à boire *f* / chanson bacchique *f*	2272
Bolero *m*	boléro *m*	2273
Burleske *f*	burlesque *f*	2274
kleine Posse *f*	petite farce *f*	2275
Cabaletta *f*	cabalette *f*	2276
Jagd *f*	chasse *f*	2277
Canarie *f*	canarie *f*	2278
Kanon *m*	canon *m*	2279
Kantate *f*	cantate *f*	2280
Kammerkantate *f*	cantate de chambre *f*	2281
Kirchenkantate *f*	cantate d'église *f*	2282
weltliche Kantate *f*	cantate profane *f*	2283
Choralkantate *f*	cantate sur un choral *f*	2284
Gesang *m* / (Kirchen-)Lied *n*	cantique *m*	2285
Kantilene *f*	cantilène *f*	2286
Karnevalslied *n*	chanson de carnaval *f*	2287
Arbeitslied *n*	chant de travail *m*	2288
Weihnachtslied *n*	chant de Noël *m*	2289
Grabgesang *m*	chant funèbre *m*	2290
Zigeunerlied *n*	chant gitan *m*	2291
Studentenlied *n*	chanson d'étudiant *m*	2292
Gregorianischer Choral *m*	plain-chant *m* / chant grégorien *m*	2293
Brautlied *n*	chant nuptial *m*	2294
Lied *n* / Kanzone *f*	chanson *f*	2295
Abendlied *n*	chant du soir *m*	2296
Kinderlied *n*	chanson enfantine *f*	2297
Schlager *m*	chanson à la mode *f* / chansonnette *f*	2298
Volkslied *n*	chanson populaire *f*	2299
Kanzonette *f*	canzonette *f*	2300
Capriccio *n*	caprice *m*	2301
Carmagnole *f* / Revolutionsgesang *m*	carmagnole *f*	2302
Carole *f*	carole *f*	2303
Kassation *f*	cassation *f*	2304
Kavatine *f*	cavatine *f*	2305
Chaconne *f*	chaconne *f*	2306
Musical *n*	comédie musicale *f*	2307
lyrische Komödie *f*	comédie lyrique *f*	2308

2309	concerto *m*	concerto
2310	concerto con quattro strumenti solisti *m*	quadruple concerto
2311	concerto doppio *m*	double concerto
2312	concerto per orchestra *m*	concerto for orchestra
2313	concerto per organo *m*	organ concerto
2314	concerto per pianoforte *m*	piano concerto
2315	concerto per violino *m*	violin concerto
2316	concerto sacro *m*	sacred concerto
2317	concerto sinfonico *m*	symphony concert
2318	concerto triplo *m*	triple concerto
2319	concerto vocale *m*	vocal concert
2320	consolazione *f*	consolation
2321	contraddanza *f*	country dance
2322	corale *m*	choral / chorale
2323	corrente *f*	courante
2324	cotillon *m*	cotillon
2325	czarda(s) *f*	czardas
2326	danza concertante *f*	concert dance
2327	danza delle streghe *f*	witches' dance
2328	danza dei morti *f* / danza macabra *f*	dance of death
2329	danza gitana *f*	gipsy dance
2330	danza popolare *f* / danza folcloristica *f*	folk dance
2331	danza rustica *f*	peasant dance
2332	danza slava *f*	Slavic dance
2333	danza spagnola *f*	Spanish dance
2334	danza ungherese *f*	Hungarian dance
2335	decimino *m*	work for ten players
2336	divertimento *m*	divertimento
2337	dramma lirico *m*	operatic / lyric drama
2338	dramma musicale *m*	music drama
2339	duetto *m* / duo *m*	duet
2340	egloga *f*	eclogue
2341	elegia *f*	elegy
2342	epilogo	epilogue
2343	fanfara *f*	fanfare / flourish
2344	fantasia *f*	fantasia / fancy

Konzert *n*	concerto *m*	2309
Quadrupelkonzert *n*	quadruple concerto *m*	2310
Doppelkonzert *n*	double concerto *m*	2311
Konzert für Orchester *n*	concerto pour orchestre *m*	2312
Orgelkonzert *n*	concerto pour orgue *m*	2313
Klavierkonzert *n*	concerto pour piano *m*	2314
Violinkonzert *n*	concerto pour violon *m*	2315
geistliches Konzert *n*	concert de musique sacrée *m*	2316
Sinfoniekonzert *n*	concert symphonique *m*	2317
Tripelkonzert *n*	triple concerto *m*	2318
Gesangskonzert *n*	concert vocal *m*	2319
Consolation *f* / Tröstung *f*	consolation *f*	2320
Kontretanz *m*	contredanse *f*	2321
Choral *m*	choral *m*	2322
Courante *f*	courante *f*	2323
Kotillon *m*	cotillon *m*	2324
Csárdás *m*	csardas *f*	2325
konzertanter Tanz *m*	danse concertante *f*	2326
Hexentanz *m*	dance des sorcières *f*	2327
Totentanz *m*	danse macabre *f*	2328
Zigeunertanz *m*	danse gitane *f*	2329
Volkstanz *m*	danse folklorique *f* / danse populaire *f*	2330
Bauerntanz *m*	danse champêtre *f* / danse paysanne *f* / villageoise *f*	2331
slawischer Tanz *m*	danse slave *f*	2332
spanischer Tanz *m*	danse espagnole *f*	2333
ungarischer Tanz *m*	danse hongroise *f*	2334
Dezett *n*	dixtuor *m*	2335
Divertimento *n* / „Unterhaltung" *f*	divertissement *m*	2336
lyrisches Drama *n*	drame lyrique *m*	2337
Musikdrama *n*	drame musical *m*	2338
Duett *n* / Duo *n*	duo *m*	2339
Hirtengedicht *n* / Ekloge *f*	églogue *f*	2340
Elegie *f*	élégie *f*	2341
Epilog *m* / Ausklang *m*	épilogue *m*	2342
Fanfare *f* / Tusch *m*	fanfare *f*	2343
Fantasie *f*	fantaisie *f*	2344

2345	farandola *f*	farandole
2346	farsa *f*	farce
2347	finale *m*	finale
2348	foglio d'album *m*	album leaf
2349	follia *f*	folia
2350	francese *f*	French dance
2351	fuga *f*	fugue
2352	fughetta *f*	fughetta
2353	furlana *f* / forlana *f*	forlana / furlana
2354	gagliarda *f*	galliard
2355	galanteria *f*	galanteries
2356	galoppo *m*	galop
2357	gavotta *f*	gavotte
2358	giga *f*	jig
2359	girotondo *m*	round dance
2360	gopak *m*	gopak
2361	improvviso *m*	impromptu
2362	inglese *f*	English dance
2363	inno *m*	hymn / anthem / hymn of praise
2364	inno nazionale *m*	national anthem
2365	interludio *m*	interlude
2366	intermezzo *m* / intermedio *m*	interlude
2367	intrada *f* / entrata *f*	intrada
2368	introduzione *f*	introduction
2369	invenzione *f*	invention
2370	istampita *f* / estampida *f*	estampie
2371	lai *m*	lay
2372	lamento *m*	lament
2373	lancieri *m pl*	lanciers
2374	landa *f*	lands
2375	lavolta *f* / volta *f*	volta
2376	leggenda *f*	legend
2377	litania *f*	litany
2378	madrigale *m*	madrigal
2379	maggiolata *f*	may song
2380	marcia *f*	march
2381	marcia funebre *f*	funeral march
2382	marcia nuziale *f*	wedding march
2383	marcia trionfale *f*	triumphal march
2384	marinesca *f*	sailor-like dance

Farandole *f*	farandole *f*	2345
Farce *f* / Posse *f*	farce *f*	2346
Schlussstück *n*	final *m*	2347
Albumblatt *n*	feuille d'album *f*	2348
Folia *f*	folie *f*	2349
Française *f*	française *f*	2350
Fuge *f*	fugue *f*	2351
Fughette *f* / kleine Fuge *f*	fughette *f*	2352
Forlana *f* / Friauler *m*	forlane *f*	2353
Gagliarde *f*	gaillarde *f*	2354
Galanterie *f*	galanteries *f pl*	2355
Galopp *m*	galop *m*	2356
Gavotte *f*	gavotte *f*	2357
Gigue *f*	gigue *f*	2358
Reigen *m*	ronde *f*	2359
Hopak *m*	gopak *m*	2360
Impromptu *n*	impromptu *m*	2361
Anglaise *f*	anglaise *f*	2362
Hymne *f* / Lobgesang *m*	hymne *m*	2363
Nationalhymne *f*	hymne national *m*	2364
Zwischenspiel *n*	entr'acte *m* / interlude *m*	2365
Zwischenspiel *n*	intermède *m*	2366
Intrade *f*	entrée *f*	2367
Einleitung *f*	introduction *f*	2368
Invention *f*	invention *f*	2369
Estampie *f*	estampie *f*	2370
Leich *m*	lai *m*	2371
Klage *f*	lamentation *f*	2372
Lancers *m Pl*	lanciers *m pl* / quadrille à la cour *f*	2373
Lande *f*	lande *f*	2374
Volta *f*	volte *f*	2375
Legende *f*	légende *f*	2376
Litanei *f*	litanie *f*	2377
Madrigal *n*	madrigal *m*	2378
Mailied *n*	chant de mai *m*	2379
Marsch *m*	marche *f*	2380
Trauermarsch *m*	marche funèbre *f*	2381
Hochzeitsmarsch *m*	marche nuptiale *f*	2382
Triumphmarsch *m*	marche triomphale	2383
Matelote *f* / Matrosentanz *m*	marinière *f* / matelote *f*	2384

2385	mascherata *f*	masque
2386	mattinata *f*	morning music / aubade
2387	mazurca *f*	mazurka
2388	melodramma *m*	melodrama
2389	messa *f*	mass
2390	messa dei defunti *f* / Requiem *m* / messa di (da) Requiem *f*	mass for the dead / requiem mass
2391	minuetto *m*	minuet
2392	mistero *m*	liturgical drama
2393	momento musicale *m*	"musical moment"
2394	monodramma *m*	monodrama
2395	moresca *f*	morris dance
2396	moto perpetuo *m* / perpetuum mobile (L)	perpetual motion
2397	mottetto *m*	motet
2398	nenia *f* / lamento funebre *m*	nenia / funeral lament
2399	ninna nanna *f*	lullaby / cradle song
2400	nonetto *m*	nonet
2401	notturno *m*	nocturne
2402	novelletta *f*	novelette
2403	ochetus *m*	hocket
2404	offertorio *m*	offertory
2405	opera *f*	opera
2406	opera buffa *f*	comic opera
2407	opera comica *f*	comic opera
2408	opera corale *f*	choral work
2409	opera seria *f*	serious opera
2410	operetta *f*	operetta
2411	oratorio *m*	oratorio
2412	ottetto *m*	octet
2413	ouverture *f* / sinfonia *f*	overture
2414	ouverture d'opera *f*	operatic overture
2415	ouverture da concerto *f*	concert overture
2416	parafrasi *f*	paraphrase
2417	parodia *f*	parody
2418	passacaglia *f*	passacaglia
2419	passepied *m*	passepied
2420	passione *f*	passion
2421	pasticcio *m*	pasticcio / pastiche
2422	pastorale *f*	pastoral

Maskenspiel *n* / Maskerade *f*	mascarade *f*	2385
Morgenständchen *n*	aubade *f*	2386
Mazurka *f*	mazurka *f*	2387
Melodram *n* / Melodrama *n*	mélodrame *m*	2388
Messe *f*	messe *f*	2389
Totenmesse *f* / Requiem *n*	messe des morts *f*	2390
Menuett *n*	menuet *m*	2391
liturgisches Drama *n*	drame liturgique *m*	2392
„musikalischer Augenblick" *m* / Moment musical *m*	moment musical *m*	2393
Monodram *n*	monodrame *m*	2394
Moreske *f* / Moriskentanz *m*	mauresque *f*	2395
durchlaufend bewegt	mouvement perpétuel *m*	2396
Motette *f*	motet *m*	2397
Nänie *f* / Totenklage *f*	nénie *f*	2398
Wiegenlied *n*	berceuse *f*	2399
Nonett *n*	nonet *m*	2400
Notturno *n* / Nachtstück *n*	nocturne *m*	2401
Novellette *f*	novelette *f*	2402
Hoketus *m*	hoquet *m*	2403
Offertorium *n*	offertoire *m*	2404
Oper *f*	opéra *m*	2405
heitere Oper *f*	opéra bouffe *m*	2406
komische Oper *f*	opéra comique *m*	2407
Chorwerk *n*	œuvre chorale *f*	2408
ernste Oper *f*	opéra sérieux *m*	2409
Operette *f*	opérette *f*	2410
Oratorium *n*	oratorio *m*	2411
Oktett *n*	octuor *m*	2412
Ouvertüre *f*	ouverture *f*	2413
Opernouvertüre *f*	ouverture d'opéra *f*	2414
Konzertouvertüre *f*	ouverture de concert *f*	2415
Paraphrase *f* / Umspielung *f*	paraphrase *f*	2416
Parodie *f*	parodie *f*	2417
Passacaglia *f*	passacaille *f*	2418
Passepied *m*	passepied *m*	2419
Passion *f*	passion *f*	2420
Flickoper *f*	pastiche *m*	2421
Pastorale *f* / Hirtenstück *n*	pastorale *f* / pastourelle *f*	2422

2423	pavana *f* / padovana *f*	pavan
2424	perigordino *m*	perigourdine
2425	pezzo caratteristico *m*	character piece
2426	pezzo da concerto *m*	concert piece
2427	pezzo lirico *m*	lyric piece
2428	poema *f*	poem
2429	poema sinfonico *m*	symphonic poem
2430	polacca *f*	polonaise
2431	polca *f*	polka
2432	postludio *m*	postlude
2433	pot-pourri *m*	pot-pourri / medley
2434	preambulo *m*	preamble
2435	preludio *m*	prelude
2436	prologo *m*	prologue
2437	quadriglia *f*	quadrille
2438	quartetto *m*	quartet
2439	quartetto d'archi *m*	string quartet
2440	quintetto *m*	quintet
2441	quintetto per (di) fiati *m*	wind quintet
2442	quodlibet *m* / messanza *f*	quodlibet
2443	rapsodia *f*	rhapsody
2444	recitativo *m*	recitative
2445	recitativo accompagnato *m*	accompanied recitative
2446	recitativo secco *m*	recitative with continuo accompaniment ("dry")
2447	ricercare *m*	ricercar
2448	rigaudon *m*	rigadoon
2449	ritornello *m*	ritornello
2450	romanza *f*	romance
2451	romanza senza parole *f*	song without words
2452	rondò *m*	rondo
2453	salmo *m*	psalm
2454	sarabanda *f*	sarabande
2455	sardana *f*	sardana
2456	scherzino *m* / scherzetto *m*	little scherzo
2457	scozzese *f*	Scottish dance
2458	serenata *f*	serenade
2459	sestetto *m*	sextet
2460	settimino *m*	septet
2461	siciliana *f*	siciliana
2462	sinfonia *f*	symphony

Pavane *f*	pavane *f*	2423
Perigourdine *f*	périgourdine *f*	2424
Charakterstück *n*	pièce de charactère *f*	2425
Konzertstück *n*	morceau de concert *m*	2426
Lyrisches Stück *n*	pièce lyrique *f*	2427
Poem *n* / Gedicht *n*	poème *m*	2428
sinfonische Dichtung *f*	poème symphonique *m*	2429
Polonaise *f*	polonaise *f*	2430
Polka *f*	polka *f*	2431
Nachspiel *n*	postlude *m*	2432
Potpourri *n*	pot-pourri *m*	2433
Präambel *f*	préambule *m*	2434
Präludium *n* / Vorspiel *n*	prélude *m*	2435
Prolog *m*	prologue *m*	2436
Quadrille *f*	quadrille *f*	2437
Quartett *n*	quatuor *m*	2438
Streichquartett *n*	quatuor à cordes *m*	2439
Quintett *n*	quintette *m*	2440
Bläserquintett *n*	quintette à vent *m*	2441
Quodlibet *n*	quodlibet *m* / fricassée *f*	2442
Rhapsodie *f*	rhapsodie *f*	2443
Rezitativ *n*	récitatif *m*	2444
begleitetes Rezitativ *n*	récitatif accompagné *m*	2445
Rezitativ nur mit Continuo („trocken") *n*	récitatif seulement avec continuo ("sec") *m*	2446
Ricercar *n*	ricercare *m*	2447
Rigaudon *m*	rigaudon *m*	2448
Ritornell *n*	ritournelle *f*	2449
Romanze *f*	romance *f*	2450
Lied ohne Worte *n*	romance sans paroles *f*	2451
Rondo *n*	rondo *m* / rondeau *m*	2452
Psalm *m*	psaume *m*	2453
Sarabande *f*	sarabande *f*	2454
Sardane *f*	sardane *f*	2455
kleines Scherzo *n*	petit scherzo *m*	2456
Ecossaise *f* (schottischer Tanz)	écossaise *f*	2457
Ständchen *n*	sérénade *f*	2458
Sextett *n*	sextuor *m*	2459
Septett *n*	septuor *m*	2460
Siciliano *m*	sicilienne *f*	2461
Sinfonie *f*	symphonie *f*	2462

2463	sinfonia concertante *f*	sinfonia concertante
2464	sogno *m*	dream
2465	sonata *f*	sonata
2466	sonata da camera *f*	chamber sonata
2467	sonata da chiesa *f*	church sonata
2468	sonata per pianoforte *f*	piano sonata
2469	sonatina *f*	sonatina
2470	stanza *f*	stanza
2471	studio *m*	study
2472	studio da concerto *m*	concert study
2473	studio di virtuosità *m*	virtuosity / virtuoso study
2474	studio trascendentale *m*	transcendental study
2475	suite francese *f*	French suite
2476	suite inglese *f*	English suite
2477	tarantella *f*	tarantella
2478	tema con variazioni *m*	theme with variations
2479	tenzone *m*	tenson
2480	terzetto *m* / trio *m*	trio
2481	tirolese *f*	tyrolienne
2482	tortiglione *m*	tourdion
2483	tragedia lirica *f*	lyric tragedy
2484	umoresca *f*	humoresque
2485	valzer *m*	waltz
2486	valzer viennese *m*	Viennese waltz
2487	variazione *f*	variation
2488	versetto *m*	verset
2489	vespri *m pl*	vespers
2490	villanella *f* / villanesca *f*	villanella
2491	zingaresca *f*	gipsy dance

Konzertante Sinfonie *f*	symphonie concertante *f*	2463
Träumerei *f* / Traum *m*	rêverie *f* / rêve *m*	2464
Sonate *f*	sonate *f*	2465
Kammersonate *f*	sonate de chambre *f*	2466
Kirchensonate *f*	sonate d'église *f*	2467
Klaviersonate *f*	sonate pour piano *f*	2468
Sonatine *f*	sonatine *f*	2469
Stanza *f*	stance *f*	2470
Etüde *f*	étude *f*	2471
Konzertetüde *f*	étude concertante *f* / étude de concert *f*	2472
virtuose Etüde *f*	étude de virtuosité *f*	2473
Transzendentaletüde *f*	étude transcendentale *f*	2474
Französische Suite *f*	suite française *f*	2475
Englische Suite *f*	suite anglaise *f*	2476
Tarantella *f*	tarentelle *f*	2477
Thema mit Variationen *n*	thème avec variations *m*	2478
Tenzone *f*	tenson *m*	2479
Terzett *n* / Trio *n*	trio *m*	2480
Tiroler Ländler *m* / Tiroler Lied *n*	tyrolienne *f*	2481
Tourdion *m*	tordion *m*	2482
Lyrische Tragödie *f*	tragédie lyrique *f*	2483
Humoreske *f*	humoresque *f*	2484
Walzer *m*	valse *f*	2485
Wienerwalzer *m*	valse viennoise *f*	2486
Variation *f* / Veränderung *f*	variation *f*	2487
Versett *n*	verset *m*	2488
Vesper *f*	vêpres *f pl*	2489
Villanella *f*	villanesque *f*	2490
Zigeunertanz *m* / Zigeunerlied *n*	tzigane *f*	2491

Le seguenti composizioni musicali
portano lo stesso nome in tutte le
lingue.

The following compositions bear
the same term in all languages.

2492	Alabado	2529	Extravaganza
2493	Alalá	2530	Fado
2494	Alborada	2531	Fandango
2495	Alegrias	2532	Farruca
2496	Angelito	2533	Flamenco
2497	Aragonaise	2534	Frottola
2498	Arioso	2535	Furiant
2499	Ayre	2536	Giustiniana
2500	Baborák	2537	Glee
2501	Badinage	2538	Greghesca
2502	Badinerie	2539	Guajira
2503	Batuque	2540	Guaracha
2504	Bergerette	2541	Habanera
2505	Bluette	2542	Halling
2506	Brunette	2543	Hey
2507	Bulerias	2544	Highland fling
2508	Cachucha	2545	Hornpipe
2509	Calata	2546	Horo
2510	Cancan	2547	Hupfauf
2511	Cantigas	2548	Jabadao
2512	Catch	2549	Jabo
2513	Cebell	2550	Jacara
2514	Chiarantana	2551	Jaleo
2515	Cinquepace	2552	Jarabe
2516	Colinda	2553	Jota
2517	Concertino	2554	Koleda
2518	Concerto grosso	2555	Kolo
2519	Contrás	2556	Kujawiak
2520	Corrido	2557	Ländler
2521	Cueca	2558	Lesginka
2522	Cumbia	2559	Lied
2523	Danzón	2560	Loure
2524	Diferencia	2561	Malagueña
2525	Doina	2562	Manfredina
2526	Double	2563	Manseque
2527	Dumka	2564	Manta
2528	Duo	2565	Monferrina

Die folgenden musikalischen
Kompositionen tragen in allen
Sprachen den gleichen Namen.

Les compositions musicales
suivantes portent le même nom
dans toutes les langues.

2566	Muñeira	2601	Sinfonietta
2567	Murciana	2602	Singspiel
2568	Musette	2603	Soleà
2569	Oberek	2604	Solfeggetto
2570	Obertas	2605	Springtanz
2571	Ode	2606	Stornello
2572	Palotas	2607	Strambotto
2573	Partita	2608	Strathspey
2574	Passamezzo	2609	Styrienne
2575	Pastourelle	2610	Suite
2576	Penillion	2611	Tambourin
2577	Petenera	2612	Tiento
2578	Piva	2613	Tirana
2579	Polo	2614	Toccata
2580	Polska	2615	Tombeau
2581	Redowa	2616	Tonadilla
2582	Reel	2617	Tourbillon
2583	Rejdovak	2618	Trepak
2584	Réjouissance	2619	Tresca
2585	Requiem	2620	Trescone
2586	Rheinländer	2621	Trezza
2587	Rispetto	2622	Trio
2588	Romanesca	2623	Trotto
2589	Ronda	2624	Tumba
2590	Rondeau	2625	Varsovienne
2591	Rondeña	2626	Vaudeville
2592	Rueda	2627	Veneziana
2593	Ruggiero	2628	Villancico
2594	Saeta	2629	Villotta
2595	Sainete	2630	Virelai
2596	Saltarello	2631	Voluntary
2597	Scherzo	2632	Zamacueco
2598	Schuhplattler	2633	Zapateado
2599	Sevillana	2634	Zarzuela
2600	Shanty	2635	Zortzico

Il linguaggio di ogni giorno

Every day language

Verbi

Verbs

2636	abbassare	to lower
2637	abbassare l'intonatura / abbassare l'accordatura	to tune down
2638	abbellire	to embellish
2639	abbreviare	to shorten
2640	accelerare	to accelerate
2641	accentuare	to stress
2642	accompagnare	to accompany
2643	accordare	to tune
2644	adattare	to adapt
2645	affrettare	to hasten
2646	aggiungere	to add
2647	allargare	to widen
2648	allontanarsi	to go away
2649	allungare	to lengthen
2650	alterare	to alter
2651	alternare	to alternate
2652	alzare	to raise
2653	alzare l'intonatura / alzare l'intonazione	to tune up
2654	ampliare	to enlarge
2655	animare	to animate
2656	annunciare	to announce
2657	applaudire	to applaud
2658	aprire	to open
2659	armonizzare	to harmonize
2660	arpeggiare	to play arpeggios
2661	articolare	to articulate
2662	ascoltare	to listen
2663	aspettare	to wait
2664	aumentare	to augment
2665	balbettare	to stammer
2666	ballare	to dance
2667	battere	to beat
2668	battere il tempo	to beat the time
2669	borbottare	to mumble

Die tägliche Sprache

Le langage de tous les jours

Verben

Verbes

senken / erniedrigen	baisser / abaisser	2636
herunterstimmen / tiefer stimmen	baisser l'accord / baisser l'intonation	2637
verschönern	embellir	2638
abkürzen	abréger	2639
beschleunigen	accélérer	2640
betonen	accentuer	2641
begleiten	accompagner	2642
einstimmen / stimmen	accorder	2643
bearbeiten	adapter	2644
beeilen	hâter	2645
hinzufügen	ajouter	2646
erweitern	élargir	2647
sich entfernen	s'éloigner	2648
verlängern	allonger	2649
alterieren	altérer	2650
alternieren / abwechseln	alterner	2651
erhöhen	hausser	2652
hinaufstimmen / höher stimmen	monter l'intonation / monter l'accord	2653
erweitern	agrandir	2654
beleben	animer	2655
ankündigen / ansagen	annoncer	2656
klatschen	applaudir	2657
öffnen	ouvrir	2658
harmonisieren	harmoniser	2659
arpeggieren	arpéger	2660
deutlich aussprechen	articuler	2661
zuhören / anhören / horchen	écouter	2662
warten	attendre	2663
vergrößern / steigern	augmenter	2664
stottern	balbutier	2665
tanzen	danser	2666
schlagen	battre	2667
Takt schlagen	battre la mesure	2668
murmeln	grommeler	2669

2670	brontolare	to grumble
2671	bussare	to knock
2672	buttare	to throw
2673	cadere / cascare	to fall down
2674	calare	to let down
2675	calmare	to calm
2676	cambiare / mutare	to change
2677	cantare	to sing
2678	capire	to understand
2679	cedere	to give in
2680	cercare	to seek / to look for
2681	chiaccherare	to chat
2682	chiedere	to ask
2683	chiudere	to shut / to close
2684	commuovere	to move
2685	comporre	to compose
2686	concatenare	to link together
2687	concentrarsi	to concentrate
2688	contare	to count
2689	continuare	to continue
2690	copiare	to copy
2691	coprire	to cover
2692	correggere	to correct
2693	creare	to create
2694	crescere	to grow
2695	criticare	to criticize
2696	dare dei concerti	to give concerts
2697	declamare	to declaim
2698	dedicare	to dedicate
2699	descrivere	to describe
2700	dimenticare	to forget
2701	diminuire	to diminish
2702	dirigere	to conduct
2703	dividere	to divide
2704	elaborare / rifinire	to elaborate
2705	elogiare / lodare	to praise
2706	entrare	to enter / to appear
2707	entrare in scena	to appear on stage
2708	esagerare	to exagerate
2709	eseguire	to perform

brummen	grogner	2670
klopfen	frapper	2671
werfen	jeter	2672
fallen / stürzen	tomber	2673
sinken / herablassen	faire descendre	2674
beruhigen	calmer	2675
wechseln / ändern	changer	2676
singen	chanter	2677
verstehen	comprendre	2678
nachgeben / nachlassen	céder	2679
suchen	chercher	2680
plaudern / tratschen	bavarder	2681
fragen	demander	2682
schließen / abschließen	fermer	2683
rühren	émouvoir	2684
komponieren	composer	2685
anknüpfen	enchaîner	2686
sich konzentrieren	se concentrer	2687
zählen	compter	2688
fortsetzen / fortfahren	continuer	2689
kopieren / abschreiben	copier	2690
bedecken	couvrir	2691
korrigieren	corriger	2692
erschaffen	créer	2693
wachsen / zunehmen / anwachsen	croître / grandir	2694
tadeln / kritisieren	critiquer	2695
konzertieren	donner des concerts	2696
deklamieren	déclamer	2697
widmen	dédier	2698
beschreiben	décrire	2699
vergessen	oublier	2700
vermindern / abnehmen	diminuer	2701
dirigieren	diriger	2702
teilen	diviser	2703
ausarbeiten	élaborer / fignoler	2704
loben	louer	2705
eintreten	entrer	2706
auftreten	entrer en scène	2707
übertreiben	exagérer	2708
ausführen / vortragen	exécuter	2709

2710	esercitare	to practise
2711	esordire	to make one's début
2712	espirare	to breathe out
2713	esprimere	to express
2714	essere fuori tempo	to be out of tempo
2715	essere in ritardo	to be late
2716	esultare	to exult
2717	fare	to make / to do
2718	felicitare	to congratulate
2719	fermare	to stop
2720	festeggiare	to celebrate
2721	finire	to finish
2722	fischiare	to whistle
2723	forzare	to force
2724	fraseggiare	to phrase
2725	frenare	to hold back / to brake
2726	graduare	to shade / to graduate
2727	grattare	to scratch
2728	gridare	to shout / to scream
2729	guidare / condurre	to lead / to guide
2730	imitare	to imitate
2731	imparare	to learn
2732	improvvisare	to improvise
2733	incominciare / attaccare	to begin / to strike up
2734	incrociare	to cross
2735	indicare	to indicate
2736	insegnare	to teach
2737	insistere	to insist
2738	interpretare	to interpret / to perform
2739	interrompere	to interrupt
2740	inspirare	to inhale
2741	intonare	to intone
2742	introdurre	to introduce
2743	invertire	to invert
2744	lavorare	to work
2745	legare	to tie / to slur
2746	leggere	to read
2747	marcare	to mark
2748	mentire	to lie
2749	mettere	to put

üben	exercer	2710
debütieren	débuter	2711
ausatmen	expirer	2712
ausdrücken	exprimer	2713
aus dem Takt sein	être hors du tempo	2714
zu spät kommen	être en retard	2715
jubeln	exulter	2716
machen / tun	faire	2717
beglückwünschen / gratulieren	féliciter	2718
abbrechen / anhalten	arrêter	2719
feiern	fêter	2720
enden	finir	2721
pfeifen	siffler	2722
forcieren	forcer	2723
phrasieren	phraser	2724
bremsen	freiner	2725
abstufen	nuancer / graduer	2726
kratzen	gratter	2727
schreien / aufschreien	crier	2728
führen	guider / conduire	2729
imitieren / nachahmen	imiter	2730
lernen	apprendre	2731
improvisieren / extemporieren	improviser	2732
anfangen / einsetzen / beginnen	commencer / attaquer	2733
kreuzen	croiser	2734
zeigen	indiquer	2735
lehren / unterrichten	enseigner	2736
beharren	insister	2737
interpretieren	interpréter	2738
unterbrechen	interrompre	2739
einatmen	inspirer	2740
anstimmen	entonner	2741
einführen / einleiten	introduire	2742
umkehren	inverser	2743
arbeiten	travailler	2744
binden	lier	2745
lesen	lire	2746
markieren	marquer	2747
lügen	mentir	2748
setzen / legen / stellen	mettre	2749

2750	mettere in scena	to stage
2751	migliorare	to improve
2752	misurare	to measure
2753	moderare	to moderate
2754	modificare	to modify
2755	mostrare	to show
2756	muoversi	to move
2757	orchestrare	to orchestrate
2758	parlare / dire	to speak / to talk / to say
2759	partecipare	to take part
2760	passare	to pass
2761	pensare	to think
2762	perfezionarsi	to improve
2763	plagiare	to plagiarize
2764	portare	to carry / to fetch
2765	posare / porre	to lay down
2766	precipitare	to precipitate / to hurry
2767	pregare	to beg / to pray
2768	preludiare	to prelude
2769	prendere	to take
2770	preparare	to prepare
2771	presentare	to present
2772	prestare	to lend
2773	progredire	to progress
2774	prolungare	to prolong
2775	pronunciare	to pronounce
2776	proporre	to propose
2777	provare	to try
2778	raccontare	to tell
2779	raccorciare / ridurre	to shorten / to reduce
2780	raddoppiare	to double
2781	raggruppare	to group
2782	rallentare	to slow down
2783	recitare	to recite
2784	registrare / incidere	to record / to tape
2785	rendere	to give back
2786	respirare	to breathe
2787	restare / rimanere	to stay / to remain
2788	richiamare	to recall

inszenieren	mettre en scène	2750
verbessern	améliorer	2751
messen	mesurer	2752
mäßigen	modérer	2753
abändern	modifier	2754
zeigen	montrer	2755
sich bewegen	se mouvoir / remuer	2756
orchestrieren	orchestrer	2757
sprechen / sagen	parler / dire	2758
teilnehmen	participer	2759
überleiten / übergehen	passer	2760
denken	penser	2761
sich vervollkommnen / sich weiterbilden	se perfectionner	2762
abschreiben / plagiieren	plagier	2763
tragen / bringen	porter	2764
niederlegen / hinlegen	poser	2765
überstürzen	précipiter	2766
bitten / beten	prier	2767
präludieren	préluder	2768
nehmen	prendre	2769
vorbereiten	préparer	2770
vorstellen	présenter	2771
leihen	prêter	2772
fortschreiten	progresser	2773
verlängern	prolonger	2774
aussprechen	prononcer	2775
vorschlagen	proposer	2776
probieren / versuchen	essayer	2777
erzählen	raconter	2778
verkürzen	réduire / raccourcir	2779
verdoppeln	doubler	2780
zusammenstellen	grouper	2781
verlangsamen	ralentir	2782
vortragen / vorzutragen	réciter	2783
(auf Tonträger) aufnehmen / mitschneiden	enregistrer / graver	2784
zurückgeben	rendre	2785
atmen	respirer	2786
bleiben / verweilen	rester	2787
zurückrufen	rappeler	2788

2789	ricominciare	to recommence / to start again
2790	ricordarsi	to remember
2791	ridere	to laugh
2792	riflettere	to think over
2793	rilassarsi / distendersi	to relax
2794	rimbalzare	to bounce
2795	rimbombare	to resound
2796	rinforzare	to reinforce
2797	rinviare	to adjourn / to put off
2798	ripetere	to rehearse / to repeat
2799	riprendere	to retake
2800	risolvere	to resolve
2801	rispondere	to answer
2802	risuonare	to replay
2803	ritardare	to delay
2804	ritenere	to hold back
2805	ritmare	to emphasize the rhythm
2806	rovesciare	to upset / to overturn
2807	saltare	to jump
2808	saltare al posto di un'altro	to understudy / to take over a part
2809	sapere / conoscere	to know
2810	sbagliare / equivocarsi	to mistake / to make a mistake
2811	scrivere	to write
2812	scrivere delle note / scrivere della musica	to notate
2813	seguire	to follow
2814	semplificare	to simplify
2815	sentire	to feel / to hear
2816	separare	to separate
2817	sfiorare	to touch lightly
2818	singhiozzare	to sob
2819	smettere / cessare	to stop
2820	smorzare	to subdue
2821	soffiare	to blow
2822	sognare	to dream
2823	sopprimere	to suppress
2824	sorridere	to smile
2825	sospirare	to sigh
2826	sostituire / rimpiazzare	to substitute

wieder beginnen	recommencer	2789
sich erinnern	se souvenir	2790
lachen	rire	2791
nachdenken / überdenken	réfléchir	2792
lockern / entspannen	se relaxer / se détendre	2793
zurückprallen	rebondir	2794
dröhnen / widerhallen	retentir	2795
verstärken	renforcer	2796
verschieben / vertagen	renvoyer / ajourner	2797
proben / wiederholen	répéter	2798
wieder anfangen / wieder aufnehmen	reprendre	2799
auflösen	résoudre	2800
antworten	répondre	2801
erneut spielen	rejouer	2802
verzögern	retarder	2803
zurückhalten	retenir	2804
rhythmisieren	rhythmer	2805
umkehren	renverser	2806
springen / überspringen	sauter	2807
einspringen	remplacer au pied levé	2808
wissen / kennen	savoir / connaître	2809
(sich) irren / sich täuschen	se tromper / faire une faute	2810
schreiben	écrire	2811
notieren / Noten schreiben	noter / écrire de la musique	2812
folgen	suivre	2813
vereinfachen	simplifier	2814
hören / fühlen	ressentir	2815
trennen	séparer	2816
streifen	effleurer	2817
schluchzen	sangloter	2818
aufhören	cesser	2819
dämpfen	atténuer	2820
blasen	souffler	2821
träumen	rêver	2822
aufheben	supprimer	2823
lächeln	sourir	2824
seufzen	soupirer	2825
ersetzen	substituer / remplacer	2826

2827	sparire	to disappear
2828	spegnere	to extinguish
2829	spiegare	to explain
2830	spingere	to push
2831	staccare	to undo
2832	stare	to stay
2833	stonare / steccare	to be out of tune / to waver in pitch / to strike a false note
2834	strappare	to tear
2835	strimpellare	to strum
2836	strumentare	to score
2837	studiare	to study
2838	suddividere	to subdivide
2839	suggerire	to prompt
2840	suonare / toccare	to play / to touch
2841	suonare a memoria	to play by heart
2842	suonare a orecchio	to play by ear
2843	suonare a prima vista / leggere a prima vista	to play at sight / to sight-read
2844	tacere	to be silent
2845	tagliare	to cut
2846	tenere	to keep / to hold
2847	tenere il tempo	to keep time
2848	terminare / concludere	to end
2849	tirare	to pull
2850	togliere / levare	to take away / to remove
2851	tornare / ritornare	to return
2852	trascinare / trascicare	to drag
2853	trasportare / spostare	to transpose
2854	trattare	to treat
2855	tremare	to tremble
2856	trovare	to find
2857	udire	to hear
2858	unire / congiungere	to connect / to join
2859	urlare	to howl
2860	variare	to vary
2861	vedere / guardare	to see / to look
2862	vibrare	to vibrate
2863	vociare	to yell
2864	voltare / girare	to turn

verschwinden	disparaître	2827
auslöschen	éteindre	2828
erklären	expliquer	2829
stoßen / treiben	pousser	2830
abstoßen / lostrennen	détacher	2831
bleiben	rester	2832
detonieren / falsch spielen	détonner / jouer faux	2833
reißen	arracher	2834
klimpern	tapoter	2835
instrumentieren	instrumenter	2836
studieren / lernen	étudier	2837
unterteilen	subdiviser	2838
vorsagen / soufflieren	souffler	2839
spielen / greifen / berühren	jouer / toucher	2840
auswendig spielen	jouer par cœur	2841
nach Gehör spielen	jouer d'oreille	2842
vom Blatt spielen	déchiffrer / jouer à vue	2843
schweigen	se taire	2844
schneiden	couper	2845
halten / aushalten	tenir	2846
Takt halten	garder la mesure	2847
beendigen / abschließen	terminer	2848
ziehen	tirer	2849
wegnehmen	enlever / lever / ôter	2850
zurückkommen / zurückkehren	revenir	2851
schleppen	traîner	2852
transponieren	transposer	2853
behandeln	traiter	2854
zittern	trembler	2855
finden	trouver	2856
hören	entendre	2857
verbinden / anschließen	unir / joindre	2858
heulen	hurler	2859
abändern / verändern	varier	2860
sehen / schauen	voir / regarder	2861
vibrieren / schwingen / erklingen	vibrer	2862
grölen / brüllen	vociférer	2863
umblättern / wenden	tourner	2864

	Piccola raccolta di parole	**A small collection of words**
2865	abbonamento *m*	subscription
2866	accademia di musica *f*	music school / college
2867	abbondante	abundant
2868	abile	able
2869	accessori *m pl*	accessories / props
2870	accentuazione *f*	accentuation
2871	accompagnamento *m*	accompaniment
2872	accordato	tuned
2873	accordatura *f*	tuning
2874	acustica *f*	acoustics
2875	acustica ambientale *f*	acoustics (of a hall/room)
2876	addio!	farewell!
2877	adesso / ora	now
2878	agenzia di concerti *f*	concert agency
2879	allievo *m* / allieva *f* / alunno *m* / alunna *f*	pupil
2880	almeno	at least
2881	altezza *f*	height
2882	alto	high
2883	amante della musica *m + f* / melomane *m + f*	music lover
2884	a mente / a memoria	by heart
2885	annotazione *f*	annotation
2886	antico	antique
2887	antologia *f*	anthology
2888	apice *m* / punto culminante *m*	climax / apex
2889	apparecchi imitanti voci animali *m pl*	animal sound-effects
2890	applauso *m*	applause
2891	archi *m pl*	string section
2892	arrangiamento *m* / adattamento *m*	arrangement / adaptation
2893	arte *f*	art
2894	artistico	artistic / artistry
2895	ascoltatore *m* / ascoltatrice *f*	listener
2896	ascolto *m*	hearing
2897	assordante	deafening
2898	attacco *m*	cue

Kleine Wörtersammlung

Petite collection de mots

Abonnement *n*	abonnement *m*	2865
Musikhochschule *f* / Musikakademie *f*	école supérieure de musique *f*	2866
reichlich	abondant	2867
geschickt / fähig zu	habile	2868
Requisiten *n Pl*	accessoires *m pl*	2869
Betonung *f*	accentuation *f*	2870
Begleitung *f*	accompagnement *m*	2871
gestimmt	accordé	2872
Stimmung (eines Instrumentes) *f*	accordage *m*	2873
Akustik *f*	acoustique *f*	2874
Raumakustik *f*	acoustique ambiante *f* / acoustique d'un local *f*	2875
Lebe wohl!	adieu!	2876
jetzt	maintenant	2877
Konzertagentur *f*	agence de concerts	2878
Schüler *m* / Schülerin *f*	élève *m* + *f*	2879
wenigstens	au moins	2880
Höhe *f*	hauteur *f*	2881
hoch	haut	2882
Musikliebhaber *m* / Musiklieb- haberin *f*	amateur de musique *m* / mélomane *m* + *f*	2883
auswendig	par cœur	2884
Anmerkung *f* / Notiz *f*	annotation *f* / notice *f*	2885
altertümlich	antique / ancien	2886
Sammelwerk *n*	anthologie *f*	2887
Höhepunkt *m*	point culminant *m*	2888
Tierstimmeneffekte *m Pl*	effects d'animaux *m pl*	2889
Beifall *m*	applaudissement *m*	2890
Streicher *m Pl*	cordes *f pl*	2891
Arrangement *n* / Bearbeitung *f*	arrangement *m* / adaptation *f*	2892
Kunst *f*	art *m*	2893
künstlerisch	artistique	2894
Hörer *m* / Hörerin *f*	auditeur *m* / auditrice *f*	2895
Gehör *n*	écoute *m*	2896
betäubend	assourdissant	2897
Einsatz *m*	entrée *f*	2898

2899	attento	attentive
2900	attenzione!	take care!
2901	atto *m*	act
2902	audizione *f*	audition
2903	autore *m*	author
2904	avanzato	advanced
2905	bacchetta *f*	stick / baton
2906	ballo *m* / danza *f*	dance
2907	ballo di società *m* / ballo di sala *m*	ballroom dance
2908	bambino prodigio *m*	infant prodigy
2909	banda *f* / fanfara *f*	brass band / wind band
2910	banda di ottoni *f*	brass band
2911	banda militare *f*	military band
2912	barocco *m*	baroque
2913	basso	low / bass
2914	basta!	that's enough!
2915	bellezza *f*	beauty
2916	bello / bella	beautiful
2917	biglietto *m* / ingresso *m*	ticket
2918	biglietto in omaggio *m*	complimentary ticket
2919	bis (L)	encore
2920	botteghino *m* / biglietteria *f*	box office
2921	brano *m* / pezzo *m*	piece
2922	bravissimo!	very good!
2923	cacofonia *f*	cacophony
2924	calcare le scene	to tread the stage
2925	cambiamento *m*	change
2926	cambio di scena *m*	change of set
2927	camerino *m*	green-room
2928	canzone a successo *f*	hit
2929	capolavoro *m*	masterpiece
2930	cappella *f*	chapel
2931	caratteristico	characteristic
2932	carnevale *m*	carnival
2933	carta da musica *f*	music-paper
2934	cartellone *m*	poster / playbill
2935	casa editrice di musica *f*	music publishing house
2936	catalogo *m*	catalogue / catalog

aufmerksam	attentif	2899
Achtung! / pass auf!	attention!	2900
Akt *m* / Aufzug *m*	acte *m*	2901
Probespiel *n*	audition *f* / essai *m*	2902
Autor *m*	auteur *m*	2903
fortgeschritten	avancé	2904
Taktstock *m* / Dirigentenstab *m*	baguette *f*	2905
Tanz *m*	danse *f*	2906
Gesellschaftstanz *m*	danse de societé *f* / danse de salon *f*	2907
Wunderkind *n*	enfant prodige *m*	2908
Blasmusik *f* / Fanfare *f*	fanfare *f* / corps de musique *m*	2909
Blechblasorchester *n*	fanfare de cuivres *f*	2910
Militärkapelle *f*	musique militaire *f* / harmonie *f*	2911
Barock *m*	baroque *m*	2912
niedrig / tief	bas	2913
genug!	assez!	2914
Schönheit *f*	beauté *f*	2915
schön	beau / belle	2916
Eintrittskarte *f*	billet *m* / billet d'entrée *m*	2917
Freikarte *f*	billet de faveur *m* / billet gratuit *m*	2918
noch einmal! / Zugabe! *f*	encore!	2919
Theaterkasse *f* / Konzertkasse *f*	bureau de location *m*	2920
Stück *n*	morceau *m* / pièce *f*	2921
sehr gut!	très bien!	2922
Kakophonie *f* / Missklang *m*	cacophonie *f*	2923
auf die Bühne gehen	monter sur les planches	2924
Abwechslung *f* / Änderung *f*	changement *m*	2925
Umbau *m*	changement de décor *m*	2926
Künstlerzimmer *n*	foyer des artistes *m*	2927
Erfolgsschlager *m*	tube *m*	2928
Meisterwerk *n*	chef-d'œuvre *m*	2929
Kapelle *f*	chapelle *f*	2930
charakteristisch	caractéristique	2931
Karneval m / Fastnacht *f* / Fasching *m*	carnaval *m*	2932
Notenpapier *n*	papier à musique *m*	2933
Plakat *n* / Spielplan *m*	affiche *f*	2934
Musikverlag *m*	maison d'édition musicale *f*	2935
Verzeichnis *n*	catalogue *m*	2936

2937	celebre / famoso	famous
2938	centro uditivo *m*	listening centre
2939	certo / sicuro	certain / sure
2940	chiesa *f*	church
2941	chiuso	closed
2942	ciclo *m*	cycle
2943	cielo *m*	sky
2944	classico	classic
2945	classicismo *m*	classicism
2946	collaborazione *f*	collaboration
2947	collezione *f* / raccolta *f*	collection
2948	colore *m* / colorito *m* / timbro *m*	tone-colour / timbre / colour
2949	colto	cultivated
2950	commedia *f*	comedy
2951	comparsa *m + f* / figurante *m + f*	bit player / extra
2952	complesso *m*	ensemble
2953	completamente / totalmente	completely
2954	completo	complete
2955	composizione *f*	composition
2956	comprimario *m*	supporting role
2957	comune	common
2958	concerto *m*	concert / recital
2959	concerto privato *m*	house concert / private concert
2960	concorso musicale *m*	musical competition / musical contest
2961	conservatorio *m*	conservatoire / conservatory
2962	consonante *f*	consonant
2963	contenuto *m*	contents
2964	continuità *f*	continuity
2965	contrario *m*	contrary
2966	contrasto *m*	contrast
2967	coreografia *f*	choreography
2968	corpo di ballo *m*	chorps de ballet
2969	corretto	correct
2970	cosa *f*	thing
2971	costume *m*	costume / dress
2972	creativo	creative

berühmt	célèbre / fameux	2937
Hörzentrum *n*	centre auditif *m*	2938
gewiss / sicher	certain / sûr	2939
Kirche *f*	église *f*	2940
geschlossen	fermé	2941
Zyklus *m*	cycle *m*	2942
Himmel *m*	ciel *m*	2943
klassisch	classique	2944
Klassik *f*	classicisme *m*	2945
Mitwirkung *f*	collaboration *f*	2946
Sammlung *f*	collection *f* / recueil *m*	2947
Klangfarbe *f* / Tonfarbe *f* / Farbe *f* / Schattierung *f*	timbre *m* / couleur *f* / nuance *f*	2948
gebildet	cultivé	2949
Komödie *f*	comédie *f*	2950
Komparse *m* / Komparsin *f* / Statist *m* / Statistin *f*	figurant *m* / figurante *f*	2951
Ensemble *n*	ensemble *m*	2952
in vollständiger Weise / gänzlich	complètement / entièrement	2953
vollständig	complet	2954
Komposition *f* / Vertonung *f*	composition *f*	2955
Nebenrolle *f*	rôle secondaire *m*	2956
gemeinsam	commun	2957
Konzert *n*	concert *m* / récital *m*	2958
Hauskonzert *n*	concert privé *m*	2959
Musikwettbewerb *m*	concours de musique *m* / compétition musicale *f* / concours musical *m*	2960
Konservatorium *n*	conservatoire *m*	2961
Konsonant *m*	consonne *f*	2962
Inhalt *m*	contenu *m*	2963
Kontinuität *f*	continuité *f*	2964
Gegenteil *n*	contraire *m*	2965
Kontrast *m*	contraste *m*	2966
Choreographie *f*	chorégraphie *f*	2967
Ballettkorps *n*	corps de ballet *m*	2968
korrekt	correct	2969
Ding *n*	chose *f*	2970
Kostüm *n*	costume *m*	2971
schöpferisch	créatif	2972

2973	critica *f*	criticism
2974	debutto *m* / esordio *m*	début
2975	dedica *f*	dedication
2976	destra (a)	right (on the)
2977	dialogo *m*	dialogue
2978	diapason *m*	tuning fork
2979	diapason à fiato *m*	pitch pipe
2980	diapason da camera *m*	concert pitch
2981	dietro le quinte	behind the scenes
2982	difetto *m*	fault
2983	differenza *f*	difference
2984	difficile	difficult
2985	difficoltà *f*	difficulty
2986	dilettante *m*	dilettante / amateur / layman
2987	dinamica *f*	dynamics
2988	direttore ospite *m*	guest conductor
2989	direzione *f*	management
2990	diritti d'autore *m pl*	royalties
2991	diritti d'esecuzione *m pl*	performing rights
2992	diritto d'autore *m*	copyright
2993	discoteca *f*	discotheque
2994	discreto	discreet
2995	disposizione dell'orchestra *f*	orchestral layout
2996	distanza *f*	distance
2997	distribuzione *f*	cast
2998	diteggiatura *f*	fingering
2999	divertente	funny / amusing
3000	dramma *m*	drama
3001	durata *f*	duration
3002	eccellente	excellent
3003	eccetera / etc	and so on
3004	ecco	here
3005	edizione *f*	edition / issue
3006	edizione completa *f*	complete edition
3007	educazione dell'orecchio *f* / ascolto *m*	aural training
3008	effetto *m*	effect / result
3009	efficace	effective

Kritik *f*	critique *f*	2973
Debüt *n*	début *m*	2974
Widmung *f*	dédicace *f*	2975
rechts	droite (á)	2976
Dialog *m*	dialogue *m*	2977
Stimmgabel *f*	diapason à branches *m*	2978
Stimmpfeife *f*	diapason à bouche *m*	2979
Kammerton *m*	diapason de chambre *m*	2980
hinter der Bühne	derrière les coulisses	2981
Fehler *m* / Mangel *m*	défaut *m*	2982
Unterschied *m*	différence *f*	2983
schwierig / schwer	difficile	2984
Schwierigkeit *f*	difficulté *f*	2985
Dilettant *m* / Liebhaber *m* / Laie *m*	dilettante *m* / amateur *m*	2986
Dynamik *f*	dynamique *f* / nuances *f pl*	2987
Gastdirigent *m*	chef invité *m*	2988
Direktion *f* / Leitung *f*	direction *f*	2989
Tantiemen *f Pl*	droits d'auteur *m pl* / tantièmes *m pl*	2990
Aufführungsrecht *n*	droits d'execution *m pl*	2991
Urheberrecht *n*	droit d'auteur *m*	2992
Diskothek *f*	discothèque *f*	2993
ziemlich gut / diskret	passable / discret	2994
Orchesteranordnung *f*	disposition de l'orchestre *f*	2995
Abstand *m* / Distanz *f*	distance *f*	2996
Besetzung *f*	distribution *f*	2997
Fingersatz *m* / Applikatur *f*	doigté *m*	2998
unterhaltend / vergnüglich	divertissant / amusant	2999
Drama *n*	drame *m*	3000
Dauer *f* / Spieldauer *f*	durée *f*	3001
ausgezeichnet	excellent	3002
und so weiter / usw.	et ainsi de suite	3003
hier / da	voici / voilà	3004
Ausgabe *f* / Auflage *f*	édition *f* / tirage *m*	3005
Gesamtausgabe *f*	édition complète *f*	3006
Gehörbildung *f*	éducation de l'oreille *f*	3007
Effekt *m* / Wirkung *f* / Eindruck *m*	effet *m*	3008
wirkungsvoll	efficace	3009

3010	eguaglianza *f*	equality
3011	entrata *f*	entrance
3012	entrata degli artisti *f*	the stage door
3013	epoca *f*	epoch / era
3014	esaurito / completo / pienone *m*	sold out / full house
3015	esecuzione *f*	performance
3016	esempio *m*	example
3017	esercizio *m*	exercise
3018	esercizio per le dita *m*	finger exercise
3019	esordiente *m* + *f* / principiante *m* + *f*	beginner
3020	esposizione *f*	exhibition
3021	espressionismo *m*	expressionism
3022	estensione *f*	range / extension
3023	estetica *f*	aesthetics
3024	estratto *m*	excerpt
3025	eterno	eternal
3026	eufonia	euphony
3027	euritmia *f*	eurhythmics
3028	facile	easy
3029	facilità *f*	facility
3030	fantasma *m* / spettro *m*	ghost / apparition
3031	favola *f* / fiaba *f*	fairy tale / fable
3032	fedele all'originale	faithful to the original
3033	felice	happy / merry
3034	festa *f* / gala *m*	holiday / festival / party / gala
3035	festival musicale *m*	music festival
3036	fiasco *m*	failure / flop
3037	fiati *m pl*	wind section
3038	fiato *m*	breath
3039	figurazione *f*	figuration
3040	filarmonica / filarmonico	philharmonic
3041	filo *m*	thread / wire
3042	finto	feigned
3043	foglio *m*	sheet
3044	folclore *m*	folklore
3045	folletto *m*	elf
3046	fonetica *f*	phonetics

Deutsch	Français	Nr.
Gleichheit *f*	égalité *f*	3010
Eingang *m* / Eintritt *m* / Orchestereinsatz *m*	entrée *f*	3011
Künstlereingang m	entrée des artistes *f*	3012
Epoche *f* / Zeitabschnitt *m*	époque *f*	3013
ausverkauft / vergriffen	épuisé / complet	3014
Ausführung *f* / Vortrag *m*	exécution *f*	3015
Beispiel *n*	exemple *m*	3016
Übung *f*	exercice *m*	3017
Fingerübung *f*	exercice pour les doigts *m*	3018
Anfänger *m* / Anfängerin *f*	débutant *m* / débutante *f*	3019
Ausstellung *f*	exposition *f*	3020
Expressionismus *m*	expressionisme *m*	3021
Umfang *m* / Raum *m* / Ausdehnung *f*	étendue *f*	3022
Ästhetik *f*	esthétique *f*	3023
Ausschnitt *m* / Auszug *m*	extrait *m*	3024
ewig	éternel	3025
Euphonie *f* / Wohlklang *m*	euphonie *f*	3026
Eurhythmie *f*	eurythmie *f*	3027
leicht	facile	3028
Leichtigkeit *f*	facilité *f*	3029
Gespenst *n* / (Geister-)Erscheinung *f*	fantôme *m* / apparition *f*	3030
Fabel *f* / Märchen *n*	fable *f* / conte *m*	3031
werkgetreu	fidèle à l'original	3032
glücklich	heureux	3033
Fest *n* / Gala *f*	fête *f* / gala *m*	3034
Musikfest(spiel) *n*	festival de musique *m*	3035
Misserfolg *m* / Durchfall *m*	échec *m* / four *m*	3036
Bläser *m Pl*	vents *m pl*	3037
Atem *m*	souffle *m*	3038
Darstellung *f*	figuration *f*	3039
philharmonisch	philharmonique	3040
Faden *m* / Garn *n* / Draht *m*	fil *m*	3041
vorgetäuscht / fingiert	simulé / feint	3042
Papierblatt *n* / Bogen *m*	feuille *f*	3043
Folklore *f*	folklore *m*	3044
Troll *m* / Poltergeist *m*	lutin *m* / follet *m*	3045
Phonetik *f* / Lautkunde *f*	phonétique *f*	3046

3047	foresta f / bosco m	forest
3048	formato m	format
3049	forza f / intensità sonora f	strength of tone / intensity
3050	fossa dell'orchestra f / golfo mistico m	orchestra box / orchestral pit
3051	frammento m	fragment
3052	fuori / all'aperto	outside / open air
3053	galleria f / loggione m	balcony / gallery
3054	generalmente	generally
3055	genere m	genre
3056	geniale	ingenious
3057	genio m	genius
3058	gesto m / cenno m	gesture / wave
3059	graduazione f	gradation
3060	gratis / gratuito	free / gratuitous
3061	gregoriano	Gregorian
3062	idea f	idea
3063	ideale	ideal
3064	il sipario si abbassa	the curtain goes down
3065	il sipario si alza	the curtain rises / goes up
3066	il sipario si apre	the curtain opens
3067	il sipario si chiude	the curtain closes
3068	illuminazione f	lighting
3069	immagine sonora f	sound picture
3070	impercettibile	imperceptible
3071	importante / considerevole	important
3072	impossibile	impossible
3073	impreciso / inesatto	inaccurate / inexact
3074	impreparato	unprepared
3075	impressionismo m	impressionism
3076	improvvisazione f	improvisation
3077	in bocca al lupo	good luck / break a leg
3078	inatteso	unexpected
3079	incerto	uncertain
3080	inchino m	bow / curtsey
3081	incompleto	incomplete
3082	indicazione metronomica f	metronome mark(ing)
3083	indipendenza f	independence

Wald *m* / Tann *m*	forêt *f* / bois *m*	3047
Format *n*	format *m*	3048
Intensität des Klanges *f*	intensité du son *f* / puissance *f*	3049
Orchestergraben *m*	fosse d'orchestre *f*	3050
Fragment *n* / Bruchstück *n*	fragment *m*	3051
draußen / im Freien	dehors / en plein air	3052
Galerie *f*	galerie *f* / poulailler *m* / paradis *m*	3053
im Allgemeinen	en général	3054
Gattung *f*	genre *m*	3055
genial	génial	3056
Genius *m* / Genie *n*	génie *m*	3057
Gebärde *f* / Geste *f*	geste *m*	3058
Abstufung *f*	graduation *f*	3059
gratis / unentgeltlich	gratuit	3060
gregorianisch	grégorien	3061
Idee *f*	idée *f*	3062
ideal / vollkommen	idéal	3063
der Vorhang fällt	le rideau se baisse	3064
der Vorhang hebt sich	le rideau se lève	3065
der Vorhang öffnet sich	le rideau s'ouvre	3066
der Vorhang schließt sich	le rideau se ferme	3067
Beleuchtung *f*	éclairage *m*	3068
Klangbild *n*	image sonore *f*	3069
unmerklich / unvernehmlich	imperceptible	3070
wichtig / bedeutend / beträchtlich	important / considerable	3071
unmöglich	impossible	3072
ungenau	imprécis / inexact	3073
unvorbereitet	non préparé	3074
Impressionismus *m*	impressionisme *m*	3075
Improvisation *f*	improvisation *f*	3076
Hals- und Beinbruch / toi, toi, toi	trois fois merde	3077
unerwartet	inattendu	3078
unsicher	incertain / douteux	3079
Verbeugung *f* / Verneigung *f*	révérence *f*	3080
unvollständig	incomplet	3081
Metronomangabe *f*	indication métronomique *f*	3082
Unabhängigkeit *f*	indépendance *f*	3083

3084	ineseguibile	unplayable
3085	inferiore	lower / inferior
3086	inizio *m* / principio *m*	beginning
3087	integrale *f*	complete works
3088	interpretazione *f*	interpretation
3089	interprete *m* + *f*	performer / interpreter
3090	interruzione *f* / pausa *f*	interruption / intermission
3091	intervallo *m*	intermission
3092	intesa *f*	agreement / entente
3093	intuizione *f*	intuition
3094	invariabile	invariable
3095	irregolare	irregular
3096	ispirazione *f*	inspiration
3097	larghezza *f*	width / breadth
3098	leggio *m*	music stand / desk
3099	legni *m pl* / strumentini *m pl*	woodwind
3100	legno *m*	wood
3101	lettera *f*	letter
3102	lezione *f*	lesson
3103	lezione collettiva *f*	group lesson
3104	libro *m* / volume *m*	book / volume
3105	luci della ribalta	limelights
3106	malgrado / nonostante	although / even
3107	maschera *f*	mask
3108	maschera *m+f*	usher *m* / usherette *f*
3109	mecenate *m*	maecenas / patron
3110	meraviglioso / stupendo	marvellous / wonderful
3111	messa in scena *f*	production / staging
3112	metronomo *m*	metronome
3113	modello *m*	model / pattern
3114	moderno	modern
3115	musa *f*	muse
3116	musica *f*	music
3117	musica a programma *f*	programme music
3118	musica a quarti di tono *f*	quarter-tone music
3119	musica aleatoria *f*	aleatoric music
3120	musica antica *f*	ancient music

Deutsch	Français	Nr.
unausführbar / unspielbar	inexécutable	3084
niedriger / unter	inférieur	3085
Anfang *m*	début *m* / commencement *m*	3086
Gesamtwerk	l'œuvre intégrale *f*	3087
Interpretation *f* / Gestaltung *f* / Deutung *f*	interprétation *f*	3088
Interpret *m* / Ausführender *m*	interprète *m* + *f*	3089
Unterbrechung *f*	interruption *f*	3090
Pause *f*	entracte *m*	3091
Einklang *m* / Überein-stimmung *f*	entente *f*	3092
Eingebung *f*	intuition *f*	3093
unveränderlich	invariable	3094
unregelmäßig	irrégulier	3095
Inspiration *f* / Einfall *m*	inspiration *f*	3096
Breite *f*	largeur *f*	3097
Notenpult *n* / Notenständer *m*	lutrin *m* / pupitre *m*	3098
Holzbläser *m Pl*	bois *m pl*	3099
Holz *n*	bois *m*	3100
Buchstabe *m* / Brief *m*	lettre *f*	3101
Lektion *f* / Unterricht *m*	leçon *f*	3102
Gruppenunterricht *m*	cours collectif *m*	3103
Buch *n* / Band *m*	livre *m* / volume *m*	3104
Rampenlicht	feux de la rampe	3105
trotzdem / ungeachtet	malgré	3106
Maske *f*	masque *m*	3107
Platzanweiser *m* / Platzanweiserin *f*	ouvreur *m* / ouvreuse *f*	3108
Mäzen *m* / Förderer *m*	mécène *m*	3109
wunderbar / erstaunlich	merveilleux / étonnant	3110
Inszenierung *f*	mise en scène *f*	3111
Metronom *m*	métronome *m*	3112
Muster *n* / Vorbild *n*	modèle *m*	3113
modern	moderne	3114
Muse *f*	muse *f*	3115
Musik *f*	musique *f*	3116
Programmmusik *f*	musique à programme *f*	3117
Vierteltonmusik *f*	musique en quarts de ton *f* / musique microtonale *f*	3118
aleatorische Musik *f*	musique aléatoire *f*	3119
alte Musik *f*	musique ancienne *f*	3120

3121	musica assoluta *f* / musica pura *f*	absolute music
3122	musica classica *f*	classical music
3123	musica concreta *f*	musique concrète
3124	musica contemporanea *f*	contemporary music
3125	musica corale *f* / musica per coro *f*	choral music
3126	musica d'ambiente *f*	mood music
3127	musica d'avanguardia *f*	avantgarde music
3128	musica da ballo *f*	dance music
3129	musica da caccia *f*	hunting music
3130	musica da camera *f*	chamber music
3131	musica da chiesa *f* / musica liturgica *f*	church music
3132	musica da consumo *f* / musica d'uso *f*	functional music
3133	musica da salotto *f*	salon music
3134	musica da tavola *f*	table music
3135	musica dell'avvenire *f*	music of the future
3136	musica descrittiva *f*	descriptive music
3137	musica di corte *f*	court music
3138	musica di gatti *f*	cater wauling / shivaree
3139	musica di sottofondo *f*	background music
3140	musica della Passione *f*	passion music
3141	musica di Natale	Christmas music
3142	musica di scena *f* / musica scenica *f*	incidental music
3143	musica dodecafonica *f*	dodecaphonic music / twelve-tone music
3144	musica drammatica *f*	dramatic music
3145	musica elettronica *f*	electronic music
3146	musica esotica *f*	exotic music
3147	musica familiare *f* / musica domestica *f*	domestic music
3148	musica funebre *f*	funeral music
3149	musica leggera *f*	light music / entertainment music
3150	musica lirica *f*	operatic music
3151	musica meccanica *f*	mechanical music
3152	musica militaire *f*	military music
3153	musica nella (della) strada *f*	street music

absolute Musik *f*	musique pure *f*	3121
klassische Musik *f* / E-Musik *f*	musique classique *f*	3122
konkrete Musik *f*	musique concrète *f*	3123
zeitgenössische Musik *f* / neue Musik *f*	musique contemporaine *f*	3124
Chormusik *f*	musique chorale *f*	3125
Stimmungsmusik *f*	musique d'ambiance	3126
avantgardistische Musik *f*	musique d'avant-garde *f*	3127
Tanzmusik *f*	musique de danse *f*	3128
Jagdmusik *f*	musique de chasse *f*	3129
Kammermusik *f*	musique de chambre *f*	3130
Kirchenmusik *f*	musique d'église *f* / musique liturgique *f*	3131
Gebrauchsmusik *f*	musique fonctionelle *f*	3132
Salonmusik *f*	musique de salon *f*	3133
Tafelmusik *f*	musique de table *f*	3134
Zukunftsmusik *f*	musique d'avenir *f*	3135
Programmmusik *f*	musique descriptive *f*	3136
Hofmusik *f*	musique de cour *f*	3137
Katzenmusik *f*	charivari *m*	3138
Hintergrundmusik *f*	musique de fond *f*	3139
Passionsmusik *f*	musique de la Passion *f*	3140
Weihnachtsmusik *f*	musique de Noël *f*	3141
Bühnenmusik *f*	musique de scène *f*	3142
Dodekaphonie *f* / Zwölfton-musik *f*	dodécaphonie *f* / musique dodécaphonique *f*	3143
dramatische Musik *f*	musique dramatique *f*	3144
elektronische Musik *f*	musique électronique *f*	3145
exotische Musik *f*	musique exotique *f*	3146
Hausmusik *f*	musique domestique *f*	3147
Trauermusik *f*	musique funèbre *f*	3148
leichte Musik *f* / Unterhaltungs-musik *f* / U-Musik *f*	musique légère *f*	3149
Opernmusik *f*	musique lyrique *f*	3150
mechanische Musik *f*	musique méchanique *f*	3151
Militärmusik *f*	musique militaire *f*	3152
Straßenmusik *f*	musique de rue *f*	3153

3154	musica orchestrale *f*	orchestral music
3155	musica per balletto *f*	ballet music
3156	musica per banda *f*	wind music / band music
3157	musica per film *f*	film music
3158	musica per la scuola *f*	school music
3159	musica per strumenti a corda *f*	music for strings
3160	musica per strumenti a fiato *f*	wind music
3161	musica popolare *f* / musica folcloristica *f*	folk music / popular music
3162	musica profana *f*	secular music
3163	musica puntillistica *f*	pointillist music
3164	musica religiosa *f*	religious music
3165	musica rinascimentale *f*	renaissance music
3166	musica sacra *f*	sacred music
3167	musica seria *f*	serious music
3168	musica seriale *f*	serial music
3169	musica sinfonica *f*	symphonic music
3170	musica sperimentale *f*	experimental music
3171	musica strumentale *f*	instrumental music
3172	musica turca *f*	Turkish music
3173	musica tzigana *f*	gipsy music
3174	musica vocale *f*	vocal music
3175	musicale	musical
3176	musicalità *f*	musicality
3177	musicista di professione *m + f*	professional musician
3178	musicologia *f*	musicology
3179	musicoterapia *f*	music therapy
3180	muto	dumb / mute
3181	narratore *m*	narrator
3182	naturale	natural
3183	necessario	necessary
3184	noioso	boring
3185	nostalgia *f*	homesickness
3186	nota falsa *f* / stecca *f*	wrong note / false note
3187	notevole	remarkable
3188	numero *m*	number
3189	nuova versione *f*	new version
3190	nuovo	new

Orchestermusik *f*	musique d'orchestre *f*	3154
Ballettmusik *f*	musique de ballet *f*	3155
Blasmusik *f* / Harmoniemusik *f*	musique pour harmonie *f*	3156
Filmmusik *f*	musique de film *f*	3157
Schulmusik *f*	musique scolaire *f*	3158
Musik für Streichinstrumente *f* / Musik für Saiteninstrumente *f*	musique pour instruments à cordes *f*	3159
Blasmusik *f*	musique pour instruments à vent *f*	3160
Volksmusik *f* / volkstümliche Musik *f*	musique folklorique *f* / musique populaire *f*	3161
weltliche Musik *f*	musique profane *f*	3162
punktuelle Musik *f*	pointillisme musical *m*	3163
geistliche Musik *f*	musique religieuse *f*	3164
Renaissancemusik *f*	musique de la Renaissance *f*	3165
Kirchenmusik *f*	musique sacrée *f*	3166
ernste Musik *f* / E-Musik *f*	musique sérieuse *f*	3167
serielle Musik *f*	musique sérielle *f*	3168
Orchestermusik *f*	musique symphonique *f*	3169
experimentelle Musik *f*	musique expérimentale *f*	3170
Instrumentalmusik *f*	musique instrumentale *f*	3171
Janitscharenmusik *f*	musique turque *f*	3172
Zigeunermusik *f*	musique tzigane *f*	3173
Vokalmusik *f*	musique vocale *f*	3174
musikalisch	musical	3175
Musikalität *f*	musicalité *f*	3176
Berufsmusiker *m* / Berufs-musikerin *f*	musicien professionel *m* + *f*	3177
Musikwissenschaft *f*	musicologie *f*	3178
Musiktherapie *f*	musicothérapie *f*	3179
stumm	muet	3180
Sprecher *m*	récitant *m*	3181
natürlich	naturel	3182
nötig	nécessaire	3183
langweilig	ennuyeux	3184
Heimweh *n*	nostalgie *f*	3185
falsche Note *f* / Misston *m*	fausse note *f* / canard *m*	3186
bemerkenswert	remarcable / notable	3187
Nummer *f* / Zahl *f*	numéro *m*	3188
Neufassung *f*	nouvelle version *f*	3189
neu	neuf	3190

3191	nuvola *f*	cloud
3192	omaggio *m*	homage
3193	onorario *m*	fee / salary
3194	opera *f* / opus (L)	work
3195	orchestra *f*	orchestra
3196	orchestra da ballo *f*	dance band
3197	orchestra da camera *f*	chamber orchestra
3198	orchestra d'archi *f*	string orchestra
3199	orchestra d'opera *f* / dell'opera *f*	opera orchestra
3200	orchestra da salotto *f*	salon orchestra
3201	orchestra della radio *f*	radio orchestra
3202	orchestra sinfonica *f*	symphony orchestra
3203	ordine *m*	order
3204	orecchio assoluto *m*	absolute pitch / perfect pitch
3205	organico (strumentale) *m*	instrumentation / ensemble
3206	organologia *f*	organology
3207	originale	original
3208	ottoni *m pl*	brass
3209	pagina *f*	page
3210	palco *m*	box
3211	palpito *n*	heart beat
3212	pantomima *f*	pantomime
3213	paragone *m* / confronto *m*	comparison
3214	parola *f*	word
3215	parrucca *f*	wig
3216	partitura *f* / spartito *m*	score
3217	partitura per il direttore *f*	full score
3218	partitura tascabile *f*	pocket score / miniature score
3219	passaggio *m* / passo *m*	passage
3220	passo *m*	step
3221	paura dinanzi al pubblico *f*	stage fright
3222	pedagogia *f*	pedagogy
3223	percettibile / percepibile	perceptible
3224	perfetto	perfect
3225	perfezione *f*	perfection
3226	pezzo imposto *m*	compulsory piece
3227	perpetuo	perpetual
3228	pettinatura *f* / acconciatura *f*	hairdo / hair style
3229	plagio *m*	plagiarism

Wolke *f*	nuage *m*	3191
Huldigung *f*	hommage *m*	3192
Gage *f*	cachet *m*	3193
Werk *n*	œuvre *f*	3194
Orchester *n*	orchestre *m*	3195
Tanzorchester *n*	orchestre de danse *m*	3196
Kammerorchester *n*	orchestre de chambre *m*	3197
Streichorchester *n*	orchestre à cordes *m*	3198
Opernorchester *n*	orchestre d'opéra *m* / de l'opéra *m*	3199
Salonorchester *n*	orchestre de salon *m*	3200
Rundfunkorchester *n*	orchestre de la radio *m*	3201
Sinfonieorchester *n*	orchestre symphonique *m*	3202
Ordnung *f* / Reihenfolge *f*	ordre *m*	3203
absolutes Gehör *n*	oreille absolue *f*	3204
Besetzung *f*	distribution *f*	3205
Musikinstrumentenkunde *f*	organologie *f*	3206
original	original	3207
Blechinstrumente *n Pl*	cuivres *m pl*	3208
Seite *f* / Blatt *n*	page *f*	3209
Loge *f*	loge *f*	3210
Herzschlag *m*	battement de coeur *m*	3211
Pantomime *f*	pantomime *f*	3212
Vergleich *m*	comparaison *f*	3213
Wort *n*	parole *f*	3214
Perücke *f*	perruque *f*	3215
Partitur *f*	partition *f*	3216
Dirigierpartitur *f*	partition de direction *f*	3217
Taschenpartitur *f*	partition de poche *f*	3218
Passage *f* / Stelle *f* / Tonfolge *f*	passage *m* / trait *m*	3219
Schritt *m*	pas *m*	3220
Lampenfieber *n*	trac *m*	3221
Pädagogik *f*	pédagogie *f*	3222
wahrnehmbar / hörbar	perceptible	3223
perfekt / vollkommen	parfait	3224
Vollendung *f*	perfection *f*	3225
Pflichtstück *m*	morceau imposé *m*	3226
fortwährend	perpétuel	3227
Frisur *f*	coiffure *f*	3228
Plagiat *n*	plagiat *m*	3229

3230	platea *f*	stalls
3231	podio *m* / pedana *f*	rostrum
3232	popolare	popular
3233	posizione *f*	position
3234	posto *m*	place / seat
3235	posto a sedere *m*	seat / place
3236	posto in piedi *m*	standing-room
3237	postumo	posthumous
3238	prassi d'esecuzione *f* / pratica d'esecuzione *f*	performing practice
3239	preclassicismo *m*	pre-classical period
3240	prefazione *f*	preface
3241	preghiera *f*	prayer
3242	preparato	prepared
3243	presenza *f*	presence
3244	prima *f*	first night / opening night
3245	prima esecuzione *f*	first performance
3246	prima esecuzione mondiale *f* / creazione *f*	world première
3247	prima edizione *f*	first edition
3248	prima volta *f*	first time
3249	primitivo	primitive
3250	primo leggio *m*	principal
3251	primo violino *m* / spalla *f*	leader / concertmaster
3252	profano	profane / secular
3253	progetto *m*	project / plan
3254	programma *m*	programme / playbill
3255	progresso *m*	progress
3256	prolungamento *f*	prolongation
3257	promotore *m*	promoter
3258	proporzione *f*	proportion
3259	proscenio *m*	frontstage
3260	prossima volta *f*	next time
3261	prova *f* / ripetizione *f*	rehearsal / coaching
3262	prova generale *f*	final rehearsal
3263	provvisorio	provisional / temporary
3264	prudenza *f*	prudence
3265	pseudonimo *m*	pseudonym / pen-name

Parkett *n*	fauteuils d'orchestre *m pl* / parterre *m*	3230
Podium *n* / Podest *n*	podium *m* / estrade *f*	3231
volkstümlich / populär	populaire	3232
Lage *f* / Stellung *f*	position *f*	3233
Platz *m* / Sitz *m*	place *f*	3234
Sitzplatz *m*	place assise *f*	3235
Stehplatz *m*	place debout *f*	3236
hinterlassen / nachgelassen	posthume	3237
Aufführungspraxis *f*	pratique de l'exécution *f*	3238
Vorklassik *f*	période pré-classique *f*	3239
Vorwort *n* / Einleitung *f*	préface *f*	3240
Gebet *n*	prière *f*	3241
präpariert / vorbereitet	préparé	3242
Ausstrahlung *f*	rayonnement *m*	3243
Premiere *f* / erste Vorstellung *f*	première *f*	3244
Uraufführung *f*	première représentation *f*	3245
Welterstaufführung *f*	première exécution mondiale *f* / création *f*	3246
Erstdruck *m*	première édition *f*	3247
erstes Mal	première fois	3248
urtümlich / primitiv	primitif	3249
Stimmführer *m* / Stimmführerin *f*	chef de pupitre *m* / chef d'attaque *m*	3250
Konzertmeister *m* / Konzertmeisterin *f* /Primarius *m*	premier violon solo *m*	3251
profan / weltlich / laienhaft	profane	3252
Projekt *m*	projet *m*	3253
Programm *n*	programme *m*	3254
Fortschritt *m*	progrès *m*	3255
Verlängerung *f*	prolongation *f*	3256
Veranstalter *m*	promoteur *m*	3257
Verhältnis *n*	proportion *f*	3258
Vorbühne *f*	l'avant-scène *f*	3259
nächstes Mal	prochaine fois *f*	3260
Probe *f* / Korrepetition *f*	répétition *f*	3261
Generalprobe *f*	répétition générale *f*	3262
provisorisch / vorläufig	provisoire	3263
Vorsicht *f*	prudence *f*	3264
Pseudonym *n* / Künstlername *m*	pseudonyme *m*	3265

3266	pubblico *m* / pubblico	audience / public
3267	pulito / netto	clean / neat / tidy
3268	punta *f*	point
3269	quadro musicale *m* / immagine musicale *f*	tone painting / musical imagery
3270	quinte *f pl*	wings
3271	raccolta di canzoni *f* / canzoniere *m*	songbook
3272	radiodiffusione *f*	broadcasting
3273	rappresentazione *f* / recita *f*	performance
3274	realtà *f*	reality
3275	regia *f*	stage direction
3276	regola *f*	rule
3277	regolare	regular
3278	repertorio *m* / avviso teatrale *m*	repertory / repertoire playbill
3279	replica *f*	repeat performance
3280	respirazione *f* / respiro	breathing
3281	retro	back / backwards
3282	retroscena *m*	backstage
3283	revisione *f*	revision
3284	ribalta *f*	footlights
3285	richiamo *m*	curtain call
3286	ridotto *m*	foyer / lobby
3287	riduzione *f* / adattamento *m*	reduction
3288	riduzione per pianoforte *f*	piano score
3289	riflettore *m*	spotlight
3290	rima *f*	rhyme
3291	rimbombo *m*	echo effect
3292	Rinascimento *m*	Renaissance
3293	rinviato	postponed
3294	riposo *m*	rest
3295	ripieno *m* / violino di fila *m*	ripieno violinist / section violinist
3296	rituale	ritual
3297	riverbero *m*	reverberation
3298	rivista *f*	magazine / review
3299	romanticismo *m*	romanticism
3300	rotto / spezzato	broken
3301	ruolo *m* / parte *f*	role / part

Publikum *n* / öffentlich	public *m* / publique	3266
sauber / reinlich	propre / net	3267
Kopf *m* / Spitze *f*	pointe *f*	3268
Tonmalerei *f*	image musicale *f* / peinture sonore *f*	3269
Kulisse *f*	coulisses *f pl*	3270
Liedersammlung *f*	recueil de chansons *m*	3271
Rundfunk *m*	radiodiffusion *f*	3272
Aufführung *f* / Darbietung *f* / Vorstellung *f*	représentation *f*	3273
Realität *f*	réalité *f*	3274
Regie *f* / Spielleitung *f*	régie *f*	3275
Regel *f*	règle *f*	3276
regelmäßig	régulier	3277
Repertoire *n* / Spielplan *m*	répertoire *m* / affiche *f*	3278
Wiederholung *f*	reprise *f* / réplique *f*	3279
Atmung *f*	respiration *f*	3280
rückwärts	en arrière	3281
Hinterbühne *f*	coulisses *f pl*	3282
Revision *f*	révision *f*	3283
Rampe *f*	rampe *f*	3284
herausklatschen / hervorklatschen	rappel *m*	3285
Foyer *n*	foyer *m*	3286
Reduktion *f* / Übertragung *f*	réduction *f*	3287
Klavierauszug *m*	partition pour piano *f*	3288
Scheinwerfer *m*	projecteur *m*	3289
Reim *m*	rime *f*	3290
Halleffekt *m* / Echo *n*	effet d'écho *m*	3291
Renaissance *f*	Renaissance *f*	3292
verschoben	renvoyé	3293
Ruhe *f*	repos *m*	3294
Ripienist *m* / Tuttigeiger *m*	ripièniste *m* / violon de file *m*	3295
rituell	rituel	3296
Rückstrahlung *f*	réverbération *f*	3297
Revue *f* / Zeitschrift *f*	revue *f*	3298
Romantik *f*	romantisme *m*	3299
gebrochen / zerbrochen	cassé / brisé	3300
Rolle *f* / Partie *f*	rôle *m* / partie *f*	3301

3302	ruolo principale *m*	main part
3303	saggezza *f*	wisdom
3304	saggio *m*	concert / audition
3305	sala da ballo *f*	ball room
3306	sala da concerto *f*	concert-hall
3307	salto *m*	jump / leap / skip
3308	santo	saint / holy
3309	sbagliato / falso / errato	wrong
3310	sbaglio *m* / errore *m*	mistake / error
3311	scambio *m*	exchange
3312	scatola *f*	box
3313	scelta *f* / selezione *f*	choice / selection
3314	scena *f* / palcoscenico *m*	scene / stage
3315	scenario *m*	scenery / set
3316	scenografia *f*	scenography
3317	scherzo *m*	joke
3318	schizzo *m* / abbozzo *m*	sketch / draft
3319	scorretto	incorrect
3320	scrittura *f* / contratto *m*	engagement / contract
3321	scuola *f*	school
3322	scuola di balletto *f*	ballet school
3323	scuola di coro *f*	choir school
3324	scuola di musica *f*	music school
3325	scuola viennese *f*	Viennese school
3326	scusa (i)	sorry
3327	segnale d'intervallo *m*	interval sign
3328	seguito *m*	continuation
3329	semplificato / facilitato	simplified
3330	senso *m*	sense
3331	sfumatura *f* / dettaglio *m*	shading / detail
3332	sguardo *m* / occhiata *f*	look / glance
3333	sillaba *f*	syllable
3334	silenzio *m* / silenzio!	silence / keep quiet!
3335	simbolo *m*	symbol
3336	simultaneo / contemporaneamente	simultaneous / at the same time
3337	sinistra (a)	left
3338	siparietto *m*	act curtain

Hauptrolle *f*	rôle principal *m*	3302
Weisheit *f*	sagesse *f*	3303
Vorspiel *n*	essai *m* / audition *f*	3304
Ballsaal *m*	salle de danse *f*	3305
Konzertsaal *m*	salle de concert *f*	3306
Sprung *m*	saut *m*	3307
heilig	saint	3308
falsch	faux	3309
Fehler *m* / Irrtum *m*	faute *f* / erreur *f*	3310
Tausch *m*	échange *m*	3311
Schachtel *f*	boîte *f*	3312
Wahl *f* / Auswahl *f*	choix *m* / sélection *f*	3313
Bühne *f* / Szene *f*	scène *f* / planches *f pl*	3314
Bühnenbild *n* / Ausstattung *f*	scénario *m* / décor *m*	3315
Bühnenmalerei *f*	l'art du décor *m* / scénographie *f*	3316
Scherz *m*	plaisanterie *f*	3317
Entwurf *m* / Skizze *f*	esquisse *f* / ébauche *f* / brouillon *m*	3318
unkorrekt / fehlerhaft	incorrect	3319
Engagement *n* / Vertrag *m*	engagement *m* / contrat *m*	3320
Schule *f*	école *f*	3321
Ballettschule *f*	école de ballet *f* / école de danse classique *f*	3322
Chorschule *f*	maîtrise *f*	3323
Musikschule *f*	école de musique *f*	3324
Wiener Schule *f*	école viennoise *f*	3325
Entschuldigung	pardon / je m'excuse	3326
Pausenzeichen *n*	signal d'entracte *m*	3327
Fortsetzung *f*	suite *f*	3328
vereinfacht / leichter gemacht	simplifié / facilité	3329
Sinn *m*	sens *m*	3330
Schattierung *f* / Detail *n*	nuance *f* / détail *m*	3331
Blick *m*	regard *m* / coup d'œil *m*	3332
Silbe *f*	syllabe *f*	3333
Schweigen *n* / Ruhe!	silence *m* / taisez-vous!	3334
Symbol *n*	symbole *m*	3335
gleichzeitig	simultané / en même temps	3336
links	gauche (á)	3337
Aktvorhang *m*	rideau d'avant-scène *m*	3338

3339	sipario *m* / telone *m*	curtain
3340	soffio *m* / alito *m*	breath / puff
3341	solista *m* + *f*	soloist
3342	sonorità *f*	sonority
3343	sordo	deaf
3344	sorpresa *f*	surprise
3345	sostituto *m* / sostituta *f*	stand in / understudy
3346	sotto la direzione di ...	under the direction of ...
3347	spada *f*	sword / épée
3348	speciale	special
3349	speranza *f*	hope
3350	spettacolo *m*	performance / show
3351	spia *f*	peep-hole
3352	squillo *m*	ring
3353	stagione *f*	season
3354	stagione concertistica *f*	concert season
3355	stagione teatrale *f*	season
3356	stampa *f*	press
3357	stampa musicale *f*	musical press
3358	stato d'animo *m* / atmosfera *f*	mood
3359	stella *f*	star
3360	stile *m*	style
3361	stonato / scordato	out of tune / mistuned
3362	storia della musica *f*	history of music
3363	storico	historical
3364	straordinario / eccezionale	extraordinary / exceptional
3365	strapuntino *m*	folding seat
3366	strumentale	instrumental
3367	strumentazione variabile *f*	alternative scoring
3368	strumento *m*	instrument
3369	strumento accompagnatore *m*	accompanying instrument
3370	strumenti ad arco *m pl*	bowed stringed instruments
3371	strumenti a corda *m pl*	stringed instruments
3372	strumenti a fiato *m pl*	wind instruments
3373	strumenti a fiato di legno *m pl* / i legni *m pl*	woodwind instruments
3374	strumenti a fiato di ottone *m pl* / gli ottoni *m pl*	brass instruments

Theatervorhang *m*	rideau *m*	3339
Blasen *n* / Luftstoß *m* / Hauch *m*	souffle *m*	3340
Solist *m* / Solistin *f*	soliste *m* + *f*	3341
Klangfülle *f*	sonorité *f*	3342
taub	sourd	3343
Überraschung *f*	surprise *f*	3344
Stellvertreter *m* / Stellvertreterin *f*	remplaçant *m* / remplaçante *f*	3345
unter der Leitung von ...	sous la direction de ...	3346
Schwert *n* / Degen *m*	épée *f*	3347
spezial	spécial	3348
Hoffnung *f*	espoir *m*	3349
Vorstellung *f* / Schauspiel *n*	spectacle *m*	3350
Guckloch *n*	judas *m*	3351
Schall *m*	sonnerie *f*	3352
Saison *f* / Jahreszeit *f*	saison *f*	3353
Konzertsaison *f*	saison de concerts *f*	3354
Spielzeit *f*	saison théâtrale *f*	3355
Presse *f*	presse *f*	3356
Notendruck *m*	typographie musicale *f* / presse musicale *f*	3357
Stimmung *f*	climat *m* / atmosphère *f*	3358
Stern *m*	étoile *f*	3359
Stil *m*	style *m*	3360
verstimmt	désaccordé	3361
Musikgeschichte *f*	histoire de la musique *f*	3362
historisch	historique	3363
außerordentlich / außergewöhnlich	extraordinaire / exceptionnel	3364
Klappsitz *m*	strapontin *m*	3365
instrumental	instrumental	3366
variable Besetzung *f*	instrumentation variable *f*	3367
Instrument *n*	instrument *m*	3368
Begleitinstrument *n*	instrument accompagnateur *m*	3369
Streichinstrumente *n Pl*	cordes *f pl* / instruments à cordes *m pl*	3370
Saiteninstrumente *n Pl*	instruments à cordes *m pl*	3371
Blasinstrumente *n Pl*	instruments à vent *m pl*	3372
Holzblasinstrumente *n Pl*	les bois *m pl*	3373
Blechblasinstrumente *n Pl*	les cuivres *m pl*	3374

3375	strumenti a percussione *m*	percussion instruments
3376	strumenti a pizzico *m pl*	plucked instruments
3377	strumenti a tastiera *m pl*	keyboard instruments
3378	strumenti traspositori *m pl*	transposing instruments
3379	strumento a tastiera *m*	keyboard instrument
3380	strumento di fondamento *m* / strumento di basso continuo *m*	continuo instrument
3381	strumento melodico *m*	melodic instrument
3382	strumento ritmico *m*	rhythmic instrument
3383	strumento solistico *m*	solo instrument
3384	successo *m*	success
3385	sulla scena	on the stage
3386	sullo sfondo	in the background
3387	superfluo	superfluous
3388	superiore	superior / upper
3389	supplemento *m* / complemento *m*	supplement
3390	supplente *m+f* / aggiunto *m*	substitute / stopgap
3391	talento *m*	talent
3392	teatrale	theatrical
3393	teatro *m*	theatre (E) / theater (Am.)
3394	tecnica *f*	technique
3395	tecnica delle dita *f*	finger action
3396	televisione *f*	television
3397	temperamento *m*	temperament
3398	temporale *m*	thunderstorm
3399	tensione *f*	tension
3400	teoria musicale *f*	theory of music
3401	teoria degli affetti *f*	theory of emotional expression
3402	testo *m*	text
3403	tetralogia *f*	tetralogy
3404	tip-tap *m*	tap dance / step dance
3405	traduzione *f*	translation
3406	tragedia *f*	tragedy
3407	trama *f* / intreccio *m*	action / plot
3408	trascrizione *f*	transcription
3409	trasmissione *f*	broadcast / telecast
3410	travestimento *m*	disguise

Schlaginstrumente *n Pl*	instruments à percussion *m pl*	3375
Zupfinstrumente *n Pl*	instruments à cordes pincées *m pl*	3376
Tasteninstrumente *n Pl*	instruments à clavier m *pl*	3377
transponierende Instrumente *n Pl*	instruments transpositeurs *m pl*	3378
Tasteninstrument *n*	instrument à clavier *m*	3379
Generalbassinstrument *n*	instrument jouant la partie de basse *m*	3380
Melodieinstrument *n*	instrument mélodique *m*	3381
Rhythmusinstrument *n*	instrument rythmique *m*	3382
Soloinstrument *n*	instrument solo *m* / instrument soliste *m*	3383
Erfolg *m*	succès *m*	3384
auf der Bühne	sur la scène	3385
im Hintergrund	sur le fond	3386
überflüssig	superflu	3387
über / höher / ober	supérieur	3388
Ergänzung *f*	supplément *m* / complément *m*	3389
Stellvertreter *m* / Aushilfe *f*	suppléant *m* / supplémentaire *m+f*	3390
Begabung *f*	talent *m*	3391
theatralisch	théâtral	3392
Theater *n*	théâtre *m*	3393
Technik *f*	technique *f*	3394
Fingertechnik *f*	technique des doigts *f*	3395
Fernsehen *n*	télévision *f*	3396
Temperatur *f* / Temperament *n*	tempérament *m*	3397
Gewitter *n*	orage *m*	3398
Spannung *f*	tension *f*	3399
Musiktheorie *f*	théorie musicale *f*	3400
Affekttheorie *f* / Affekten-lehre *f*	théorie de l'expression des émotions *f*	3401
Text *m*	texte *m*	3402
Tetralogie *f*	tétralogie *f*	3403
Stepptanz *m*	claquettes *f pl*	3404
Übersetzung *f*	traduction *f*	3405
Tragödie *f*	tragédie *f*	3406
Handlung *f*	action *f*	3407
Transkription *f* / Übertragung *f*	transcription *f*	3408
Sendung *f*	émission *f*	3409
Verkleidung *f*	déguisement *m*	3410

3411	trilogia *f* / trittico *m*	trilogy / triptych
3412	tuono *m*	thunder
3413	udito *m*	hearing
3414	uscita *f*	exit
3415	varietà *f*	variety
3416	varietà *f*	vaudeville (theatre) / music hall
3417	vento *m*	wind
3418	veramente	really
3419	verismo *m*	verismo / realism
3420	versione *f*	version
3421	versione originale *f*	original version
3422	verso *m*	verse / line
3423	vicino / presso	near / close
3424	vista *f*	sight
3425	vocale *f*	vocal / vowel
3426	volontà *f*	will
3427	zingaro *m* / zingara *f*	gipsy

Il corpo umano   The human body

3428	anca *f*	haunch / hip
3429	articolazione *f*	joint
3430	avambraccio *m*	forearm
3431	bocca *f*	mouth
3432	braccio *m*	arm
3433	capelli *m pl*	hair
3434	collo *m*	neck
3435	cuore *m*	heart
3436	denti *m pl*	teeth
3437	diaframma *m*	diaphragm
3438	dito *m*	finger
3439	dorso della mano *m*	back of the hand
3440	faccia *f*	face
3441	falange *f*	phalanx
3442	faringe *f*	pharynx
3443	fronte *f*	forehead
3444	gamba *f*	leg
3445	ginocchio *m*	knee
3446	gola *f*	throat

Trilogie *f* / Triptychon *m*	trilogie *f* / triptyque *m*	3411
Donner *m*	tonnerre *m*	3412
Gehör *n*	ouïe *f*	3413
Ausgang *m*	sortie *f*	3414
Vielfältigkeit *f*	variété *f*	3415
Varieté *n*	variété *m* / café-concert *m*	3416
Wind *m*	vent *m*	3417
wirklich	vraiment	3418
Verismo *m* / Verismus *m*	vérisme *m*	3419
Version *f* / Fassung *f*	version *f*	3420
Urtext *m*	version originale *f*	3421
Vers *m*	vers *m*	3422
nahe	près	3423
Sicht *f*	vue *f*	3424
Vokal *m* / Selbstlaut *m*	vocal *f* / voyelle *f*	3425
Wille *m*	volonté *f*	3426
Zigeuner *m* / Zigeunerin *f*	bohémien *m*/-ne *f* / tzigane *m* + *f*	3427

Der menschliche Körper   Le corps humain

Hüfte *f*	hanche *f*	3428
Gelenk *n*	articulation *f*	3429
Unterarm *m*	avant-bras *m*	3430
Mund *m*	bouche *f*	3431
Arm *m* / Oberarm *m*	bras *m*	3432
Haare *n Pl*	cheveux *m pl*	3433
Hals *m*	cou *m*	3434
Herz *n*	coeur *m*	3435
Zähne *m Pl*	dents *f pl*	3436
Zwerchfell *n*	diaphragme *m*	3437
Finger *m*	doigt *m*	3438
Handrücken *m*	dos de la main *m*	3439
Gesicht *n*	visage *m*	3440
Fingerglied *n* / Finger-knochen *m*	phalange *f*	3441
Rachenhöhle *f*	pharynx *m*	3442
Stirn *f*	front *m*	3443
Bein *n*	jambe *f*	3444
Knie *n*	genou *m*	3445
Kehle *f* / Rachen *m*	gorge *f*	3446

3447	gomito *m*	elbow
3448	guancia *f*	cheek
3449	indice *m*	forefinger
3450	labbro *m*	lip
3451	laringe *f*	larynx
3452	lingua *f*	tongue
3453	mano *f*	hand
3454	mascella *f*	jaw
3455	mento *m*	chin
3456	mignolo *m*	little finger
3457	muscolo *m*	muscle
3458	naso *m*	nose
3459	nervo *m*	nerve
3460	nuca *f*	nape of the neck
3461	occhio *m*	eye
3462	orecchio *m*	ear
3463	osso *m*	bone
3464	palato *m*	palate
3465	palmo della mano *m*	palm of the hand
3466	pancia *f*	tummy
3467	petto *m*	breast
3468	piede *m*	foot
3469	pollice *m*	thumb
3470	polmoni *m pl*	lungs
3471	polpastrello *m*	fingertips
3472	polso *m*	pulse
3473	polso *m*	wrist
3474	sangue *m*	blood
3475	schiena *f* / dorso *m*	back
3476	sedere *m*	backside
3477	spalla *f*	shoulder
3478	stomaco *m*	stomach
3479	tallone *m*	heel
3480	testa *f*	head
3481	torace *m*	thorax
3482	trachea *f*	windpipe
3483	unghia *f*	nail
3484	vena *f*	vein

Ellbogen *m*	coude *m*	3447
Wange *f*	joue *f*	3448
Zeigefinger *m*	index *m*	3449
Lippe *f*	lèvre *f*	3450
Kehlkopf *m*	larynx *m*	3451
Zunge *f*	langue *f*	3452
Hand *f*	main *f*	3453
Kiefer *m* / Kinnlade *f*	mâchoire *f*	3454
Kinn *n*	menton *m*	3455
kleiner Finger *m*	petit doigt *m*	3456
Muskel *m*	muscle *m*	3457
Nase *f*	nez *m*	3458
Nerv *m*	nerf *m*	3459
Genick *n* / Nacken *m*	nuque *f*	3460
Auge *n*	œil *m*	3461
Ohr *n*	oreille *f*	3462
Knochen *m*	os *m*	3463
Gaumen *m*	palais *m*	3464
Handfläche *f*	paume de la main *f*	3465
Bauch *m*	ventre *m*	3466
Brust *f*	poitrine *f*	3467
Fuß *m*	pied *m*	3468
Daumen *m*	pouce *m*	3469
Lungen *f Pl*	poumons *m pl*	3470
Fingerkuppe *f*	bout du doigt *m*	3471
Puls *m*	pouls *m*	3472
Handgelenk *n*	poignet *m*	3473
Blut *n*	sang *m*	3474
Rücken *m*	dos *m*	3475
Gesäß *n*	derrière *m*	3476
Schulter *f* / Achsel *f*	épaule *f*	3477
Magen *m*	estomac *m*	3478
Ferse *f*	talon *m*	3479
Kopf *m*	tête *f*	3480
Brustkorb *m*	thorax *m*	3481
Luftröhre *f*	trachée *f*	3482
Nagel *m*	ongle *m*	3483
Ader *f*	veine *f*	3484

	I mestieri	**The professions**
3485	accompagnatore *m* / accompagnatrice *f*	accompanist
3486	accordatore *m* / accordatrice *f*	tuner
3487	arpista *m+f*	harpist
3488	arrangiatore *m* / arrangiatrice *f*	arranger
3489	artista *m+f*	artist
3490	attore *m* / attrice *f*	actor *m* / actress *f*
3491	ballerino *m* / ballerina *f*	dancer / ballerina
3492	batterista *m+f*	drummer
3493	cantante *m+f*	singer / vocalist
3494	chitarrista *m+f*	guitarist
3495	clarinettista *m+f*	clarinettist / clarinetist
3496	clavicembalista *m+f*	harpsichordist
3497	compositore *m* / compositrice *f*	composer
3498	concertista *m+f*	concert artist
3499	contrabbassista *m+f*	double bass player / bass player
3500	copista *m+f*	copyist
3501	coreografo *m+f*	choreographer
3502	coreologo *m+f*	choreologist
3503	corista *m+f*	chorus singer / chorister
3504	cornista *m+f*	horn player
3505	critico musicale *m+f*	music critic
3506	direttore d'orchestra *m+f*	conductor
3507	fagottista *m+f*	bassoonist
3508	flautista *m+f*	flutist / flautist
3509	incisore *m+f*	engraver
3510	insegnante *m+f* / professore *m* / professoressa *f*	teacher / professor
3511	liutaio *m+f*	violin maker

Die Berufe

Les métiers

Begleiter *m* / Begleiterin *f*	accompagnateur *m* / accompagnatrice *f*	3485
Stimmer *m* / Stimmerin *f*	accordeur *m+f*	3486
Harfenist *m* / Harfenistin *f*	harpiste *m+f*	3487
Bearbeiter *m* / Bearbeiterin *f*	arrangeur *m+f*	3488
Künstler *m* / Künstlerin *f*	artiste *m+f*	3489
Schauspieler *m* / Schauspielerin *f*	acteur *m* / actrice *f* / comédien *m* / comédienne *f*	3490
Tänzer *m* / Tänzerin *f* / Balletttänzer *m* / Balletttänzerin *f*	danseur *m* / danseuse *f*	3491
Schlagzeuger *m* / Schlagzeugerin *f*	batteur *m+f*	3492
Sänger *m* / Sängerin *f*	chanteur *m* / chanteuse *f* / cantatrice *f*	3493
Gitarrist *m* / Gitarristin *f*	guitariste *m+f*	3494
Klarinettist *m* / Klarinettistin *f*	clarinettiste *m+f*	3495
Cembalist *m* / Cembalistin *f*	claveciniste *m+f*	3496
Komponist *m* / Komponistin *f* / Tondichter *m* / Tondichterin *f*	compositeur *m*	3497
ausübender Künstler *m* / ausübende Künstlerin *f*	concertiste *m+f*	3498
Kontrabassist *m* / Kontrabassistin *f*	contrebassiste *m+f*	3499
Kopist *m* / Kopistin *f*	copiste *m+f*	3500
Choreograph *m* / Choreographin *f*	chorégraphe *m+f*	3501
Choreologe *m* / Choreologin *f*	choréologue *m+f*	3502
Chorsänger *m* / Chorsängerin *f*	choriste *m+f*	3503
Hornist *m* / Hornistin *f*	corniste *m+f*	3504
Musikkritiker *m* / Musikkritikerin *f*	critique musical *m+f*	3505
Dirigent *m* / Dirigentin *f* / Kapellmeister *m* / Kapellmeisterin *f*	chef d'orchestre *m+f*	3506
Fagottist *m* / Fagottistin *f*	basson *m+f*	3507
Flötist *m* / Flötistin *f*	flûtiste *m+f*	3508
Stecher *m* / Stecherin *f*	graveur *m* / graveuse *f*	3509
Lehrer *m* / Lehrerin *f* / Professor *m* / Professorin *f*	instituteur *m* / institutrice *f* / professeur *m+f*	3510
Geigenbauer *m* / Geigenbauerin *f*	luthier *m+f*	3511

3512	maestro di ballo *m+f*	ballet master
3513	musicista *m+f*	musician
3514	musicologo *m+f*	musicologist
3515	oboista *m+f*	oboist
3516	organista *m+f*	organist
3517	pianista *m+f*	pianist
3518	professore d'orchestra *m* / professoressa d'orchestra *f*	orchestralist
3519	regista *m+f*	director / producer
3520	ripetitore / maestro sostituto *m+f*	coach
3521	sassofonista *m+f*	saxophonist
3522	suggeritore *m* / suggeritrice *f*	prompter
3523	tecnico del suono	sound engineer
3524	timpanista *m+f*	timpanist
3525	tromba *m+f*	trumpeter / trumpetist
3526	trombone *m+f*	trombonist
3527	violinista *m+f*	violinist
3528	violista *m+f*	violist
3529	violoncellista / cellista *m+f*	cellist

Ballettmeister *m* / Ballettmeisterin *f*	maître de ballet *m* / maîtresse de ballet *f*	3512
Musiker *m* / Musikerin *f*	musicien *m* / musicienne *f*	3513
Musikwissenschaftler *m* / Musikwissenschaftlerin *f*	musicologue *m+f*	3514
Oboist *m* / Oboistin *f*	hautboiste *m+f*	3515
Organist *m* / Organistin *f*	organiste *m+f*	3516
Pianist *m* / Pianistin *f*	pianiste *m+f*	3517
Orchestermusiker *m* / Orchestermusikerin *f*	musicien d'orchestre *m* / musicienne d'orchestre *f*	3518
Regisseur *m* / Regisseurin *f* / Spielleiter *m* / Spielleiterin *f*	régisseur	3519
Korrepetitor *m* / Korrepetitorin *f*	répétiteur *m* / répétitrice *f*	3520
Saxophonist *m* / Saxophonistin *f*	saxophoniste *m + f*	3521
Souffleur *m* / Souffleuse *f*	souffleur *m* / souffleuse *f*	3522
Tonmeister *m* / Tonmeisterin *f*	ingénieur du son *m+f*	3523
Pauker *m* / Paukerin *f*	timbalier *m+f*	3524
Trompeter *m* / Trompeterin *f*	trompette *m+f*	3525
Posaunist *m* / Posaunistin *f*	trombone *m+f* / tromboniste *m+f*	3526
Geiger *m* / Geigerin *f*	violiniste *m+f*	3527
Bratschist *m* / Bratschistin *f*	altiste *m+f*	3528
Cellist *m* / Cellistin *f*	violoncelliste *m+f*	3529

Anhang
Appendice
Appendix
Appendice

Terminologie française | Terminologia francese

Terminologie française	Terminologia francese
à peine ralenti	appena rallentato
à toute vitesse	a tutta velocità
animez progressivement	animate progressivamente
attaques profondes	attacchi profondi
au dessous du mouvement	più lento del tempo primo
aussi légèrement que possible	il più leggermente possibile
avec beaucoup d'entrain	con molto brio
avec de brusques oppositions d'extrême violence et de passionnée douceur	con repentinee opposizioni di estrema violenza e di dolcezza appassionata
avec plus d'abandon	con più abbandono
avec la même humeur du début	con lo stesso stato d'animo dell'inizio
avec un doux flottement	dolcemente fluente
avec un profond ennui	con una noia profonda
avec une douceur cachée	con una dolcezza nascosta
avec une élégance grave et lente	con una lenta e grave eleganza
avec une émotion naissante	con un'emozione nascente
avec une étrangeté subite	con una repentinea stranezza
avec une expression intense	con un'espressione intensa
avec une fausse douceur	con una falsa dolcezza
avec une grâce capricieuse	con una grazia capricciosa
avec une grâce dolente	con una grazia dolente
avec une grande douceur	con una grande dolcezza
avec une grande émotion	con una grande emozione
avec une joie de plus en plus tumultueuse	con una gioia sempre più tumultuosa
avec une joie voilée	con una gioia velata
avec une légèreté fantasque mais précise	con una leggerezza fantasiosa ma precisa
avec une passion naissante	con una passione nascente
avec une volupté dormante	con una voluttà dormente
baigné de pédales	bagnato di pedali
beaucoup de pédale en la changeant très souvent	molto pedale, cambiandolo spessissimo
bien égal	molto uguale

French specialist terms

Französische Fachausdrücke

hardly slower	kaum verlangsamt
very quickly	mit größter Geschwindigkeit
animate progressively	nach und nach beleben
deep touch	tiefe Anschläge
in a slower tempo	in langsamerem Zeitmaß
as lightly as possible	so leicht wie möglich
with much liveliness	mit viel Lebhaftigkeit / mit Schwung
with sudden contrasts of extreme violence and passionate softness	mit Gegensätzen äußerster Heftigkeit und leidenschaftlicher Sanftheit
with more abandon	mit mehr Hingabe
with the same mood as at the beginning	in der gleichen Stimmung wie am Anfang
smoothly flowing	sanft fließend
with profound boredom	mit tiefer Langeweile
with hidden gentleness	mit verborgener Sanftheit
with a dignified and slow elegance	mit würdevoller und langsamer Eleganz
with growing emotion	mit aufkommender Erregung
with sudden strangeness	mit plötzlicher Seltsamkeit
with an intense expression	mit intensivem Ausdruck
with false sweetness	mit falscher Sanftmut
with capricious grace	mit launischer Anmut
with plaintive grace	anmutig klagend
with great tenderness	mit großer Zartheit
with a great emotion	mit großer Gemütsbewegung
with ever-increasing tumultuous joy	mit immer stürmischerer Freude
with restrained joy	mit verhaltener Freude
with an odd lightness but precise	mit wunderlicher, aber präziser Leichtigkeit
with growing passion	mit aufkommender Leidenschaft
with sleepy voluptuousness	mit schläfriger Wollust
full of pedals	mit sehr viel Pedal
much pedal, very often changing	viel Pedal, sehr oft wechselnd
very even	sehr gleichmäßig

changer souvent (la pédale)	cambiare spesso (il pedale)
claque *f*	pubblico pagato per applaudire
claquement doux et mouillé	un colpetto dolce e bagnato
comme de loin	come da lontano
comme des souffles frais	come dei zeffiri freschi
comme un fond de paysage	come lo sfondo di un paesaggio
comme une causerie	come una conversazione
comme un cri	come un grido
comme une buée irisée	come un leggero vapore iridato
comme un murmure confus	come un mormorio confuso
comme une ombre mouvante	come un'ombra movente
comme un regret	come un rimpianto
comme un lointain tumulte	come un tumulto lontano
comme une sonnerie de cors	come uno squillo di corni
d'un air songeur et triste	in maniera sognante e triste
commencer un peu en dessous du movement	incominciare un poco sotto il tempo
d'un bout à l'autre	da capo fino in fondo
d'un petit pas égal	d'un piccolo passo uguale
d'un rhythme las	con un ritmo stanco (lasso)
d'un rhythme libre	il ritmo libero
d'un seul doigt	con un dito solo
d'une sonorité pleine	con una sonorità piena
dans le style d'une sarabande	nello stile di una sarabanda
dans un goût burlesque	in modo burlesco
dans un halo de pédales	in un alone di pedali
dans un murmure	in un mormorio
dans un sentiment intime	con un sentimento intimo
dans une sonorité claire	con una sonorità chiara
d'une voix vivante	a viva voce
dans une sonorité harmonieuse et lointaine	con una sonorità armoniosa e distante
de plus en plus brouillé	sempre più confuso
de plus loin	da più lontano
de très loin	da molto lontano
doucement contenu	dolcemente rattenuto
doucement timbré	dolcemente sonoro
durant tout le morceau	durante tutto il pezzo

change often (the pedal)	das Pedal oft wechselnd
professional clapper audience	bezahlter Beifallklatscher
damp and gentle tapping	weicher, verschwommener Anschlag
as from far away	wie aus der Ferne
like a fresh breeze	wie eine frische Brise
with a country background	wie ein ländlicher Hintergrund
like a chat	wie ein Geplauder
like a cry	wie ein Schrei
like a rainbow-coloured mist	wie ein regenbogenfarbiger Dunst
like a confusing murmur	wie ein verworrenes Gemurmel
like a moving shadow	wie ein gleitender Schatten
like a regret	wie ein Bedauern
like tumult from far away	wie ein Tumult aus der Ferne
like a sound of horns	wie Hörnerklang
wistfully and sad	nachdenklich und traurig
start in a little slower tempo	in einem etwas langsameren Zeitmaß beginnend
from the beginning to the end	vom Anfang bis zum Schluss
in little, even pace	mit einem kleinen, gleichmäßigen Schritt
in a tired rhythm	mit müdem Rhythmus
in a free rhythm	in freiem Rhythmus
with only one finger	nur mit einem Finger
with a full sound	mit einem vollen Klang
in the style of a sarabande	im Stil einer Sarabande
in a burlesque style	in burlesker Weise
with a gentle touch of pedals	mit einem Hauch von Pedal
in a murmur	gemurmelt
with intimate feeling	mit innigem Gefühl
with a clear sound	mit hellem Klang
with lively voice	mit lebhafter Stimme
with a harmonious sound from far away	mit einem harmonischen Klang aus der Ferne
more and more confused	immer wirrer
from further away	von weiter her
from very far away	von sehr weit her
gently restrained	sacht zurückgehalten
with a gentle timbre	mit einer sanften Klangfarbe
during the whole piece	während des ganzen Stücks

en animant toujours davantage	sempre più animando
en demi-teinte	in mezza tinta
en diminuant graduellement	diminuendo gradualmente
en donnant à la basse une sonorité cristalline et dégagée	dando al basso una sonorità cristallina e disinvolta
en général sans nuances	generalmente senza dinamica
en se rapprochant	avvicinandosi
enveloppé de pédales	avvolto di pedale
frapper les accords sans lourdeur	suonare gli accordi senza pesantezza
gardez la pédale	tenete il pedale
intimement doux	intimamente dolce
jamais assez	mai abbastanza
joyeusement animé	allegramente animato
joyeux et emporté	gioioso ed impetuoso
jusqu'à la fin en se perdant	perdendosi fino al fine
la ligne d'en haut	la voce superiore in fuori
la mesure précédente	la battuta precedente
la moitié moins vite	la metà meno svelto
le chant un peu en dehors	il canto un poco in fuori
le reste	il resto
le thème en dehors	il tema in rilievo
les arpèges serrés	gli arpeggi stretti
les petites notes doivent être frappées sur le temps	le notine in battere
lâchez	allentate
librement déclamé	liberamente declamato
marquez le thème	marcate il tema
mettre beaucoup de pédale	mettere molto pedale
pédale à chaque accord	pedale ad ogni accordo
pédale à chaque mesure	pedale ad ogni battuta
pédale forte sur chaque temps	il pedale destro su ogni battuta
petite reprise	piccola ripresa
plus lent qu'au début	più lento del principio
plus pénétrant	più penetrante
plutôt lent	piuttosto lento
point trop vite	non troppo presto

more and more animated	mehr und mehr belebt
with light colour	mit halber (schwacher) Färbung
gradually becoming softer	schrittweise leiser werdend
giving the bass a crystalline and unconstrained timbre	dem Bass einen kristalklaren und ungezwungenen Klang gebend
generally without shading	im Allgemeinen ohne Abstufungen
approaching	sich nähernd
enveloped by pedals	in Pedalklang gehüllt
sound in unison without any weight	die Akkorde ohne Gewicht anschlagen
keep the pedal down	das Pedal halten
intimately gentle	innig sanft
never enough	nie genug
joyfully animated	freudig belebt
gaily and impetuously	fröhlich und ungestüm
allowing to die out	sich bis zum Schluss verlierend
the upper voice stressed	die obere Stimme hervorgehoben
the preceding measure	der vorhergehende Takt
half the speed	halb so schnell
the melody a little stressed	die Melodie etwas hervorgehoben
the rest	der Rest
the theme stressed	das Thema hervorgehoben
the arpeggios hurried	die Arpeggien eng gedrängt
the small notes on the beat	die kleinen Noten auf den Schlag
let slacken	nachlassen
freely recited / declaimed	frei deklamiert
mark the theme	das Thema mit Nachdruck
use plenty of pedal	viel Pedal nehmen
pedal on each chord	Pedal auf jeden Akkord
pedal on each measure	Pedal auf jeden Takt
sustaining pedal on each time	rechtes Pedal auf jede Taktzeit
short reprise	kleine Reprise
more slowly than at the beginning	langsamer als am Anfang
more penetrating	durchdringender
rather slowly	eher langsam
not too fast	nicht zu schnell

presque plus rien	quasi più niente
profondément expressif	profondamente espressivo
rallentissez beaucoup	rallentato molto
relâche *f*	oggi riposo
reprendre sans refrapper	riprendere senza ribattere
respectez scrupuleusement ce doigté	rispettate scrupolosamente questa diteggiatura
retro	fuori moda
revenez au premier mouvement	tornate al tempo primo
revenir au tempo initial	tornare al tempo iniziale
rêveusement lent	lento sognante
richement coloré	riccamento colorito
sans accentuation	senza accenti
sans aucun	senza nessun
sans aucune accentuation	senza nessuna accentuazione
sans décomposer	senza decomporre
sans dureté	senza durezza
sans expression	senza espressione
sans hâte	senza fretta
sans interrompre	senza interrompere
sans lourdeur	senza pesantezza
sans nuances	senza dinamica
sans presser ni ralentir	senza accelerare ne rallentare
sans sécheresse	senza secchezza
sensiblement plus...	sensibilmente più…
sourdement agité	cupamente agitato
sourdine durant toute la pièce	la sordina durante tutto il pezzo
sortant de la brume	uscendo dalla foschia/nebbia
tout à fait	del tutto
très allant	con molto brio
très calme	molto calmo
très chaleureux	molto caloroso
très décidé	molto deciso
très effilé	molto sottile
très fondu	molto fuso
très franc	molto schietto
très intense	molto intenso

almost nothing anymore	beinahe nichts mehr
with deep expression	mit tiefem Ausdruck
slow down a lot	verlangsamen Sie sehr
no performance today	heute keine Vorstellung
take back without touching again	nochmals niederdrücken, ohne anzuschlagen
follow this fingering exactly	peinlich genau diesen Fingersatz beachten
oldfashioned	altmodisch
go back to the first tempo	zum ersten Zeitmaß zurückkehren
come back to the initial tempo	zum Anfangszeitmaß zurückkehren
dreamily slow	träumerisch langsam
richly coloured	reichlich gefärbt
without accentuation	ohne Betonung
without any	ohne jegliche
without any accentuation	ohne jegliche Betonung
without decomposing	ohne den Takt zu zerlegen
without hardness	ohne Härte
without expression	ohne Ausdruck
without haste	ohne Eile
without interrupting	ohne zu unterbrechen
without heaviness	ohne Schwerfälligkeit
no differences in the dynamics	ohne Unterschied in der Dynamik
neither hurry nor slow down	weder eilen noch verlangsamen
without dryness	ohne Trockenheit
considerably more...	spürbar mehr...
gloomily agitated	düster bewegt
soft pedal throughout the whole piece	Dämpfer während des ganzen Stücks
appearing out of the fog	aus dem Nebel auftauchend
entirely	ganz und gar
very lively	sehr lebhaft
very calm	sehr ruhig
very cordial	sehr warmherzig
very decided	sehr bestimmt
very slender	sehr schlank
very melted	sehr verschmolzen
very sincere	sehr aufrichtig
very intense	sehr intensiv

très lointain	molto lontano
uniformément articulé	uniformemente articolato
un peu appuyé	un poco appoggiato
un peu élargi	un poco allargato
un peu en dehors	un poco in fuori
un peu en valeur	un poco in risalto
un peu languissant	un poco languido
un peu plus lent qu'au début	un poco più lento dell'inizio
un peu plus à l'aise	un poco più comodo
un peu plus intense	un poco più intenso
un peu plus las	un poco più lasso
un peu plus vif	un poco più vivo
un tant-soit-peu	pochissimo / appena

Deutsche Fachausdrücke   Terminologia tedesca

aber immer fließend	ma sempre scorrevole
aber stets ernst und gewichtig	ma sempre serio e con molta importanza
abwechslungsreich	ricco di cambiamenti
allmählich abnehmen und ins erste Zeitmaß zurückgehen	diminuire poco a poco e ritornare al tempo primo
allmählich bewegter	poco a poco più mosso
allmählich etwas zurückhalten	progressivamente un poco ritenuto
allmählich ins schnelle Zeitmaß	passare poco a poco al tempo rapido
allmählich verbreitern	allargare poco a poco
ängstlich erregt	ansiosamente eccitato
Anmerkung für den Dirigenten	nota per il direttore d'orchestra
bedeutend langsamer	considerabilmente più lento
beständig zunehmen	aumentando costantemente (sempre crescendo)
bühnenreif	pronto per la scena
das gleiche Gleiten eines langsamen Walzers nachahmend	imitando il movimento scivolante di un valzer lento
die Begleitung fast durchweg leise	l'accompagnamento quasi sempre piano

very distant	sehr entfernt
evenly articulated	gleichmäßig artikuliert
somewhat supported	etwas gestützt
somewhat enlarged	etwas gedehnt
somewhat stressed	etwas herausgehoben
somewhat stressed	etwas hervorgehoben
somewhat languishing	etwas schmachtend
somewhat slower than at the beginning	etwas langsamer als am Anfang
somewhat comfortably	etwas gemächlicher
somewhat more intensively	etwas intensiver
somewhat more tired	etwas müder
somewhat more lively	etwas lebendiger
only just	ein ganz kleines bisschen

German specialist terms   Terminologie allemande

but always flowing	mais toujours fluide
but always serious and weighty	mais toujours sérieux et avec beaucoup d'importance
full of changes	plein de changements
gradually diminishing and going back to the first tempo	diminuer peu à peu et revenir au premier mouvement
moving ahead little by little	peu à peu plus animé
gradually holding back a little	retenir un peu progressivement
gradually moving into the fast tempo	passer peu à peu au tempo rapide
gradually broadening	en élargissant peu à peu
anxiously excited	craintivement excité
note for the conductor	note pour le chef d'orchestre
considerably slower	considérablement plus lent
continually growing	en augmentant constamment
ready for the stage	prêt pour la scène
imitating the sliding motion of a slow waltz	en imitant le mouvement glissant d'une valse lente
almost always a soft accompaniment	l'accompagnement presque toujours piano

die Einleitung ein wenig breiter	l'introduzione un poco più ampia
die Taste tonlos niederdrücken	premere il tasto senza farlo suonare
dieser Teil ist durchweg sehr leise zu spielen	questa parte deve essere suonata sempre dolcemente
doch nie übereilt	ma mai precipitosamente
dreimal so langsam	tre volte più lento
durch die untere Oktave zu verstärken	da rinforzare con l'ottava inferiore
durchaus phantastisch und leidenschaftlich vorzutragen	eseguire in maniera fantasiosa e appassionata
durchweg die gleiche Geschwindigkeit	sempre la stessa velocità
durchweg mit dem Dämpferpedal zu spielen	sempre col pedale sinistro
durchweg sehr zart und schlicht	sempre dolcissimo e semplice
ein wenig voran	avanzare un poco
entsprechend / gemäß	adeguato / conformemente
erreicht / gewonnen	raggiunto
etwas fließender, aber sehr ausdrucksvoll	un poco più rapido ma molto espressivo
etwas unbeholfen vorzutragen	va interpretato in modo piuttosto goffo
fest und bestimmt beginnend, dann allmählich wieder etwas lebhafter	incominciare fermo e deciso poi nuovamente un poco animato
folgt sofort der nächste Satz	attacca subito il tempo seguente
frisch und munter	vivo e vegeto
gefühlvoll	pieno di sentimento
genau doppelt so schnell	esattamente due volte più rapido
Grillen	propositi capricciosi
hanebüchen	un poco rude / rozzo
Hauptzeitmaß	il tempo principale
hier ist ein festes Zeitmaß erreicht	quì è stato raggiunto un tempo costante
hier wieder eine Pause, jedoch nicht so lang wie die erste	quì nuovamente una pausa, però non così lunga come la prima
hinabstürzend / herabstürzend	precipitando
immer ein wenig abziehen	sempre un poco diminuendo

the introduction a little broader	l'introduction un peu plus ample
to press the key without making a sound	enfoncer la touche sans la faire parler
this part has to be performed throughout very softly	cette partie doit être jouée toujours très doucement
but never rushed	mais sans jamais bousculer
three times slower	trois fois plus lent
to be reinforced with the lower octave	doit être renforcé par l'octave inférieure
to be absolutely performed with fantasy and passion	à exécuter de façon fantasque et passionnée
always the same tempo throughout	jouer continuellement à la même vitesse
always to be played with the soft pedal	toujours avec la pédale gauche
always very sweetly and simple	toujours très doux et simple
to go ahead a little	avancer un peu
according to / in proportion to	selon / conforme
reached	atteint
a little more quickly but very expressive	un peu plus rapide, mais très expressif
to be performed in a rather clumsy way	à interpréter d'une façon un peu gauche
beginning firm and decided, then gradually again a little more lively	commencer d'une façon ferme et décidée, puis peu à peu à nouveau plus animé
the next movement follows immediately	enchaîner tout de suite le mouvement suivant
fresh and lively	frais et dispos
full of feelings	plein de sentiment
exactly twice as fast	exactement deux fois plus vite
whims / silly ideas	un petit vélo dans la tête (Cortot: propos capricieux)
a little rough	un peu rude / grossier
the main tempo	le tempo principal
here a steady tempo is reached	ici on atteint une vitesse constante
here again a rest, but not as long as the first one	ici une nouvelle pause, mais pas aussi longue que la première
tumbling	en précipitant (précipiter)
always diminishing a little	en diminuant toujours un peu

immer frei deklamierend	sempre declamando liberamente
immer gut gehalten	sempre ben tenuto
immer mehr zurückhalten	sempre più ritenuto
immer noch beschleunigen	ancora accelerando (accelerare sempre di più)
immer so leise als möglich	sempre il più piano possibile
immerfort, immerzu	sempre, continuamente
in das nächste Zeitmaß übergehen	passare al tempo seguente
in das Tempo des Anfangs übergehen	passare alla velocità del tempo iniziale
in ruhigem, gleichmäßigem Zeitmaß	con un'andatura calma e regolare
in sich hineinhorchend	ascoltandosi internamente
in starr durchlaufender eintöniger Bewegung	con un movimento continuamente rigido e monotono
in wechselnder Taktart	con un tempo mutevole
ins erste Zeitmaß übergehen	passare al tempo primo
ins Hauptzeitmaß zurückgehen	ritornare al tempo principale
jeden Lauf etwas langsam beginnen	incominciare ogni passaggio un poco lentamente
kleine Noten mitspielen	suonare anche le notine
lassen / weglassen	lasciare
merklich	sensibilmente più...
mit akzentuiertem Ton	con un tono ben accentuato
mit äußerster Zartheit	con la massima dolcezza
mit fröhlichem Ausdruck	con un'espressione allegra
mit gänzlich gedämpfter Stimme	a bassa voce
mit geheimnisvoll schwermütigem Ausdruck	con un'espressione piena di mistero e di malinconia
mit gesteigertem Ausdruck	con un'espressione crescente
mit gutem Humor	di buon umore
mit höchster Kraft	con la massima forza
mit innigem Ausdruck	con un sentimento intimo (interno)
mit inniger Empfindung	con un'intensa espressione interna (intima)
mit schmerzlichem Ausdruck	con un'espressione dolorosa

always declaiming freely	en déclamant toujours librement
always well held	toujours bien tenu
holding back more and more	retenir toujours plus
still accelerating	accélérer de plus en plus
always as soft as possible	toujours aussi piano que possible
always	continuellement, toujours
to go on the the next tempo	passer au tempo suivant
to go on to the speed of the initial tempo	dans le mouvement du début
with a quite steady tempo	dans un mouvement calme et régulier
listening to oneself inwardly	en s'écoutant intérieurement
with a stiff and monotonous movement	dans un mouvement toujours rigide et monotone
with a changing meter	en changeant de tempo
to go on into the first tempo	passer au premier tempo
to go on to the main tempo	revenir au tempo principal
to begin each passage a little more slowly	commencer chaque passage un peu lentement
also play the grace notes	jouer aussi les petites notes
to let	laisser
noticeably more…	sensiblement plus…
with an accentuated sound	avec un ton bien accentué
with extreme sweetness	avec la plus extrême tendresse
with a cheerful expression	avec une expression joyeuse
in a very low voice	à voix basse
with an expression full of mistery and melancholy	avec une expression pleine de mystère et de mélancolie
with increasing expression	avec une expression croissante
with good humor	de bonne humeur
with greatest power	avec la plus grande force
with intimate sentiments	dans un sentiment d'intimité expressive
with intense intimate feeling	dans un profond sentiment d'intimité
with grievous expression	avec une expression douloureuse

mit Schwermut und Trauer vorzutragen	eseguire con malinconia e tristezza
mit verständigem Pedalgebrauch	con un uso ragionevole del pedale
mit viel innerlicher Bewegung	con un profondo e intenso sentimento intimo
munter, aber immer gemächlich	allegro ma sempre comodo
musizieren	suonare insieme
nach und nach belebter	poco a poco più animato
nach und nach immer schneller	poco a poco sempre più veloce
nicht unbedingt nötig	non è assolutamente necessario
noch ruhiger als am Anfang	ancora più calmo dell'inizio
ohne im Geringsten hervorzutreten	senza mettersi assolutamente in evidenza
ohne Rücksicht	senza riguardo
ohne Unterbrechung weiter	continuare senza interruzioni
reuig andächtig	pentendosi piosamente
schattenhaft	ombreggiato (ombroso)
schnarren	come una raganella
schreitend	avanzando solennemente
schrittmäßig	passo a passo
sehr innig zu spielen	da eseguire intimamente
sehr stürmisch und stets drängend	molto impetuoso e sempre accelerando
schmerzlich leidenschaftlich, doch nicht schneller	dolorosamente appassionato ma non più presto
so schnell wie möglich	il più presto possibile
stets streng im Zeitmaß	senza alcuna licenza
stets zunehmen und vorangehen	sempre andando e crescendo
Traumeswirren	sogni confusi
übernehmen	assumere / adossarsi
umstimmen	cambiare l'accordatura
unbeholfen / täppisch / anmutlos	goffo / sgraziato
unmerklich / in unmerkbarer Weise	impercettibilmente
Urlicht	luce divina
von hier bis zum Schluss	da adesso fino alla fine
allmählich langsamer werden	rallentare progressivamente

to be performed with melancholy and sorrow	interpréter avec mélancolie et douleur
with reasonable use of the pedal	avec un usage raisonnable de la pédale
with deep and intense intimate expression	avec beaucoup d'émotion intérieure
lively, but always comfortable	gai, mais toujours à l'aise
to play together	faire de la musique d'ensemble
little by little more animated	peu à peu plus animé
gradually getting faster	accélerer de plus en plus
not absolutely necessary	n'est pas absolument nécessaire
even calmer than at the beginning	encore plus calme qu'au début
without coming forward at all	surtout ne pas se mettre en valeur
without consideration	sans égard
to continue without interruption	continuer sans interruption
repentant devoted	en se repentant pieusement
shadowy	ombragé
like a rattle	comme une crécelle
going forward solemnly	en avançant solennellement
step by step	pas-à-pas
to be performed in a very intimate way	à exécuter d'une façon très intime
very impetuous and always speeding up	très fougueux et en accélerant continuellement
painfully passionate, but not faster	douloureusement passionné, mais jamais plus vite
as fast as possible	le plus rapidement possible
always strictly a tempo	toujours strictement en mesure
always moving on and increasing	en augmentant et en avançant de façon continue
confused dreams	rêve confus (Cortot: hallucinations)
to take on / to take over	assumer / se charger de
to change the tuning	changer l'accordage
clumsy / awkward	maladroit / disgracieux
imperceptible	imperceptiblement
divine light	lumière divine
from here to the end, getting gradually slower	dès maintenant jusqu'à la fin ralentir peu à peu

vorwärtstreiben / vorwärtsdrängen	spingere (procedere)
weit ausspannen	ampliando molto
wie ein Gespräch	come una conversazione
wie ein Kondukt	come un convoglio funebre
wie eine Vogelstimme	come il canto di un uccello
wie im Vorspiel	come nel preludio
wie überhörend	come se non si sentisse
wieder das alte Zeitmaß, aber stets vorwärtsgehen	nuovamente il tempo precedente ma sempre andando speditamente
ziemlich lebhaft, immer noch beschleunigen	vivo assai, continuando sempre ad accelerare
zurücktreten	passare in secondo piano

pushing	pousser (avancer)
extending widely	en amplifiant beaucoup
like a conversation	comme une conversation
like a funeral procession	comme un convoi funèbre
like a bird's song	comme le chant d'un oiseau
as in the prelude	comme dans le prélude
as if one does not hear	comme si on n'entendait pas
again in the former tempo, but always pushing	à nouveau le tempo précédant, mais en avançant sans arrêt
quite lively, still accelerating	assez vif, toujours en accélérant
to pass in the second ground	passer au deuxième plan

English and American specialist terms

Terminologia inglese ed americana

all along	tutto il tempo
along	lungo
as fast as possible	il più presto possibile
a shade slower	una sfumatura più lento
as if coming from a distance	come da lontano
at a brisk pace	tempo animato
awkwardly	maldestramente
back to first speed / back to pattern	tornando al tempo
back to refrain	tornando al ritornello
becoming ferocious	diventando selvaggio
boisterously	tempestoso
bouncy	rimbalzante
brassy	come degli ottoni
brightly	brillantemente
bring out the melody	far risaltare la melodia
bubbly	spumante
bumpily	sobbalzando
buzz along	sempre ronzando
casually	casualmente
choppily	mutevole
chug along	sciolto / rilassato
clap hands	battere le mani
clashing	rumoroso
crisp	vivo / frizzante
cussedly	ostinato
dazzling	abbagliante / radioso
delicately	delicatamente
devised	improvvisato / escogitato
doggedly	ostinato
dragging	trascinato
driving tempo	andando
drowsily	sonnolento
dryly	seccamente
early	presto
eloquently	eloquentemente
evenly	in modo uguale
explosive	esplosivo

Englische und amerikanische Fachausdrücke

Terminologie anglaise et américaine

die ganze Zeit	tout le temps
entlang	le long
so schnell wie möglich	aussi vite que possible
eine Nuance langsamer	une nuance plus lent
wie aus weiter Ferne	comme au lointain
in forscher Gangart	d'un mouvement animé
ungeschickt / unbeholfen	maladroitement
zurück zum Anfangstempo	en retournant au mouvement
zurück zum Refrain	revenez au refrain
wild werdend	en devenant sauvage
stürmisch	tempétueux
hüpfend	bondissant
wie Blechinstrumente	comme des cuivres
glanzvoll / strahlend	brillamment
Melodie hervorheben	faire ressortir la mélodie
sprudelnd	pétillant
holprig	en sautant
dahinsummend	en bourdonnant sans arrêt
gelegentlich	par hasard
wechselhaft	changeant
lässig gehend	relaxé
in die Hände klatschen	battre des mains
lärmend	bruyant
frisch	pétillant
stur	obstiné
delikat / zart	délicatement
glänzend / blendend	radieux
improvisiert	improvisé
hartnäckig	obstiné
schleppend	traînant
vorantreibendes Tempo	en allant
verschlafen / schläfrig	d'un air endormi
trocken	sèchement
frühzeitig / baldig	tôt
redegewandt	éloquement
gleichmäßig	de façon égale
explosiv	explosif

fade out	svanire
fading	perdendosi
fair	bello
fairly	abbastanza
final ending	parte finale
flexibly	flessibile
frenchy	alla francese
gaily	gaiamente
gaily moving	movendo allegramente
gay but strict	gioioso ma preciso
gentle	garbato
gently flowing	dolcemente scorrevole
gliding	scorrevole
gossipy	pettegolo
gradually picking up speed	accelerando poco a poco
groovy	vitale
hammer it out	molto chiaro e martellato
handclapping	battendo le mani
happily	felicemente
heavily	pesantemente
"homespun style"	stile "casalingo"
hungrily	affamato
in a grand manner	con grandezza
in an easy going manner	in maniera comoda
in a pensive mood	pensieroso
in a song-like manner	come una canzone
in a steady pace	d'un passo uguale
in a straightforward manner	avanzando in modo deciso
jogging along	correndo leggermente
jokingly	scherzando
jolly	ameno
jumping	saltando
just a little faster	solo un poco più presto
just a little slower	solo un poco più lento
keep moving	sempre mosso
langorously	languidamente
lazily	pigramente
left hand loud	la mano sinistra forte

ausklingen / ausblenden	expirer
ausklingend	en se perdant
schön / hell	beau
ziemlich	assez
Schlussteil *m*	partie finale
flexibel	flexible
kokett	à la française
fröhlich / frech	gaîment
fröhlich bewegend	joyeusement animé
fröhlich, aber exakt	joyeux mais exact
sanft	affable
sanft dahinfließend	en s'écoulant doucement
gleitend	alerte
geschwätzig	bavard
allmählich schneller werdend	en accélerant peu à peu
fit / vital	en pleine forme
sehr scharf hervorheben	très clair et martelé
in die Hände klatschen	en battant des mains
glücklich	heureux
schwer	lourdement
„hausgemacht" / schlicht	style "maison"
hungrig	affamé
elegant / großzügig	avec beaucoup d'envergure (ou: de style)
auf unbeschwerte Art	de façon decontractée
in einer nachdenklichen Stimmung	d'humeur pensive
wie ein Lied	comme une chanson
mit gleichmäßigem Schritt	d'une allure égale
entschieden vorwärtsgehen	en avançant d'une façon déçidée
locker dahinlaufend	en courant légèrement
spaßend / scherzend	en plaisantant
vergnügt	jovial
springend	en sautant
nur ein wenig schneller	seulement un peu plus vite
nur ein wenig langsamer	seulement un peu plus lent
immer weiter bewegen	toujours en mouvement
schmachtend	langoureusement
träge	paresseusement
linke Hand laut	la main gauche appuyée

leisurely	comodamente
let it ring	lasciare risuonare
like a hymn	come un inno
like a prayer	come una preghiera
lilting	cantando melodiosamente
lively jumping	saltando gioiosamente
lumbering	pesantemente
meditatively	meditativo
menacingly	minacciosamente
mighty	potente
moderately fast	moderatamente rapido
moody	lunatico
mournfully	tristemente
moving along	sempre movendo
no speed limit	senza limite di velocità
notice the expression	osservate i segni dinamici
optional ending	fine facoltativa
pattern (rhythm)	modello (ritmo)
patterned	misurato
perky	vispo / gaio
picking up	riprendendo
plodding	faticosamente
pound it out	fare risaltare
quick four	tempo veloce a quattro
quietly moving	andando tranquillamente
quite	piuttosto
real	vero
reflective	riflessivo
restrained waltz tempo	ritmo di valzer ritenuto
reverently	riverente
rhythmically	ritmicamente
right hand soft	la mano destra leggera
rippling	mormorando / gorgogliando
rolling along	ondulando tutto il tempo
rolling motion	movimento ondulante
seadreamy	sognante / "sogno marittimo"

mit Muße / entspannt	decontracté
lass es klingen	laisser résonner
wie eine Hymne	comme un hymne
wie ein Gebet	comme une prière
trällernd / beschwingt singend	en chantant mélodieusement / fredonnant
lebhaft hüpfend	en sautant joyeusement
schwerfällig	pesant
besinnlich / nachdenklich	méditatif
drohend	de façon menaçante
mächtig	puissant
mäßig schnell	modérément rapide
launenhaft	lunatique
trauervoll	tristement
durchgehend bewegt	en mouvement continu
ohne Tempobeschränkung	sans limitation de vitesse
beachte die Ausdrucksvermerke	observez les nuances
möglicher (freigestellter) Schluss	fin facultative
Muster (Rhythmus)	modèle (rythme)
gegliedert / gemessen	mesuré
keck / flott	pimpant / hardi
wieder aufnehmend	en reprenant
mühsam	lourdement / traînant
hervorhebend / heftig anschlagend	mettre en évidence
schneller Vierertakt	mouvement rapide à quatre temps
ruhig gehend	en allant tranquillement
ziemlich	plutôt
wirklich / echt	vrai
nachdenklich	réfléchi
zurückhaltendes Walzertempo	rythme de valse retenu
ehrfurchtsvoll	révérent
rhythmisch	rythmiquement
rechte Hand leise	la main droite légère
murmelnd	en murmurant / gargouillant
dahinströmend	en ondulant tout le long
rollende Bewegung	mouvement ondulant
träumerisch / „wie ein Meerestraum"	rêveur / "rêve maritime"

shuffling	strascicando
skip	salto / balzo
slinky	furtivamente
slow doo-wop tempo	tempo lento di "scat"
slowly but moving	lentamente però andando
snappish	beffardo
solidly	solidamente
somewhat	alquanto
somewhat hurrying	un poco affrettando
sophisticated	sofisticato
spooky	spiritato
sprightly	brioso
stamp out	estinguendo
stately tempo	maestoso
steadily	fermamente
steady walking	camminando regolarmente
stealthy	furtivo
steaming	a tutto vapore
strained	teso
strict	preciso
stroll along	passeggiando
strong and forceful	forte e potente
strut	pavoneggiandosi
strutting tempo	con andatura solenne
subtle	sottile / astuto
swaying	oscillando
swishing	sibilando
take time	prendete tempo
tempo "disturb the neighbours"	tempo "disturba i vicini"
the top voice	la voce superiore
to interlude	all'interludio
very rhythmically	ben ritmato
waddling	ondeggiando / scodinzolando
weeping willow	salice piangente
well contrasted	ben contrastato
whistfully	meditabondo
with a back beat	accento sul tempo debole
with a clear tone	con un suono chiaro
with a fling	rilassato
with a full rich tone	con una sonorità ricca e piena

schleppend / schlurfend	traînant
Sprung	saut / bond
verstohlen	furtivement
langsames „scat"-Tempo	tempo lent de "scat"
langsam, aber mit Bewegung	lentement mais avec allant
schnippisch	narquois
fest / solide	solidement
ein wenig	quelque peu
etwas eilend	légèrement pressant
spitzfindig / raffiniert	sophistiqué
spukhaft / gespenstisch	hanté
spritzig	vif
verlöschend	en éteignant
imposant	majestueux
stetig	fermement
gleichmäßig gehend	en marchant régulièrement
verstohlen	furtif
mit Volldampf	à toute vapeur
angespannt	tendu
strikt	rigoureux
dahinschlendern	en se promenant
stark und kräftig	fort et puissant
einherstolzierend	en se pavanant
feierlich	d'allure solennel
subtil	subtil
schwankend	en oscillant
schwirrend	en sibilant
sich Zeit lassen	prenez votre temps
Tempo „störe die Nachbarn"	tempo "dérange les voisins"
die obere Stimme	la voix supérieure
zum Zwischenspiel gelangen	à l'interlude
sehr rhythmisch	très rythmique
watschelnd	en dandinant
Trauerweide	saule pleureur
mit deutlichem Gegensatz	bien contrasté
nachdenklich	d'un air songeur
Betonung auf der schwachen Taktzeit	les accents sur les temps faibles
mit einem klaren Ton	avec un ton clair
lässig hingeworfen	décontracté
mit einem vollen, reichen Ton	avec une sonorité riche et pleine

with a gentle motion	tranquillamente mosso
with a Glenn Miller flavour	con un profumo di Glenn Miller
with a lilt	allegramente ritmato
with ambition	con ambizione
with an easy flow	scorrendo tranquillamente
with a steady insistence	con grande insistenza
with a singing tone	con un suono cantabile
with a springing touch	con un tocco saltellante
with a steady pulse	con un impulso ritmico regolare
with a warm expression	con un'espressione intensa
with bad humor	di cattivo umore
with dash	con slancio
with deep feeling	con profonda espressione
with drive	con impulso
with dry humour	con un'umore secco
with feeling	con sentimento
with firm step	d'un passo deciso
with full tone	con un suono pieno
with good humour	di buon umore
with great expression	con grande espressione
with great warmth	con grande calore
with imagination	con immaginazione
with inflections of plainsong	con delle inflessioni di canto gregoriano
with much precision	molto preciso
with pity	con pietà
with quiet dignity	con una tranquilla dignità
with regained strength	con recuperata forza
with simple tenderness	con semplice tenerezza
with sincere sympathy	con sincera simpatia
with spiritual feeling	con sentimento spirituale
with sport	giocoso
with steady heavy motion	pesante e regolare
with sure rhythm	con un ritmo sicuro

mit sanfter Bewegung	avec un mouvement calme
mit einem Hauch von Glenn Miller	avec un parfum de Glenn Miller
mit einem flotten Rhythmus	rythmé allégrement
ehrgeizig	avec ambition
ruhig dahinfließend	en s'écoulant tranquillement
mit gleichbleibendem Nachdruck	avec une grande insistance
mit singendem Klang	d'un ton chantant
mit hüpfendem Anschlag	avec un toucher sautillant
mit gleichmäßigem Puls	avec une pulsation réguliére
mit warmem Ausdruck	avec une intense expression
mit schlechter Laune	de mauvaise humeur
mit Schwung	avec élan
sehr gefühlvoll	avec une profonde expression
mit Schwung / intensiv rhythmisch	avec de l'entrain
mit trockenem Humor	avec un humour sec
mit Gefühl	avec sentiment
mit festem Schritt	d'un pas décidé
mit vollem Klang	avec un son plein
mit guter Laune	de bonne humeur
sehr ausdrucksvoll	avec une grande expression
mit viel Wärme	avec beaucoup de chaleur
mit Phantasie	avec imagination
mit gregorianischen Schattierungen	avec des nuances de plain-chant
sehr genau	avec beaucoup de précision
mitleidig	avec pitié
mit stiller Würde	avec une tranquille dignité
mit neuer Kraft	avec une vigueur retrouvée
mit schlichter Zärtlichkeit	avec simple tendresse
mit herzlicher Sympathie	avec sincère sympathie
mit andächtigem Gefühl	avec un sentiment spirituel
mit Spaß / mit Vergnügen	avec enjouement
mit stetiger, heftiger Bewegung	pesant et régulier
mit sicherem Rhythmus	avec un rythme sur

Jazz, Rock, Pop

all-star band	complesso jazz / formato da musicisti noti
background	sottofondo
backline	gli strumenti e gli accessori sulla scena
band	complesso jazz o rock
bandleader	il capo del complesso
barrelhouse piano style	pianoforte con suono metallico
beat (1960)	"colpo"; stile musicale
Bebop (1940)	uno stile di jazz
big band	grande complesso
blues ending	finale di Blues
Blues (1912)	una delle forme principali del jazz (schema di 12 battute)
Boogie-Woogie (1928)	stile pianistico (schema di 12 battute)
bounce	ritmo rimbalzante
break	interruzione e pausa
bridge	ponte
call and response	principio: appello e risposta
chorus	ritornello (schema di 32 battute)
combo	piccolo complesso
comeback	il ritorno
commercial	commerciale
Cool Jazz (1948)	jazz "freddo"
country blues (1850)	blues autentico
country music	musica campestre
creative music (1970)	sostituisce la parola jazz
crooner	cantante con voce sentimentale
cue	gesto o segno per attacca
dirty tones	suoni "sporchi"/ strascicati
disco music (1975)	musica in voga nelle discoteche
Dixieland (1920)	jazz suonato dai bianchi
double time / duple time	tempo doppio
drive	impulso
featuring	nel ruolo principale

Jazz, Rock, Pop

Jazz, Rock, Pop

Jazzensemble aus berühmten Musikern	formation de jazz avec des musiciens connus
Hintergrund	musique de fond
gesamtes Instrumentarium und Zubehör auf der Bühne	les instruments et les accessoires sur la scène
Musikgruppe Jazz oder Rock	formation de jazz ou de rock
Leiter einer Musikgruppe	chef de l'ensemble
Klavierstil mit klirrendem Klang	piano avec un son métallique
„Schlag"; Musikrichtung	"coup"; style de musique
ein Jazzstil	un style de jazz
große Musikgruppe	grande formation
Blues-Schlusswendung	final de Blues
eine der Hauptformen des Jazz (Grundschema: 12 Takte)	une des principales formes du jazz (schéma de 12 mesures)
ein pianistischer Stil (Grundschema: 12 Takte)	style pianistique (schéma de 12 mesures)
hüpfender Rhythmus	rythme rebondissant
Unterbrechung und Pause	interruption et pause
Überleitung	pont / passage
Ruf-Antwort-Prinzip	principe: appel-réponse
Grundmelodie; Refrain (Grundschema: 32 Takte)	refrain (schéma de 32 mesures)
kleine Musikgruppe	petit ensemble
Wiederkehr	le retour
kommerziell	commercial
„kühler" Jazz	jazz "froid"
authentischer Blues	blues authentique
ländliche Musik	musique champêtre
ersetzt das Wort Jazz	remplace le mot jazz
Sänger mit sanfter Stimme / Schnulzensänger	chanteur avec voix sentimentale
Hinweis für Einsatz	geste ou signe pour attaque
„dreckige" Töne, schleifend	sons "sales", traînants
Diskomusik	musique en vogue dans les discothèques
Jazz, von Weißen gespielt	jazz joué par les blancs
Verdopplung des Tempos	tempo double
Schwung / Antrieb	impulsion
in der Hauptrolle	dans le rôle principal

feeling	sentimento
Folk-Rock (1965)	fusione dei due generi
Free Jazz (1960)	jazz "libero"
Funk (1950/1970)	stile di jazz, in seguito di Pop
Fusion (1970)	fusione di generi musicali o di culture differenti
gimmick	un trucco
Gospelsong (1930)	canto religioso dei neri
growl	cantare e soffiare al tempo stesso
Hard Rock (1970)	rock "duro"
head arrangement	improvvisazione "concordata"
headline	la melodia o il testo che rimane nella memoria
Heavy Metal (1970)	hard rock
Hillbilly (1900)	musica campestre eseguita dai bianchi negli S.U.
hit	un grande successo
hit-parade	la parata dei successi
hit song	canzonetta a successo
Honky Tonk music (1900)	musica eseguita nelle bettole
hot (1925)	uno dei primi jazz
hot jazz (1925)	jazz "caldo" tradizionale
house rent party / skiffle	festa privata con musica
Intro	2, 4 o 8 battute d'introduzione
Jam Session	concerto spontaneo, improvvisato
Jazz (1880)	forma musicale afroamericana
Jubilee	musica afroamericana religiosa
juke box / music box	juke-box
jungle style (1920)	stile "giungla"
latin american music	musica sudamericana
lead	melodia principale
light show	l'illuminazione dello spettacolo
live	dal vivo
locked hands style / block chords	melodia suonata parallelamente con le due mani

Gefühl	sentiment
Fusion der zwei Stile	fusion des deux genres
„freier" Jazz	jazz "libre"
ein Jazzstil, später Popstil	un style de jazz, ensuite de Pop
in der Popmusik Verschmelzung verschiedener Kulturen	fusion de cultures ou genres différents de musique
ein Kniff	un truc
religiöser Gesang der Schwarzen	chant religieux des noirs
Singen und Blasen gleichzeitig	chanter et souffler en même temps
„harter" Rock	rock "dur"
vereinbarte Improvisation	improvisation "décidée"
der „Aufhänger", Musik und Text	la mélodie ou le texte qui restent dans la mémoire
harter Rock	hard rock
ländliche Volksmusik der Weißen in den USA	musique champêtre produite par des blancs aux E.U.
großer Erfolg	un grand succès, un tube
Schlagerparade	la parade des succès
erfolgreicher Schlager	chanson à succès
Country-Musik in Western-Bars	musique exécutée dans une gargote
einer der frühesten Jazzstile	un des premiers jazz
„heißer" Jazz, traditionell	jazz "chaud" traditionnel
Privatfest mit Musik	fête privée avec de la musique
2, 4 oder 8 Takte Einleitung (Kurzform für Introduktion)	2, 4 ou 8 mesures d'introduction
zwanglose Zusammenkunft von Jazzmusikern zu gemeinsamem Spielen	concert spontané, bœuf
afroamerikanische Musikform	forme musicale afroaméricaine
afroamerikanische geistliche Musik	musique afroaméricaine religieuse
Musikbox / Musikautomat	jukebox
„Urwald"-Stil, Dschungelstil	style "jungle"
lateinamerikanische Musik	musique sudaméricaine
führende Melodie	mélodie principale
Konzertlichtgestaltung	l'éclairage du spectacle
Direktübertragung	sur le vif
auf dem Klavier Melodie mit beiden Händen parallel spielen	mélodie jouée parallèlement avec les deux mains au piano

loft jazz / midwest jazz	jazz non commerciale, praticato negli scantinati
long playing / LP	microsolco
Mainstream (1940)	jazz moderato
marching band / street band	antiche bande americane
medium	tempo moderato
musical	commedia musicale
music hall	varietà
Negro Spiritual	musica religiosa dei neri americani
New Orleans / Old Time Jazz (1900)	prima forma del jazz
New Wave (1975)	altra forma di Rock
off beat	l'accento sui tempi deboli / contrattempo
off pitch / off key	fuori dal tono giusto
on beat	l'accento in battere
paradiddle	figura ritmica per il batterista
play party	serata danzante con canti ma senza strumenti
Pop Music (1960)	sintesi tra la canzone e il Rock
power	potenza
Progressive Jazz (1945)	sviluppo del "Big band"
Punk Rock	musica di stile provocativo
Ragtime (1870)	stile pianistico
Rap	ritmi parlati
Reggae (1965)	forma musicale giamaicana
revival	ripresa, rinascita
rhythm section	sezione ritmica
Rhythm and Blues (1940)	uno stile di jazz
riff	brevi motivi ripetuti
rim shot	tecnica particolare di percussione
Rock (1965)	continuazione del Rock'n'Roll e del beat
Rockabilly (1950)	origine del Rock'n'Roll
scat	canto sillabato

nicht vermarktete Musik, in Kellern gespielt	jazz non commercial, pratiqué dans les cantines
Langspielplatte	microsillon
gemäßigter Jazz	jazz modéré
frühere USA-Marschmusik	anciennes fanfares américaines
mittleres Tempo	tempo modéré
Musical / musikalische Komödie	comédie musicale
Varieté	variété / café-concert
geistliche Musik der Afroamerikaner	musique religieuse des noirs
erste Form des schwarzen Jazz	première forme de jazz
eine Form von Rock	autre forme de Rock
Betonung auf dem schwachen Schlag	l'accent sur les temps faibles
weg von der exakten Tonhöhe	à côté du ton exact
Betonung auf dem starken Schlag	l'accent sur les temps forts
ein rhythmisches Element für den Schlagzeuger	un élément rythmique pour le batteur
Tanzabend mit Gesang, aber ohne Instrumente	soirée dansante avec des chants, mais sans instruments
Synthese zwischen Schlager und Rock	synthèse entre la chanson et le rock
Kraft, Stärke	puissance
eine Weiterentwicklung der „Big Band"	un développement du "Big Band"
Punk, provokativer Musikstil	musique provocative, choquante
ein Klavierstil	style pianistique
gesprochener Rhythmus	rythmes parlés
Musikform aus Jamaika	forme musicale de la Jamaique
Wiederaufleben	reprise, renaissance
Rhythmusgruppe	section rythmique
ein Jazzstil	un style de jazz
kleine wiederholte Figuren	brefs motifs répétés
Trommelschlag besonderer Art (auf den Rand)	technique particulière de percussion
Fortsetzung von Rock'n'Roll und Beat	continuation du Rock'n'Roll et de la musique beat
frühe Spielart des Rock'n'Roll	origine du Rock'n'Roll
Silbengesang	syllabes chantées

section	sezione
shout (1930)	stile vocale "urlato"
shuffle	motivo ritmico
ska (1950)	forma ritmica
smear	tipo di portamento
Soft Rock (1970)	rock morbido
Soul (1950)	"anima", musica pop afroamericana
sound	sonorità
square dance	ballo popolare in uso negli S.U.
standard	pezzo di repertorio
steel band	piccoli complessi diffusi a Trinidad, composti di strumenti a percussione ricavati da basi di bidoni
stomp	forma ritmica
straight	esecuzione fedele all'originale
sweet music	musica dolce
Swing (1930)	stile di jazz
syncopated music	musica sincopata
tag / ending	coda; alcune battute aggiunte
talkbox	scatola parlante
tap-dance / step dance	tip-tap
Third Stream (1950)	sintesi tra il jazz e la musica contemporanea
timing	senso del tempo
two beat	accenti uguali su uno e tre
uptempo	tempo molto veloce
verse	strofa
walking bass	un motivo "camminante" al basso
West Coast Jazz (1950)	jazz "bianco" in California
work songs	canti degli schiavi al lavoro

(Instrumenten-)Gruppe	section
„schreiender" Vokalstil	style vocal "hurlé"
eine Rhythmusfigur	un motif rythmique
eine rhythmische Form	une forme rythmique
Verschleifen der Töne	genre de "portamento"
„sanfter" Rock	rock doux
„Seele", afroamerikanische Popmusik	"âme", musique pop des noirs
Klang	sonorité
berühmter Volkstanz aus den USA	danse populaire répandue aux E.U.
bekanntes, älteres Stück	morceau de répertoire
ein Schlagzeugensemble karibischen Ursprungs, auf leeren Benzin- oder Ölfässern spielend	un ensemble de percussionistes des Caraïbes (Trinidad) jouant sur des instruments fabriqués à partir de fonds de barils de pétrole
eine rhythmische Form	une forme rythmique
originalgetreu musizieren	exécution fidèle à l'original
sanfte Musik	musique douce
ein Jazzstil	un style de jazz
synkopierte Musik	musique syncopée
Schlusswendung	mesures finales ajoutées
Sprechkasten (E-Gitarre)	boîte parlante (guitare éléctronique)
Steptanz	claquettes
Synthese von Jazz und Neuer Musik	synthèse entre le jazz et la musique contemporaine
„Timing" / richtiges Zeitgefühl	sens du temps
gleich starke Betonung auf eins und drei	accents égaux sur un et trois
sehr rasches Tempo	mouvement très rapide
Strophe	strophe / couplet
laufende Bassfigur	motif "allant" à la basse
„weißer" Jazz in Kalifornien	jazz "blanc" en Californie
Arbeitslieder der Sklaven	chant des esclaves au travail

Danze
(Le seguenti danze portano lo
stesso nome in tutte le lingue)

Dances
(The following dances bear the
same term in all languages)

Baion	Charleston
Bamba	Conga
Batucada	Dirty dance
Beguine	English waltz
Big apple	Foxtrott
Black bottom	Guaracha
Boogie-Woogie	Highlife
Bossa nova	Hully Gully
Boston	Hustle
Bounce	Java
Break dance	Jitterbug
Cakewalk	Jive
Calipso	Joropo
Carioca	Kasatschok
Cha-cha-cha	Lambada

Tänze
(Die folgenden Tänze tragen in
allen Sprachen den gleichen
Namen)

Danses
(Les danses suivants portent le
même nom dans toutes les
langues)

Lambeth walk	Raspa
Letkiss	Rock'n'Roll
Lindy-Hop	Rumba
Machiche	Salsa
Madison	Samba
Mambo	Shake
Merengue	Shimmy
Milonga	Sirtaki
Musette	Slowfox
Onestep	Slop
Pachanga	Surf
Pasodoble	Tango
Quickstep	Twist
Ramble	Twostep
Ranchera	Valse hésitation

100 composizioni celebri

Questa lista è stata redatta all'unico scopo di soddisfare la curiosità del lettore desideroso di conoscere la traduzione di un titolo particolare nelle varie lingue. Quindi non rappresenta una graduatoria sul valore musicale dei brani inseriti.

100 famous works

This list has been prepared with the purpose of satisfying the curiosity of the reader who wishes to understand the title of a particular piece in various languages. The list does not reflect any specific artistic criteria.

Bach, J.S.

Il clavicembalo ben temperato	The Welltempered Clavier
L'arte della fuga	The Art of Fugue
L'oratorio di Natale	Christmas Oratorio
L'offerta musicale	The Musical Offering

Bartók, Béla

Il mandarino meraviglioso	The Miraculous Mandarin

Beethoven, L. van

La consacrazione della casa	The Consecration of the House
Le creature di Prometeo	The Creatures of Prometheus
Sonata al chiaro di luna	Moonlight Sonata

Bellini, Vincenzo

La sonnambula	The Sleepwalker

Berlioz, Hector

La dannazione di Faust	Faust's Damnation

Bizet, Georges

I pescatori di perle	The Pearl Fishers

Boieldieu, François

La dama bianca	The White Lady

Borodin, Aleksandr

Nelle steppe dell'Asia centrale	In the Steppes of Central Asia

Boulez, Pierre

Il martello senza padrone	The Hammer without Master

100 berühmte Kompositionen

Diese Liste wurde allein mit dem Ziel zusammengestellt, die Wissbegier des Lesers, der die Übersetzung eines Titels in den verschiedenen Sprachen erfahren möchte, zu befriedigen. Eine künstlerische Bewertung der aufgeführten Kompositionen ist damit nicht intendiert.

100 œuvres célèbres

Cette liste a été rédigée dans l'unique but de satisfaire la curiosité du lecteur désireux de connaître la traduction d'un titre dans les differentes langues. Ainsi la liste ne reflète aucun critère artistique sur la valeur des titres insérés.

Bach, J.S.

Das Wohltemperierte Klavier	Le clavecin bien tempéré
Die Kunst der Fuge	L'art de la fugue
Das Weihnachtsoratorium	L'oratorio de Noël
Das Musikalische Opfer	L'offrande musicale

Bartók, Béla

Der wunderbare Mandarin	Le mandarin merveilleux

Beethoven, L. van

Die Weihe des Hauses	La consécration de la maison
Die Geschöpfe des Prometheus	Les créatures de Prométhée
Mondscheinsonate	Sonate au clair de lune

Bellini, Vincenzo

Die Nachtwandlerin	La somnambule

Berlioz, Hector

Faust's Verdammnis	La damnation de Faust

Bizet, Georges

Die Perlenfischer	Les pêcheurs de perles

Boieldieu, François

Die weiße Dame	La dame blanche

Borodin, Aleksandr

Eine Steppenskizze aus Mittelasien	Dans le steppes de l'Asie centrale

Boulez, Pierre

Der Hammer ohne Meister	Le marteau sans maître

Cimarosa, Domenico
Il matrimonio segreto   The Clandestine Marriage

Débussy, Claude
Il mare   The Sea
L'angolo dei bambini   Children's Corner
La scatola dei balocchi   The Toy's Box
Preludio al pomeriggio di un   Prelude to the Afternoon of a
fauno   Faun

De Falla, Manuel
Il cappello a tre punte   The Three-cornered Hat
La danza del fuoco   The Fire Dance
L'amore stregone   Love the Wizard
La vita breve   Life is Short
Notti nei giardini di Spagna   Nights in the Gardens of Spain

Donizetti, Gaetano
La figlia del reggimento   The Daughter of the Regiment
L'elisir d'amore   The Love Potion

Dukas, Paul
L'apprendista stregone   The Sorcerer's Apprentice

Dvořák, Antonín
Sinfonia dal nuovo mondo   New World Symphony

Händel, G.F.
Il fabbro armonioso   The Harmonious Blacksmith

Haydn, Joseph
La creazione   The Creation
Le stagioni   The Seasons

Khatschaturjan, Aram
La danza delle spade   Sabre Dance

Lehár, Franz
Il paese del sorriso   The Land of Smiles
La vedova allegra   The Merry Widow

Cimarosa, Domenico
Die heimliche Ehe   Le mariage secret

Débussy, Claude
Das Meer   La mer
Die Ecke der Kinder   Le coin des enfants
Die Spielzeugkiste   La boite à joujoux
Präludium zum Nachmittag   Prélude à l'après-midi d'un
eines Fauns   faune

De Falla, Manuel
Der Dreispitz   Le tricorne
Feuertanz   La danse du feu
Liebeszauber   L'amour sorcier
Ein kurzes Leben   La vie brève
Nächte in spanischen Gärten   Nuits dans les jardins
                                 d'Espagne

Donizetti, Gaetano
Die Regimentstochter   La fille du régiment
Der Liebestrank   L'élixir d'amour

Dukas, Paul
Der Zauberlehrling   L'apprenti sorcier

Dvořák, Antonín
Symphonie aus der Neuen Welt   Symphonie du nouveau monde

Händel, G.F.
Grobschmied-Variationen   Le forgeron harmonieux

Haydn, Joseph
Die Schöpfung   La création
Die Jahreszeiten   Les saisons

Khatschaturjan, Aram
Säbeltanz   La danse du sabre

Lehár, Franz
Das Land des Lächelns   Le pays du sourire
Die lustige Witwe   La veuve joyeuse

Liszt, Franz
Anni di pellegrinaggio   Years of Pilgrinage

Mahler, Gustav
Il canto della terra   The Song of the Earth

Mendelssohn Bartholdy, Felix
Il sogno di una notte di mezza   Midsummer Night's Dream
estate
La filatrice   Spinning Song
Mare tranquillo e viaggio felice   Calm Sea and Prosperous
                                          Voyage

Monteverdi, Claudio
L'incoronazione di Poppea   The Coronation of Poppea

Mozart, W.A.
Cosi fan tutte   All Women do it
Il flauto magico   The Magic Flute
Il ratto dal serraglio   The Elopement from the Harem
La finta giardiniera   The Pretended Garden-Girl
La marcia turca   The Turkish March
Le nozze di Figaro   The Marriage of Figaro

Mussorgsky, Modest
Quadri di un esposizione   Pictures at an Exhibition
Una notte sul monte calvo   Night on the Bare Mountain

Nicolai, Otto
Le allegre comari di Windsor   The Merry Wives of Windsor

Offenbach, Jacques
I conti di Hoffmann   The Tales of Hoffmann
Orfeo all'inferno   Orpheus in the Underworld

Pergolesi, Giovanni Battista
La serva padrona   The Maid as Mistress

Liszt, Franz
Pilgerjahre   Années de pèlerinage

Mahler, Gustav
Das Lied von der Erde   Le chant de la terre

Mendelssohn Bartholdy, Felix
Der Sommernachtstraum   Le Songe d'une nuit d'été

Das Spinnerlied   La fileuse
Meeresstille und glückliche   Mer tranquille et voyage
Fahrt   heureux

Monteverdi, Claudio
Die Krönung der Poppea   Le couronnement de Poppée

Mozart, W.A.
So machen es alle (Frauen)   Comme elles sont toutes
Die Zauberflöte   La flûte enchantée
Die Entführung aus dem Serail   L'enlèvement au serail
Die Gärtnerin aus Liebe   La prétendue jardinière
Türkischer Marsch   La marche turque
Figaros Hochzeit   Les noces de Figaro

Mussorgsky, Modest
Bilder einer Ausstellung   Tableaux d'une exposition
Eine Nacht auf dem kahlen   Une nuit sur le mont-chauve
Berge

Nicolai, Otto
Die lustigen Weiber von   Les joyeuses commères de
Windsor   Windsor

Offenbach, Jacques
Hoffmanns Erzählungen   Les contes d'Hoffmann
Orpheus in der Unterwelt   Orphée aux enfers

Pergolesi, Giovanni Battista
Die Magd als Herrin   La servante maîtresse

Prokofjew, Sergej
L'amore delle tre melarance   The Love for Three Oranges
Pierino ed il lupo   Peter and the Wolf

Puccini, Giacomo
Il tabarro   The Cloak

Ravel, Maurice
L'ora spagnola   The Spanish Hour

Respighi, Ottorino
Le fontane di Roma   The Fountains of Rome

Rimskij-Korsakow, Nikolaj
Il gallo d'oro   The Golden Cockerel
Il volo del calabrone   Flight of the Bumble Bee
La grande Pasqua russa   The Russian Easter

Rossini, Gioachino
Il barbiere di Siviglia   The Barber of Seville
La Cenerentola   Cinderella
La gazza ladra   The Thievish Magpie

Schönberg, Arnold
La mano felice   The Lucky Hand

Schubert, Franz
Il viaggio d'inverno   The Winter Journey
La bella mugnaia   The Fair Maid of the Mill
La morte e la fanciulla   Death and the Maiden
La trota   The Trout
L'incompiuta   The Unfinished (Symphony)

Schumann, Robert
Amor di poeta   Poet's Love
Amore e vita di donna   Woman's Love and Live
Scene infantili   Scenes from Childhood

Sinding, Christian A.
Mormorio di primavera   Rustle of Spring

Prokofjew, Sergej
Die Liebe zu den drei Orangen   L'amour des trois oranges
Peter und der Wolf   Pierre et le loup

Puccini, Giacomo
Der Mantel   La houppelande

Ravel, Maurice
Die spanische Stunde   L'heure espagnole

Respighi, Ottorino
Römische Brunnen   Les fontaines de Rome

Rimskij-Korsakow, Nikolaj
Der goldene Hahn   Le coq d'or
Der Hummelflug   Le vol du bourdon
Russische Ostern   La grande Pâques russe

Rossini, Gioachino
Der Barbier von Sevilla   Le barbier de Séville
Aschenbrödel   Cendrillon
Die diebische Elster   La pie voleuse

Schönberg, Arnold
Die glückliche Hand   La main heureuse

Schubert, Franz
Die Winterreise   Le voyage d'hiver
Die schöne Müllerin   La belle meunière
Der Tod und das Mädchen   La mort et la jeune fille
Die Forelle   La truite
Die Unvollendete (Symphonie)   La symphonie inachevée

Schumann, Robert
Dichterliebe   Amour de poète
Frauenliebe und -leben   Amour et vie de femme
Kinderszenen   Scènes d'enfants

Sinding, Christian A.
Frühlingsrauschen   Le gazouillement du printemps

Smetana, Bedřich
La mia patria   My Country
La sposa venduta   The Bardered Bride

Strauß, Johann (Sohn)
Il bel Danubio blu   The Beautiful Blue Danube
Il pipistrello   The Bat

Strauss, Richard
Il cavaliere della rosa   The Rose Cavalier
La donna senz'ombra   The Woman without a Shadow
Morte e trasfigurazione   Death and Transfiguration
Una vita d'eroe   A Hero's Life

Strawinsky, Igor
Il bacio della fata   The Fairy's Kiss
La carriera di un libertino   The Rake's Progress
La sagra della primavera   Rite of Spring
La storia del soldato   The Soldier's Tale
L'uccello di fuoco   The Firebird
L'usignolo   The Nightingale

Tschaikowsky, Peter I.
Il lago dei cigni   Swan Lake
La bella addormentata nel   The Sleeping Beauty
bosco
Lo schiaccianoci   The Nutcracker
Romeo e Giulietta   Romeo and Juliet

Verdi, Giuseppe
Il trovatore   The Troubadour
I vespri siciliani   The Sicilian Vespers
La forza del destino   The Force of Destiny
Un ballo in maschera   A Masked Ball

Vivaldi, Antonio
Le quattro stagioni   The Four Seasons

Smetana, Bedřich
Mein Vaterland   Ma patrie
Die verkaufte Braut   La fiancée vendue

Strauß, Johann (Sohn)
An der schönen blauen Donau   Le beau Danube bleu
Die Fledermaus   La chauve-souris

Strauss, Richard
Der Rosenkavalier   Le chevalier à la rose
Die Frau ohne Schatten   La femme sans ombre
Tod und Verklärung   Mort et transfiguration
Ein Heldenleben   Une vie de héros

Strawinsky, Igor
Der Kuss der Fee   Le baiser de la fée
Die Karriere eines Wüstlings   La carrière d'un libertin
Das Frühlingsopfer   Le sacre du printemps
Die Geschichte vom Soldaten   L'histoire du soldat
Der Feuervogel   L'oiseau de feu
Die Nachtigall   Le rossignol

Tschaikowsky, Peter I.
Schwanensee   Le lac des cygnes
Dornröschen   La belle au bois dormant

Der Nussknacker   Casse-noisette
Romeo und Julia   Roméo et Juliette

Verdi, Giuseppe
Der Troubadour   Le trouvère
Die Sizilianische Vesper   Les vêpres siciliennes
Die Macht des Schicksals   La force du destin
Ein Maskenball   Le bal masqué

Vivaldi, Antonio
Die vier Jahreszeiten   Les quatre saisons

Wagner. Richard

I maestri cantori di Norimberga	The Mastersingers of Nuremberg
Il vascello fantasma	The Flying Dutchman
L'anello del Nibelungo	The Nibelung's Ring

Weber, Karl Maria v.

Il franco cacciatore	The Freeshooter
L'invito al valzer	Invitation to the Dance

Weill, Kurt

L'opera da tre soldi	The Threepenny Opera

I nomi di persone come Carmen, Tosca, Lohengrin etc. sono invariabili.

Names of persons like Carmen, Tosca, Lohengrin etc. are invariable.

Wagner. Richard

Die Meistersinger von Nürnberg	Les Maîtres chanteurs de Nuremberg
Der fliegende Holländer	Le vaisseau fantôme
Der Ring des Nibelungen	L'anneau du Nibelung

Weber, Karl Maria v.

Der Freischütz	Le franc-tireur
Aufforderung zum Tanz	L'invitation à la valse

Weill, Kurt

Die Dreigroschenoper	L'opéra de quat'sous

Personennamen wie Carmen, Tosca, Lohengrin usw. bleiben unverändert.

Les noms de personnes comme Carmen, Tosca, Lohengrin etc. sont invariables.

Opera

Parole spesso utilizzate – scelta

abbracciare	to hug
abito *m* / vestito *m* / costume *m*	suit / dress / costume
accanito / impietoso / senza pietà / spietato	ruthless / pitiless / merciless
accasciato / spossato / sfinito / esausto /stremato	worn out / crushed / exhausted /. dejected
affranto	broken-hearted
affrontare / sfidare	to face / to brave / to challenge
aiuto!	help!
albero *m*	tree
amico *m* / compagno *m*	friend / fellow / comrade
ammazzare / uccidere	to kill
anello *m*	ring
anno *m*	year
arma *f*	weapon
asino *m*	donkey
assassino *m*	killer / murderer
autunno *m*	autumn / fall (Am.)
avaro / taccagno	avaricious / stingy
avvicinarsi	to approach / to get near
azzurro / celeste	sky-blue
babbo *m* / padre *m*	father
bacio *m*	kiss
balia *f*	nurse / nanny
bambola *f*	doll
bandiera *f* / stendardo *m*	flag / banner
barba *f*	beard
barca *f* / nave *f* / battello *m*	rowing boat / boat
benedire	to bless
bere / tracannare	to drink
bestia *f* / animale *m*	beast / animal
bianco	white
bicchiere *m* / calice *m* / coppa *f*	glass / goblet
blu	(dark) blue
bottiglia *f*	bottle

Opera

Frequently used words – choice

Oper

Opéra

Häufig gebrauchte Wörter – Auswahl

Mots fréquemment utilisés – choix

umarmen	embrasser
Anzug *m* / Kleid *n* / Tracht *f*	habit *m* / robe *f* / costume *m*
verbissen / unbarmherzig / ohne Mitleid / erbarmungslos	acharné / sans pitié / impitoyable
entkräftet / erschöpft / entmutigt	épuisé / abattu
niedergeschlagen	accablé / brisé
entgegentreten / herausfordern	affronter / faire face / défier
Hilfe!	à l'aide! / au secours!
Baum *m*	arbre *m*
Freund *m* / Gefährte *m* / Kamerad *m*	ami *m* / compagnon *m* / camarade *m*
töten / umbringen	tuer
Ring *m*	bague *f* / anneau *m*
Jahr *n*	an *m* / année *f*
Waffe *f*	arme *f*
Esel *m*	âne *m*
Mörder *m*	assassin *m* / meurtrier *m*
Herbst *m*	automne *m*
geizig / habgierig	avare
sich nähern	s'approcher
hellblau / himmelblau	azur / bleu ciel
Vater *m*	père *m*
Kuss *m*	baiser *m*
Amme *f*	nourrice *f*
Puppe *f*	poupée *f*
Fahne *f* / Flagge *f* / Banner *n*	drapeau *m* / étendard *m*
Bart *m*	barbe *f*
Kahn *m* / Boot *n* / Schiff *m*	barque *f* / bateau *m*
segnen	bénir
trinken	boire
Tier *n*	bête *f* / animal *m*
weiß	blanc
Glas *m* / Kelch *m*	verre *m* / calice *m* / coupe *f*
blau	bleu
Flasche *f*	bouteille *f*

brancolare / annaspare	to grope / to reel
brigante *m* / bandito *m* / masnadiere *m*	bandit / highwayman
bruciare	to burn
brutto	ugly
buffone *m* / pagliaccio *m*	buffoon / clown
bugia *f* / bugiardo *m*	lie / liar
calunnia *f*	slander / libel
camera *f* / stanza *f*	room
canaglia *f* / furfante *m* / mascalzone *m*	rogue / scoundrel / villain
candela *f* / cero *m*	candle
casa *f* / palazzo *m*	house / palace
catena *f*	chain
cattivo / malvagio	bad / wicked / mean
cavallo *m* / cavalcare	horse / to ride
chiesa *f* / duomo *m*	church / cathedral
cieco	blind
cigno *m*	swan
cipiglio (con) / accigliato	scowling / frowning
combattimento *m* / battaglia *f*	fight / battle
comprare	to buy
con te	with you
condannare	to sentence
conte *m* / duca *m*	count / earl / duke
contrabbandiere *m*	smuggler
coppia *f*	couple
corona *f*	crown / coronet
corte *f*	court
crepuscolo *m*	twilight / dusk
crimine *m* / delitto *m*	crime / offense (Am.)
croce *f*	cross
culla *f*	cradle
dea *f*	goddess
depresso / scoraggiato	depressed / discouraged
detto …	called …
diavolo *m* / demonio *m*	devil / demon
difendere	to defend

tappen / haspeln / taumeln	avancer à tâtons / tâtonner / tituber
Räuber *m* / Bandit *m*	brigand *m* / bandit *m*
brennen	brûler
hässlich	laid
Narr *m* / Possenreißer *m*	bouffon *m* / pitre *m*
Lüge *f* / Lügner *m*	mensonge *m* / menteur *m*
Verleumdung *f*	calomnie *f*
Zimmer *n*	chambre *f*
Schurke *m* / Gauner *m*	canaille *f* / vaurien *m* / fripouille *f*
Kerze *f*	bougie *f* / cierge *m*
Haus *n* / Palast *m*	maison *f* / palais *m*
Kette *f*	chaîne *f*
böse / schlecht / gemein	mauvais / méchant
Pferd *n* / reiten	cheval *m* / chevaucher / monter à cheval
Kirche *f* / Dom *m*	église *f* / cathédrale *f*
blind	aveugle
Schwan *m*	cygne *m*
mit finsterer Miene / stirnrunzelnd	d'un air sombre / renfrogné
Kampf *m* / Gefecht *n* / Schlacht *f*	combat *m* / lutte *f* / bataille *f*
kaufen	acheter
mit dir	avec toi
verurteilen	condamner
Graf *m* / Herzog *m*	comte *m* / duc *m*
Schmuggler *m*	contrebandier *m*
Paar *n*	couple *m*
Krone *f* / Kranz *m*	couronne *f*
Hof *m*	cour *f*
Dämmerung *f*	crépuscule *m*
Verbrechen *n* / Vergehen *n*	crime *m* / délit *m*
Kreuz *n*	croix *f*
Wiege *f*	berceau *m*
Göttin *f*	déesse *f*
niedergeschlagen / mutlos	déprimé / découragé
genannt …	dit …
Teufel *m* / Dämon *m*	diable *m* / démon *m*
verteidigen	défendre

Dio	God
disarmato	disarmed / unarmed
domestica *f* / serva *f*	maid / servant
donna *f*	woman
dormire	to sleep
dubbio / sospetto / ambiguo	doubtful / suspicious
eroe *m*	hero
esecrabile / odioso / spregevole / scellerato	hateful / contemptible / loathsome / despicable
estate *f*	summer
età *f*	age
evadere / fuggire / scappare	to escape / to flee / to run away
evviva	hurrah
fanfarone *m* / gradasso *m*	braggart / boaster
fannullone *m* / bighellone *m*	idler / loafer
fata *f*	fairy
fedele / leale	faithful / loyal
ferito	wounded / injured
figlio *m* / figlia *f*	son / daughter
finestra *f*	window
fingere / far finta	to pretend / to feign
fiore *m*	flower
folla *f* / massa *f*	crowd / throng
folletto *m* / spiritello *m*	sprite / elf / goblin
fontana *f* / fonte *f*	fountain / spring
forca *f* / patibolo *m*	gibbet / gallows
foresta *f* / bosco *m*	forest / wood
fortuna *f* / sfortuna *f*	luck / bad luck
frate *m* / monaco *m*	friar / monk
fratello *m* / sorella *f*	brother / sister
freccia *f*	arrow
frusta *f*	whip / lash
fucile *m*	rifle / gun
fulmine *m* / lampo *m*	lightning / thunderbolt
geloso	jealous
giallo	yellow
gioiello *m*	jewel
giorno *m*	day
giovane	young
giurare	to swear

Gott	Dieu
entwaffnet / unbewaffnet	désarmé / sans armes
Magd *f* / Dienerin *f*	domestique *m* / servante *f*
Frau *f*	femme *f*
schlafen	dormir
zweifelhaft / verdächtig	douteux / suspect / ambigu
Held *m*	héros *m*
fluchwürdig / hassenswert / verachtenswert	exécrable / odieux / méprisable
Sommer *m*	été *m*
Alter *n*	âge *m*
entkommen / fliehen / weglaufen	s'évader / échapper / s'enfuir
hoch lebe …	hourra / vive …
Angeber *m* / Prahler *m*	fanfaron *m*
Faulenzer *m* / Faulpelz *m*	fainéant *m* / paresseux *m*
Fee *f*	fée *f*
treu / lauter / loyal	fidèle / loyal
verwundet / verletzt	blessé
Sohn *m* / Tochter *f*	fils *m* / fille *f*
Fenster *n*	fenêtre *f*
vortäuschen / heucheln	feindre / faire semblant
Blume *f*	fleur *f*
Menge *f* / Masse *f*	foule *f* / masse *f*
Kobold *m*	lutin *m* / esprit *m*
Brunnen *m* / Quelle *f*	fontaine *f* / source *f*
Galgen *m*	gibet *m* / potence *f*
Wald *m*	forêt *f* / bois *m*
Glück *n* / Unglück *n*	chance *f* / malchance *f*
Mönch *m*	moine *m*
Bruder *m* / Schwester *f*	frère *m* / sœur *f*
Pfeil *m*	flèche *f*
Peitsche *f*	fouet *m*
Gewehr *n*	fusil *m*
Blitz *m*	foudre *f* / éclair *m*
eifersüchtig	jaloux
gelb	jaune
Schmuckstück *n* / Juwel *n*	bijou *m* / joyau *m*
Tag *m*	jour *m*
jung	jeune
schwören	jurer

giustizia *f*	justice
gloria *f*	glory
grotta *f* / caverna *f* / antro *m*	cave / cavern
guarito / sano	recovered / healthy
guerra *f*	war
ignobile / infame	ignoble / infamous
innamorato	in love
incontrare	to meet
infedele	unfaithful
ingannare / truffare / imbrogliare	to deceive / to swindle / to cheat
ingiusto	unjust / unfair
insulto *m* / ingiuria *f* / oltraggio *m*	insult / abuse / offence
intorno / attorno	around
intrigare / cospirare / complottare	to intrigue / to conspire / to plot
inverno *m*	winter
istigare / aizzare / fomentare	to instigate / to stir up
lacrima *f*	tear
ladro *m*	thief
lavare	to wash
letto *m*	bed
libertà *f*	freedom / liberty
litigare / bisticciare	to quarrel / to squabble
luna *f*	moon
lutto *m*	mourning
maledetto / dannato	cursed / damned
mamma *f* / madre *f*	mum / mother
mangiare	to eat
mare *m*	sea
marito *m* / sposo *m*	husband / bridegroom
mattina *f*	morning
medico *m* / dottore *m*	doctor
mellifluo / melenso / sdolcinato	mawkish / honeyed
mezzanotte *f*	midnight
mezzogiorno *m*	midday / noon
moglie *f* / sposa *f*	wife / bride
montagna *f* / monte *m*	mountain
navigare	to sail

Gerechtigkeit *f*	justice *f*
Ruhm *n*	gloire *f*
Grotte *f* / Höhle *f*	grotte *f* / caverne *f*
genesen / gesund	guéri / sain
Krieg *m*	guerre *f*
unehrenhaft / niederträchtig / schändlich	ignoble / infâme
verliebt	amoureux
treffen / begegnen	rencontrer
untreu	infidèle
betrügen / schwindeln / täuschen	tromper / escroquer
ungerecht	injuste
Beschimpfung *f* / Schmähung *f* / Beleidigung *f*	insulte *f* / injure *f* / outrage *m*
umher / herum	autour
intrigieren / verschwören / anzetteln	intriguer / conspirer / comploter
Winter *m*	hiver *m*
anstiften / hetzen / schüren	inciter / pousser à / ourdir
Träne *f*	larme *f*
Dieb *m*	voleur *m*
waschen	laver
Bett *m*	lit *m*
Freiheit *f*	liberté *f*
streiten / zanken	se disputer / se quereller
Mond *m*	lune *f*
Trauer *f*	deuil *m*
verflucht / verdammt	maudit / damné
Mama *f* / Mutter *f*	maman *f* / mère *f*
essen	manger
Meer *n*	mer *f*
Ehemann *m* / Bräutigam *m*	mari *m* / époux *m*
Morgen *m* / Vormittag *m*	matin *m*
Arzt *m*	médecin *m* / docteur *m*
süßlich / schnulzig	mielleux / doucereux
Mitternacht *f*	minuit *m*
Mittag *m*	midi *m*
Ehefrau *f* / Braut *f*	femme *f* / épouse *f* / mariée *f*
Berg *m*	montagne *f*
zur See fahren	naviguer

nebbia *f*	mist
nel frattempo	in the meantime
nemico *m*	enemy / foe
nero	black
neve *f*	snow
notte *f*	night
nozze *f.pl.* / matrimonio *m*	wedding / marriage
nuvola *f* / nube *f*	cloud
odiare / detestare	to hate / to detest
offrire	to offer
onesto / disonesto	honest / dishonest
onore *m*	honour
ora *f*	hour
osare	to dare
padrone *m* / capo *m*	master / boss / leader
pagare	to pay
pallido / cereo	pale / wan / waxed
pane *m*	bread
patria *f*	native country / fatherland
pazzo / demente / matto	crazy / mad / insane
penna *f* / piuma *f*	pen / feather
per fortuna	fortunately
per sempre / eternamente	for ever
perdere / vinto *m* / perdente *m*	to lose / loser
perdonare	to forgive
pericolo *m*	danger
piazza *f*	square
pietra *f* / sasso *m*	stone
pioggia *f*	rain
pomeriggio *m*	afternoon
porta *f*	door
potere *m*	power
povero / meschino	poor / miserable
prete *m*	priest
prigione *f* / carcere *m*	prison / jail
primavera *f*	spring
proibito / vietato	forbidden
pugnale *m* / coltello *m*	dagger / knife
purtroppo	unfortunately
ragazzo *m* / ragazza *f*	boy / girl

Nebel *m*	brouillard *m*
inzwischen	entre-temps
Feind *m*	ennemi *m*
schwarz	noir
Schnee *m*	neige *f*
Nacht *f*	nuit *f*
Hochzeit *f* / Trauung *f* / Ehe *f*	noces *f.pl.* / mariage *m*
Wolke *f*	nuage *m*
hassen / verabscheuen	haïr / détester
anbieten	offrir
ehrlich / unehrlich	honnête / malhonnête
Ehre *f*	honneur *m*
Stunde *f*	heure *f*
wagen	oser
Chef *m* / Anführer *m*	patron *m* / chef *m*
zahlen / bezahlen	payer
blass / kreidebleich	pâle / cireux
Brot *n*	pain *m*
Vaterland *n*	patrie *f*
verrückt / wahnsinnig / schwachsinnig	fou / insensé / dément
Füllfeder *f* / Feder *f*	plume *f*
zum Glück	heureusement
für immer / für ewig	pour toujours
verlieren / Verlierer *m*	perdre / perdant *m*
verzeihen	pardonner
Gefahr *f*	danger *m*
Platz *m*	place *f*
Stein *m*	pierre *f* / caillou *m*
Regen *m*	pluie *f*
Nachmittag *m*	après-midi *m*
Tür *f*	porte *f*
Macht *f*	pouvoir *m*
arm / armselig	pauvre / misérable
Priester *m* / Pfarrer *m*	prêtre *m*
Gefängnis *n* / Kerker *m*	prison *f*
Frühling *m*	printemps *m*
verboten	interdit / défendu
Dolch *m* / Messer *n*	poignard *m* / couteau *m*
leider	malheureusement
Junge *m* / Mädchen *n*	garçon *m* / fille *f*

rancore *m* / astio *m*	rancour / grudge
rapire	to kidnap
re *m* / regina *f*	king / queen
ricatto *m*	blackmail
rivolta *f*	revolt
rosso	red
schiavo *m*	slave
sconfitta *f*	defeat
sconvolto	dismayed / upset
segreto / celato	secret / clandestine
sera *f* / serata *f*	evening
soldato *m*	soldier
sole *m*	sun
sparare	to shoot
spia *f*	spy
sporco / sudicio	dirty / filthy
sposarsi	to get married / to marry
stupido / scemo / cretino / idiota	stupid / silly / fool / idiot
svenire	to faint
tappeto *m*	carpet
tavola *f*	table
terra *f*	earth
ti amo	I love you
tomba *f* / sepolcro *m*	grave / tomb / sepulchre
traditore *m*	traitor
tranello *m* / insidia *f* / agguato *m* / imboscata *f*	trap / snare / ambush
trono *m*	throne
ubriaco / ebbro	drunk / inebriated
uccello *m*	bird
umiliare / mortificare	to humble
uomo *m*	man
vano / inutile	vain / useless
vantarsi	to boast
vecchio / anziano	old / elderly
veleno *m*	poison
vendere	to sell
verde	green
vergogna *f*	shame
verità *f*	truth

Groll *m*	rancœur *f*
entführen	enlever
König *m* / Königin *f*	roi *m* / reine *f*
Erpressung *f*	chantage *m*
Aufstand *m*	révolte *f*
rot	rouge
Sklave *m*	esclave *m*
Niederlage *f*	défaite *f*
verstört / erschüttert / bestürzt	bouleversé
geheim / heimlich	secret / clandestin
Abend *m*	soir *m* / soirée *f*
Soldat *m*	soldat *m*
Sonne *f*	soleil *m*
schießen	tirer / faire feu
Spion *m*	espion *m*
schmutzig / dreckig	sale
heiraten	épouser / se marier
dumm / blöd / Dummkopf *m* / Idiot *m*	stupide / bête / crétin *m* / idiot *m*
in Ohnmacht fallen	s'évanouir
Teppich *m*	tapis *m*
Tisch *m*	table *f*
Erde *f*	terre *f*
ich liebe dich	je t'aime
Grab *n* / Gruft *f*	tombe *f* / tombeau *m*
Verräter *m*	traître *m*
Falle *f* / Hinterhalt *m*	piège *m* / embuscade *f*
Thron *m*	trône *m*
betrunken / berauscht	ivre / saoûl
Vogel *m*	oiseau *m*
demütigen / erniedrigen	humilier / abaisser
Mann *m*	homme *m*
vergeblich / unnötig	vain / inutile
prahlen	se vanter
alt / betagt	vieux / âgé
Gift *m*	poison *m*
verkaufen	vendre
grün	vert
Scham *f* / Schande *f*	honte *f*
Wahrheit *f*	vérité *f*

272 | Opera:
Parole spesso utilizzate – scelta | Opera:
Frequently used words – choice

vero	true
viaggio *m*	journey
vigliacco / vile	cowardly / craven
villaggio *m* / paese *m* / città *f*	village / country / town
vinto	defeated
vita *f*	life
vittoria *f*	victory
voltarsi / girarsi	to turn / to pivot
zerbinotto *m* / farfallone *m* / bellimbusto *m*	fop / coxcomb / dandy

wahr	vrai
Reise *f*	voyage *m*
feige	lâche
Dorf *n* / Land *n* / Stadt *f*	village *m* / pays *m* / ville *f*
besiegt	vaincu
Leben *n*	vie *f*
Sieg *m*	victoire *f*
sich umdrehen / sich umwenden	se retourner / se tourner
Luftikus *m* / Stutzer *m* / Geck *m*	bellâtre *m* / gandin *m*

Indice alfabetico
Index
Register
Index

A (D, E)	2214	a mezza voce (I)	637
a ballata (I)	914	à mi-voix (F)	614, 637
a bassa voce (I)	635	a misura (I)	720
a battuta (I)	720	a molte parti (I)	1861
a beneplacito (I)	718	à nouveau (F)	1686
a bocca chiusa (I)	636	à peine (F)	1639
à bouche fermée (F)	636	a piacere (I)	719
a cappella (I)	1612	a più voci (I)	1861
a capriccio (I)	917	à pleine voix (F)	647
à côté (F)	1613	à plusieurs parties (F)	1861
à défaut de (F)	1719	à plusieurs voix (F)	1861
à deux (F)	1616	à quatre mains (F)	456
à deux claviers manuels (F)	455	à quatre voix (F)	1862
à deux voix (F)	1859	a quattro mani (I)	456
A double flat (E)	2218	a quattro voci (I)	1862
A double sharp (E)	2217	à sa place (F)	1628, 1729
à doubles cordes (F)	1649	A sharp (E)	2215
a due (I)	1616	a tempo (I)	720
a due manuali (I)	455	a tre voci (I)	1863
a due voci (I)	1859	à trois voix (F)	1863
a due volte (I)	1617	à un (seul) clavier manuel (F)	458
a fior di labbro (I)	1618	a un manuale (I)	458
A flat (E)	2216	a very little (E)	1848
a forma aperta (I)	1860	a voce piena (I)	647
à l'aise (F)	1053	à voix basse (F)	635, 876
à l'allemande (F)	949	a volontà (I)	719
à l'octave (F)	1621	à volonté (F)	724
à l'unisson (F)	2181	à votre gré (F)	718
à la blanche (F)	1622	ab initio (L)	1611
à la corde (F)	82	ab inizio (I)	1611
à la fin (F)	1619	abaisser (F)	2636
à la hausse (F)	84	abändern (D)	2754, 2860
à la hongroise (F)	956	abandoning oneself (E)	915
a la maniera (I)	946	abbandonandosi (I)	915
à la manière de (F)	946	abbandonatamente (I)	916
à la partie finale (F)	1623	abbandono (con) (I)	916
à la renverse (F)	2106	abbassando (I)	891
à la turque (F)	950	abbassare (I)	2636
à la tzigane (F)	951	abbassare l'accordatura (I)	2637
a little (E)	1849	abbassare l'intonatura (I)	2637
a little bit (E)	1826	abbastanza (I)	1610
a little less (E)	1777	abbellimento (I)	1864
a little more (E)	1778, 1850	abbellire (I)	2638
a lungo (I)	1730	abbellito (I)	1865
a memoria (I)	2884	abbonamento (I)	2865
a mente (I)	2884	abbondante (I)	2867

abbozzo (I)	3318	absteigend (D)	1957
abbrechen (D)	2719	abstoßen (D)	2831
abbreviare (I)	2639	Abstrakte (D)	453
abbreviation (E)	1866	Abstrich (D)	86
abbreviatura (I)	1866	abstufen (D)	2726
abbreviazione (I)	1866	Abstufung (D)	3059
abdämpfen (D)	389	abtaktig (D)	1998
Abendlied (D)	2296	abtasten (D)	570
aber (D)	1732	abundant (E)	2867
aber nicht zu sehr (D)	1733	abusive (E)	1291
abgesetzt (D)	111	abwärts (D)	1717
abgestoßen (D)	877	abwechseln (D)	2651
abgewechselt (D)	1632	abwechselnd (D)	1631, 1853
abile (I)	2868	Abwechslung (D)	2925
abilità (con) (I)	1092	accademia di musica (I)	2866
abkürzen (D)	2639	accanto (I)	1613
able (E)	2868	accarezzando (I)	918
abmildernd (D)	893	accarezzevole (I)	918
abmischen (D)	534	accarezzevolmente (I)	918
abnehmen (D)	2701	accelerando (I)	785
abnehmend (D)	900, 908	accelerare (I)	2640
abondant (F)	2867	accelerated (E)	786
Abonnement (D)	2865	accelerato (I)	786
abonnement (F)	2865	accéléré (F)	786
about (E)	1654	accélérer (F)	2640
above (E)	1726	accent (E, F)	1867
above all (E)	1815	accent principal (F)	1868
abprallendes Stakkato (D)	106	accent secondaire (F)	1869
abréger (F)	2639	accento (I)	1867
abréviation (F)	1866	accento principale (I)	1868
abschließen (D)	2683, 2848	accento secondario (I)	1869
Abschluss (D)	1936	accentuare (I)	2641
abschreiben (D)	2690, 2763	accentuated (E)	841
abschwächend (D)	894, 909	accentuated beat (E)	2156
abschweifend (D)	1109	accentuation (E, F)	2870
absinkend (D)	891, 898	accentuato (I)	841
absolu (F)	1643	accentuazione (I)	2870
absolument (F)	1642	accentué (F)	841
absolut (D)	1643	accentuer (F)	2641
absolute (E)	1643	acceso (I)	1274
absolute music (E)	3121	accessoires (F)	2869
absolute Musik (D)	3121	accessori (I)	2869
absolute pitch (E)	3204	accessories (E)	2869
absolutely (E)	1642	acchetandosi (I)	892
absolutes Gehör (D)	3204	acciaccatura (I)	1870
Abstand (D)	2001, 2996	acciaccatura doppia (I)	1871

accident (F)	1872	accordo perfetto (I)	1877
accidental (E)	1872	accordo spezzato (I)	1878
accidente (I)	1872	accouplement (F)	407
accolade (F)	1873	accrescendo (I)	880
accollatura (I)	1873	accuratamente (I)	921
accompagnamento (I)	2871	accuratezza (con) (I)	922
accompagnando (I)	1614	accurato (I)	921
accompagnare (I)	2642	Achse (D)	437
accompagnateur (F)	3485	Achsel (D)	3477
accompagnatore (I)	3485	Achtel (D)	2227
accompagnatrice (F, I)	3485	Achtelpause (D)	2234
accompagnement (F)	2871	Achtung! (D)	2900
accompagner (F)	2642	acoustics (E)	2874
accompanied recitative (E)	2445	acoustics (of a hall/room)	
accompaniment (E)	2871	(E)	2875
accompanist (E)	3485	acoustique (F)	2874
accompanying (E)	1614	acoustique ambiante (F)	2875
accompanying instrument (E)	3369	acoustique d'un local (F)	2875
acconciatura (I)	3228	acquietandosi (I)	892
accoppiamento (I)	407	act (E)	2901
accoramento (con) (I)	919	act curtain (E)	3338
accoratamente (I)	920	acte (F)	2901
accorato (I)	920	acteur (F)	3490
accord (F)	1874	action (E)	431, 451, 471
accord brisé (F)	1878	action (E, F)	3407
accord de passage (F)	1875	action d'octavier (F)	245
accord de séptième de		actor (E)	3490
dominante (F)	1876	actress (E)	3490
accord parfait (F)	1877	actrice (F)	3490
accordage (F)	2873	acustica (I)	2874
accordare (I)	2643	acustica ambientale (I)	2875
accordato (I)	2872	acuto (I)	1615
accordatore (I)	3486	ad libitum (L)	724
accordatrice (I)	3486	adage (F)	722
accordatura (I)	2873	adagietto (I)	721
accordé (F)	2872	adagino (I)	721
accordéon (F)	395	adagio (I)	722
accordéon à boutons (F)	396	adagissimo (I)	723
accordéon à clavier (F)	397	adaptation (E, F)	2892
accorder (F)	2643	adapter (F)	2644
accordeur (F)	3486	adattamento (I)	2892, 3287
accordion (E)	395	adattare (I)	2644
accordo (I)	1874	addio! (I)	2876
accordo di passaggio (I)	1875	addolcendo (I)	893
accordo di settima di		addolorato (I)	1119
dominante (I)	1876		

Ader (D)	59, 3484	affrettato (I)	725
adesso (I)	2877	affreux (F)	1364
adieu! (F)	2876	afono (I)	638
adiratamente (I)	923	after (E)	1691
adirato (I)	924	afterwards (E)	1690
adorazione (con) (I)	925	again (E)	1636, 1686
adoringly (with adoration)		against (E)	1673
(E)	925	agence de concerts (F)	2878
adornamento (I)	2051	agenzia di concerti (I)	2878
adornando (I)	926	agevole (I)	936
adornato (I)	927	agevolezza (con) (I)	937
adorned (E)	927	aggiungere (I)	2646
adorning (E)	926	aggiunto (I)	3390
advanced (E)	2904	aggiustamente (I)	938
aeolian (E)	1970	aggradevole (I)	1241
aéré (F)	928	aggravamento (I)	1897
aereo (I)	928	aggressiv (D)	1007
aesthetics (E)	3023	aggressive (E)	1007
affabile (I)	929	aggressivo (I)	1007
affable (E, F)	929	agiatamente (I)	939
affannato (I)	930	agile (E, F, I)	940
affanno (con) (I)	931	agilement (F)	940
affannosamente (I)	931	agilità (con) (I)	941
affannoso (I)	931	agilmente (I)	940
affecté (F)	932	agitated (E)	942
affected (E)	932, 1309	agitato (I)	942
affectionately (E)	934	agitazione (con) (I)	942
affectueusement (F)	934	agité (F)	942, 1503
affectueux (F)	935	agogic (E)	1879
Affektenlehre (D)	3401	agogica (I)	1879
affektiert (D)	932	Agogik (D)	1879
Affekttheorie (D)	3401	agogique (F)	1879
affettato (I)	932	agrandir (F)	2654
affetto (con) (I)	933	agréable (F)	1241
affettuosamente (I)	934	agreeable (E)	1241
affettuoso (I)	935	agreement (E)	3092
affiche (F)	2934, 3278	agrément (F) (F)	1864
affievolendo (I)	894	agressif (F)	1007
affine (I)	2092	agreste (I)	943
affinità (I)	2093	aigri (F)	961
afflicted (E)	1335	aigu (F)	1615
affligé (F)	1335	aiguille (phono) (F)	547
afflitto (I)	1335	aimable (F)	959
afflizione (con) (I)	919	air (E, F)	2252
affrettando (I)	787	air à vocalises (F)	2256
affrettare (I)	2645	air avec colorature (F)	2256

air d'opéra (F)	2254	all (D, E)	1836, 1839
air de bravoure (F)	2255	all the force (E)	1837
air de concert (F)	2253	all'antica (I)	944
air de cour (F)	2257	all'aperto (I)	3052
air de fête (F)	1178	all'improvvista (I)	1620
air-passage (E)	201	all'ongarese (I)	956
airy (E)	928	all'ottava (I)	1621
Ais (D)	2215	all'ungherese (I)	956
aisé (F)	936	alla breve (I)	1622
aisément (F)	939	alla coda (I)	1623
Aisis (D)	2217	alla contadina (I)	945
ajourner (F)	2797	alla corda (I)	82
ajouter (F)	2646	alla maniera di (I)	946
Akkord (D)	1874	alla marcia (I)	947
Akkordeon (D)	395	alla meglio (I)	1624
Akkordzither (D)	4	alla militare (I)	948
Akt (D)	2901	alla punta d'arco (I)	83
Aktvorhang (D)	3338	alla tedesca (I)	949
Akustik (D)	2874	alla turca (I)	950
Akzent (D)	1867	alla zingara (I)	951
al centro (I)	373	alla zoppa (I)	952
al fine (I)	1619	allargando (I)	812
al luogo (I)	1729	allargare (I)	2647
al rigore di tempo (I)	1626	allargato (I)	1630
al segno (I)	1627	allarmato (I)	953
al suo posto (I)	1628	alle (D)	1838
al tallone (I)	84	allegramente (I)	954
al tempo precedente (I)	1629	allègre (F)	728
Alabado (D, E, F, I)	2492	allégrement (F)	954
Alalá (D, E, F, I)	2493	allegretto (I)	726
alarmé (F)	953	allegrezza (con) (I)	955
alarmed (E)	953	allegria (con) (I)	955
alba (I)	2248	allegrissimo (I)	727
Alborada (D, E, F, I)	2494	allegro (I)	728
album leaf (E)	2348	allegro assai (I)	727
Albumblatt (D)	2348	allein (D)	1811
alcune (I)	1787	allemanda (I)	2249
aleatoric music (E)	3119	Allemande (D)	2249
aleatorische Musik (D)	3119	allemande (E, F)	2249
Alegrias (D, E, F, I)	2495	allentando (I)	813
alerte (F)	1522	alles (D)	1839
aletta (I)	234	allettando (I)	1318
aliquot string (E)	50	allieva (I)	2879
Aliquotsaite (D)	50	allievo (I)	2879
alito (I)	3340	allmählich (D)	1774
alive (E)	1602	allmählich mehr (D)	1776

allmählich schneller werdend (D)	810
allmählich weniger (D)	1775
allonger (F)	2649
allontanando (I)	895
allontanandosi (I)	895
allontanarsi (I)	2648
allumé (F)	1274
allungando (I)	814
allungare (I)	2649
alluring (E)	1318
almand (E)	2249
almeno (I)	2880
Almglocken (D)	250
almglocken (E, F)	250
almgloken (I)	250
almost (E)	1789
almost like a fantasy (E)	1414
almost nothing (E)	869
alone (E)	1811
alpenhorn (E)	133
Alphorn (D)	133
alphorn (E)	133
alquanto (I)	1625
already (E)	1705
als ob (D)	1789
also (E)	1635
Alt (D)	602
Altblockflöte (D)	145
alte Musik (D)	3120
alterare (I)	2650
Alteration (D)	1872
alteration (E)	1872
altération (F)	1872
alterato (I)	1880
alterazione (I)	1872
altéré (F)	1880
altered (E)	1880
altérer (F)	2650
alterieren (D)	2650
alteriert (D)	1880
alternando (I)	1631
alternare (I)	2651
alternate (E)	1853
alternate (E)	1632
alternating (E)	1631
alternative scoring (E)	3367
alternatively (E)	1631
alternativement (F)	1853
alternato (I)	1632
alterné (F)	1632
alterner (F)	2651
alternieren (D)	2651
alternierend (D)	1631
altero (I)	957
altertümlich (D)	2886
altezza (I)	2881
altezza del suono (I)	1881
Altflöte (D)	150
although (E)	3106
altiste (F)	3528
Altistin (D)	602
Altklarinette (D)	126
alto (E, F, I)	28, 602, 2882
alto clarinet (E)	126
alto clef (E)	1924
alto flute (E)	150
alto recorder (Am.)	145
alto saxophone (E)	168
altoparlante (I)	481
altrimenti (I)	1633
altro (I)	1634
Altsaxophon (D)	168
Altschlüssel (D)	1924
alunna (I)	2879
alunno (I)	2879
always (E)	1798
always more animated (E)	805
always the same (E)	1799
alzando (I)	881
alzare (I)	2652
alzare l'intonatura (I)	2653
alzare l'intonazione (I)	2653
am Frosch (D)	84
am Rand (D)	387
am Steg (D)	116
amabile (I)	959
amabilità (con) (I)	958
amante della musica (I)	2883
amaramente (I)	960
amareggiato (I)	961
amarezza (con) (I)	962

amaro (I)	963	
amateur (E, F)	2986	
amateur de musique (F)	2883	
Amboss (D)	291	
âme (F)	33	
améliorer (F)	2751	
ameno (I)	1388	
amer (F)	963	
amèrement (F)	960	
amiable (E)	959	
amore (con) (I)	964	
amorevole (I)	965	
amorevolmente (I)	966	
amorosamente (I)	966	
amoroso (I)	965	
amorti (F)	875	
amortissement du bruit (F)	561	
ampiezza (con) (I)	482, 967	
ampio (I)	968, 1515	
ample (F)	968	
ampliando (I)	882	
ampliare (I)	2654	
amplificateur (F)	483	
amplificatore (I)	483	
amplifier (E)	483	
amplifying (E)	882	
Amplitude (D)	482	
amplitude (E, F)	482	
ampolloso (I)	969	
ampoulé (F)	969	
amusant (F)	2999	
amusing (E)	2999	
an der Bogenspitze (D)	83	
an der Saite (D)	82	
an seinem Platz (Oktavierung aufgehoben) (D)	1729	
an seiner Stelle (D)	1628	
an Stelle von (D)	1718	
anacrouse (F)	1882	
anacrusi (I)	1882	
anacrusis (E)	1882	
Anakrusis (D)	1882	
analisi (I)	1883	
Analyse (D)	1883	
analyse (F)	1883	
analysis (E)	1883	

anca (I)	3428	
anche (F, I)	191, 209, 1635	
anche battante (F)	192	
anche double (F)	193	
ancia (I)	191	
ancia battente (I)	192	
ancia doppia (I)	193	
ancien (F)	2886	
ancient music (E)	3120	
ancora (I)	1636	
ancora una volta (I)	1637	
and so on (E)	3003	
andächtig (D)	1095, 1418	
andamento (I)	1884	
andando (I)	788	
andante (I)	729	
andantino (I)	730	
anderenfalls (D)	1633	
anderer (D)	1634	
ändern (D)	2676	
Änderung (D)	2925	
anelante (I)	970	
anello (I)	194	
anello del pollice (I)	195	
Anfang (D)	3086	
anfangen (D)	2733	
anfangend (D)	1665	
Anfänger (D)	3019	
Anfängerin (D)	3019	
Anfangstempo (D)	778	
anflehend (D)	1540	
angelic (E)	971	
angelico (I)	971	
angélique (F)	971	
Angelito (D, E, F, I)	2496	
angemessen (D)	1706	
angemessenes Zeitmaß (D)	777	
angenehm (D)	1241, 1388	
angestrengt (D)	833	
Anglaise (D)	2362	
anglaise (F)	2362	
angoissant (F)	973	
angoscia (con) (I)	972	
angosciosamente (I)	973	
angoscioso (I)	973	
angreifend (D)	1007	

angry (E)	924, 991	Ansprache (D)	100
ängstlich (D)	1378	anstimmen (D)	2741
angstvoll (D)	973, 1377	Anstoß (D)	236
anguished (E)	973	Anstrich (D)	87
angustia (con) (I)	931	answer (E)	2099
anhalten (D)	2719	antecedent (E)	1885, 2082
Anhang (D)	1655	antécédent (F)	1885, 2082
anhören (D)	2662	antecedente (I)	1885
anima (con) (I)	33, 408, 974	antérieur (F)	1782
animal sound-effects (E)	2889	anteriore (I)	1782
animando (I)	789	anthem (E)	2363
animare (I)	2655	anthologie (F)	2887
animated (E)	731	anthology (E)	2887
animato (I)	731	anticipation (E, F)	1886
animé (F)	731	anticipazione (I)	1886
animer (F)	2655	antico (I)	2886
animo (con) (I)	975	antienne (F)	2250
animoso (I)	976	antifona (I)	2250
anknüpfen (D)	1646, 2686	antike Cymbeln (D)	277
ankündigen (D)	2656	Antiphon (D)	2250
anmaßend (D)	992, 1594	antiphon (E)	2250
Anmerkung (D)	2885	antique (E, F)	2886
anmutig (D)	1245	antique cymbals (E)	277
annähernd (D)	1640	Antizipation (D)	1886
anneau (F)	194	antologia (I)	2887
anneau du pouce (F)	195	Antwort (D)	2099
annoncer (F)	2656	antworten (D)	2801
annotation (E, F)	2885	anvil (E)	291
annotazione (I)	2885	anwachsen (D)	2694
annuler (F)	489	anwachsend (D)	885
annullare (I)	489	anxieusement (F)	931, 978
annunciare (I)	2656	anxieux (F)	979
another time (E)	1844	anxious (E)	931, 979
anrufend (D)	1040, 1405	anxiously (E)	978
ansagen (D)	2656	äolisch (D)	1970
ansante (I)	970	apathetic (E)	980
Ansatz (D)	208, 244	apathique (F)	980
Ansatz der Stimme (D)	613	apathisch (D)	980
Anschlag (D)	471	apatico (I)	980
anschließen (D)	2858	aperto (I)	1638
anschließend (D)	1690	apertura (I)	196
anschwellend (D)	885	aperture (E)	196
ansia (con) (I)	977	apex (E)	2888
ansietà (con) (I)	977	aphone (F)	638
ansiosamente (I)	978	apice (I)	2888
ansioso (I)	979	aplani (F)	1518

apparecchi imitanti voci animali (I)	2889	arcata in su (I)	87
appareils générateurs d'effets (F)	578	archeggiamento (I)	88
apparition (E, F)	3030	archet (F)	34
appassionatamente (I)	981	archetto (I)	34
appassionato (I)	981	archi (I)	2891
appeasing (E)	906	archiluth (F)	1
appeau (F)	312	archlute (E)	1
appena (I)	1639	arcigno (I)	983
appenato (I)	982	arciliuto (I)	1
applaudir (F)	2657	arco (I)	34
applaudire (I)	2657	ardemment (F)	985
applaudissement (F)	2890	ardent (E, F)	984
applause (E)	2890	ardente (I)	984
applauso (I)	2890	ardentemente (I)	985
Applikatur (D)	2998	ardently (E)	985
appoggiando (I)	842	arditamente (I)	986
appoggiare (I)	639	arditezza (con) (I)	987
appoggiato (I)	843	ardito (I)	988
appoggiatura (I)	1887	ardore (con) (I)	989
appoggiatura doppia (I)	1888	arduous (E)	1529
appoggiature (F)	1887	argentino (I)	1527
appoggiature double (F)	1888	aria (E, I)	2252
appoggio (sulla maschera) (I)	640	aria concertante (I)	2253
appogiature brève (F)	1870	aria d'opera (I)	2254
apprendre (F)	2731	aria di bravura (I)	2255
appropriate speed (E)	777	aria di coloratura (I)	2256
approssimativo (I)	1640	aria di corte (I)	2257
approximately (E)	1640	aria-like (E)	2259
approximatif (F)	1640	Arie (D)	2252
appui du souffle (F)	640	arietta (I)	2258
appuntino (I)	1641	ariette (F)	2258
appuyé (F)	843	arioso (I)	928, 2259
appuyer (F)	639	Arioso (D, E, F, I)	2498
âpre (F)	996	Arm (D)	3432
après (F)	1690	arm (E)	3432
aprire (I)	2658	armatura di chiave (I)	1889
arabesca (I)	2251	armature (F)	1889
Arabeske (D)	2251	Armgewicht (D)	467
arabesque (E, F)	2251	armonia (I)	1890
Aragonaise (D, E, F, I)	2497	armonica (I)	251
arbeiten (D)	2744	armonica a bocca (I)	117
Arbeitslied (D)	2288	armonica a vetro (I)	251
arcata (I)	85	armonico (I)	1891
arcata in giù (I)	86	armonio (I)	390
		armoniosamente (I)	990
		armonioso (I)	990

armonizzare (I)	2659
armure de la clé (F)	1889
armweight (E)	467
arpa (I)	2
arpa a doppio movimento (I)	3
arpa a pedali (I)	2
arpégé (F)	457
arpège (F)	1892
arpéger (F)	2660
arpeggiare (I)	2660
arpeggiated (E)	457
arpeggiato (I)	457
arpeggieren (D)	2660
arpeggiert (D)	457
Arpeggio (D)	1892
arpeggio (E, I)	1892
arpista (I)	3487
arrabbiato (I)	991
arraché (F)	113
arracher (F)	2834
Arrangement (D)	2892
arrangement (E, F)	2892
arranger (E)	3488
arrangeur (F)	3488
arrangiamento (I)	2892
arrangiatore (I)	3488
arrangiatrice (I)	3488
arrêter (F)	2719
arroganza (con) (I)	992
arsi (I)	1893
Arsis (D)	1893
arsis (E, F)	1893
art (E, F)	2893
art du chant (F)	641
art of singing (E)	641
art vocal (F)	641
arte (I)	2893
arte del canto (I)	641
artful (E)	1215
articolando (I)	844
articolare (I)	2661
articolato (I)	845
articolazione (I)	3429
articulated (E)	845
articulating (E)	844
articulation (F)	3429

articulé (F)	845
articuler (F)	2661
artificial (E)	993
artificiale (I)	993
artificiel (F)	993
artificioso (I)	993
artikulierend (D)	844
artikuliert (D)	845
artist (E)	3489
artista (I)	3489
artiste (F)	3489
artistic (E)	2894
artistico (I)	2894
artistique (F)	2894
artistry (E)	2894
arzillo (I)	994
As (D)	2216
as (E)	1659
as above (E)	1662
as before (E)	1661
as if (E)	1789
as it is (E)	1663
as loud as possible (E)	865
as much as (E)	1788
as much as possible (E)	1712
as soft as possible (E)	866
as the beginning (E)	1660
as well as possible (E)	1624
as you like (E)	718
ascendant (F)	1894
ascendente (I)	1894
ascending (E)	1894
ascoltare (I)	2662
ascoltatore (I)	2895
ascoltatrice (I)	2895
ascolto (I)	2896, 3007
Ases (D)	2218
aspettare (I)	2663
aspiratamente (I)	1427
aspirated attack (E)	646
asprezza (con) (I)	995
aspro (I)	996
assai (I)	1610, 1744
asse per lavare (I)	252
assez (F)	1610
assez! (F)	2914

assieme (I)	1725	attack (E)	236
associazione corale (I)	642	"attack!" (E)	1645
assolo (I)	1811	attack with the tongue (E)	239
assolutamente (I)	1642	attaque (F)	236, 471, 1645
assoluto (I)	1643	attaque dure (F)	645
assordante (I)	1644, 2897	attaque murmurée (F)	646
assottigliando (I)	896	attaquer (F)	2733
assourdissant (F)	1644, 2897	attendre (F)	2663
Ästhetik (D)	3023	attentif (F)	2899
astuccio (I)	35	attention! (F)	2900
at ease (E)	936	attentive (E)	2899
at least (E)	2880	attento (I)	2899
at once (E)	1822	attenuando (I)	897
at one's pleasure (E)	719, 724	atténuer (F)	2820
at the edge (E)	387	attenzione! (I)	2900
at the frog (E)	84	atto (I)	2901
at the heel (E)	84	attore (I)	3490
at the octave (E)	1621	attrezzature ritmiche (I)	484
at the point (E)	83	attrice (I)	3490
at the preceding pace (E)	1629	attristé (F)	919
at the same time (E)	1847, 3336	au centre frappé (F)	373
atelier (F)	551	au lieu de (F)	1718
Atem (D)	3038	au même mouvement (F)	756
Atembehandlung (D)	693	au moins (F)	2880
atemlos (D)	930	au mouvement (F)	720
Atempause (D)	624	au mouvement antérieur (F)	776
Atemstütze (D)	640	au mouvement précédent (F)	1629
Atemtechnik (D)	693	au premier plan (F)	1722
ätherisch (D)	1157	au signe (F)	1627
atmen (D)	2786	au talon (F)	84
atmend (D)	1427	au tempo précédent (F)	776
atmosfera (I)	3358	aubade (song at dawn)	
atmosphère (F)	3358	(E, F)	2248, 2386
Atmung (D)	3280	aube (F)	2248
atonal (D, E, F)	1895	auch (D)	1635
atonale (I)	1895	aucun (F)	1751
atone (F)	643	audace (I)	997
atono (I)	643	audacemente (I)	998
atroce (I)	1550	audacia (con) (I)	999
attacca (I)	1645	audacieusement (F)	998
attacca subito (I)	1646	audacieux (F)	997
attaccare (I)	2733	audacious (E)	997
attacco (I)	236, 471, 2898	audaciously (E)	998
attacco dolce (I)	644	audible (E, F)	1840
attacco duro (I)	645	audience (E)	3266
attacco sul fiato (I)	646	auditeur (F)	2895

audition (E, F)   2902, 3304
auditrice (F)   2895
audizione (I)   2902
auf (D)   1814, 1821
auf betrübte Weise (D)   1334
auf das (D)   1821
auf der (D)   1821
auf der Bühne (D)   3385
auf der Saite (D)   82
auf die (D)   1821
auf die Bühne gehen (D)   2924
auf dieselbe Art (D)   1697, 1750
auf gewohnte Weise (D)   1810
auf lebhafte Weise (D)   784
Aufbau (D)   2139
auffallend (D)   1598
Aufführung (D)   3273
Aufführungspraxis (D)   3238
Aufführungsrecht (D)   2991
aufgebracht (D)   923, 991, 1144
aufgeregt (D)   1125
aufgeweckt (D)   1091
aufheben (D)   2823
aufhören (D)   2819
Auflage (D)   3005
auflösen (D)   2800
auflösend (D)   901
Auflösung (einer Dissonanz)
  (D)   2098
Auflösungszeichen (D)   1906
aufmerksam (D)   2899
Aufnahme (D)   554
Aufnahmestudio (D)   551
(auf Tonträger) aufnehmen
  (D)   2784
aufregend (D)   1125
aufreizend (D)   1297
aufrichtig (D)   1500
Aufsatz (D)   212
Aufsatzbogen (D)   219
Aufschlag (D)   1999
aufschlagendes Rohrblatt (D)   192
Aufschnitt (D)   196
aufschreien (D)   2728
aufschreiend (D)   1580
aufsteigend (D)   1894

Aufstrich (D)   87
Auftakt (D)   1882, 1999
auftreten (D)   2707
aufwärts (D)   1726
Aufzeichnung (D)   554
Aufzug (D)   2901
Auge (D)   3461
augmentation (E, F)   1897
augmenté (F)   1896
augmented (E)   1896
augmenter (F)   2664
augmenting (E)   880
aumentando (I)   883
aumentare (I)   2664
aumentato (I)   1896
aumentazione (I)   1897
aural training (E)   3007
aus dem Takt sein (D)   2714
ausarbeiten (D)   2704
ausatmen (D)   2712
ausatmend (D)   832
ausdehnend (D)   817
Ausdehnung (D)   3022
ausdrücken (D)   2713
Ausdrucksbezeichnung (D)   2114
ausdrucksvoll (D)   1150
ausführen (D)   2709
Ausführender (D)   3089
Ausführung (D)   3015
Ausgabe (D)   3005
Ausgang (D)   593, 3414
ausgedehnt (D)   968, 1304, 1530
ausgehalten (D)   1831
ausgelöscht (D)   848
ausgenommen (D)   1694
ausgewogen (D)   1008
ausgezeichnet (D)   3002
aushalten (D)   2846
Aushilfe (D)   3390
Ausklang (D)   2342
ausklingen lassend (D)   822
auslachend (D)   1031
ausladend (D)   968
auslöschen (D)   2828
auslöschend (D)   910
Auslöser (D)   441

Ausnahme (D)	1695
Ausschnitt (D)	3024
ausschwingen (D)	98
Außenstimme (D)	2054
außergewöhnlich (D)	3364
außerhalb (D)	1716
außerordentlich (D)	3364
äußerst (D)	1698
äußerst... (D)	1711
Aussetzung (eines bezifferten Basses) (D)	2091
aussi (F)	1635
Aussprache (D)	621
aussprechen (D)	2775
Ausstattung (D)	3315
Ausstellung (D)	3020
Ausstrahlung (D)	3243
ausübende Künstlerin (D)	3498
ausübender Künstler (D)	3498
ausverkauft (D)	3014
Auswahl (D)	3313
Ausweichung (D)	2025
auswendig (D)	2884
auswendig spielen (D)	2841
Auszug (D)	3024
autant (F)	1827
autant que (F)	1788
autentico (I)	1898
auteur (F)	2903
authentic (E)	1898
authentic cadence (E)	1914
authentique (F)	1898
authentisch (D)	1898
authentische Kadenz (D)	1914
author (E)	2903
authoritarian (E)	1000
autoarpa (I)	4
autoharp (E)	4
Autor (D)	2903
autore (I)	2903
autoritaire (F)	1000
autoritär (D)	1000
autoritario (I)	1000
autre (F)	1634
autrement (F)	1633
auxiliary note (E)	2039

avambraccio (I)	3430
avancé (F)	2904
avant (F)	1783
avant de (F)	1784
avant que (F)	1784
avant-bras (F)	3430
avantgarde music (E)	3127
avantgardistische Musik (D)	3127
avanti (I)	790
avanzando (I)	790
avanzato (I)	2904
avec (F)	1666
avec abandon (F)	916
avec accablement (F)	1461
avec adoration (F)	925
avec adresse (F)	1092
avec affectation (F)	1309
avec affection (F)	933
avec agilité (F)	941
avec agitation (F)	942
avec agrément (F)	1388
avec aisance (F)	937, 1521
avec allant (F)	738
avec allégresse (F)	955
avec amabilité (F)	958
avec âme (F)	974
avec amertume (F)	962
avec amour (F)	964
avec ampleur (F)	967
avec amusement (F)	1110
avec angoisse (F)	972
avec anxiété (F)	977
avec âpreté (F)	995
avec ardeur (F)	989
avec arrogance (F)	992
avec assurance (F)	1002
avec audace (F)	999
avec beaucoup de liberté (F)	737
avec bonheur (F)	1226
avec bravoure (F)	1012
avec calme (F)	1023
avec candeur (F)	1028
avec caractère (F)	1034
avec célérité (F)	734
avec chaleur (F)	1025
avec charme (F)	1166

avec clarté (F)	1042	avec exaltation (F)	1143
avec cœur (F)	1065	avec expansion (F)	1148
avec colère (F)	1047	avec expression (F)	1149
avec confiance (F)	1179	avec extase (F)	1151
avec constance (F)	1385	avec facétie (F)	1158
avec conviction (F)	1058	avec faiblesse (F)	1070
avec convoitise (F)	1010	avec fantaisie (F)	1162
avec coquetterie (F)	1046	avec faste (F)	1487
avec courage (F)	975	avec fatigue (F)	1168
avec crainte (F)	1555	avec fermeté (F)	1171
avec décision (F)	1072	avec férocité (F)	1174
avec dédain (F)	1464	avec ferveur (F)	1176
avec déférence (F)	1444	avec feu (F)	1214
avec défi (F)	1490	avec fierté (F)	1181
avec dégoût (F)	1428	avec finesse (F)	1184
avec délicatesse (F)	1079	avec flexibilité (F)	1187
avec délice (F)	1084	avec fluidité (F)	1188
avec délire (F)	1083	avec force (F)	1193
avec dérision (F)	1031	avec fougue (F)	1255
avec désarroi (F)	1496	avec fourberie (F)	1215
avec désespoir (F)	1105	avec fracas (F)	1534
avec désinvolture (F)	1101	avec fraîcheur (F)	1204
avec désir (F)	1089, 1603	avec franchise (F)	1197
avec détermination (F)	1094	avec frémissements (F)	1202
avec deux baguettes (F)	377	avec frénésie (F)	1203, 1502
avec dextérité (F)	1092	avec froideur (F)	1199
avec dignité (F)	1096	avec fureur (F)	1217
avec diligence (F)	1097	avec gaîté (F)	1221
avec discrétion (F)	1099	avec galanterie (F)	1224
avec douceur (F)	1114, 1343	avec gentillesse (F)	1230
avec douleur (F)	1111, 1118	avec goût (F)	1249
avec dureté (F)	1122	avec grâce (F)	1245
avec effroi (F)	1377	avec grandeur (F)	1242
avec élan (F)	1501	avec gravité (F)	1244, 1482
avec élégance (F)	1127	avec hardiesse (F)	987
avec élévation (F)	1129	avec hâte (F)	735
avec émotion (F)	1130	avec horreur (F)	1416
avec emphase (F)	1133	avec humour (F)	1577
avec emportement (F)	1217	avec imagination (F)	1251
avec énergie (F)	1131	avec impatience (F)	1253
avec enthousiasme (F)	1136	avec impétuosité (F)	1255
avec entrain (F)	1600	avec indifférence (F)	1266
avec envie (F)	1603	avec indolence (F)	1269
avec esprit (F)	1523	avec innocence (F)	1279
avec essor (F)	1501	avec inquiétude (F)	1281
avec exactitude (F)	1145	avec insistance (F)	1285

avec insolence (F)   1286
avec inspiration (F)   1153
avec ironie (F)   1294
avec ivresse (F)   1124
avec joie (F)   1235
avec l'archet (F)   94
avec la main (F)   378
avec la plus haute
    virtuosité (F)   1056
avec la pointe de l'archet (F)   83
avec la voix (F)   1657
avec langueur (F)   1302
avec lassitude (F)   1528
avec le / - la / - les (F)   1666
avec le bois (F)   95
avec légèreté (F)   1306
avec lenteur (F)   736
avec lustre (F)   1320
avec maintien (F)   1400
avec maîtrise (F)   1323
avec mélancolie (F)   1325
avec mépris (F)   1106
avec modération (F)   1340
avec mollesse (F)   1341
avec moquerie (F)   1457
avec mouvement (F)   738
avec noblesse (F)   1354
avec nonchalance (F)   1355
avec obstination (F)   1366
avec paix (F)   1370
avec panache (F)   1181
avec passion (F)   1373
avec peine (F)   1168
avec persévérance (F)   1385
avec plaisir (F)   1110
avec pompe (F)   1398
avec préciosité (F)   1429
avec précipitation (F)   739
avec précision (F)   1403
avec promptitude (F)   743
avec prudence (F)   1410
avec pureté (F)   1411
avec quelques licences (F)   740
avec raffinement (F)   1421
avec rage (F)   1415
avec raideur (F)   1434

avec rancune (F)   1441
avec rapidité (F)   741
avec recherche (F)   1429
avec recueillement (F)   1417
avec regret (F)   1440
avec résignation (F)   1424
avec résolution (F)   1442
avec respect (F)   1365, 1444
avec ressentiment (F)   1441
avec rigueur (F)   742
avec sensibilité (F)   1471
avec sentiment (F)   1475
avec sérénité (F)   1480
avec sévérité (F)   1484
avec sillets (F)   74
avec simplicité (F)   1470
avec sobriété (F)   1505
avec soin (F)   922
avec solennité (F)   1509
avec sourdine (F)   96, 459
avec stupeur (F)   1537
avec suffisance (F)   1539
avec sûreté (F)   1498
avec tendresse (F)   1546
avec tièdeur (F)   1548
avec timidité (F)   1554
avec tranquillité (F)   1564
avec transport (F)   1136
avec tristesse (F)   1574
avec un doigt (F)   1667
avec vaillance (F)   1582
avec véhémence (F)   1586
avec vélocité (F)   744
avec vénération (F)   1588
avec verve (F)   1014
avec vigueur (F)   1592
avec violence (F)   1595
avec virtuosité (F)   1596
avec vivacité (F)   1600
avec volonté (F)   1605
avec volubilité (F)   1607
avec zèle (F)   1609
avide (F)   1011
avido (I)   1011
avvilito (I)   1461
avviso teatrale (I)   3278

avvivando (I)	791
awake (E)	1091
awkward (E)	1239
axe (F)	437
Ayre (D, E, F, I)	2499
B (D, E)	1905, 2219, 2221
B double flat (E)	2223
B double sharp (E)	2222
B flat (E)	2221
B sharp (E)	2220
Baborák (D, E, F, I)	2500
baby grand (E)	403
baccanale (I)	2260
Bacchanal (D)	2260
bacchanal (E)	2260
bacchanale (F)	2260
bacchetta (I)	347, 2905
bacchetta da tamburo (I)	348
bacchetta di cuoio (I)	349
bacchetta di feltro (I)	350
bacchetta di legno (I)	351
bacchetta di spugna (I)	352
bacchetta imbottita (I)	353
bacchetta per piatti (I)	354
bacchetta per timpani (I)	355
bacchette (I)	279
back (E)	60, 1684, 3281, 3475
back of the hand (E)	3439
background music (E)	3139
backside (E)	3476
backstage (E)	3282
backwards (E)	1684, 2106, 3281
Badinage (D, E, F, I)	2501
Badinerie (D, E,F, I)	2502
bagatella (I)	2261
Bagatelle (D)	2261
bagatelle (E, F)	2261
bagpipe (E)	162, 189
baguette (F)	347, 2905
baguette d'éponge (F)	352
baguette de bois (F)	351
baguette de cuir (F)	349
baguette de cymbales (F)	354
baguette de feutre (F)	350
baguette de tambour (F)	348
baguette de timbales (F)	355
baguette rembourrée (F)	353
baguettes de percussion (F)	279
baguettes entrechoquées (F)	279
baîller (F)	683
baisser (F)	2636
baisser l'accord (F)	2637
baisser l'intonation (F)	2637
balai de jazz (F)	322
balais (F)	370
balalaica (I)	5
Balalaika (D)	5
balalaika (E, F)	5
balancé (F)	1008
balanced (E)	1008
balbettando (I)	1001
balbettare (I)	2665
balbutier (F)	2665
balcony (E)	3053
baldanza (con) (I)	1002
baldanzoso (I)	1002
Balg (D)	428
ball room (E)	3305
ballabile (I)	1068
ballad (E)	2262
Ballade (D)	2262
ballade (F)	2262
ballare (I)	2666
ballata (I)	2262
ballerina (E, I)	3491
ballerino (I)	3491
ballet (E, F)	2263
ballet de cour (F)	2264
ballet master (E)	3512
ballet music (E)	3155
ballet school (E)	3322
Ballett (D)	2263
Ballettkorps (D)	2968
Ballettmeister (D)	3512
Ballettmeisterin (D)	3512
Ballettmusik (D)	3155
balletto (I)	2263
balletto di corte (I)	2264
Ballettschule (D)	3322
Balletttänzer (D)	3491
Balletttänzerin (D)	3491
ballo (I)	2906

ballo di sala (I)	2907	barilotto (I)	197
ballo di società (I)	2907	Bariton (D)	599
ballo tedesco (I)	2265	baritone (E)	119, 599
ballroom dance (E)	2907	baritone clef (E)	1922
Ballsaal (D)	3305	baritone saxophone (E)	166
balzato (I)	89	Baritonhorn (D)	119
balzellato (I)	90, 108	baritono (I)	599
bambino prodigio (I)	2908	Baritonsaxophon (D)	166
bamboo brasilene (E)	342	Baritonschlüssel (D)	1922
bamboo scraper (E)	311	Barkarole (D)	2266
bambou brésilien (F)	342	barmherzig (D)	1392
Bambusraspel (D)	311	barocco (I)	2912
Bambusschüttelrohr (D)	342	Barock (D)	2912
Band (D)	3104	baroque (E, F)	2912
band music (E)	3156	barra (I)	2134
banda (I)	2909	barré (E, F, I)	91
banda di frequenza (I)	485	barre (F)	39, 41
banda di ottoni (I)	2910	Barré (Quergriff bei	
banda militare (I)	2911	Gitarre/Laute) (D)	91
Bandbreite (D)	519	barre de mesure (F)	2134
bande de fréquences (F)	485	barre transversale (F)	2176
bande magnétique (F)	537	barrel socket (E)	197
Bandgeschwindigkeit (D)	595	barrel-organ (E)	478
Bandoneon (D)	391	barrette (F)	232
bandoneon (E, I)	391	barsch (D)	1017
bandonéon (F)	391	barsche Stimme (D)	706
bandpass filter (E)	512	baryton (F)	599
Bandpassfilter (D)	512	bas (F)	2913
bandwidth (E)	519	bass (E)	600, 2913
bange (D)	979	Bass (D)	600
bangend (D)	931, 978	bass clarinet (E)	124
Banjo (D)	6	bass clef (E)	1923
banjo (E, F, I)	6	bass drum (E)	289
banquette (F)	443	bass drum pedal (E)	367
bar (E)	1902, 2018	bass flute (E)	150
bar number (E)	2046	bass player (E)	3499
bar-line (E)	2134	bass recorder (E)	144
barbare (F)	1003	bass saxophone (E)	167
barbarisch (D)	1003	bass string (E)	45
barbaro (I)	1003	bass trumpet (E)	175
barbarous (E)	1003	bass tuba (E)	186
barcarola (E, I)	2266	bass-bar (E)	41
barcarolle (F)	2266	Bass-Buffo (D)	601
barcollando (I)	1004	bassa danza (I)	2267
baril (F)	197	Bassbalken (D)	41
barillet (F)	197	Bassblockflöte (D)	144

basse (F)	600	battitoia (I)	357
basse bouffe (F)	601	battle (E)	2268
basse chiffrée (F)	1899	battre (F)	2667
basse continue (F)	1900	battre la mesure (F)	2668
basse contrainte (F)	1901	battuta (I)	1902
Basse danse (D)	2267	battuta composta (I)	1903
basse danse (E, F)	2267	battuta semplice (I)	1904
basse obstinée (F)	1901	Batuque (D, E, F, I)	2503
bassethorn (E)	134	Bauch (D)	3466
Bassetthorn (D)	134	Bauerntanz (D)	2331
bassin (F)	229	bäurisch (D)	945
Bassklarinette (D)	124	bavarder (F)	2681
basso (I)	600, 2913	be quiet (E)	1823
basso buffo (E, I)	601	beam (E)	2134, 2176
basso cifrato (I)	1899	beaming (E)	1420
basso continuo (I)	1900	bearbeiten (D)	2644
basso numerato (I)	1899	Bearbeiter (D)	3488
Basso ostinato (D)	1901	Bearbeiterin (D)	3488
basso ostinato (I)	1901	Bearbeitung (D)	2892
basson (F)	141, 3507	bearing (E)	1400
bassoon (E)	141	beat (E)	374, 487, 542, 1902
bassoonist (E)	3507	beater (E)	347
Basssaxophon (D)	167	beating reed (E)	192
Bassschlüssel (D)	1923	beato (I)	1005
Basstrompete (D)	175	beau (F)	2916
Basstuba (D)	120, 186	beau chant (F)	648
basta! (I)	2914	beaucoup (F)	1744
bastante (I)	1647	beauté (F)	2915
bataille (F)	2268	beautiful (E)	2916
baton (E)	2905	beautiful singing (E)	648
battaglia (I)	2268	beauty (E)	2915
battaglio (I)	356	bebend (D)	696, 878, 1201
battant (F)	356	Bebung (D)	879
battement (F) 374, 487, 542, 2027		bec (F)	198, 438
battement de coeur (F)	3211	bécarre (F)	1906
battente (I)	356	becco (I)	198
battere (I)	2667	Becken (D)	303
battere il tempo (I)	2668	Beckenschlägel (D)	354
batteria (I)	253	becoming calmer (E)	892
batteria elettronica (I)	486	becoming more animated (E)	789
batterie (F)	253	bedächtig (D)	1387, 1401
batterista (I)	3492	bedecken (D)	2691
battery (E)	1892	bedeckt (D)	379
batteur (F)	317, 3492	bedeutend (D)	3071
battimento (I)	487	bedrängend (D)	799
battito (I)	374	bedrohlich (D)	1316

beeilen (D)	2645
beeilend (D)	807
beendet (D)	1702
beendigen (D)	2848
beffardo (I)	1006
before (E)	1783, 1784
Begabung (D)	3391
begierig (D)	1011
begin (E)	1645
beginne (D)	1645
beginnen (D)	2733
beginner (E)	3019
beginning (E)	1665, 3086
begleiten (D)	2642
begleitend (D)	1614
Begleiter (D)	3485
Begleiterin (D)	3485
begleitetes Rezitativ (D)	2445
Begleitinstrument (D)	3369
Begleitung (D)	2871
beglückwünschen (D)	2718
Begrenzer (D)	520
behäbig (D)	1393
behaglich (D)	1052
behände (D)	940
behandeln (D)	2854
beharren (D)	2737
beherzt (D)	976
behind the scenes (E)	2981
Beifall (D)	2890
Bein (D)	3444
beinahe (D)	1789
Beispiel (D)	3016
bekümmert (D)	982
bel canto (I)	648
beleben (D)	2655
belebend (D)	789
belebt (D)	731
beleidigend (D)	1291
beleidigt (D)	1359
Beleuchtung (D)	3068
beliebig (D)	1699
bell (E)	200, 212, 257
bell down (E)	247
bell in the air (E)	237
bell stroke (E)	375

bell tree (E)	300
bell up (E)	237
bella (I)	2916
belle (F)	2916
bellezza (I)	2915
bellicose (E)	1007
bellicoso (I)	1007
belliqueux (F)	1007
bello (I)	2916
bellows (E)	428
belly (E)	77
below (E)	1717
bemerkenswert (D)	3187
bémol (F)	1905
bemolle (I)	1905
ben (I)	1648
ben ritmato (I)	846
bene (I)	1648
Benzinfass (D)	331
bequadro (I)	1906
bequem (D)	936, 1053
berauschend (D)	1124, 1271
berceuse (F)	2399
bereits (D)	1705
bergamasca (I)	2269
bergamask (E)	2269
bergamasker Tanz (D)	2269
bergamasque (F)	2269
Bergerette (D, E, F, I)	2504
berstend (D)	1460
Berufsmusiker (D)	3177
Berufsmusikerin (D)	3177
beruhigen (D)	2675
beruhigend (D)	815
berühmt (D)	2937
berühren (D)	2840
besänftigend (D)	906
beschaulich (D)	1057
bescheiden (D)	1576
beschleunigen (D)	2640
beschleunigend (D)	785
beschleunigt (D)	786
Beschluss (D)	1936
beschreiben (D)	2699
beschreibend (D)	1088
Besen (D)	370

Besetzung (D)	2997, 3205	billet gratuit (F)	2918
beside (E)	1613	binaire (F)	1907
beständig (D)	1061	binario (I)	1907
bestimmt (D)	1093	binary (E)	1907
bestürzt (D)	1496	binary form (E)	1981
betäubend (D)	2897	Bindebogen (D)	2004
beten (D)	2767	binden (D)	2745
betend (D)	1405	bindend (D)	1758
betonen (D)	2641	biniou (F)	189
betonend (D)	842, 884	bird pipe (E)	312
betont (D)	841	Birne (D)	197
Betonung (D	1867, 2870	bis (D)	1809
betörend (D)	1263	bis (L)	2919
beträchtlich (D)	3071	bis zu (D)	1703
betrübt (D)	920	bis zum (D)	1703
beunruhigend (D)	1280	bis zum Ende (D)	1619
beunruhigt (D)	953, 1281	bis zum Schlussteil (D)	1623
bevor (D)	1784	bis zum Zeichen (D)	1627, 1704
bewegend (D)	795	bisbigliando (arpa) (I)	92
beweglich (D)	1339	bisbigliare (I)	649
bewegt (D)	738, 759, 1050	bischero (I)	36
Bewegung (D)	1745	biscroma (I)	2229
bezaubert (D)	1262	biseau (F)	196, 408
beziffern (D)	1931	bissig (D)	1344
bezifferter Bass (D)	1899	bit player (E)	2951
Bezifferung (D)	1932	biting (E)	1344
bezüglich (Paralleltonart)		bitonalità (I)	1908
(D)	2092	Bitonalität (D)	1908
bichord (E)	1649	bitonalité (F)	1908
bicordo (I)	1649	bitonality (E)	1908
bieco (I)	1561	bitten (D)	2767
bien (F)	1648	bitter (D, E)	963
bien comme il faut (F)	1641	bitterly (E)	960
bien en mesure (F)	720	bizarre (E, F)	1009
bien rythmé (F)	846	bizzarro (I)	1009
bienheureux (F)	1005	blanche (F)	2225
big (E)	1710	blasen (D)	2821, 3340
big drum (E)	289	Bläser (D)	3037
biglietteria (I)	2920	Bläserquintett (D)	2441
biglietto (I)	2917	Blasinstrumente (D)	3372
biglietto in omaggio (I)	2918	Blasmusik (D)	2909, 3156, 3160
bilancia (I)	409	Blatt (D)	3209
bilanciato (I)	1008	blättere um (D)	1857
billet (F)	2917	Blechblasinstrumente (D)	3374
billet d'entrée (F)	2917	Blechblasorchester (D)	2910
billet de faveur (F)	2918	Blechinstrumente (D)	3208

bleiben (D)   2787, 2832
blendend (D)   1492
Blick (D)   3332
blissful (E)   1005
blitzend (D)   1212
bloc de bois (F)   254
block (E)   408
block chords (E)   4031
block cinese (I)   254
Blockflöte (D)   152
blood (E)   3474
blühend (D)   1436
„blühender" Kontrapunkt (D) 1942
Bluette (D, E, F, I)   2505
Blume (Verzierung) (D)   1978
Blut (D)   3474
bocal (F)   202
bocca (I)   3431
bocchino (I)   199
Boden (D)   60
body (E)   361, 416
bodyweight (E)   468
Bogen (D)   34, 221, 3043
Bogenführung (D)   85
Bogenhaare (D)   55
Bogenstrich (D)   85
bohémien/-ne (F)   3427
Bohrung (D)   425
bois (F)   3047, 3099, 3100
boîte (F)   3312
boîte à musique (F)   475
boîte expressive (F)   417
boiteux (F)   952
bold (E)   1002
boldly (E)   986
Bolero (D)   2273
bolero (E, I)   2273
boléro (F)   2273
bombarda (I)   118
bombarde (E, F)   118
bombardino (I)   119
bombardon (E, F)   120
Bombardon (D)   120
bombardone (I)   120
bombastic (E)   969, 1439
Bomhard (D)   118

bondi (F)   89
bondissant (F)   1456
bone (E)   3463
bones (E)   334
Bongo (D)   255
bongo (E, I)   255
Bongotrommel (D)   255
bonnet (F)   200
book (E)   3104
borbottando (I)   1016
borbottare (I)   2669
bord (F)   366
bordone (I)   1909
bordoniera (I)   358
Bordun (D)   1909
Bordunsaite (D)   49
bore (E)   425
boring (E)   3184
borry (E)   2270
bosco (I)   3047
boshaft (D)   1327
botteghino (I)   2920
bottone (I)   37, 410
bottoni dei registri (I)   411
bouché (F)   238
bouche (F)   3431
bouncing (E)   89, 90, 108
bound (E)   854
bourdon (E, F)   1909
bourée (E)   2270
Bourrée (D)   2270
bourrée (F, I)   2270
bousculé (F)   761
bout du doigt (F)   3471
bouton (F)   37, 410
boutons de registres (F)   411
bow (E)   34, 3080
bowed stringed instruments
  (E)   3370
bowing (E)   85
box (E)   3210, 3312
box office (E)   2920
boys' choir (E)   663
braccio (I)   3432
brace (E)   1873
bracket (E)   1873

braking (E)	819	brillant (F)	1013
bramosia (con) (I)	1010	brillante (I)	1013
bramoso (I)	1011	Brille (D)	194
brando (I)	2271	brilliant (E)	1013
Branle (D)	2271	brindisi (I)	2272
branle (E, F)	2271	bring forward (E)	1716
brano (I)	2921	bring out (E)	1716
bransle (F)	2271	bringen (D)	2764
bras (F)	3432	brio (con) (I)	1014
brass (E)	3208	brioso (I)	1015
brass band (E)	2909, 2910	brisé (F)	3300
brass instruments (E)	3374	brisk (E)	1597
brassy overblowing (E)	245	briskly (E)	954
Bratsche (D)	28	broad (E)	751
Bratschist (D)	3528	broadcast (E)	3409
Bratschistin (D)	3528	broadcasting (E)	3272
Brautlied (D)	2294	broadened (E)	1630
brave (E)	976	broadening (E)	812
bravissimo! (I)	2922	broadly (E)	1304
Bravourarie (D)	2255	broderie (F)	1864, 2051
bravura (con) (I)	1012	broken (E)	3300
bravura aria (E)	2255	broken chord (E)	1878
breadth (E)	3097	brontolando (I)	1016
break a leg (E)	3077	brontolare (I)	2670
breast (E)	3467	brosse (F)	322
breath (E)	3038, 3340	brouillon (F)	3318
breath control (E)	693	Bruchstück (D)	3051
breath support (E)	640	bruit (F)	566
breathing (E)	1427, 3280	brûlant (F)	984
breathing pause (E)	624	brüllen (D)	2863
breathless (E)	930	brumeux (F)	1348
bref (F)	1650	Brummeisen (D)	315
breit (D)	751	brummen (D)	2670
Breite (D)	3097	brummend (D)	1016
breiter werdend (D)	812	Brummtopf (D)	273
bremsen (D)	2725	Brunette (D, E, F, I)	2506
bremsend (D)	819	bruscamente (I)	1017
brennend (D)	985	brusco (I)	1017
Brettchenklapper (D)	334	brüsk (D)	1017
breve (I)	1650	brusque (E, F)	1017
bridal song		brusquement (F)	1017
(wedding song) (E)	2294	Brust (D)	3467
bridge (E)	65, 2072	Brustkorb (D)	3481
Brief (D)	3101	Bruststimme (D)	710
brief (E)	1650	brutal (D, E, F)	1018
bright (E)	1317	brutale (I)	1018

bruyamment (F)	1448	Cabaletta (D)	2276
bruyant (F)	1448	cabaletta (E, I)	2276
Buch (D)	3104	cabalette (F)	2276
Buchstabe (D)	3101	cabasa (E)	256
bucolico (I)	1374	Cabaza (D)	256
buffet (F)	416	cabaza (I)	256
buffo (I)	1049	caccavella (I)	273
Bügelhorn (D)	154	caccia (I)	2277
bugle (F)	132	caché (F)	1748
bugle à pistons (F)	154	cachet (F)	3193
Bühne (D)	3314	Cachucha (D, E, F, I)	2508
Bühnenbild (D)	3315	cacofonia (I)	2923
Bühnenmalerei (D)	3316	cacophonie (F)	2923
Bühnenmusik (D)	3142	cacophony (E)	2923
Bulerias (D, E, F, I)	2507	cadence (E, F)	1910
bull roarer (E)	293	cadence finale (F)	1912
Bund (D)	76	cadence interrompue (F)	1916
bündig (D)	1669	cadence parfaite (F)	1914
bureau de location (F)	2920	cadence plagale (F)	1915
buree (E)	2270	cadence rompue (F)	1911
burlando (I)	1019	cadence suspendue (F)	1913, 1916
burlesca (I)	2274	cadencing (E)	1651
burlescamente (I)	1020	cadential (E)	1651
burlesco (I)	1020	cadentiel (F)	1651
Burleske (D)	2274	cadenza (E, I)	1910
burlesque (E, F)	2274	cadenza d'inganno (I)	1911
burletta (I)	2275	cadenza evitata (I)	1911
burning (E)	1275	cadenza finale (I)	1912
burrascoso (I)	1542	cadenza imperfetta (I)	1913
bursting (E)	1460	cadenza perfetta (I)	1914
bussare (I)	2671	cadenza plagale (I)	1915
but (E)	1732	cadenza sospesa (I)	1916
but not too much (E)	1733	cadenzale (I)	1651
butt (E)	221	cadenzante (I)	1651
buttare (I)	2672	cadere (I)	2673
button accordion (E)	396	cadre (F)	360, 450
by heart (E)	2884	caesura (E)	1920
by step (E)	1939	café-concert (F)	3416
C (D, E)	2189	caisse (F)	267, 416
C clef (E)	1925	caisse claire (F)	332
C double flat (E)	2193	caisse de résonance (F)	40
C double sharp (E)	2192	caisse roulante (F)	268
C flat (E)	2191	calando (I)	898
C sharp (E)	2190	calante (I)	898
C-Schlüssel (D)	1925	calare (I)	650, 2674
ça suit (F)	1796	Calata (D, E, F, I)	2509

calcando (I)	884
calcare le scene (I)	2924
calculateur (F)	504
caldaia (I)	359
caldamente (I)	1021
caldo (I)	1022
calebasse (F)	256
câlin (F)	918
calling (E)	1040
calm (E)	1024, 1401
calma (con) (I)	1023
calmamente (I)	1023
calmando (I)	815
calmandosi (I)	816
calmare (I)	2675
calme (F)	1024
calmement (F)	1024
calmer (F)	2675
calming (E)	815
calming down (E)	816
calmly (E)	1023
calmo (I)	1024
calore (con) (I)	1025
calorosamente (I)	1026
caloroso (I)	1026
cambia (I)	1747
cambiamento (I)	2925
cambiamento di posizione (I)	93
cambiamento di tempo (I)	1917
cambiando (I)	1652
cambiare (I)	2676
cambiata (F)	2040
cambio della voce (I)	616
cambio di misura (I)	1917
cambio di scena (I)	2926
cambio di tonalità (I)	1918
camera d'aria (I)	201
camerino (I)	2927
camminando (I)	792
campana (I)	200, 257
campanaccio (I)	258
campane doriche (I)	259
campane in alto (I)	237
campane tubolari (I)	260
campanella (I)	262
campanelli (I)	261

campanelli a tastiera (I)	264
campanelli della messa (I)	263
campanello (I)	262
campestre (I)	943
canal pour l'air (F)	201
canale (I)	412, 488
canard (F)	3186
canaria (I)	2278
Canarie (D)	2278
canarie (F)	2278
canary (E)	2278
Cancan (D)	2510
cancan (E, F, I)	2510
cancellare (I)	489
candid (E)	1027
candidamente (I)	1027
candide (F)	1027
candidement (F)	1027
candidly (E)	1027
candido (I)	1027
candore (con) (I)	1028
cangiando (I)	1652
canna (I)	413
canna ad ancia (I)	414
canna labiale (I)	415
canne de tambour major (F)	363
canon (E, F)	2279
canone (I)	2279
canoro (I)	651
cantabile (I)	1029
cantando (I)	1030
cantante (I)	3493
cantare (I)	2677
cantare a prima vista (I)	652
cantare giusto (I)	653
cantata (E, I)	2280
cantata da camera (I)	2281
cantata da chiesa (I)	2282
cantata profana (I)	2283
cantata su un corale (I)	2284
cantate (F)	2280
cantate d'église (F)	2282
cantate de chambre (F)	2281
cantate profane (F)	2283
cantate sur un choral (F)	2284
cantatrice (F)	3493

canticchiare (I)	654
canticle (E)	2285
cantico (I)	2285
Cantigas (D, E, F, I)	2511
cantilena (E, I)	2286
cantilène (F)	2286
cantino (I)	38
cantique (F)	2285
canto carnascialesco (I)	2287
canto di lavoro (I)	2288
canto di Natale (I)	2289
canto fermo (I)	1919
canto funebre (I)	2290
canto gitano (I)	2291
canto goliardico (I)	2292
canto gregoriano (I)	2293
canto nuziale (I)	2294
canto parlato (I)	655
Cantus firmus (D)	1919
cantus firmus (E, F)	1919
canzonando (I)	1031
canzone (I)	2295
canzone a successo (I)	2928
canzone della sera (I)	2296
canzone infantile (I)	2297
canzone moderna (I)	2298
canzone popolare (I)	2299
canzonet (E)	2300
canzonetta (I)	2298, 2300
canzonette (F)	2300
canzoniere (I)	3271
caparbio (I)	1032
capelli (I)	3433
capire (I)	2678
capodaste (F)	39
capolavoro (I)	2929
capotasto (E, I)	39
cappella (I)	2930
cappello cinese (I)	300
Capriccio (D)	2301
capriccio (E, I)	2301
capricciosamente (I)	1033
capriccioso (I)	1033
caprice (F)	2301
capricieusement (F)	917, 1033
capricieux (F)	1033
capricious (E)	917, 1033
capsula (I)	202
capsule (F)	202
caractéristique (F)	2931
carattere (con) (I)	1034
caratteristico (I)	2931
cardboard mute (E)	224
careful (E)	921
carefully (E)	921
carelessly (E)	1355
caressing (E)	918
carezzevole (I)	918
caricato (I)	1035
cariglione (I)	479
carillon (E, F, I)	265, 266, 475
carillon à clavier (F)	266
carillon a tastiera (I)	266
carino (I)	1036
carmagnola (I)	2302
Carmagnole (D)	2302
carmagnole (E, F)	2302
carnaval (F)	2932
carnevale (I)	2932
carnival (E)	2932
carnival song (E)	2287
carol (E)	2303
carola (I)	2303
Carole (D)	2303
carole (F)	2303
carried over (E)	868
carrying over (E)	867
carrying the voice (E)	619
carta da musica (I)	2933
cartellone (I)	2934
cartridge (E)	498
casa editrice di musica (I)	2935
cascare (I)	2673
case (E)	35, 231, 416
casque d'écoute (F)	495
cassa (I)	267, 416
cassa armonica (I)	40
cassa chiara (I)	268, 332
cassa di risonanza (I)	40
cassa espressiva (I)	417
cassa rullante (I)	268
cassation (E, F)	2304

cassazione (I)	2304	celeste (I)	1039
cassé (F)	3300	celestiale (I)	1039
cassette recorder (E)	553	celia (con) (I)	1158
cassettophone (F)	553	Cellist (D)	3529
cast (E)	2997	cellist (E)	3529
castagnette (I)	269	cellista (I)	3529
castagnette con manico (I)	270	Cellistin (D)	3529
castagnette di metallo (I)	271	Cembalist (D)	3496
castagnette spagnole (I)	272	Cembalistin (D)	3496
castagnettes (F)	269	Cembalo (D)	393
castagnettes à manches (F)	270	cennamella (I)	121
castagnettes de métal (F)	271	cenno (I)	3058
castagnettes espagnoles (F)	272	centre auditif (F)	2938
castanets (E)	269	centre pin (E)	437
castigato (I)	1340, 1506	centro uditivo (I)	2938
casto (I)	1037	cercare (I)	2680
castrat (F)	656	cerchio (I)	360
castrato (E, I)	656	cerone (I)	658
catalog (E)	2936	certain (E, F)	2939
catalogo (I)	2936	certo (I)	2939
catalogue (E, F)	2936	cervelas (F)	163
Catch (D, E, F, I)	2512	Ces (D)	2191
catégories de voix (F)	659	Ceses (D)	2193
catena (I)	41	cessare (I)	2819
catena di trilli (I)	657	cesser (F)	2819
catene (I)	274	cesser de vibrer (F)	98
cater wauling (E)	3138	cesura (I)	1920
cauto (I)	1409	césure (F)	1920
cavalleresco (I)	1038	cetra (I)	7
cavatina (E, I)	2305	cetra da tavolo (I)	8
cavatine (F)	2305	Chaconne (D)	2306
cavigliere (I)	42	chaconne (E, F)	2306
CD (Abk. für		chacun (F)	1759
Compact Disc) (D, E)	581	chagrin (F)	1335
Cebell (D, E, F, I)	2513	chagriné (F)	920
cedendo (I)	899	chain of trills (E)	657
céder (F)	2679	chaîne (F)	488
cedere (I)	2679	chaînes (F)	274
célèbre (F)	2937	chains (E)	274
celebre (I)	2937	chaleureusement (F)	1021, 1026
celeramente (I)	732	chaleureux (F)	1026
celere (I)	732	chalumeau (F)	121, 190
Celesta (D)	392	chamber cantata (E)	2281
celesta (E, I)	392	chamber music (E)	3130
célesta (F)	392	chamber orchestra (E)	3197
céleste (F)	1039	chamber sonata (E)	2466

champêtre (F)	943	chapel (E)	2930
change (E, F)	1747, 2925	chapelle (F)	2930
change of finger (E)	470	chaque (F)	1759
change of meter (E)	1917	chaque fois (F)	1760
change of set (E)	2926	character piece (E)	2425
change of time (E)	1917	characteristic (E)	2931
changeable (E)	1339	charakteristisch (D)	2931
changement (F)	2925	Charakterstück (D)	2425
changement de décor (F)	2926	chargé (F)	1035
changement de mesure (F)	1917	charged (E)	1035
changement de position (F)	93	charitable (F)	1392
changement de temps (F)	1917	charivari (F)	3138
changement de tonalité (F)	1918	charleston (I)	275
changer (F)	2676	charleston cymbal (E)	307
changing (E)	1652	Charleston-Becken (D)	307
changing note (E)	2040	Charlestonmaschine (D)	275
channel (E)	412, 488	charmant (F)	1036
chanson (F)	2295	charmé (F)	1262
chanson à boire (F)	2272	charmed (E)	1262
chanson à la mode (F)	2298	charming (E)	1036, 1263
chanson bacchique (F)	2272	chasse (F)	2277
chanson d'étudiant (F)	2292	chaste (E, F)	1037
chanson de carnaval (F)	2287	chaud (F)	1022
chanson enfantine (F)	2297	che (I)	1653
chanson populaire (F)	2299	cheek (E)	3448
chansonnette (F)	2298	cheeky (E)	1486
chant de mai (F)	2379	cheerful (E)	728, 1311
chant de Noël (F)	2289	cheerfully (E)	955
chant de travail (F)	2288	cheerily (E)	994
chant du soir (F)	2296	chef d'attaque (F)	3250
chant funèbre (F)	2290	chef d'orchestre (F)	3506
chant gitan (F)	2291	chef de chœur (F)	674
chant grégorien (F)	2293	chef de pupitre (F)	3250
chant nuptial (F)	2294	chef invité (F)	2988
chant parlé (F)	655	chef-d'œuvre (F)	2929
chantant (F)	1029	chercher (F)	2680
chanter (F)	2677	chest voice (E)	710
chanter à vue (F)	652	chevaleresque (F)	1038
chanter juste (F)	653	chevalet (F)	65
chanter trop bas (F)	650	cheveux (F)	3433
chanter trop haut (F)	671	cheville (F)	36
chanterelle (F)	38	chevillier (F)	42
chanteur (F)	3493	chevroter (F)	697
chanteuse (F)	3493	chiaccherare (I)	2681
chantonner (F)	654	chiamando (I)	1040
chapeau chinois (F)	300	chiaramente (I)	1041

Chiarantana (D, E, F, I)	2514	chœur de garçons (F)	663
chiarezza (con) (I)	1042	chœur de radio (F)	661
chiaro (I)	1043	chœur mixte (F)	667
chiave (I)	203, 1921	chœur parlé (F)	668
chiave dell'acqua (I)	204	choice (E)	3313
chiave di baritono (I)	1922	choir (E)	660, 667
chiave di basso (I)	1923	choir school (E)	3323
chiave di contralto (I)	1924	choirmaster (E)	674
chiave di do (I)	1925	choix (F)	3313
chiave di mezzosoprano (I)	1926	Chor (D)	660
chiave di soprano (I)	1927	Choral (D)	2322
chiave di tenore (I)	1928	choral (E)	2322
chiave di violino (I)	1929	choral (F)	2322
chiedere (I)	2682	choral cantata (E)	2284
chiesa (I)	2940	choral conductor (E)	674
chiffrage (F)	1932	choral music (E)	3125
chiffrer (F)	1931	choral society (E)	642
child's voice (E)	714	choral speaking (E)	668
childish (E)	1272	choral work (E)	2408
children's choir (E)	663	chorale (E)	2322
chin (E)	3455	Choralkantate (D)	2284
chin-rest (E)	62	chord (E)	1874
chinese block (E)	254	Chordirigent (D)	674
chinese cymbals (E)	305	chorégraphe (F)	2967, 3501
chinesische Becken (D)	305	Choreograph (D)	3501
chiocciola (I)	68	choreographer (E)	3501
chitarra (I)	10	Choreographie (D)	2967
chitarra battente (I)	11	Choreographin (D)	3501
chitarra elettrica (I)	490	choreography (E)	2967
chitarra hawaiana (I)	12	Choreologe (D)	3502
chitarra jazz (I)	11	Choreologin (D)	3502
chitarrista (I)	3494	choreologist (E)	3502
chiudere (I)	2683	choréologue (F)	3502
chiusa del trillo (I)	1930	choriste (F)	3503
chiuso (I)	238, 2941	chorister (E)	3503
chivalrous (E)	1038	Chormusik (D)	3125
chocalho (E)	276	chorps de ballet (E)	2968
chocallo (I)	276	Chorsänger (D)	3503
Chocolo (D)	276	Chorsängerin (D)	3503
chocolo (E, F)	276	Chorschule (D)	3323
chœur (F)	54, 660	chorus (E)	660
chœur d'église (F)	662	chorus singer (E)	3503
chœur d'enfants (F)	663	Chorwerk (D)	2408
chœur d'hommes (F)	666	chose (F)	2970
chœur d'opéra (F)	664	chrétien (F)	1063
chœur de femmes (F)	665	christian (E)	1063

christlich (D)	1063
Christmas music (E)	3141
Christmas song (E)	2289
chromatic (E)	1947
chromatic timpano (E)	338
chromaticism (E)	1948
Chromatik (D)	1948
chromatique (F)	1947
chromatisch (D)	1947
chromatische Pauke (D)	338
chromatisme (F)	1948
Chrotta (D)	16
chrotta (F)	16
chuchoter (F)	649
church (E)	2940
church cantata (E)	2282
church choir (E)	662
church mode (E)	2022
church music (E)	3131
church sonata (E)	2467
ciaccona (I)	2306
ciaramella (I)	121
ciascuno (I)	1759
ciclo (I)	2942
ciel (F)	2943
cielo (I)	2943
cifrare (I)	1931
cifratura (I)	1932
cilindro (I)	418
cilindro rotativo (I)	205
cimbali (I)	277
cimbalini (I)	278
cimbalom (E, I)	9
cinelle (I)	303
cinetico (I)	1044
cinétique (F)	1044
Cinquepace (D, E, F, I)	2515
cinquième mouvement (F)	2089
circa (I)	1654
circle of fifths (E)	1933
circolando (I)	733
circolo delle quinte (I)	1933
circulating (E)	733
Cis (D)	2190
Cisis (D)	2192
Cister (D)	7
cistre (F)	7
cithare (F)	8
cithare d'amateur (F)	4
cittern (E)	7
civettando (I)	1045
civetteria (con) (I)	1046
civettuolo (I)	1046
clair (F)	1043
clairement (F)	1041
clapper (E)	321, 356
claquettes (F)	3404
clarinet (E)	122
clarinetist (E)	3495
clarinette (F)	122
clarinette alto (F)	126
clarinette basse (F)	124
clarinette contrebasse (F)	125
clarinettist (E)	3495
clarinettista (I)	3495
clarinettiste (F)	3495
clarinetto (I)	122
clarinetto basso (I)	124
clarinetto contrabbasso (I)	125
clarinetto contralto (I)	126
clarinetto piccolo (I)	123
classi vocali (I)	659
classic (E)	2944
classical music (E)	3122
classicism (E)	2945
classicisme (F)	2945
classicismo (I)	2945
classico (I)	2944
classique (F)	2944
clavecin (F)	393
claveciniste (F)	3496
claves (E, F, I)	279
clavicembalista (I)	3496
clavicembalo (I)	393
clavichord (E)	394
clavicorde (F)	394
clavicordo (I)	394
clavier (F)	447
claviers éléctroniques (F)	577
clé (F)	203, 1921
clé d'eau (F)	204
clé d'ut (F)	1925

clé d'ut première ligne (F)   1927
clé d'ut quatrième ligne (F)   1928
clé d'ut seconde ligne (F)   1926
clé d'ut troisième ligne (F)   1924
clé de fa quatrième ligne (F)   1923
clé de fa troisième ligne (F)   1922
clé de sol (F)   1929
clean (E)   3267
clear (E)   1043
clear voice (E)   707
clearly (E)   1041, 1352
clef (E, F)   1921
clément (F)   1271
clemente (I)   1271
climat (F)   3358
climax (E)   2888
cloche (F)   257
cloche de vache (F)   258
cloches doriennes (F)   259
cloches tubulaires (F)   260
clochette (F)   262
clochettes pour la messe (F)   263
close (E)   3423
close position (E)   2075
close to the bridge (E)   116
closed (E)   2941
cloud (E)   3191
clumsy (E)   1239
coach (E)   3520
coaching (E)   3261
coarse (E)   1246
coda (I)   1655
codetta (I)   1934
coeur (F)   3435
coi (I)   1666
coiffure (F)   3228
coinvolto (I)   1656
col (I)   1666
col legno (I)   95
colachon (F)   13
colascione (E, I)   13
Colascione (D)   13
cold (E)   1200
coldly (E)   1198
coléreusement (F)   923
coléreux (F)   1292

Colinda (D, E, F, I)   2516
coll'arco (I)   94
colla (I)   1666
colla punta d'arco, -di arco/-
    dell'arco (I)   83
colla voce (I)   1657
collaboration (E, F)   2946
collaborazione (I)   2946
colle (I)   1666
collection (E, F)   2947
college (E)   2866
collera (con) (I)   1047
collezione (I)   2947
collo (I)   3434
colofonia (I)   43
colonna sonora (I)   491
colonne sonore (F)   491
colophane (F)   43
colorato (I)   1048
coloratura (E, I)   669
coloratura aria (E)   2256
coloratura soprano (E)   629
colorature (F)   669
coloré (F)   1048
colore (I)   2948
colorito (I)   2948
colossale (I)   1232
colour (E)   2948
coloured (E)   1048
colpo (I)   374, 1658
colpo d'arco (I)   85
colpo del battaglio (I)   375
colpo di lingua (I)   239
colpo di lingua semplice (I)   240
colpo di tamburo (I)   376
colto (I)   2949
comando del suono (I)   492
come (I)   1659
come al principio (I)   1660
come prima (I)   1661
come sopra (I)   1662
come stà (I)   1663
come una cadenza (I)   1664
comédie (F)   2950
comédie lyrique (F)   2308
comédie musicale (F)   2307

comédien (F)	3490
comédienne (F)	3490
comedy (E)	2950
Comes (D)	2099
comfortable (E)	939
comfortably (E)	1052
comic opera (E)	2406, 2407
comical (E)	1049
comico (I)	1049
cominciando (I)	1665
comique (F)	1049
comma (E, F, I)	1935
commande du son (F)	492
comme (F)	1659
comme au début (F)	1660
comme avant (F)	1661
comme plus haut (F)	1662
comme une aria (F)	2259
comme une ballade (F)	914
comme une cadence (F)	1664
comme une danse paysanne (F)	945
comme une sonnerie (F)	1527
commedia (I)	2950
commedia musicale (I)	2307
commedia per musica (I)	2308
commence (F)	1645
commencement (F)	3086
commencer (F)	2733
commodément (F)	1052
commodo (I)	1053
common (E)	2957
common chord (E)	1877
commosso (I)	1050
commovente (I)	1051
commun (F)	2957
commuovere (I)	2684
comodamente (I)	1052
comodo (I)	1053
compact (E, F)	1087
compact disc (E)	581
comparaison (F)	3213
comparison (E)	3213
comparsa (I)	2951
compatto (I)	1087
compétition musicale (F)	2960
compiacente (I)	1231
compiacenza (con) (I)	1230
compiacevole (I)	1231
complaisant (F)	1231
complément (F)	3389
complemento (I)	3389
complesso (I)	2952
complet (F)	2954, 3014
completamente (I)	2953
complete (E)	2954
complete edition (E)	3006
complete works (E)	3087
completely (E)	2953
complètement (F)	2953
completo (I)	2954, 3014
complimentary ticket (E)	2918
comporre (I)	2685
composer (E)	3497
composer (F)	2685
compositeur (F)	3497
composition (E, F)	2955
compositore (I)	3497
compositrice (I)	3497
composizione (I)	2955
compound time (E)	1903
comprendre (F)	2678
compresseur (F)	493
compressing (E)	884
compressor (E)	493
compressore (I)	493
comprimario (I)	2956
compter (F)	2688
comptez (F)	1670
compulsory (E)	1758
compulsory piece (E)	3226
Computer (D)	504
computer (E)	504
computer music (E)	536
Computermusik (D)	536
comune (I)	2957
con (I)	1666
con celerità (I)	734
con due bacchette (I)	377
con fretta (I)	735
con la mano (I)	378
con la voce (I)	1657

con lentezza (I)	736	concerto (E, F, I)	2309, 2958
con molta libertà (I)	737	concerto con quattro	
con moto (I)	738	strumenti solisti (I)	2310
con movimento (I)	738	concerto doppio (I)	2311
con precipitazione (I)	739	concerto for orchestra (E)	2312
con prestezza (I)	741	Concerto grosso (D, E, F, I)	2518
con prontezza (I)	743	concerto per orchestra (I)	2312
con qualche licenza (I)	740	concerto per organo (I)	2313
con rapidità (I)	741	concerto per pianoforte (I)	2314
con rigore (I)	742	concerto per violino (I)	2315
con somma bravura (I)	1056	concerto pour orchestre (F)	2312
con sordina (I)	96, 459	concerto pour orgue (F)	2313
con sordino (I)	96	concerto pour piano (F)	2314
con speditezza (I)	743	concerto pour violon (F)	2315
con tutta la forza (I)	847	concerto privato (I)	2959
con un dito (I)	1667	concerto sacro (I)	2316
con velocità (I)	744	concerto sinfonico (I)	2317
concatenare (I)	2686	concerto triplo (I)	2318
concencieux (F)	1060	concerto vocale (I)	2319
concentrarsi (I)	2687	concis (F)	1669
concentrated (E)	1054	concise (E)	1669
concentrato (I)	1054	conciso (I)	1669
concentré (F)	1054	concitato (I)	942
concert (E, F)	2958, 3304	concitazione (con) (I)	942
concert agency (E)	2878	concludere (I)	2848
concert aria (E)	2253	conclusion (E, F)	1936
concert artist (E)	3498	conclusione (I)	1936
concert dance (E)	2326	concorso musicale (I)	2960
concert de musique sacrée		concours de musique (F)	2960
(F)	2316	concours musical (F)	2960
concert overture (E)	2415	condenser microphone (E)	529
concert piece (E)	2426	condotta delle parti (I)	1937
concert pitch (E)	2980	condotta delle voci (I)	1938
concert privé (F)	2959	conductor (E)	3506
concert season (E)	3354	conduire (F)	2729
concert study (E)	2472	conduite des voix (F)	1938
concert symphonique (F)	2317	condurre (I)	2729
concert vocal (F)	2319	confident (E)	1522
concert-hall (E)	3306	confortante (I)	1055
concertant (F)	1668	confronto (I)	3213
concertante (E, I)	1668	confuso (I)	1102
Concertino (D)	2517	Conga (D)	280
concertino (E, F, I)	2517	conga (E, F, I)	280
concertista (I)	3498	congiungere (I)	2858
concertiste (F)	3498	congiunto (I)	1939
concertmaster (E)	3251	conjoint (F)	1939

conjunct (E)	1939	continua (I)	1671
connaître (F)	2809	continuamente (I)	1672
conoscere (I)	2809	continuare (I)	2689
conscientious (E)	1060	continuation (E)	3328
consecutives (E)	2141	continuellement (F)	1672
conseguente (I)	2099	continuer (F)	2689
consequent (E)	2099	continuez (F)	1671
conséquent (F)	2099	continuità (I)	2964
conservatoire (E, F)	2961	continuité (F)	2964
conservatorio (I)	2961	continuity (E)	2964
conservatory (E)	2961	continuo (I)	1672
considerable (F)	3071	continuo instrument (E)	3380
considerevole (I)	3071	continuous (E)	1672
consolant (F)	1055	contrabass trombone (E)	182
consolante (I)	1055	contrabassoon (E)	127
Consolation (D)	2320	contrabbassista (I)	3499
consolation (E, F)	2320	contrabbasso (I)	14
consolazione (I)	2320	contrabbasso a pizzico (I)	15
console (E, F)	56, 419	contract (E)	3320
consoling (E)	1055	contraddanza (I)	2321
consolle (I)	419	contrafagotto (I)	127
consonance (E, F)	1940	contraint (F)	852
consonant (E)	2962	contraire (F)	2965
consonante (I)	2962	contraltista (I)	603
consonanza (I)	1940	contralto (E, I)	602
consonne (F)	2962	contrappunto (I)	1941
conspiring (E)	1568	contrappunto fiorito (I)	1942
constamment (F)	1798	contrappunto florido (I)	1942
constant (F)	1061	contrario (I)	2965
construction (E, F)	2139	contrary (E)	2965
construction linéaire (F)	1937	contrary motion (E)	2032
contact microphone (E)	530	Contrás (D, E, F, I)	2519
contano (I)	1670	contrast (E)	2966
contare (I)	2688	contraste (F)	2966
conte (F)	3031	contrasto (I)	2966
contemplatif (F)	1057	contrat (F)	3320
contemplative (E)	1057	contrattempo (I)	1944
contemplativo (I)	1057	contratto (I)	3320
contemporaneamente (I)	3336	contre (F)	1673
contemporary music (E)	3124	contre-chant (F)	1945
contento (I)	1422	contre-temps (F)	1944
contents (E)	2963	contrebasse (F)	14
contenu (F)	2963	contrebasse à pistons (F)	187
contenuto (I)	2963	contrebasse à pistons (F)	186
continuously (E)	1642	contrebasse jouée sans archet	
continu (F)	1672	(F)	15

contrebassiste (F)	3499
contrebasson (F)	127
contredanse (F)	2321
contrepoint (F)	1941
contrepoint fleuri (F)	1942
contresujet (F)	1943
contristato (I)	1572
contro (I)	1673
controcanto (I)	1945
contrôle du souffle (F)	693
controsoggetto (I)	1943
controtema (I)	1945
convinzione (con) (I)	1058
convulsé (F)	1059
convulsive (E)	1059
convulso (I)	1059
coperchio (I)	420
coperto (I)	379
copiare (I)	2690
copier (F)	2690
copista (I)	3500
copiste (F)	3500
copri-ancia (I)	202
coprire (I)	389
coprire (I)	2691
copyist (E)	3500
copyright (E)	2992
coquet (F)	1045
coquettish (E)	1045
coquettishly (E)	1046
coquille (F)	68
cor (F)	131
cor anglais (E, F)	136
cor de basset (F)	134
cor de chasse (F)	132
cor de postillion (F)	135
cor de vache (F)	137
cor des Alpes (F)	133
coraggio (con) (I)	975
coraggioso (I)	976
corale (I)	2322
corda (I)	44
corda d'acciaio (I)	47
corda del sol (I)	45
corda di bordone (I)	49
corda di budello (I)	46
corda di metallo (I)	48
corda di risonanza (I)	50
corda melodica (I)	51
corda simpatica (I)	52
corda vuota (I)	97
corde (F)	44
corde à vide (F)	97
corde d'acier (F)	47
corde de boyau (F)	46
corde de résonance (F)	50
corde hors manche (F)	49
corde incrociate (I)	421
corde mélodique (F)	51
corde métallique (F)	48
corde sympathique (F)	52
corde vocali (I)	670
cordes (F)	2891, 3370
cordes croisées (F)	421
cordes vocales (F)	670
cordier (F)	53
cordiera (I)	53
coreografia (I)	2967
coreografo (I)	3501
coreologo (I)	3502
corista (I)	3503
cornamusa (I)	162
cornemuse (F)	162
cornet (E, F)	128
cornet à bouquin (F)	130
cornet à pistons (F)	129
cornet de poste (F)	135
cornett (E)	130
cornetta (I)	128
cornetta a pistoni (I)	129
cornetta di postiglione (I)	135
cornetto (I)	130
cornista (I)	3504
corniste (F)	3504
corno (I)	131
corno da caccia (I)	132
corno da nebbia (I)	281
corno delle Alpi (I)	133
corno di bassetto (I)	134
corno di postiglione (I)	135
corno di toro (I)	137
corno inglese (I)	136

coro (I)	54, 660	counter melody (E)	1945
coro d'opera (I)	664	counter part (E)	1945
coro della radio (I)	661	counter subject (E)	1943
coro di chiesa (I)	662	counter voice (E)	1945
coro di fanciulli (I)	663	counter-hoop (E)	360
coro femminile (I)	665	counterpoint (E)	1941
coro maschile (I)	666	countertenor (E)	603
coro misto (I)	667	country dance (E)	2321
coro parlato (I)	668	coup (F)	374, 1658
corona (I)	1946	coup d'archet (F)	85
corpo di ballo (I)	2968	coup d'œil (F)	3332
corps (F)	233	coup de cloche (F)	375
corps de ballet (F)	2968	coup de glotte (F)	645
corps de musique (F)	2909	coup de langue (F)	239
corps de rechange (F)	219	coup de langue simple (F)	240
corps supérieur (F)	230	coup de tambour (F)	376
correct (E, F)	2969	couper (F)	2845
correggere (I)	2992	coupler (E)	407
correndo (I)	745	couplet (F)	2137
corrente (I)	745, 2323	coupure (F)	582
corretto (I)	2969	courageous (E)	976
correttore di tonalità (I)	494	courageux (F)	976
Corrido (D, E, F, I)	2520	courant (F)	745
corriger (F)	2692	Courante (D)	2323
cortesemente (I)	929	courante (E, F)	2323
corto (I)	1650	courbe inférieure (F)	80
cosa (I)	2970	courbe supérieure (F)	79
coscienzoso (I)	1060	cours collectif (F)	3103
costante (I)	1061	course (E)	54
costantemente (I)	1798	court (F)	1650
costanza (con) (I)	1385	court dance (E)	2264
costly (E)	1167	court music (E)	3137
costruzione (I)	2139	court song (E)	2257
costume (E, F, I)	2971	courteous (E)	929
cosy (E)	1053	courtois (F)	929
cotillon (E, F, I)	2324	coussin (F)	72
cou (F)	3434	coussinet (F)	423
coucou (F)	282	couvercle (F)	420
coude (F)	3447	couvert (F)	379
coulamment (F)	1462	couvrir (F)	568, 2691
coulant (F)	1462	cow horn (E)	137
coulé (F)	1871	cowbell (E)	258
couleur (F)	2948	crackling (E)	1460
coulisse (F)	217, 231	cradle song (E)	2399
coulisses (F)	3270, 3282	craintif (F)	1378
count (E)	1670	craintivement (F)	1556

crânement (F)	1002	crotchet rest (E)	2233
crapaud (F)	403	crotta (I)	16
craving (E)	1011	crowd (E)	16
creare (I)	2693	crudele (I)	672
créatif (F)	2972	cruel (E, F)	672
création (F)	3246	crumhorn (E)	138
creative (E)	2972	crushed note (E)	1870
creativo (I)	2972	crying (E)	1389
creazione (I)	3246	crystalline (E)	1062
crécelle (F)	309, 321	Csárdás (D)	2325
créer (F)	2693	Csardas (F)	2325
crépitant (F)	1460	cuckoo (E)	282
crepitante (I)	1460	cuculo (I)	282
crescendo (I)	885	cuddle (E)	918
crescere (I)	671, 2694	cue (E)	2898
crier (F)	2728	cue note (E)	2045
crini dell'arco (I)	55	Cueca (D, E, F, I)	2521
crins de l'archet (F)	55	cuffia (I)	495
cristallin (F)	1062	Cuica (D)	283
cristallino (I)	1062	cuica (E, F, I)	283
cristiano (I)	1063	cuivrer (F)	245
critica (I)	2973	cuivres (F)	3208
criticare (I)	2695	culasse (F)	221
criticism (E)	2973	cullando (I)	1064
critico musicale (I)	3505	cultivated (E)	2949
critique (F)	2973	cultivé (F)	2949
critique musical (F)	3505	Cumbia (D, E, F, I)	2522
critiquer (F)	2695	cunning (E)	1215
croche (F)	2227	cuore (I)	3435
crochet (F)	1934	cuore (con) (I)	1065
croiser (F)	2734	cup (E)	206, 229
croître (F)	2694	cupo (I)	1066
croma (I)	2227	cura (con) (I)	922
cromatico (I)	1947	curieux (F)	1067
cromatismo (I)	1948	curioso (I)	1067
cromorne (F)	138	curious (E)	1067
cromorno (I)	138	curtain (E)	3339
crook (E)	219	curtain call (E)	3285
cross (E)	2176	curtsey (E)	3080
cross-fingering (E)	242	curva della meccanica (I)	56
cross-stay (E)	232	cuscinetto (I)	206, 422
cross-strung (E)	421	cushion (E)	422
crossing hands (E)	462	custodia (I)	35
Crotales (D)	278	cut (E)	582
crotales (E, F)	278	cuvette (F)	81
crotchet (E)	2226	cycle (E, F)	2942

cycle des quintes (F)	1933
cyclic form (E)	1982
cylindre (F)	216, 418
cylindre à rotation (F)	205
Cymbal (D)	9
cymbal stick (E)	354
cymbale charleston (F)	307
cymbale suspendue (F)	308
cymbales (F)	303
cymbales antiques (F)	277
cymbales chinoises (F)	305
cymbales digitales (F)	278
cymbales sur tiges (F)	304
cymbales turques (F)	306
cymbals (E)	303
cymbalum (F)	9
Czarda(s) (I)	2325
Czardas (E)	2325
D (D, E)	2194
D double flat (E)	2198
D double sharp (E)	2197
D flat (E)	2196
D sharp (E)	2195
d'aplomb (F)	1100
d'effets (F)	578
d'une façon lyrique (F)	1313
da (D)	3004
da (I)	1674
da capo (I)	1675
da capo al fine (I)	1676
da capo al segno (I)	1677
da qui (I)	1682
daccapo (I)	1675
dactyl (E)	1949
dactyle (F)	1949
dahinfließend (D)	1462
dainty (E)	1080
Daktylos (D)	1949
dal principio (I)	1675
dal principio alla fine (I)	1678
dal segno (I)	1679
dal segno al fine (I)	1680
dämonisch (D)	1086
damper (E)	444, 1816
dämpfen (D)	246, 389, 2820
dämpfend (D)	897

Dämpfer (D)	434, 444, 1816
Dämpfer ab (D)	248
Dämpfer abnehmen (D)	1728
Dämpfer auf (D)	246
Dämpfer weg (D)	248
damping pedal (E)	434
dance (E)	2906
dance band (E)	3196
dance des sorcières (F)	2327
dance music (E)	3128
dance of death (E)	2328
dancer (E)	3491
dann (D)	1690
dans la (F)	1749
dans le (F)	1749
dans le caractère d'une marche (F)	947
dans le style ancien (F)	944
dansant (F)	1068
danse (F)	2906
danse allemande (F)	2265
danse champêtre (F)	2331
danse concertante (F)	2326
danse de salon (F)	2907
danse de societé (F)	2907
danse espagnole (F)	2333
danse folklorique (F)	2330
danse gitane (F)	2329
danse hongroise (F)	2334
danse macabre (F)	2328
danse paysanne (F)	2331
danse populaire (F)	2330
danse slave (F)	2332
danser (F)	2666
danseur (F)	3491
danseuse (F)	3491
danza (I)	2906
danza concertante (I)	2326
danza dei morti (I)	2328
danza delle streghe (I)	2327
danza folcloristica (I)	2330
danza gitana (I)	2329
danza macabra (I)	2328
danza popolare (I)	2330
danza rustica (I)	2331
danza slava (I)	2332

danza spagnola (I)	2333
danza tedesca (I)	2265
danza ungherese (I)	2334
danzante (I)	1068
Danzón (D, E, F, I)	2523
dappertutto (I)	1681
Darbietung (D)	3273
dare dei concerti (I)	2696
daring (E)	988
dark (E)	1544
Darmsaite (D)	46
Darstellung (D)	3039
darting (E)	1456
das meiste (D)	1711
dasselbe (D)	1735
dasselbe Zeitmaß (D)	756
dattilo (I)	1949
Dauer (D)	3001
Daumen (D)	3469
Daumenring (D)	195
Daumenuntersatz (D)	465
davantage (F)	1770
davanti (I)	1683
davor (D)	1683
de bonne volonté (F)	1605
de façon (F)	1720
de façon burlesque (F)	1020
de façon saillante (F)	1519
de forme ouverte (F)	1860
de la même façon (F)	1750
de manière (F)	1720
de moins en moins (F)	1775
de plus en plus (F)	1776
de plus en plus animé (F)	805
de toutes ses forces (F)	847, 1837
de/à la pointe (F)	83
deaf (E)	3343
deafening (E)	2897
debile (I)	1069
debole (I)	1069
debolezza (con) (I)	1070
debolmente (I)	1071
débonnairement (F)	1396
Debüt (D)	2974
début (E, F)	2974, 3086
débutant (F)	3019

débutante (F)	3019
débuter (F)	2711
debütieren (D)	2711
debutto (I)	2974
deceptive cadence (Am.)	1911
déchaîné (F)	1455
déchiffrer (F)	2843
déchirant (F)	1533
déchiré (F)	1299
decibel (E, I)	496
décibel (F)	496
décidé (F)	1073
decided (E)	1073
decima (I)	2247
decimino (I)	2335
decisione (con) (I)	1072
decisively (E)	1072
deciso (I)	1073
Decke (D)	77
Deckel (D)	206, 420
decken (D)	568
declaimed (E)	1075
declaiming (E)	1074
declamando (I)	1074
declamare (I)	2697
declamation (E)	673
déclamation (F)	673
declamato (I)	1075
declamazione (I)	673
déclamé (F)	1075
déclamer (F)	2697
décontracté (F)	1438
décor (F)	3315
decorating (E)	1185
découvert (F)	384
decreasing (E)	900
decreasing to nothing (E)	905
decrescendo (I)	900
décrire (F)	2699
dédaigneux (F)	1464
dedica (I)	2975
dédicace (F)	2975
dedicare (I)	2698
dedication (E)	2975
dédier (F)	2698
deep (E)	1406

deep voice (E)	708
défaut (F)	2982
deferente (I)	1444
defiant (E)	1490
deficiendo (I)	908
dégagé (F)	1310, 1522
Degen (D)	3347
degno (I)	1076
degré (F)	1992
degree (E)	1992
déguisement (F)	3410
dehnend (D)	835
dehors (F)	3052
déjà (F)	1705
Deklamation (D)	673
deklamieren (D)	2697
deklamierend (D)	1074
deklamiert (D)	1075
delayed (E)	830
delayed cadence (E)	1916
delaying (E)	820
deliberatamente (I)	1077
deliberately (E)	1077
délibérément (F)	1077
délicat (F)	1080
delicatamente (I)	1078
delicate (E)	1080
delicately (E)	1078
délicatement (F)	1078
delicatezza (con) (I)	1079
delicato (I)	1080
délicieusement (F)	1085
délié (F)	1459
delighted (E)	1422
delightfully (E)	1085
delirando (I)	1081
délirant (F)	1082
delirante (I)	1082
delirio (con) (I)	1083
delirious (E)	1082
deliroso (I)	1082
delizia (con) (I)	1084
deliziosamente (I)	1085
delusive cadence (E)	1911
demander (F)	2682
demi (F)	1738
demi force (F)	1739
demi-cadence (F)	1913
demi-pause (F)	2232
demi-soupir (F)	2234
demi-ton (F)	2117
demie (F)	1738
demisemiquaver (E)	2229
demisemiquaver rest (E)	2236
demo tape (E)	557
Demo-Aufnahme (D)	557
Demo-Band (D)	557
demoniaco (I)	1086
démoniaque (F)	1086
demonic (E)	1086
demütig (D)	1576
den Text respektieren (D)	1791
den Ton ausspinnen (D)	607
denken (D)	2761
denkend (D)	1382
dennoch (D)	1768
dense (E, F)	1087
denso (I)	1087
dent de scie (F)	497
dente di sega (I)	497
denti (I)	3436
dents (F)	3436
déplacement (F)	1819
déployé (F)	1520
dépouillé (F)	1468
depuis (F)	1674
depuis ici (F)	1682
der Vorhang fällt (D)	3064
der Vorhang hebt sich (D)	3065
der Vorhang öffnet sich (D)	3066
der Vorhang schließt sich (D)	3067
derb (D)	1246
deridendo (I)	1031
derisone (con) (I)	1006
dernier (F)	1843
dernier mouvement (F)	2180
dernière (F)	1843
dernière fois (F)	1842
dérobé (F)	768
derrière (F)	1684, 3476
derrière les coulisses (F)	2981
derselbe (D)	1735

Des (D)	2196
désaccordé (F)	3361
descant recorder (E)	147
descendant (F)	1957
descending (E)	1957
descriptif (F)	1088
descriptive (E)	1088
descriptive music (E)	3136
descrittivo (I)	1088
descrivere (I)	2699
Deses (D)	2198
désespéré (F)	1104
désespérément (F)	1103
desiderio (con) (I)	1089
désinvolte (F)	1100
desio (con) (I)	1603
désireux (F)	1011
desk (E)	3098
desolate (E)	1090
desolato (I)	1090
désolé (F)	1090
désordonné (F)	1102
desperate (E)	1104
desperately (E)	1103
dessous (F)	1817
dessus (F)	1814
destin (F)	677
destino (I)	677
destiny (E)	677
desto (I)	1091
destra (a) (I)	2976
destrezza (con) (I)	1092
détaché (F)	111, 877, 1548
detached (E)	111, 877
detached staccato (bowing) (E)	112
détacher (F)	2831
detail (E)	
Detail (D)	3331
détail (F)	3331
détendu (F)	1438
determinato (I)	1093
determinazione (con) (I)	1094
déterminé (F)	1093
determined (E)	1093
detonieren (D)	692, 2833
détonner (F)	692, 2833
dettaglio (I)	3331
dettato (I)	1950
dettato musicale (I)	1951
deutlich (D)	1108
deutlich ausgesprochen (D)	1407
deutlich aussprechen (D)	2661
deutlich getrennt (D)	112
Deutscher Tanz (D)	2265
Deutung (D)	3088
deux cordes (F)	461
deux fois (F)	1617
deuxième mouvement (F)	2113
devant (F)	1683
development (E)	2148
développement (F)	2148
dévot (F)	1095
devoto (I)	1095
devout (E)	1095
Dezett (D)	2335
Dezibel (D)	496
Dezime (D)	2247
di colpo (I)	1685
di molto (I)	1744
di nuovo (I)	1686
di più (I)	1770
di sopra (I)	1661
diabolical (E)	1273
diabolico (I)	1273
diabolique (F)	1273
diafano (I)	1567
diaframma (I)	498, 3437
Dialog (D)	2977
dialogo (I)	2977
dialogue (E, F)	2977
diapason (I)	2978
diapason à bouche (F)	2979
diapason à branches (F)	2978
diapason à fiato (I)	2979
diapason da camera (I)	2980
diapason de chambre (F)	2980
diaphragm (E)	3437
diaphragme (F)	498, 3437
diatonic (E)	1952
diatonicism (E)	1953
diatonico (I)	1952

Diatonik (D)	1953	dilettante (E, F, I)	2986
diatonique (F)	1952	diletto (con) (I)	1084
diatonisch (D)	1952	diligenza (con) (I)	1097
diatonisme (F)	1953	diluendo (I)	901
diatonismo (I)	1953	dilungando (I)	814
dicendo (I)	1372	dimenticare (I)	2700
dicht (D)	1087	diminished (E)	1955
dichterisch (D)	1397	diminishing (E)	902
dictation (E)	1950	diminué (F)	1955
dictée (F)	1950	diminuendo (I)	902
dictée musicale (F)	1951	diminuer (F)	2701
diction (E, F)	675	diminuire (I)	2701
die ganze (D)	1836	diminuito (I)	1955
die ganze Kraft (D)	1837	diminution (E, F)	1956
die Stimme heben (D)	612	diminuzione (I)	1956
die Übrigen (D)	1707	dinamica (I)	2987
dièse (F)	1954	dinamico (I)	1098
dieselbe (D)	1735	Ding (D)	2970
dieselben (D)	1708	dire (F, I)	2758
diesis (I)	1954	direction (F)	2989
dietro (I)	1684	director (E)	3519
dietro le quinte (I)	2981	Direktion (D)	2989
Diferencia (D, E, F, I)	2524	direttore d'orchestra (I)	3506
difetto (I)	2982	direttore del coro (I)	674
difference (E)	2983	direttore ospite (I)	2988
différence (F)	2983	direzione (I)	2989
different (E)	1688	dirge (E)	2290
différent (F)	1688	Dirigent (D)	3506
differenza (I)	2983	Dirigentenstab (D)	2905
difficile (F, I)	2984	Dirigentin (D)	3506
difficoltà (I)	2985	diriger (F)	2702
difficult (E)	2984	dirigere (I)	2702
difficulté (F)	2985	dirigieren (D)	2702
difficulty (E)	2985	Dirigierpartitur (D)	3217
diffusion radiophonique (F)	588	diritti d'autore (I)	2990
diffusion télévisée (F)	589	diritti d'esecuzione (I)	2991
digital (D, E)	499	diritto (I)	1687
digital techniques (E)	583	diritto d'autore (I)	2992
digitale (I)	499	Dis (D)	2195
Digitaltechnik (D)	583	discendente (I)	1957
digne (F)	1076	disco (I)	500
dignified (E)	1076	disconsolate (E)	1090
dignità (con) (I)	1096	discoteca (I)	2993
Diktat (D)	1950	discotheque (E)	2993
Diktion (D)	675	discothèque (F)	2993
Dilettant (D)	2986	discreet (E)	2994

discret (F)   2994
discreto (I)   2994
discrezione (con) (I)   1099
disdainful (E)   1464
disdegnoso (I)   1464
disguise (E)   3410
disgusto (con) (I)   1428
disinvolto (I)   1100, 1522
disinvoltura (con) (I)   1101
Disis (D)   2197
Diskothek (D)   2993
diskret (D)   2994
disordinato (I)   1102
disparaître (F)   2827
dispassionate (E)   1514
disperatamente (I)   1103
disperato (I)   1104
disperazione (con) (I)   1105
disperdere (I)   98
Disposition (D)   460
disposition (F)   460
disposition de l'orchestre (F) 2995
disposizione (I)   460
disposizione dell'orchestra
    (I)   2995
disprezzo (con) (I)   1106
disque (F)   500
disque compact (F)   581
disquieting (E)   1280
dissonance (E, F)   1958
Dissonanz (D)   1958
dissonanza (I)   1958
distacco (con) (I)   1548
distance (E, F)   2996
distant (E, F)   1107
distante (I)   1107
Distanz (D)   2996
distanza (I)   2996
distendersi (I)   2793
disteso (I)   1530
distinct (E, F)   1108
distinctement (F)   1108
distinctly (E)   1041, 1108
distintamente (I)   1108
distinto (I)   1108
distorsion (F)   501

distorsione (I)   501
distortion (E)   501
distracted (E)   1575
distressed (E)   982
distribution (F)   2997, 3205
distribuzione (I)   2997
disturbed (E)   1575
diteggiatura (I)   2998
ditirambo (I)   2272
dito (I)   3438
divagando (I)   1109
diverso (I)   1688
divertente (I)   2999
Divertimento (D)   2336
divertimento (E, I)   2336
divertimento (con) (I)   1110
divertissant (F)   2999
divertissement (F)   1884, 2336
divided (E)   1689
dividere (I)   2703
divisé (F)   1689
diviser (F)   2703
divisi (I)   1689
diviso (I)   1689
divoto (I)   1095
dixième (F)   2247
dixtuor (F)   2335
dizione (I)   675
Do (F, I)   2189
Do bémol (F)   2191
Do bemolle (I)   2191
Do dièse (F)   2190
Do diesis (I)   2190
do doppio bemolle (I)   2193
do doppio diesis (I)   2192
do double bémol (F)   2193
do double dièse (F)   2192
Docke (D)   440
dodecafonia (I)   1959
dodecaphonic music (E)   3143
dodécaphonie (F)   3143
dodécaphonisme (F)   1959
Dodekaphonie (D)   3143
doglia (con) (I)   1111
doglioso (I)   1117
doigt (F)   3438

doigté (F)	2998
doigté fourché (F)	242
Doina (D, E, F, I)	2525
dolce (I)	1112
dolcemente (I)	1113
dolcezza (con) (I)	1114
dolcissimo (I)	1115
dolendo (I)	1116
dolente (I)	1117
dolore (con) (I)	1118
doloroso (I)	1119
domestic music (E)	3147
dominant (E)	1960
dominant seventh (E)	2123
dominant seventh chord (E)	1876
Dominante (D)	1960
dominante (F, I)	1876, 1960
dominante de passage (F)	1961
dominante di passaggio (I)	1961
dominante secondaria (I)	1961
Dominantseptakkord (D)	1876
Dominantseptime (D)	2123
dondolando (I)	1120
done neatly (E)	1641
Donner (D)	3412
donner des concerts (F)	2696
Donnermaschine (D)	295
donnernd (D)	1558
dopo (I)	1690
Doppel-B (D)	1963
Doppelgriff (D)	99, 1649
Doppelkegeldämpfer (D)	223
Doppelkonzert (D)	2311
Doppelkreuz (D)	1964
Doppelloch (D)	221
Doppelpedalharfe (D)	3
Doppelpunkt (D)	2085
Doppelrohrblatt (D)	193
Doppelschlag (D)	1993
Doppelstrich (D)	1962
doppelt (D)	1691
doppelt so schnell (D)	793
doppelte Auslösung (D)	423
Doppelvorschlag (D)	1888
Doppelzunge (D)	193, 241
doppia corda (I)	99
doppia stanghetta (I)	1962
doppio (I)	1691
doppio bemolle (I)	1963
doppio colpo di lingua (I)	241
doppio diesis (I)	1964
doppio movimento (I)	793
doppio scappamento (I)	423
dorian (E)	1965
Dorian bells (E)	259
dorico (I)	1965
dorien (F)	1965
dorisch (D)	1965
dorische Glocken (D)	259
dorso (I)	3475
dorso della mano (I)	3439
dos (F)	3475
dos de la main (F)	3439
dot (E)	2084
dotted (E)	2083
dotted note (E)	2043
Double (D, E, F, I)	2526
double (E, F)	1691
doublé (F)	1993
double action harp (E)	3
double appoggiatura (E)	1888
double articulation (F)	241
double bar (E)	1962
double barre (F)	1962
double bass (E)	14
double bass clarinet (E)	125
double bass player (E)	3499
double bassoon (E)	127
double bémol (F)	1963
double cadence (F)	1993
double concerto (E, F)	2311
double corde (F)	99
double croche (F)	2228
double dièse (F)	1964
double dot (E)	2085
double échappement (F)	423
double flat (E)	1963
double joint (E)	221
double manual (E)	455
double mute (E)	223
double point (F)	2085
double reed (E)	193

double sharp (E)	1964
double stop (E)	99
double the speed (E)	793
double tonguing (E)	241
double-bass saxhorn (E)	187
double-bass trombone (E)	182
doublehopper (E)	423
doubler (F)	2780
doubling (E)	2090
douçaine (F)	139
doucement (F)	864, 1113
douloureusement (F)	1117, 1321
douloureux (F)	1119
douteux (F)	3079
doux (F)	965, 1112
down-bow (E)	86
downbeat (E)	1998
draft (E)	3318
dragged (E)	840
dragging (E)	836
Draht (D)	3041
Drama (D)	3000
drama (E)	3000
dramatic (E)	1121
dramatic music (E)	3144
dramatic soprano (E)	628
dramatique (F)	1121
dramatisch (D)	1121
dramatische Musik (D)	3144
dramatischer Sopran (D)	628
drame (F)	3000
drame liturgique (F)	2392
drame lyrique (F)	2337
drame musical (F)	2338
dramma (I)	3000
dramma lirico (I)	2337
dramma musicale (I)	2338
drammatico (I)	1121
drängend (D)	749, 794, 884
draußen (D)	3052
draw-stops (E)	411
drawing (E)	838
drawing together (E)	810
drawing together again (E)	804
drawn together (E)	809
dreadful (E)	1550

dream (E)	2464
dreaming (E)	1507
Drehleier (D)	17
Drehorgel (D)	478
Drehventil (D)	205
drei Saiten (D)	473
Dreieck (besser: Dreieck-schwingung) (D)	592
dreifach (D)	1833
Dreiklang (D)	1877, 2177
dreist (D)	1494
dreistimmig (D)	1863
dreiteilig (D)	2158
dreiteilige Form (D)	1983
dress (E)	2971
dringend (D)	811
drinking song (E)	2272
dritter Satz (D)	2161
drohend (D)	1336
dröhnen (D)	2795
dröhnend (D)	1439, 1558
droit (F)	1687
droit d'auteur (F)	2992
droite (á) (F)	2976
droits d'auteur (F)	2990
droits d'execution (F)	2991
drôle (F)	1049
drone string (E)	49
drum (E)	267, 327
drum major's baton (E)	363
drum roll (E)	382, 383
drum stick (E)	348
drumbeat (E)	376
drumhead (E)	357, 365
drummer (E)	3492
drums (E)	253
dry (E)	1465
du bout des lèvres (F)	1618
du début (F)	1611, 1675
du début à la fin (F)	1676, 1678
du début au signe (F)	1677
du signe (F)	1679
du signe à la fin (F)	1680
du tout (F)	1752
Dudelsack (D)	162
due corde (I)	461

due volte (I)	1617
duet (E)	2339
Duett (D)	2339
duetto (I)	2339
duftig (D)	1307
duina (I)	1966
dulcian (E)	139
dulciana (I)	139
dulcimer (E)	24
dull (E)	1361
Dulzian (D)	139
dumb (E)	3180
Dumka (D, E, F, I)	2527
dumpf (D)	1066
dunkel (D)	1544
dunkle Stimme (D)	708
dunstig (D)	1584
Duo (D, E, F, I)	2339, 2528
duo (F, I)	2339
Duole (D)	1966
duolet (F)	1966
duolo (con) (I)	1118
duple time (E)	2154
duplet (E)	1966
Dur (D)	2008
dur (F)	1123
durant (F)	1692
durante (I)	1692
durata (I)	3001
durata del suono (I)	1967
duration (E)	3001
durch (D)	1764
durchaus (D)	1642
durchdringend (D)	1380, 1527
Durchfall (D)	3036
Durchführung (D)	2148
Durchgang (D)	2059, 2173
Durchgangsakkord (D)	1875
Durchgangsnote (D)	2041
Durchgangston (D)	2041
durchgehend (D)	1672, 1803
durchkomponiert (D)	1860
durchlaufend bewegt (D)	2396
durchsichtig (D)	1567
durchweg (D)	1678
durée (F)	3001

durée du son (F)	1967
durezza (con) (I)	1122
dürftig (D)	1576
during (E)	1692
duro (I)	1123
dusky (E)	1066
düster (D)	1066
Dux (D)	1885, 2127
dwindling (E)	896
dying away (E)	824
dying out (E)	832
dynamic (E)	1098
dynamic mark (E)	2115
dynamic sign (E)	2115
dynamics (E)	2987
Dynamik (D)	2987
dynamique (F)	1098, 2987
dynamisch (D)	1098
dynamisches Zeichen (D)	2115
E (D, E)	2199
E double flat (E)	2203
E double sharp (E)	2202
E flat (E)	2201
E sharp (E)	2200
E-Gitarre (D)	45
E-Musik (D)	3122, 3167
each (E)	1759
ear (E)	3462
ear-deafening (E)	1644
easily (E)	1159
easy (E)	3028
ébauche (F)	3318
ebbrezza (con) (I)	1124
éblouissant (F)	1492
eccedente (I)	1896
eccellente (I)	3002
eccentric (E)	1009
eccentrico (I)	1009
eccessivamente (I)	1693
eccetera (I)	3003
eccetto (I)	1694
eccezionale (I)	3364
eccezione (I)	1695
eccitante (I)	1125
eccitato (I)	1125
ecco (I)	3004

échange (F)	3311
échappement (F)	441
échec (F)	3036
echeggiante (I)	1443
Echo (D)	502, 3291
echo (E)	502
écho (F)	502
echo effect (E)	3291
echt (D)	1413
éclairage (F)	3068
éclatant (F)	1195, 1460
éclisse (F)	58
eclogue (E)	2340
eco (I)	502
école (F)	3321
école de ballet (F)	3322
école de danse classique (F)	3322
école de musique (F)	3324
école supérieure de musique (F)	2866
école viennoise (F)	3325
Ecossaise (schottischer Tanz) (D)	2457
écossaise (F)	2457
écoute (F)	2896
écouter (F)	2662
écrire (F)	2811
écrire de la musique (F)	2812
ecstatic (E)	1152
edel (D)	1353
edge (E)	366
edition (E)	3005
édition (F)	3005
édition complète (F)	3006
edizione (I)	3005
edizione completa (I)	3006
éducation de l'oreille (F)	3007
éducation de la voix (F)	604
educazione dell'orecchio (I)	3007
educazione della voce (I)	604
effacer (F)	489
effe (I)	57
effect (E)	3008
effective (E)	3009
effects d'animaux (F)	2889
Effekt (D)	3008
Effektgerät (D)	578
effet (F)	3008
effet d'écho (F)	3291
effet sonore (F)	503
effetto (I)	3008
effetto sonoro (I)	503
efficace (F, I)	3009
effilé (F)	1147
effleurer (F)	2817
effortless (E)	1478
effrayant (F)	1570
effréné (F)	1493
effronté (F)	1486
égal (F)	1841
égalisateur (F)	510
égalité (F)	3010
église (F)	2940
egloga (I)	2340
églogue (F)	2340
eguaglianza (I)	3010
eguale (I)	1841
eher (D)	1772
ehrerbietig (D)	1444
ehrfurchtsvoll (D)	1445
eifrig (D)	1609
eigensinnig (D)	1032, 1367
Eigenton (D)	2144
eighth note (Am.)	2227
eighth note rest (Am.)	2234
eilend (D)	787
eilig (D)	725, 735
eiliger (D)	796
ein anderes Mal (D)	1844
ein bißchen (D)	1826
ein klein wenig (D)	1848
ein wenig (D)	1849
ein wenig frei (D)	768
ein wenig mehr (D)	1850
einatmen (D)	2740
einbezogen (D)	1656
Eindruck (D)	3008
eindrucksvoll (D)	1259
eine Saite (D)	474
einer Eingebung folgend (D)	1153
einfach (D)	1468
einfacher Takt (D)	1904

einfacher Zungenstoß (D)   240
Einfall (D)   3096
einfältig (D)   1028, 1278
einführen (D)   2742
Eingang (D)   509, 3011
Eingebung (D)   3093
einheitlich (D)   1579
einige (D)   1787
Einklang (D)   3092
Einlage (D)   59
einleiten (D)   2742
Einleitung (D)   2368, 3240
einmal (D)   1845
einmanualig (D)   458
Einsatz (D)   1969, 2898
einschmeichelnd (D)   1284
einschneidend (D)   1264
einsetzen (D)   2733
einspringen (D)   2808
einstimmen (D)   2643
Einstimmigkeit (D)   2026
eintönig (D)   1342
eintreten (D)   2706
Eintritt (D)   3011
Eintrittskarte (D)   2917
einzig (D)   1846
Eis (D)   2200
eisig (D)   1227
Eisis (D)   2202
Ekloge (D)   2340
ekstatisch (D)   1152
elaborare (I)   2704
elaboratore (I)   504
elaboratore musicale (I)   505
élaborer (F)   2704
élargi (F)   1630
élargir (F)   2647
elbow (E)   3447
electric guitar (E)   490
électro-acoustique (F)   506
electroacoustics (E)   506
electrodynamic microphone
    (E)   531
electromagnetic microphone
    (E)   532
electronic drums (E)   486

electronic keyboards (E)   577
electronic music (E)   3145
electronic organ (E)   539
électronique musicale (F)   508
electrophone (E)   507
électrophone (F)   507
electrophonic instrument (E)   507
élégamment (F)   1126
elegantemente (I)   1126
elegantly (E)   1126
eleganza (con) (I)   1127
elegia (I)   2341
elegiac (E)   1128
elegiaco (I)   1128
élégiaque (F)   1128
Elegie (D)   2341
élégie (F)   2341
elegisch (D)   1128
elegy (E)   2341
Elektroakustik (D)   506
elektrodynamisches
    Mikrophon (D)   531
Elektrogitarre (D)   490
elektromagnetisches
    Mikrophon (D)   532
elektronische Musik (D)   3145
elektronische Orgel (D)   539
elektronische Tasteninstrumente
    (D)   577
elektronisches Schlagzeug
    (D)   486
Elektrophon (D)   507
elettroacustica (I)   506
elettrofono (I)   507
elettronica (I)   577
elettronica musicale (I)   508
elevamento (con) (I)   1129
elevated (E)   1129
elevatezza (con) (I)   1129
elevato (I)   1129
élevé (F)   1129
élève (F)   2879
elf (E)   3045
elicon (I)   140
Ellbogen (D)   3447
elogiare (I)   2705

éloigné (F)	1107	en arrière (F)	1684, 3281
else (E)	1763	en articulant (F)	844
elusive (E)	1261	en attenuant (F)	897
embellir (F)	2638	en aucun cas (F)	1721
embellished (E)	1865	en augmentant (F)	883
embellishing (E)	1185	en avançant (F)	790
embellishment (E)	1864, 1978	en avant (F)	790
embittered (E)	961	en badinant (F)	1458
Embouchure (D)	244	en balançant (F)	1120
embouchure (E, F)	199, 208, 244	en balbutiant (F)	1001
embrasé (F)	1275	en bas (F)	1717
émission (F)	100, 3409	en berçant (F)	1064
émission originale (F)	591	en cajolant (F)	1590
emissione (I)	100	en calmant (F)	815
émouvant (F)	1051	en caressant (F)	918
émouvoir (F)	2684	en cédant (F)	899
emozione (con) (I)	1130	en chancelant (F)	1004
empfindlich (D)	1472	en changeant (F)	1652
empfindungslos (D)	1282	en chantant (F)	1030
emphasized (E)	870	en chevrottant (F)	696
emphatic (E)	1134	en cinglant (F)	872
emphatique (F)	1134	en circulant (F)	733
emphatisch (D)	1134	en colère (F)	924, 1293
emporté (F)	1256	en commençant (F)	1665
emporté (F)	1585	en comprimant (F)	884
empressé (F)	772	en conspirant (F)	1568
empty (E)	1858	en contraignant (F)	851
empty string (E)	97	en coquettant (F)	1045
ému (F)	1050	en courant (F)	745
en abaissant (F)	891	en criant (F)	1580
en accélerant (F)	785	en croissant (F)	885
en accompagnant (F)	1614	en déclamant (F)	1074
en accroissant (F)	880	en décroissant (F)	900
en adoucissant (F)	893, 907	en défaillant (F)	822
en affaiblissant (F)	894	en dehors (F)	1716
en agrandissant (F)	882	en délirant (F)	1081
en allant (F)	729, 788	en déployant (F)	889
en allongeant (F)	814	en dérobant (F)	768
en alternant (F)	1631	en descendant (F)	898
en amenuisant (F)	896	en diluant (F)	901
en amoindrissant (F)	908	en diminuant (F)	902
en amortissant (F)	909	en disant (F)	1372
en animant (F)	789	en divaguant (F)	1109
en apaisant (F)	906	en doublant le mouvement (F)	793
en appelant (F)	1040	en élargissant (F)	812, 821
en appuyant (F)	842	en élevant (F)	881

en estompant (F)	1495
en éteignant (F)	910
en évidence (F)	1716
en expirant (F)	832
en exultant (F)	1155
en faisant descendre (F)	898
en filant (F)	1182
en fleurissant (F)	1185
en folâtrant (F)	1191
en forçant (F)	873
en freinant (F)	819
en frôlant (F)	114
en froufroutant (F)	1208
en gazouillant (F)	1345
en gémissant (F)	1301
en général (F)	3054
en glissant (F)	853
en haut (F)	1726
en hésitant (F)	746
en hurlant (F)	1580
en imitant (F)	1713
en improvisant (F)	1260
en insultant (F)	1291
en invoquant (F)	1040, 1405
en jubilant (F)	1156
en marchant (F)	792
en marquant (F)	856
en martelant (F)	858
en méditant (F)	1331
en même temps (F)	1847, 3336
en mesure (F)	720
en modérant (F)	823, 912
en mourant (F)	824
en murmurant (F)	1345
en narrant (F)	1346
en ondoyant (F)	1360
en ornant (F)	926
en ôtant (F)	913
en parlant (F)	1372
en peinant (F)	833
en plaisantant (F)	1458
en plein air (F)	3052
en pleurs (F)	1389
en portant (F)	867
en poussant (F)	808
en précipitant (F)	798

en pressant (F)	787, 799
en priant (F)	1405
en procédant (F)	788
en prolongeant (F)	825
en psalmodiant (F)	1452
en racontant (F)	1419
en ralentissant (F)	826
en ranimant (F)	802
en ranimant (F)	791
en ravivant (F)	800
en réchauffant (F)	803
en récit (F)	1425
en récitant (F)	1425
en réfléchissant (F)	1382
en relâchant (F)	813, 828
en relief (F)	1723
en remettant (F)	767
en renforçant (F)	886
en reprenant (F)	767
en respirant (F)	1427
en resserrant (F)	804
en retardant (F)	829
en retenant (F)	839
en rêvant (F)	1507
en réveillant (F)	890
en réveillant (F)	888
en revenant (F)	1792
en revenant au mouvement (F)	779
en riant (F)	682
en s'abandonnant (F)	915
en s'apaisant (F)	892
en s'attardant (F)	820
en s'effaçant (F)	837
en s'éloignant (F)	895
en s'estompant (F)	837
en s'étandant (F)	817
en s'éteignant (F)	903
en s'étendant (F)	835
en s'évaporant (F)	904
en s'exténuant (F)	818
en sanglotant (F)	686
en sautillant (F)	1453
en se calmant (F)	816
en se hâtant (F)	807
en se perdant (F)	905

en se souvenant (F)	1432
en serrant (F)	810
en sifflotant (F)	717
en souffrant (F)	1116
en soupirant (F)	1513
en sourdine (F)	459
en souriant (F)	687
en style récitatif (F)	1287
en suppliant (F)	1540
en survolant (F)	1512
en talonnant (F)	794
en tenant (F)	1829
en tintinnabulant (F)	1557
en tiraillant (F)	834
en tirant (F)	838
en titubant (F)	1296
en tonnant (F)	1558
en traînant (F)	836
en tremblottant (F)	696
en vacillant (F)	1004
en valeur (F)	1723
en vibrant (F)	1591
en volant (F)	1604
enarmonico (I)	1968
enchaîner (F)	1646, 2686
enchanted (E)	1262
enchanteur (F)	1263
enclume (F)	291
encore (E, F)	1636, 2919
encore une fois (F)	1637
encore! (F)	2919
end (E)	1701
enden (D)	2721
endpin (E)	37
endroit (F)	1731
energetic (E)	1132
energia (con) (I)	1131
energico (I)	1132
énergique (F)	1132
energisch (D)	1132
enfant prodige (F)	2908
enfantin (F)	1272
enfasi (con) (I)	1133
enfatico (I)	1134
enflammé (F)	1274
enflé (F)	969
eng (D)	809
engagé (F)	1656
Engagement (D)	3320
engagement (E, F)	3320
enge Lage (D)	2075
engelhaft (D)	971, 1479
enger werdend (D)	804
Engführung (D)	2136
Englische Suite (D)	2476
Englischhorn (D)	136
English dance (E)	2362
english horn (Am.)	136
English suite (E)	2476
engraver (E)	3509
enharmonic (E)	1968
enharmonic change (E)	2130
enharmonique (F)	1968
enharmonisch (D)	1968
enharmonische Verwechslung (D)	2130
enigmatico (I)	1135, 1497
énigmatique (F)	1135
enjoué (F)	1234
enlevé (F)	1014
enlever (F)	2850
enlever la pédale gauche (F)	472
enlever la sourdine (F)	248, 1728
enlivening (E)	791
ennuyeux (F)	3184
énormément (F)	1696, 1743
enormemente (I)	1696
enormously (E)	1696
enough (E)	1610
enragé (F)	991
enraged (E)	1276
enregistrement (F)	554
enregistrement à pistes multiples (F)	555
enregistrement de démonstration (F)	557
enregistrement du son (F)	574
enregistrement original (F)	556
enregistrement radiophonique (F)	558
enregistrement télévisé (F)	559
enregistrer (F)	2784

enroué (F)	622	envolé (F)	1501
enseigner (F)	2736	éolien (F)	1970
Ensemble (D)	2952	eolifono (I)	284
ensemble (E, F)	1725, 2952, 3205	eolio (I)	1970
ensuite (F)	1690	épaule (F)	3477
entendre (F)	2857	épée (E, F)	3347
entente (E, F)	3092	epic (E)	1137
entertainment music (E)	3149	epico (I)	1137
entêté (F)	1032	épiglotte (F)	191
entfaltend (D)	889	Epilog (D)	2342
entfaltet (D)	1520	epilogo (I)	2342
entfernend (D)	895	epilogue (E)	2342
entfernt (D)	855, 1107	épilogue (F)	2342
entfesselt (D)	1455	épinette (F)	405
enthaltsam (D)	1506	épique (F)	1137
entièrement (F)	2953	episch (D)	1137
entonner (F)	2741	Episode (D)	1971
entr'acte (F)	2365	episode (E)	1971
entracte (F)	3091	épisode (F)	1971
entraînant (F)	1015	episodio (I)	1971
entrance (E)	3011	epoca (I)	3013
entrare (I)	2706	epoch (E)	3013
entrare in scena (I)	2707	Epoche (D)	3013
entrata (I) 509, 1969, 2367, 3011		époque (F)	3013
entrata degli artisti (I)	3012	épouvantable (F)	1550
entrée (F)		épuisé (F)	3014
509, 1969, 2367, 2898, 3011		equabilmente (I)	1697
entrée des artistes (F)	3012	equable (E)	1579
entrée douce (F)	644	equal (E)	1841
entrer (F)	2706	equal temperament (E)	2151
entrer en scène (F)	2707	equality (E)	3010
entrüstet (D)	1267	equalizer (E)	510
entry (E)	1969	equalizzatore (I)	510
entschieden (D)	1073, 1170	equilibrato (I)	1008
entschlossen (D)	1073	équilibré (F)	1008
Entschuldigung (D)	3326	équitablement (F)	1697
entschwindend (D)	822, 837	equitably (E)	1697
entsetzlich (D)	1364, 1550	equivocarsi (I)	2810
entspannen (D)	2793	era (E)	3013
entspannt (D)	1438	éraillé (F)	622
entusiasmo (con) (I)	1136	Erbarmen (D)	681
Entwicklung (D)	2148	erbittert (D)	961
Entwurf (D)	3318	erfinderisch (D)	1277
Entzerrer (D)	510	erflehend (D)	1258
entzündet (D)	1274	Erfolg (D)	3384
environ (F)	1654	Erfolgsschlager (D)	2928

erfreulich (D)	1388	erweiternd (D)	882
erfreut (D)	1422	erwünscht (D)	1089
Ergänzung (D)	3389	erzählen (D)	2778
ergeben (D)	1394	erzählend (D)	1346, 1419
ergreifend (D)	1533	Erzlaute (D)	1
erhaben (D)	1129, 1538	erzürnt (D)	924
erhebend (D)	881	Es (D)	2201
erhöhen (D)	2652	es folgt (D)	1796
Erhöhungszeichen (D)	1954	esacordo (I)	1972
erklären (D)	2829	esagerare (I)	2708
erklingen (D)	2862	esagerato (I)	1140
erloschen (D)	911	esaltante (I)	1141
erlöscht (D)	848, 911	esaltato (I)	1142
ermattet (D)	1305	esaltazione (con) (I)	1143
ermüdet (D)	1305	esasperato (I)	1144
erneut spielen (D)	2802	esattezza (con) (I)	1145
erniedrigen (D)	2636	esatto (I)	1146
Erniedrigungszeichen (D)	1905	esaurito (I)	3014
ernst (D)	1483	escapement (E)	423
ernste Musik (D)	3167	escapement lever (E)	441
ernste Oper (D)	2409	esecuzione (I)	3015
eroico (I)	1138	eseguire (I)	2709
erotic (E)	1139	esempio (I)	3016
erotico (I)	1139	esercitare (I)	2710
érotique (F)	1139	esercizio (I)	3017
erotisch (D)	1139	esercizio per le dita (I)	3018
errato (I)	3309	esercizio vocale (I)	605
erregt (D)	942	Eses (D)	2203
erreur (F)	3310	esile (I)	1147
error (E)	3310	esitando (I)	746
errore (I)	3310	esitante (I)	746
erschaffen (D)	2693	esordiente (I)	3019
(Geister-)Erscheinung (D)	3030	esordio (I)	2974
ersehnt (D)	1089	esordire (I)	2711
ersetzen (D)	2826	espandendosi (I)	817
erstaunlich (D)	3110	espansione (con) (I)	1148
Erstdruck (D)	3247	espiègle (F)	1327
erste Sängerin (D)	620	espirando (I)	832
erste Vorstellung (D)	3244	espirare (I)	2712
erster Satz (D)	2079	espoir (F)	3349
ersterbend (D)	824	esposizione (I)	1973, 3020
erstes Mal (D)	3248	espressione (con) (I)	1149
erstes Zeitmaß (D)	778	espressionismo (I)	3021
erwärmend (D)	803	espressivo (I)	1150
erweckend (D)	890	esprimere (I)	2713
erweitern (D)	2647, 2654	esquisse (F)	3318

essai (F)	2902, 3304
essayer (F)	2777
essential note (E)	2042
essere fuori tempo (I)	2714
essere in ritardo (I)	2715
essouflé (F)	930
estampida (I)	2370
Estampie (D)	2370
estampie (E, F)	2370
estasi (con) (I)	1151
estatico (I)	1152
estendendo (I)	817
estensione (I)	3022
estensione vocale (I)	606
estenuandosi (I)	818
esteso (I)	1530
estetica (I)	3023
esthétique (F)	3023
estinguendo (I)	903
estinguendosi (I)	903
estinto (I)	848
estomac (F)	3478
estompé (F)	1495
estrade (F)	3231
estratto (I)	3024
estremamente (I)	1698
estro (con) (I)	1153
estroso (I)	1154
esuberante (I)	1601
esultante (I)	1155
esultanza (con) (I)	1156
esultare (I)	2716
esultazione (con) (I)	1156
et ainsi de suite (F)	3003
etc (I)	3003
éteindre (F)	2828
éteint (F)	848, 911
étendu (F)	1530
étendue (F)	3022
etereo (I)	1157
eternal (E)	3025
éternel (F)	3025
eterno (I)	3025
éthéré (F)	1157
ethereal (E)	1157
étincelant (F)	1489
étoile (F)	3359
étonnant (F)	3110
étouffé (F)	96, 238
étouffer (F)	389
étouffoir (F)	444
étrange (F)	1531
être en retard (F)	2715
être hors du tempo (F)	2714
étroit (F)	809
Etüde (D)	2471
étude (F)	2471
étude concertante (F)	2472
étude de concert (F)	2472
étude de virtuosité (F)	2473
étude transcendentale (F)	2474
étudier (F)	2837
étui (F)	35
etwas (D)	1625, 1849
etwas mehr (D)	1778
etwas weniger (D)	1777
eufonia (I)	3026
eunuch flute (E)	301
Euphonie (D)	3026
euphonie (F)	3026
euphonium (E, F)	119
euphony (E)	3026
eurhythmics (E)	3027
Eurhythmie (D)	3027
euritmia (I)	3027
eurythmie (F)	3027
evanescente (I)	1584
evaporandosi (I)	904
evaporating (E)	904
éveillé (F)	1091
even (E)	1314, 1518, 3106
evening song (E)	2296
every (E)	1759
every time (E)	1760
everybody (E)	1838
everywhere (E)	1681
evirato (I)	656
ewig (D)	3025
exact (E, F)	1146
exagéré (F)	1140
exagérer (F)	2708
exaggerated (E)	1140

exaltant (F)	1141	Expressionismus (D)	3021
exalté (F)	1142	expressive (E)	1150
exalted (E)	1142	exprimer (F)	2713
exalting (E)	1141	exquisite (E)	1430
example (E)	3016	extatique (F)	1152
exasperated (E)	1144	extemporieren (D)	2732
exaspéré (F)	1144	extended position (E)	2074
excellent (E, F)	3002	extending (E)	817
excentrique (F)	1009	extension (E)	3022
except (E)	1694	extinguished (E)	848, 911
excepté (F)	1694	extinguishing (E)	903, 910
exception (E, F)	1695	extra (E)	2951
exceptional (E)	3364	extrait (F)	3024
exceptionnel (F)	3364	extraordinaire (F)	3364
excerpt (E)	3024	extraordinary (E)	3364
excessively (E)	1693	extravagant (D, E, F)	1532
excessivement (F)	1693	Extravaganza (D, E, F, I)	2529
exchange (E)	3311	extremely (E)	1698
excité (F)	1125	extremely fast (E)	762
excited (E)	1125	extremely slow (E)	723
exciting (E)	1125	extremely soft (E)	863
exécuter (F)	2709	extrèmement (F)	1698
exécution (F)	3015	extrêmement lent (F)	752
exemple (F)	3016	extrêmement lent (F)	723
exercer (F)	2710	exubérant (F)	1436, 1601
exercice (F)	3017	exultant (E)	1155
exercice pour les doigts (F)	3018	exulter (F)	2716
exercice vocal (F)	605	eye (E)	3461
exercise (E)	3017	F (D, E)	2204
exhibition (E)	3020	F double flat (E)	2208
exit (E)	3414	F double sharp (E)	2207
exitant (F)	1125	F flat (E)	2206
exotic music (E)	3146	F sharp (E)	2205
exotische Musik (D)	3146	F-Loch (D)	57
expédié (F)	774	Fa (F, I)	2204
experimental music (E)	3170	Fa bémol (F)	2206
experimentelle Musik (D)	3170	Fa bemolle (I)	2206
expirer (F)	2712	Fa dièse (F)	2205
expliquer (F)	2829	Fa diesis (I)	2205
explorer (F)	570	Fa doppio bemolle (I)	2208
Exposition (D)	1973	Fa doppio diesis (I)	2207
exposition (E, F)	1973, 3020	Fa double bémol (F)	2208
expressif (F)	1150	Fa double dièse (F)	2207
expression mark (E)	2114	Fabel (D)	3031
expressionism (E)	3021	fable (E, F)	3031
expressionisme (F)	3021	faburden (E)	1975

faccia (I)	3440	Falsett (D)	676
face (E)	3440	falsettista (I)	603
facezia (con) (I)	1158	falsetto (E, I)	676
…fach (D)	1855	falso (I)	1160, 3309
facile (F, I)	3028	falso bordone (I)	1975
facilement (F)	1159	famelico (I)	1011
facilità (I)	3029	fameux (F)	2937
facilità (con) (I)	937	famoso (I)	2937
facilitato (I)	3329	famous (E)	2937
facilité (F)	3029, 3329	fanatic (E)	1161
facility (E)	3029	fanatico (I)	1161
facilmente (I)	1159	fanatique (F)	1161
facoltativo (I)	1699	fanatisch (D)	1161
facultatif (F)	1699	fanciful (E)	1163
Faden (D)	3041	fancy (E)	2344
fading away (E)	832	Fandango (D, E, F, I)	2531
Fado (D, E, F, I)	2530	fanfara (I)	2343, 2909
Fagott (D)	141	Fanfare (D)	2343, 2909
Fagottist (D)	3507	fanfare (E, F)	2343, 2909
fagottista (I)	3507	fanfare de cuivres (F)	2910
Fagottistin (D)	3507	fantaisie (F)	2344
fagotto (I)	141	fantasia (E, I)	2344
fähig zu (D)	2868	fantasia (con) (I)	1162
Fähnchen (D)	1934	Fantasie (D)	2344
faible (F)	1069	fantasioso (I)	1163
faiblement (F)	1071	fantasma (I)	3030
failure (E)	3036	fantasque (F)	1154, 1163
faint (E)	1069	fantastic (E)	1164
faire (F)	2717	fantastico (I)	1164
faire descendre (F)	2674	fantastique (F)	1164
faire une faute (F)	2810	fantôme (F)	3030
fairy tale (E)	3031	far away (E)	855, 1107
faithful to the original (E)	3032	farandola (I)	2345
falange (I)	3441	Farandole (D)	2345
fall (E)	420	farandole (E, F)	2345
„falle ein" (D)	1645	Farbe (D)	2948
fallen (D)	2673	farbig (D)	1048
falls (D)	1793	farblos (D)	1477
falsa relazione (I)	1974	Farce (D)	2346
falsch (D)	1160, 3309	farce (E, F)	2346
falsch singen (D)	692	farceur (F)	1165
falsch spielen (D)	2833	farcical (E)	1165
falsche Note (D)	3186	fard (pour la scène) (F)	658
false (E)	1160	fare (I)	2717
false note (E)	3186	farewell! (E)	2876
false relation (E)	1974	faringe (I)	3442

Farruca (D, E, F, I)	2532	feindre (F)	685
farsa (I)	2346	feint (F)	3042
farsesco (I)	1165	felice (I)	3033
Fasching (D)	2932	felicitare (I)	2718
fascia (I)	58, 361	féliciter (F)	2718
fascino (con) (I)	1166	Fell (D)	365, 368
Fassung (D)	3420	felt (E)	424
fast (D, E)	763, 1789	felt stick (E)	350
fast nichts (D)	869	feltro (I)	424
fast unvernehmlich (D)	1618	female voice (E)	712
fast wie eine Fantasie (D)	1414	fermamente (I)	1170
Fastnacht (D)	2932	fermare (I)	2719
fastoso (I)	1167	fermata (E)	1946
fastueux (F)	1167, 1488	Fermate (D)	1946
fate vibrare (I)	1700	fermé (F)	2941
fatica (con) (I)	1168	ferme (F)	1172
faticoso (I)	1168	fermement (F)	1170
fatigué (F)	1528	fermer (F)	2683
fato (I)	677	fermezza (con) (I)	1171
faul (D)	1393	fermo (I)	1172
fault (E)	2982	fern (D)	855
fausse note (F)	3186	Fernbedienung (D)	584
fausse relation (F)	1974	Fernsehaufnahme (D)	559
fausset (F)	676	Fernsehen (D)	3396
faute (F)	3310	Fernsehübertragung (D)	589
fauteuils d'orchestre (F)	3230	féroce (F)	1173
faux (F)	1160, 3309	feroce (I)	1173
faux-bourdon (F)	1975	ferocia (con) (I)	1174
Fauxbourdon (D)	1975	ferocious (E)	1173
fauxbourdon (E)	1975	Ferse (D)	3479
favola (I)	3031	fervent (F)	1175
fearful (E)	1378	fervid (E)	1175
febbrile (I)	1169	fervido (I)	1175
fébrile (F)	1169	fervore (con) (I)	1176
fede (con) (I)	1179	Fes (D)	2206
fedele all'originale (I)	3032	Feses (D)	2208
fee (E)	3193	Fest (D)	3034
feed back (E)	550	festa (I)	3034
feeling comfortable (E)	1053	festeggiante (I)	1177
Fehler (D)	2982, 3310	festeggiare (I)	2720
fehlerhaft (D)	3319	festival (E)	3034
feierlich (D)	1508	festival de musique (F)	3035
feiern (D)	2720	festival musicale (I)	3035
feiernd (D)	1177	festive (E)	1178
feigned (E)	3042	festivo (I)	1178
fein (D)	1183	festlich (D)	1178

festoso (I)	1178	figuré (F)	1977
fête (F)	3034	figure (F)	1976
fêter (F)	2720	figured (E)	1977
feuille (F)	3043	figured bass (E)	1899
feuille d'acier (F)	292	figuriert (D)	1977
feuille d'album (F)	2348	figuring (E)	1932
feurig (D)	984, 1190	fil (F)	3041
feutre (F)	424	filando (I)	1182
feux de la rampe (F)	3105	filar la voce (I)	607
feverish (E)	1169	filarmonica (I)	3040
few (E)	1773	filarmonico (I)	3040
fiaba (I)	3031	filer le son (F)	607
fiacco (I)	1305	filet (F)	59
fiammante (I)	984	filetto (I)	59
fiasco (I)	3036	filling-in part (E)	2187
fiati (I)	3037	film music (E)	3157
fiato (I)	3038	Filmmusik (D)	3157
fickle (E)	1606	filo (I)	3041
fiddle (E)	27	Filter (D)	511
Fidel (D)	27	filter (E)	511
fidèle à l'original (F)	3032	filtre (F)	511
fiducia (con) (I)	1179	filtre passe-bande (F)	512
fieberhaft (D)	1169	filtro (I)	511
Fiedel (D)	27	filtro passabanda (I)	512
fier (F)	1363	Filz (D)	424
fieramente (I)	1180	Filzschlägel (D)	350
fierce (E)	1173	fin (F)	1183, 1701
fièrement (F)	1180	final (F)	2347
fierezza (con) (I)	1181	final cadenza (E)	1912
fiero (I)	1363	final part (E)	1655
fiery (E)	1190	final rehearsal (E)	3262
fievole (I)	1069	finale (E, I)	2347
fife (E)	142, 161	finden (D)	2856
fiffero (I)	161	fine (E, I)	1183, 1701
fifre (F)	161	finezza (con) (I)	1184
fifth (E)	2242	Finger (D)	3438
fifth movement (E)	2089	finger (E)	3438
fignoler (F)	2704	finger action (E)	3395
Figur (D)	1976	finger exercise (E)	3018
figura (I)	1976	finger-cymbals (E)	278
figurant (F)	2951	finger-hole (E)	207
figurante (F, I)	2951	fingerboard (E)	75
figuration (E, F)	1932, 3039	Fingercymbeln (D)	278
figurato (I)	1977	fingere (I)	685
figurazione (I)	3039	Fingerglied (D)	3441
figure (E)	1976	fingering (E)	2998

Fingerknochen (D)	3441
Fingerkuppe (D)	3471
Fingerloch (D)	207
Fingersatz (D)	2998
Fingertechnik (D)	3395
fingertips (E)	3471
Fingerübung (D)	3018
Fingerwechsel (D)	470
fingiert (D)	3042
finir (F)	2721
finire (I)	2721
finished (E)	1702
finito (I)	1702
fino (I)	1183
fino al (I)	1703
fino al segno (I)	1704
finster (D)	1544
finto (I)	3042
fioco (I)	700, 1147
fioreggiando (I)	1185
fiorettando (I)	1185
fioritura (I)	608, 1978
fioriture (F)	608, 1978
firm (E)	1172
firmly (E)	1170
first edition (E)	3247
first movement (E)	2079
first night (E)	3244
first performance (E)	3245
first phrase (E)	2077
first time (E)	3248
Fis (D)	2205
fisarmonica (I)	395
fisarmonica a bottoni (I)	396
fisarmonica bitonica (I)	396
fisarmonica con tastiera di pianoforte (I)	397
fischiare (I)	2722
fischiettando (I)	717
fischietto (I)	142
Fisis (D)	2207
Fistelstimme (D)	676
flabby (E)	1341
flag (E)	1934
Flageolett-Töne (D)	2145
Flamenco (D, E, F, I)	2533
flasque (F)	1341
flat (E)	1905
Flatsche (D)	301
flatté (F)	1319
flattered (E)	1319
flatterhaft (D)	1606
Flatterzunge (D)	243
flatteur (F)	1318
flautando (I)	115
flautato (I)	2145
flautist (E)	3508
flautista (I)	3508
flauto (I)	143
flauto a becco basso (I)	144
flauto a becco contralto (I)	145
flauto a becco sopranino (I)	146
flauto a becco soprano (I)	147
flauto a becco tenore (I)	148
flauto a tiro (I)	149
flauto contralto (I)	150
flauto di Pan (I)	151
flauto diritto (I)	152
flauto dolc (I)	152
flauto piccolo (I)	160
flauto traverso (I)	153
flebile (I)	1186
fleet (E)	780
fleeting (E)	1210
fleetly (E)	780
flehend (D)	1540
flessibilità (con) (I)	1187
Flexaton (D)	285
flexaton (F, I)	285
flexatone (E)	285
Flickoper (D)	2421
flicorne (F)	154
flicorno (I)	154
fliegend (D)	1604
fliegendes Staccato (D)	89
fließend (D)	1189
flink (D)	1308
floating (E)	1225
flop (E)	3036
florid counterpoint (E)	1942
florid ornaments (E)	608
florido (I)	1436

florissant (F)	1436	flying (E)	1604
floscio (I)	1341	flying above (E)	1512
Flöte (D)	143	flying away (E)	1604
Flötenuhr (D)	477	focoso (I)	1190
Flötenwerk (D)	477	fog horn (E)	281
Flötist (D)	3508	foga (con) (I)	1255
Flötistin (D)	3508	foggy (E)	1348
flott (D)	954	foglio (I)	3043
flottant (F)	1225	foglio d'album (I)	2348
flou (F)	1268	...fois (F)	1855
flourish (E)	2343	folclore (I)	3044
flourishing (E)	1436	folding seat (E)	3365
flowing (E)	1462	Folge (D)	2140
flüchtig (D)	1210	folgen (D)	2813
fluent (E)	1189	folgen Sie (D)	1797
fluente (I)	1189	folgorante (I)	1212
fluet (F)	1147	Folia (D)	2349
Flügel (D)	401	folia (E)	2349
Flügelhorn (D)	154	folie (F)	2349
flugelhorn (E)	154	folk dance (E)	2330
Flügelröhre (D)	234	folk music (E)	3161
fluide (F)	1189	folk song (E)	2299
fluidezza (con) (I)	1188	Folklore (D)	3044
fluidità (I)	1188	folklore (E, F)	3044
fluido (I)	1189	folle (I)	1192
flüssig (D)	1312	folleggiando (I)	1191
flüstern (D)	649	follement (F)	1192, 1379
flute (E)	143	follemente (I)	1192
flûte (F)	143	follet (F)	3045
flûte à bec alto (F)	145	folletto (I)	3045
flûte à bec basse (F)	144	follia (I)	2349
flûte à bec sopranino (F)	146	follow (E)	1797
flûte à bec soprano (F)	147	fonction (F)	1988
flûte à bec ténor (F)	148	fond (F)	60
flûte à coulisse (F)	149	fondamental (F)	1979
flûte alto (F)	145, 150	fondamental position (E)	2073
flûte basse (F)	150	fondamentale (I)	1979
flûte de Pan (F)	151	fondling (E)	1590
flûte douce (F)	152	fondo (I)	60
flûte droite (F)	152	fondu (F)	1218
flûte lotine (F)	149	fonetica (I)	3046
flute pipe (E)	415	foolish (E)	1192
flûte traversière (F)	153	foot (E)	3468
flutist (E)	3508	footlights (E)	3284
flûtiste (F)	3508	for (E)	1764
flutter-tonguing (E)	243	for four hands (E)	456

for singing (E)	651
for the last time (E)	1766
for the whole length (E)	1767
forcé (F)	873
forced (E)	852, 873
forceful (E)	1132
forcer (F)	2723
forchetta (I)	242
forcieren (D)	2723
forcierend (D)	851
forciert (D)	852
forcing (E)	851, 873
Förderer (D)	3109
forearm (E)	3430
forefinger (E)	3449
forehead (E)	3443
forest (E)	3047
foresta (I)	3047
forêt (F)	3047
fori (I)	425
fork (E)	78
fork fingering (E)	242
Forlana (D)	2353
forlana (E, I)	2353
forlane (F)	2353
Form (D)	1980
form (E)	1980
forma (I)	1980
forma binaria (I)	1981
forma ciclica (I)	1982
forma ternaria (I)	1983
Format (D)	3048
format (E, F)	3048
formato (I)	3048
formazione della voce (I)	604
forme (F)	1980
forme binaire (F)	1981
forme cyclique (F)	1982
forme ternaire (F)	1983
former speed (E)	776
foro (I)	207
fort (F)	849
forte (I)	849
Fortepedal (D)	433
fortfahren (D)	2689
fortgeschritten (D)	2904

fortissimo (I)	850
fortschreiten (D)	2773
fortschreitend (D)	788
Fortschreitung (D)	2081
Fortschritt (D)	3255
fortsetzen (D)	2689
Fortsetzung (D)	3328
fortwährend (D)	3227
forward (E)	790
forza (I)	3049
forza (con) (I)	1193
forzando (I)	851
forzare (I)	2723
forzato (I)	852
fosco (I)	1066
fossa dell'orchestra (I)	3050
fosse d'orchestre (F)	3050
fou (F)	1192
fouet (F)	286
fouetté (F)	88, 1209
fougeux (F)	1190
four (F)	3036
four voices (E)	1862
fourchette (F)	78
fourth (E)	2241
fourth movement (E)	2087
Foyer (D)	3286
foyer (E, F)	3286
foyer des artistes (F)	2927
fragen (D)	2682
fragile (E, F, I)	1194
Fragment (D)	3051
fragment (E, F)	3051
fragoroso (I)	1195
frail (E)	1240
frais (F)	1205
frame (E)	450
frame drum (E)	323
frammento (I)	3051
Française (D)	2350
française (F)	2350
francamente (I)	1196
francese (I)	2350
franchement (F)	1196
franchezza (con) (I)	1197
franco (I)	997

frankly (E) 1196
frantic (E) 1203
Französische Suite (D) 2475
frappé (F) 1998
frapper (F) 380, 2671
frase (I) 1984
fraseggiare (I) 2724
fraseggio (I) 1985
Frauenchor (D) 665
Frauenstimme (D) 712
frech (D) 1486
freddamente (I) 1198
freddezza (con) (I) 1199
freddo (I) 1200
free (E) 755, 3060
free and easy (E) 1459, 1522
freely (E) 1310
freezing (E) 1227
frei (D) 755
frei im Vortrag (D) 1310
Freikarte (D) 2918
freimütig (D) 1196
freiner (F) 2725
frêle (F) 1240
fremebondo (I) 1201
fremente (I) 1201
frémissant (F) 1201
fremito (con) (I) 1202
frenando (I) 819
frenare (I) 2725
French dance (E) 2350
French horn (E) 131
French suite (E) 2475
frenesia (con) (I) 1203
frenetico (I) 1203
frénétique (F) 1203
frenzied (E) 1203
fréquence (F) 513
frequency (E) 513
frequency band (E) 485
Frequenz (D) 513
frequenza (I) 513
Frequenzband (D) 485
freschezza (con) (I) 1204
fresco (I) 1205
fresh (E) 1205

fret (E) 76
fretboard (E) 75
frettando (I) 787
fretted (E) 74
fretted string (E) 51
frettoloso (I) 747
freudig (D) 1236
Friauler (D) 2353
fricassée (F) 2442
friction board (E) 333
friction drum (E) 273
friction wheel (E) 70
friedlich (D) 1369, 1396
frigio (I) 1986
frisch (D) 1205
Frisur (D) 3228
frivole (F) 1206
frivolo (I) 1206
frivolous (E) 1206
frizzante (I) 1207
frog (E) 73
fröhlich (D) 954, 1233, 1311
frohlockend (D) 1155
froid (F) 1200
froidement (F) 1198
frolicsome (E) 1191
from (E) 1674
from here (E) 1682
from the beginning (E) 1611, 1675
from the beginning to the end (E) 1676
from the beginning to the sign (E) 1677
from the sign (E) 1679
from the sign to the end (E) 1680
fromm (D) 1394
front (F) 3443
fronte (I) 3443
frontstage (E) 3259
Frosch (D) 73
frotter (F) 386
Frottola (D, E, F, I) 2534
früher (D) 1783
frullato (I) 243
frusciando (I) 1208

frusta (I)	286	funny (E)	2999
frustato (I)	1209	funzione (I)	1988
fuga (I)	2351	fuoco (con) (I)	1214
fugace (F, I)	1210	fuocoso (I)	1190
fugal episode (E)	1884	fuori (I)	3052
fugato (I)	1987	für (D)	1764
Fuge (D)	2351	für die ganze Dauer (D)	1767
Fugen-Zwischenspiel (D)	1884	für Gesang (D)	651
fugenartig (D)	1987	furbescamente (I)	1215
fughetta (E, I)	2352	furbo (I)	1215
Fughette (D)	2352	furchtbar (D)	1570
fughette (F)	2352	fürchterlich (D)	1364
fugue (E, F)	2351	furchtlos (D)	1290
fugué (F)	1987	furchtsam (D)	1378, 1556
fühlen (D)	2815	furente (I)	1216
führen (D)	2729	furia (con) (I)	1217
Führer (D)	1885	Furiant (D, E, F, I)	2535
Führung der Stimme (D)	613	furibond (F)	1216
fulgido (I)	1211	furibondo (I)	1216
fulgurant (F)	1212	furieux (F)	1216, 1276
full (E)	1769	furioso (I)	1216
full house (E)	3014	furious (E)	1216
full of live (E)	1014	furlana (E, I)	2353
full of pep (E)	1015	furore (con) (I)	1217
full organ (E)	426, 464	fuso (I)	1218
full score (E)	3217	Fuß (Harfe) (D)	81, 3468
Füllstimme (D)	2187	Fußmaschine (D)	367
fulminant (F)	1212	Fußstück (D)	215
fulminante (I)	1212	fût (F)	359, 361
fulminating (E)	1212	futile (I)	1206
function (E)	1988	fuyant (F)	1210
functional music (E)	3132	G (D, E)	2209
fundamental (E)	1979, 2143	G double flat (E)	2213
funèbre (F)	1213	G double sharp (E)	2212
funebre (I)	1213	G flat (E)	2211
funeral lament (E)	2398	G sharp (E)	2210
funeral march (E)	2381	G-Saite (D)	45
funeral music (E)	3148	Gabel (D)	78
funereal (E)	1213	Gabelbecken (D)	271
funereo (I)	1213	Gabelgriff (D)	242
funeste (F)	1321	Gage (D)	3193
funesto (I)	1321	gagliarda (I)	2354
Fünfliniensystem (D)	2063	Gagliarde (D)	2354
fünfter Satz (D)	2089	gagliardo (I)	1219
funkelnd (D)	1489	gagner (F)	702
Funktion (D)	1988	gähnen (D)	683

gai (F)	1222, 1233	Garn (D)	3041
gaiamente (I)	1220	garniture (F)	422
gaiezza (con) (I)	1221	gasping (E)	970
gaillard (F)	1219	Gastdirigent (D)	2988
gaillarde (F)	2354	Gattung (D)	3055
gaily (E)	1220	gauche (á) (F)	3337
gaîment (F)	1220	gaudio (con) (I)	1226
gaio (I)	1222	Gaumen (D)	3464
Gala (D)	3034	gavotta (I)	2357
gala (E, F, I)	3034	gavotte (E, F)	2357
galamment (F)	1223	Gavotte (D)	2357
galant (D, F)	1223	gay (E)	1222
galante (I)	1223	Gebärde (D)	3058
galanteria (con) (I)	1224, 2355	Gebet (D)	3241
Galanterie (D)	2355	gebieterisch (D)	1254
galanteries (E, F)	2355	gebildet (D)	2949
Galerie (D)	3053	Gebrauchsmusik (D)	3132
galerie (F)	3053	gebrochen (D)	3300
gallant (E)	1223	gebrochener Akkord (D)	1878
galleggiante (I)	1225	gebunden (D)	854
galleria (I)	3053	gedämpft (D)	875
gallery (E)	3053	gedankenvoll (D)	1383
galliard (E)	2354	gedeckt (D)	238
galop (E, F)	2356	gedehnt (D)	1530
Galopp (D)	2356	Gedicht (D)	2428
galoppo (I)	2356	gedrängt (D)	806
gamba (I)	3444	geebnet (D)	1518
Gambe (D)	29	gefällig (D)	1231
gambo (I)	1989	gefühllos (D)	1283
gamme (F)	2109	gefühlvoll (D)	3711
gamme par tons (F)	2110	gegen (D)	1673
ganz (D)	1839	Gegenbewegung (D)	2032
ganz richtig (D)	1641	Gegensatz (D)	1943
Ganze (D)	2224	Gegenschlagzunge (D)	192
ganze Pause (D)	2231	Gegenstimme (D)	1945
gänzlich (D)	2953	Gegenteil (D)	2965
Ganzschluss (D)	1914	Gegenthema (D)	1943
Ganzton (D)	2170	Gegenzeit (Betonung auf dem	
Ganztonleiter (D)	2110	schlechten Taktteil) (D)	1944
gar (D)	1744	gehalten (D)	1831
gar nichts (D)	1752	gehämmert (D)	463
garbato (I)	959	gehauchter Einsatz (D)	646
garbo (con) (I)	958	Gehäuse (D)	416
garder la mesure (F)	2847	geheimnisvoll (D)	1337, 1497
gardez (F)	1830	gehend (D)	729, 792
gardez la pédale (F)	3604	gehetzt (D)	798

Gehör (D)	2896, 3413
Gehörbildung (D)	3007
gehüpft (Bogenstrich) (D)	90, 108
Geige (D)	30
Geigenbauer (D)	3511
Geigenbauerin (D)	3511
Geiger (D)	3527
Geigerin (D)	3527
Geistererscheinung (D)	3030
geisterhaft (D)	1517
geistesverwirrt (D)	1082
geistlich (D)	1525
geistliche Musik (D)	3164
geistliches Konzert (D)	2316
geistreich (D)	1523, 1524
geistvoll (D)	1524
gekünstelt (D)	993
gelassen (D)	1438
geläufig (D)	774
Gelenk (D)	3429
gelido (I)	1227
gemächlich (D)	939
gemäßigt (D)	758
gemebondo (I)	1228
gemeinsam (D)	2957
gemendo (I)	1228
gemessen (D)	1742
gemischt (D)	1741
gemischte Stimmen (D)	716
gemischter Chor (D)	667
gémissant (F)	1228
gemurmelt (D)	1345
gemütlich (D)	939
gemütlos (D)	1283
gemütsbewegend (D)	935
gemütvoll (D)	974
genau (D)	1146, 1641
genau im Takt (D)	938
general pause (E)	2061
Generalbass (D)	1899, 1900
Generalbassinstrument (D)	3380
generally (E)	3054
Generalpause (D)	2061
Generalprobe (D)	3262
générateur (F)	514
générateur de sons sinussoidaux (F)	515
Generator (D)	514
generator (E)	514
generatore (I)	514
generatore di suoni sinusiodali (I)	515
genere (I)	3055
généreux (F)	1229
generoso (I)	1229
generous (E)	1229
genial (D)	3056
génial (F)	3056
geniale (I)	3056
Genick (D)	3460
Genie (D)	3057
génie (F)	3057
genio (I)	3057
Genius (D)	3057
genius (E)	3057
genou (F)	3445
genre (E, F)	3055
gentilezza (con) (I)	1230
gentilmente (I)	1231
gentiment (F)	1231
gently (E)	1113
genug (D)	1610
genug! (D)	2914
genügend (D)	1610, 1647
gepeitscht (D)	88, 1209
gequält (D)	1559
gerade (D)	1687
gerader Takt (D)	2154
geräumig (D)	1515
Geräusch (D)	566
geräuschvoll (D)	1448
„geraubt" (D)	768
gereizt (D)	1298
gerissen (D)	113
German dance (E)	2265
German flute (E)	153
gerührt (D)	1050
Ges (D)	2211
gesammelt (D)	1418
Gesamtausgabe (D)	3006
Gesamtwerk (D)	3087

Gesang (D)	2285	getting less (E)	908
gesanglich (D)	1029	getting slower (E)	826
Gesangskonzert (D)	2319	gewaltig (D)	1402
Gesangskunst (D)	641	gewaltsam (D)	1594
Gesangspartitur (D)	618	gewichtig (D)	1399
Gesangstechnik (D	694	gewiss (D)	2939
Gesangsübung (D)	605	gewissenhaft (D)	1060
Gesangverein (D)	642	Gewitter (D)	3398
gesangvoll (D)	1029	gewitterhaft (D)	1542
Gesäß (D)	3476	gewöhnlich (D)	1762
gesättigt (D)	1357	gewohnt (D)	1810
geschickt (D)	2868	geworfen (D)	101
geschlagen (D)	862	geziert (D)	932, 1309
geschleppt (D)	840	gezupft (D)	104
geschlossen (D)	2941	gezwickt (D)	104
geschmeichelt (D)	1319	ghastly (E)	1517
geschmeidig (D)	1375	ghiribizzoso (I)	1154
geschwätzig (D)	3836	ghironda (I)	17
geschwind (D)	775	ghost (E)	3030
Gesellschaftstanz (D)	2907	ghostly (E)	1517
Geses (D)	2213	già (I)	1705
gesetzt (D)	1401	giambo (I)	1990
Gesicht (D)	3440	gierig (D)	1011
gespannt (D)	1551	giga (I)	2358
Gespenst (D)	3030	gigantesco (I)	1232
gespenstisch (D)	1517	gigantesque (F)	1232
gesprungen (D)	107	gigantic (E)	1232
Gestalt (D)	1980	Gigue (D)	2358
Gestaltung (D)	3088	gigue (F)	2358
Geste (D)	3058	ginocchio (I)	3445
geste (F)	3058	giocondo (I)	1233
gestimmt (D)	2872	giocoso (I)	1234
gesto (I)	3058	gioia (con) (I)	1235
gestochen (D)	103	gioioso (I)	1236
gestopft (D)	238	gioviale (I)	1237
gestoßen (D)	691	gipsy (E)	3427
gesture (E)	3058	gipsy dance (E)	2329, 2491
gestützt (D)	843	gipsy music (E)	3173
gesucht (D)	1430	gipsy song (E)	2291
geteilt (D)	1689	giradischi (I)	516
getragen (D)	691, 868	girare (I)	2864
getrennt (D)	111, 1806	girotondo (I)	2359
getrillert (D)	1832	Gis (D)	2210
gettato (I)	101	Gisis (D)	2212
getting exhausted (E)	818	Gitarre (D)	10
getting faster (E)	785	Gitarrist (D)	3494

Gitarristin (D)	3494
giù (I)	1717
giubilante (I)	1155, 1238
giubilo (con) (I)	1238
giulivo (I)	1311
giustamente (I)	1706
Giustiniana (D, E, F, I)	2536
giusto (I)	1146, 1991
glacé (F)	1227
glacial (F)	1227
glad (E)	1311
glance (E)	3332
glänzend (D)	1013, 1211
Glasharmonika (D)	251
glass harmonica (E)	251
glatt (D)	1314
Glee (D, E, F, I)	2537
gleich (D)	1808, 1841
gleichartig (D)	1218
gleichgültig (D)	1266
Gleichheit (D)	3010
gleichmäßig (D)	1579, 1841
gleichzeitig (D)	1847, 3336
gleitend (D)	853
gli altri (I)	1707
gli ottoni (I)	3374
gli stessi (I)	1708
glissando (I)	853
glisser (F)	853
glitzernd (D)	1489
Glocke (D)	257
Glockenschlag (D)	375
Glockenspiel (D)	261, 265
glockenspiel (E)	261
gloomy (E)	1066, 1316
glorieux (F)	1138
glorioso (I)	1138
glorious (E)	1138
glorreich (D)	1138
glottal attack (E)	645
Glottisschlag (D)	645
glücklich (D)	3033
glückselig (D)	1005
glühend (D)	984, 1275
go on (E)	1645, 1671
godimento (con) (I)	1226

goffo (I)	1239
going on (E)	788
gola (I)	3446
golfo mistico (I)	3050
gomito (I)	3447
Gong (D)	287
gong (E, F, I)	287
gong cinesi (I)	288
Gongspiel (chromatisch) (D)	288
good luck (E)	3077
gopak (E, F, I)	2360
gorge (F)	3446
gorgheggio (I)	609
gorgia (I)	608
Grabgesang (D)	2290
grace-note (E)	1887
graceful (E)	1245
gracieusement (F)	1245
gracieux (F)	1245
gracile (I)	1240
gradatamente (I)	1709
gradation (E)	3059
gradevole (I)	1241
gradito (I)	1241
grado (I)	1992
gradually (E)	1709
gradually less (E)	1775
gradually more (E)	1776
gradualmente (I)	1709
graduare (I)	2726
graduation (F)	3059
graduazione (I)	3059
graduellement (F)	1709
graduer (F)	2726
grammofono (I)	517
Grammophon (D)	517
gramophone (E, F)	517
gran (I)	1710
grancassa (I)	289
grand (F)	1710
grand orgue (F)	426
grand piano (E)	401
grand'organo (I)	426
grande (I)	1710
grandezza (con) (I)	1242
grandiose (E, F)	1243

grandioso (I)	1243
grandir (F)	2694
gratis (D, I)	3060
grattare (I)	2727
gratter (F)	2727
gratuit (F)	3060
gratuito (I)	3060
gratuitous (E)	3060
gratulieren (D)	2718
grausam (D)	672
grave (F, I)	748, 1483
gravement (F)	1384
graver (F)	2784
graveur (F)	3509
graveuse (F)	3509
gravicembalo (I)	393
gravità (con) (I)	1244
gravure (F)	412
grazia (con) (I)	1245
graziös (D)	1245
grazioso (I)	1245
grease point (E)	658
great (E)	1710
great organ (E)	426
greatest (E)	1734
greedy (E)	1011
green-room (E)	2927
Greghesca (D, E, F, I)	2538
Gregorian (E)	3061
gregorianisch (D)	3061
Gregorianischer Choral (D)	2293
gregoriano (I)	3061
grégorien (F)	3061
greifen (D)	2840
grêle (F)	1147
grezzo (I)	1450
gridando (I)	1580
gridare (I)	2728
grieved (E)	920, 1119
Griffbrett (D)	75
Griffloch (D)	207
grim (E)	1561
grimmig (D)	1561
grinta (con) (I)	1034
grintoso (I)	1007
grob (D)	1246, 1450
grölen (D)	2863
(der) größte (D)	1734
grogner (F)	2670
grognon (F)	1016
grommeler (F)	2669
groove (E)	412
groppo (I)	1993
groß (D)	1710
großartig (D)	1243
grosse caisse (F)	289
große Trommel (D)	289
grossier (F)	1246
großmütig (D)	1229
grossolano (I)	1246
großzügig (D)	1229
grotesk (D)	1247
grotesque (E, F)	1247
grottesco (I)	1247
ground bass (E)	1901
group lesson (E)	3103
groupe de notes (F)	1994
groupe de sons (F)	1994
grouper (F)	2781
growing louder (E)	885
grumbling (E)	1016
Grundstellung (D)	2073
Grundton (D)	2143, 2168
Gruppenunterricht (D)	3103
gruppetto (I)	1993
gruppetto final (F)	1930
gruppo di note (I)	1994
gruppo di suoni (I)	1994
Guajira (D, E, F, I)	2539
guancia (I)	3448
Guaracha (D, E, F, I)	2540
guardare (I)	2861
Guckloch (D)	3351
guerresco (I)	1248
guerrier (F)	1248
guerriero (I)	1248
guest conductor (E)	2988
guidare (I)	2729
guider (F)	2729
guidonian hand (E)	2009
Guidonische Hand (D)	2009
guilleret (F)	994

guimbarde (F)	315	Hälfte (D)	1737
Guiro (D)	290	Hall (D)	565
guiro (E, F, I)	290	Halleffekt (D)	3291
guitar (E)	10	Halling (D, E, F, I)	2542
guitare (F)	10	Hals (D)	61, 3434
guitare de jazz (F)	11	Hals- und Beinbruch	3077
guitare électrique (F)	490	Haltebogen (D)	2006
guitare hawaïenne (F)	12	halten (D)	2846
guitarist (E)	3494	halten Sie (D)	1830
guitariste (F)	3494	haltend (D)	1829
Gurgeltriller (D)	609	Hammer (D)	364, 430
gusto (con) (I)	1249	hammer (E)	364, 430
gut (D)	1648	hammered (E)	463
gut string (E)	46	hammering (E)	858
gütig (D)	1271	hämmernd (D)	858
gutmütig (D)	1396	Hammond organ (E)	540
guttural (E, F)	610	Hammondorgel (D)	540
gutturale (I)	610	hampe (F)	1989
H (D)	2219	hanche (F)	3428
Haare (D)	3433	Hand (D)	3453
Habanera (D, E, F, I)	2541	hand (E)	3453
habile (F)	2868	hand castanets (E)	272
habituel (F)	1810	hand drum (E)	328
habituel (F)	1762	handbell (E)	262
Hackbrett (D)	24	Hände kreuzend (D)	462
hair (E)	3433	Handfläche (D)	3465
hair of the bow (E)	55	Handgelenk (D)	3473
hair style (E)	3228	Handglocke (D)	262
hairdo (E)	3228	Handharmonika (D)	395
halb (D)	1738	handle castanets (E)	270
Halbe (D)	2225	Handlung (D)	3407
halbe Kraft (D)	1739	Handrücken (D)	3439
halbe Pause (D)	2232	Handtrommel (D)	323, 328
Halbkadenz (D)	1916	hängendes Becken (D)	308
halblaut (D)	859	happy (E)	3033
halbleise (D)	860	hard (E)	1123
Halbschluss (D)	1913	hard lever (E)	427
Halbton (D)	2117	Hardanger fiddle (E)	18
haletant (F)	970	Hardanger Fiedel (D)	18
half (E)	1737, 1738	hardi (F)	976, 988
half loud (E)	859	hardiment (F)	986
half note (Am.)	2225	Harding (E)	18
half note rest (Am.)	2232	Hardingfele (I)	18
half soft (E)	860	Harfe (D)	2
half strength (E)	1739	Harfenist (D)	3487
half-close (E)	1913	Harfenistin (D)	3487

hargneux (F)	983	haunch (E)	3428
harmonic (E)	1891	Haupt-... (D)	2080
harmonic curve (E)	56	Hauptbetonung (D)	1868
harmonica (F)	117	Hauptnote (D)	2042
harmonica de verre (F)	251	Hauptrolle (D)	3302
harmonics (E)	2145	Hauptstimme (D)	2188
Harmonie (D)	1890	Hauptthema (D)	2078
harmonie (F)	1890, 2911	Hauptwerk (D)	426
Harmonielehre (D)	2175	Hauskonzert (D)	2959
Harmoniemusik (D)	3156	Hausmusik (D)	3147
harmonieusement (F)	990	hausse (F)	73
harmonieux (F)	990	hausser (F)	2652
harmonious (E)	990	haut (F)	2882
harmoniously (E)	990	haut-parleur en coffret (F)	567
harmonique (F)	1891	hautain (F)	957
harmonisch (D)	1891	hautbois (F)	156
harmoniser (F)	2659	hautbois d'amour (F)	157
harmonisieren (D)	2659	hautboiste (F)	3515
Harmonium (D)	390	haute-contre (F)	603
harmonium (E, F)	390	hauteur (F)	2881
harmony (E)	1890	hauteur du son (F)	1881
harp (E)	2	hautparleur (F)	481
harpe (F)	2	Hawaii-Gitarre (D)	12
harpe à double mouvement		Hawaiian guitar (E)	12
(F)	3	head (E)	3480
harpe à pédales simples (F)	2	head joint with beak (E)	230
harpist (E)	3487	head voice (E)	711
harpiste (F)	3487	headphone (E)	495
harpsichord (E)	393	hearing (E)	3413
harpsichordist (E)	3496	hearing (E)	2896
harsch (D)	996	heart (E)	3435
harsh (E)	996	heart beat (E)	3211
harsh voice (E)	706	heart-breaking (E)	1533
hart (D)	1123	heart-felt (E)	1476
harter Einsatz (D)	645	heartily (E)	1026
hartnäckig (D)	1367, 1543	heavenly (E)	1039
hastening (E)	787	heavy (E)	1386
hastig (D)	735, 747	Hebung (D)	1893
hasty (E)	747	Heckelphon (D)	155
hat mute (E)	222	heckelphon (I)	155
hâté (F)	725	heckelphone (E, F)	155
hâter (F)	2645	heel (E)	73, 3479
hätschelnd (D)	1590	heftig (D)	1585
Hauch (D)	3340	height (E)	2881
häufig (D)	1818	heilig (D)	3308
haughty (E)	957	heimtückisch (D)	1160

Heimweh (D)	3185	Hexachord (D)	1972
heiser (D)	622	hexachord (E)	1972
heiß (D)	985	hexacorde (F)	1972
heiter (D)	728, 1481	Hexentanz (D)	2327
heitere Oper (D)	2406	Hey (D, E, F, I)	2543
hektisch (D)	747	hi-hat pedal (E)	275
held (E)	1831	hidden (E)	1748
held back (E)	831	hidden consecutives (E)	2052
Heldentenor (D)	633	hier (D)	1786, 3004
helicon (E)	140	high (E)	2882
hélicon (F)	140	high dramatic soprano (E)	628
Helikon (D)	140	highest (E)	1813
hell (D)	1043, 1317	Highland fling (D, E, F, I)	2544
helle/klare Stimme (D)	707	Hilfslinie (D)	2149
hemidemisemiquaver (E)	2230	Himmel (D)	2943
hemidemisemiquaver rest (E)	2237	himmlisch (D)	1039
hemiola (E)	1995	hinaufstimmen (D)	2653
Hemiole (D)	1995	hinkend (D)	952
hemiolia (I)	1995	hinlegen (D)	2765
hemiolios (F)	1995	hinsterbend (D)	832
herablassen (D)	2674	hinten (D)	1684
herabstürzend (D)	3718	hinter der Bühne (D)	2981
herausfordernd (D)	1408, 1490	Hinterbühne (D)	3282
herausklatschen (D)	3285	Hintergrundmusik (D)	3139
here (E)	1786, 3004	hinterlassen (D)	3237
heroic (E)	1138	hinzufügen (D)	2646
heroic tenor (E)	633	hip (E)	3428
héroïque (F)	1138	Hirtengedicht (D)	2340
heroisch (D)	1138	Hirtenpfeife (D)	190
herunterstimmen (D)	2637	Hirtenpfeife (D)	121
hervor (D)	1716	Hirtenstück (D)	2422
hervorbringen (D)	1724	His (D)	2220
hervorgehoben (D)	870, 1723	Hisis (D)	2222
hervorklatschen (D)	3285	histoire de la musique (F)	3362
hervorstechend (D)	1724	historical (E)	3363
hervortretend (D)	1716	historique (F)	3363
Herz (D)	3435	historisch (D)	3363
herzlich (D)	1026	history of music (E)	3362
Herzschlag (D)	3211	hit (E)	2928
herzzerreißend (D)	1533	hoarse (E)	622
Heses (D)	2223	hoch (D)	2882
hésitant (F)	746	hochalteriert (D)	1896
hesitating (E)	746	hochdramatischer Sopran (D)	628
heucheln (D)	685	hochet (F)	321
heulen (D)	2859	hochmütig (D)	957
heureux (F)	3033	höchst (D)	1813

hochzeitlich (D)	1358
Hochzeitsmarsch (D)	2382
hocket (E)	2403
Hoffnung (D)	3349
höfischer Tanz (D)	2264
höfisches Lied (D)	2257
Hofmusik (D)	3137
Höhe (D)	2881
Höhepunkt (D)	2888
höher (D)	3388
höher stimmen (D)	2653
höhnisch (D)	1006
Hoketus (D)	2403
hold (D)	1589
holding (E)	1829
holding back (E)	839
holiday (E)	3034
höllisch (D)	1273
holy (E)	3308
Holz (D)	3100
Holzbläser (D)	3099
Holzblasinstrumente (D)	3373
Holzblock (D)	254
Holzschlägel (D)	351
Holzstäbe (D)	279
Holztrommel (D)	329
homage (E)	3192
homesickness (E)	3185
hommage (F)	3192
homogène (F)	1218
homogeneous (E)	1218
Homophonie (D)	2048
homophonie (F)	2048
homophony (E)	2048
Hopak (D)	2360
hope (E)	3349
hopper (E)	441
hopping (E)	1453
hoquet (F)	2403
hörbar (D)	1840, 3223
horchen (D)	2662
hören (D)	2815, 2857
Hörer (D)	2895
Hörerin (D)	2895
horizontal (D, E, F)	2050
Horn (D)	131
horn (E)	131
horn player (E)	3504
Hornist (D)	3504
Hornistin (D)	3504
Hornpipe (D, E, F, I)	2545
Horo (D, E, F, I)	2546
horrible (F)	1364
horrifying (E)	1364
Hörzentrum (D)	2938
house concert (E)	2959
housse (F)	35
how (E)	1659
however (E)	1768
hübsch (D)	1589
Hüfte (D)	3428
huitième de soupir (F)	2236
Huldigung (D)	3192
Hülse (D)	233
humble (E, F)	1576
humming (E)	636
Humoreske (D)	2484
humoresque (E, F)	2484
humoristique (F)	1578
humoristisch (D)	1578
humorous (E)	1578
Hungarian dance (E)	2334
hunt (E)	2277
hunting horn (E)	132
hunting music (E)	3129
Hupfauf (D, E, F, I)	2547
hüpfend (D)	1453
hurdy-gurdy (E)	17
hurler (F)	2859
hurried (E)	725
hurrying (E)	787
hurtig (D)	780
Huschdämpfer (D)	227
hush mute (E)	227
husky (E)	700
husten (D)	695
Hutdämpfer (D)	222
hymn (E)	2363
hymn of praise (E)	2363
Hymne (D)	2363
hymne (F)	2363
hymne national (F)	2364

i legni (I)	3373	Imitation (D)	1996
iamb (E)	1990	imitation (E, F)	1996
ici (F)	1786	imitazione (I)	1996
icy (E)	1227	imiter (F)	2730
idea (E, I)	3062	imitieren (D)	2730
ideal (D, E)	3063	immaginazione (con) (I)	1251
idéal (F)	3063	immagine musicale (I)	3269
ideale (I)	3063	immagine sonora (I)	3069
Idee (D)	3062	immediatamente (I)	1822
idée (F)	3062	immediate attack (E)	1646
idée fixe (F)	2031	immediately (E)	1822
idilliaco (I)	1250	immédiatement (F)	1822
idyllic (E)	1250	immer (D)	1798
idyllique (F)	1250	immer belebter (D)	805
idyllisch (D)	1250	immutato (I)	1714
if (E)	1793	impacciato (I)	1239
if necessary (E)	1794	imparare (I)	2731
if possible (E)	1781	imparfait (F)	1997
il più possibile (I)	1712	impatient (E, F)	1252
il più... (I)	1711	impavido (I)	1290
il sipario si abbassa (I)	3064	impaziente (I)	1252
il sipario si alza (I)	3065	impazienza (con) (I)	1253
il sipario si apre (I)	3066	imperceptible (E, F)	3070
il sipario si chiude (I)	3067	impercettibile (I)	3070
ilare (I)	1311	imperfect (E)	1997
illanguidendosi (I)	1303	imperfect cadence (E)	1913
illibato (I)	1037	imperfetto (I)	1997
illuminazione (I)	3068	impérieusement (F)	1254
im (D)	1749	impérieux (F)	1254
im Allgemeinen (D)	3054	imperioso (I)	1254
im alten Stil (D)	944	imperious (E)	1254
im Delirium (D)	1083	impertinent (E, F)	1494
im Einklang (D)	2181	impertinente (I)	1494
im Freien (D)	3052	impeto (con) (I)	1255
im gleichen Tempo (D)	756	impétueux (F)	1256
im Hintergrund (D)	3386	impetuoso (I)	1256
im Takt (D)	720	impetuous (E)	1256
im Vordergrund (D)	1722	implacabile (I)	1257
im Vorigen (D)	1782	implacable (E, F)	1257
im Zeitmaß (D)	720	implorando (I)	1540
image musicale (F)	3269	implorant (F)	1258
image sonore (F)	3069	implorante (I)	1258
imboccatura (I)	208, 244	imploring (E)	1258, 1540
imitando (I)	1713	imponente (I)	1259
imitare (I)	2730	important (E, F, I)	3071
imitating (E)	1713	imposant (F)	1259

impossibile (I)	3072
impossible (E, F)	3072
impostazione (I)	613
imprécis (F)	3073
impreciso (I)	3073
impreparato (I)	3074
impressionism (E)	3075
impressionisme (F)	3075
impressionismo (I)	3075
Impressionismus (D)	3075
impressive (E)	1259
Impromptu (D)	2361
impromptu (E, F)	2361
Improvisation (D)	3076
improvisation (E, F)	3076
improvisé (F)	1620
improvised (E)	1620
improviser (F)	2732
improvisieren (D)	2732
improvisierend (D)	1260
improvisiert (D)	1620
improvising (E)	1260
improvvisamente (I)	1715
improvvisando (I)	1260
improvvisare (I)	2732
improvvisazione (I)	3076
improvviso (I)	1715, 2361
impudent (E, F)	1494
Impuls (D)	518
impulse (E)	518
impulsion (F)	518
impulso (I)	518
in (D)	1749
in ... Weise (D)	1720
in a ... manner (E)	1720
in a ... way (E)	1720
in a ballad style (E)	914
in a dance style (E)	1068
in a hectic pace (E)	794
in a hurry (E)	747
in a lyrical way (E)	1313
in a singing style (E)	1029
in an undertone (E)	876
in battere (I)	1998
in bequemer Weise (D)	1052
in besonnener Weise (D)	1451
in bitterer Weise (D)	960
in bocca al lupo (I)	3077
in der Mitte geschlagen (D)	373
in der Oktave (D)	1621
in deutlicher Weise (D)	1108
in einfacher Weise (D)	1469
in eleganter Weise (D)	1126
in enormer Weise (D)	1696
in entschlossener Weise (D)	1077
in entzückender Weise (D)	1085
in Ermangelung von (D)	1719
in evidenza (I)	1716
in fließender Weise (D)	1188
in freier Weise (D)	1310
in fretta (I)	735
in front (E)	1683
in fugal style (E)	1987
in fuori (I)	1716
in gipsy style (E)	951
in giù (I)	1717
in gleichförmiger Weise (D)	1697
in halben Noten (D)	1622
in haste (E)	735
in heiterer Weise (D)	1220
in hervorstechender Weise (D)	1519
in herzlicher Weise (D)	934
in Hungarian style (E)	956
in keinem Fall (D)	1721
in klarer Weise (D)	1041, 1352
in kühner Weise (D)	986, 998
in langer Weise (D)	1730
in launenhafter Weise (D)	1033
in leichter Weise (D)	1159
in levare (I)	1999
in liebevoller Weise (D)	966
in lontananza (I)	1107
in luogo di (I)	1718
in mancanza di (I)	1719
in maniera (I)	1720
in many parts (E)	1861
in mäßiger Weise (D)	757
in misura (I)	720
in modo (I)	1720
in närrischer Weise (D)	1191
in nessun caso (I)	1721

in no case (E)	1721
in old style (E)	944
in order to finish (E)	1765
in pain (E)	1117
in place of (E)	1718
in primo piano (I)	1722
in Raserei (D)	1083
in rilievo (I)	1723
in risalto (I)	1724
in ruhiger Weise (D)	1368
in sanfter Weise (D)	1113
in schneller Weise (D)	765
in schwacher Weise (D)	1071
in stile recitativo (I)	1287
in stolzer Weise (D)	1180
in strenger Weise (D)	1790
in su (I)	1726
in tempo (I)	720
in the (E)	1749
in the absence of (E)	1719
in the background (E)	3386
in the foreground (E)	1722
in the manner of (E)	946
in the same way (E)	1750
in the style of German dance (E)	949
in time (E)	720
in trauriger Weise (D)	1573
in Turkish style (E)	950
in two (E)	1616
in unison (E)	2181
in vollständiger Weise (D)	2953
in warmherziger Weise (D)	1021
in zarter Weise (D)	1078
in zwei Zählzeiten (D)	1616
inaccurate (E)	3073
inafferando (I)	1261
inalterato (I)	1714
inattendu (F)	3078
inatteso (I)	3078
inbrünstig (D)	1175
incalzando (I)	794
incalzante (I)	749
incantato (I)	1262
incantatoire (F)	1263
incantevole (I)	1263
incanto (con) (I)	1263
incertain (F)	3079
incerto (I)	3079
inchangé (F)	1714
inchino (I)	3080
incidental music (E)	3142
incidere (I)	2784
incisif (F)	1264
incisive (E)	1264
incisivo (I)	1264
incisore (I)	3509
incollerito (I)	1047
incominciare (I)	2733
incomplet (F)	3081
incomplete (E)	3081
incompleto (I)	3081
incomprensibile (I)	1261
incorrect (E, F)	3319
incostante (I)	1339, 1606
increasing (E)	883
incrociare (I)	2734
incudine (I)	291
indebolendo (I)	894
indécis (F)	1265
indeciso (I)	1265
indépendance (F)	3083
independence (E)	3083
index (F)	3449
indicare (I)	2735
indication de la mesure (F)	2153
indication métronomique (F)	3082
indicazione metronomica (I)	3082
indice (I)	3449
indietro (I)	1684
indifferent (E)	1266
indifférent (F)	1266
indifferente (I)	1266
indifferenza (con) (I)	1266
indignantly (E)	1267
indignato (I)	1267
indigné (F)	1267
indipendenza (I)	3083
indiquer (F)	2735
indistinctly (E)	1268
indistinguibile (I)	1268

indistinto (I)	1268
indocile (I)	1270
indolent (E, F)	1269
indolente (I)	1269
indolenza (con) (I)	1269
indomabile (I)	1270
indomitable (E)	1270
indomito (I)	1270
indomptable (F)	1270
indugiando (I)	820
indulgent (F)	1271
indulgente (I)	1271
inebriante (I)	1124
inesatto (I)	3073
ineseguibile (I)	3084
inexact (E, F)	3073
inexécutable (F)	3084
infant prodigy (E)	2908
infantile (F, I)	1272
inférieur (F)	3085
inferior (E)	3085
inferiore (I)	3085
infernal (E, F)	1273
infernale (I)	1273
infiammato (I)	1274
inflamed (E)	1274
inflated (E)	969
inflection (E)	611
inflessione (I)	611
inflexion (F)	611
infocato (I)	1275
infuriato (I)	1276
ingegnoso (I)	1277
ingénieur du son (F)	3523
ingénieux (F)	1277
ingenious (E)	1277, 3056
ingénu (F)	1278
ingenuo (I)	1278
ingenuous (E)	1278
inglese (I)	2362
ingratiating (E)	1284
ingresso (I)	2917
Inhalt (D)	2963
inizio (I)	3086
innalzare la voce (I)	612
Innenstimme (D)	2056

inner part (E)	2056
innerlich (D)	1289
innerst (D)	1289
innig (D)	1289
inno (I)	2363
inno nazionale (I)	2364
innocenza (con) (I)	1279
input (E)	509
inquiet (F)	1281
inquiétant (F)	1280
inquietante (I)	1280
inquieto (I)	1281
ins vorige Zeitmaß zurückkehrend (D)	1629
insaisissable (F)	1261
insano (I)	1192
insegnante (I)	3510
insegnare (I)	2736
insensibile (I)	1282
insensibilmente (I)	1283
insensible (E, F)	1282
insensiblement (F)	1283
insensitively (E)	1283
insieme (I)	1725
insinuant (F)	1284
insinuante (I)	1284
insistenza (con) (I)	1285
insister (F)	2737
insistere (I)	2737
insolente (I)	1286
insolenza (con) (I)	1286
inspirare (I)	2740
Inspiration (D)	3096
inspiration (E, F)	3096
inspirer (F)	2740
instituteur (F)	3510
institutrice (F)	3510
Instrument (D)	3368
instrument (E, F)	3368
instrument à clavier (F)	3379
instrument accompagnateur (F)	3369
instrument de percussion électronique (F)	486
instrument jouant la partie de basse (F)	3380

instrument mélodique (F)   3381
instrument rythmique (F)   3382
instrument soliste (F)   3383
instrument solo (F)   3383
instrumental (D, E, F)   3366
instrumental music (E)   3171
Instrumentalmusik (D)   3171
instrumentation (E, F) 2138, 3205
instrumentation variable (F) 3367
instrumenter (F)   2836
instrumentieren (D)   2836
Instrumentierung (D)   2138
instruments à clavier (F)   3377
instruments à cordes (F)
                              3370, 3371
instruments à cordes pincées
    (F)   3376
instruments à percussion (F) 3375
instruments à vent (F)   3372
instruments transpositeurs
    (F)   3378
insultando (I)   1291
inszenieren (D)   2750
Inszenierung (D)   3111
intavolatura (I)   2000
integrale (I)   3087
intense (E)   1288
intense (F)   1288
intensif (F)   1288
intensità sonora (I)   3049
Intensität des Klanges (D)   3049
intensité du son (F)   3049
intensité du son (F)   598
intensity (E)   598
intensity (E)   3049
intensiv (D)   1288
intensivo (I)   1288
intenso (I)   1288
intérieur (F)   1289
interligne (F)   2133
interlude (E)   2366
interlude (E)   2365
interlude (F)   2365
interludio (I)   2365
intermède (F)   2366
intermedio (I)   2366

intermezzo (I)   2366
intermission (E)   3091
intermission (E)   3090
interno (I)   1289
intero (I)   2224
Interpret (D)   3089
interpretare (I)   2738
Interpretation (D)   3088
interpretation (E)   3088
interprétation (F)   3088
interpretazione (I)   3088
interprète (F)   3089
interprete (I)   3089
interpreter (E)   3089
interpréter (F)   2738
interpretieren (D)   2738
interrompere (I)   2739
interrompre (F)   2739
interruption (E)   3090
interruption (F)   3090
interruzione (I)   3090
interval (E)   2001
interval sign (E)   3327
Intervall (D)   2001
intervalle (F)   2001
intervallo (I)   3091
intervallo (I)   2001
intesa (I)   3092
intimate (E)   1289
intime (F)   1289
intimo (I)   1289
intonare (I)   2741
Intonation (D)   2002
intonation (E)   2002
intonation (F)   2002
intonazione (I)   2002
intrada (E)   2367
intrada (I)   2367
Intrade (D)   2367
intreccio (I)   3407
intrepid (E)   1290
intrépide (F)   1290
intrepido (I)   1290
introduction (E)   2368
introduction (F)   2368
introduire (F)   2742

introdurre (I)	2742
introduzione (I)	2368
intuition (E)	3093
intuition (F)	3093
intuizione (I)	3093
invariabile (I)	3094
invariable (E)	3094
invariable (F)	3094
invectivant (F)	1291
Invention (D)	2369
invention (E)	2369
invention (F)	2369
invenzione (I)	2369
inverser (F)	2743
inversion (E)	2107
inversion (F)	2107
inverted mordent (E)	2029
invertire (I)	2743
invettivando (I)	1291
invocando (I)	1040, 1405
invocating (E)	1040
invoking (E)	1405
involved (E)	1656
inward (E)	1289
ionian (E)	2003
ionico (I)	2003
ionien (F)	2003
ionisch (D)	2003
ira (con) (I)	1415
iracondo (I)	1292
irascibile (I)	1292
irascible (E, F)	1292
irato (I)	1293
ironia (con) (I)	1294
ironical (E)	1295
ironico (I)	1295
ironique (F)	1295
ironisch (D)	1295
iroso (I)	1293
irregolare (I)	3095
irregular (E)	3095
irrégulier (F)	3095
(sich) irren (D)	2810
irrequieto (I)	1281
irreredend (D)	1081
irrésolu (F)	1296
irresolute (E)	1296
irresoluto (I)	1296
irritant (F)	1297
irritante (I)	1297
irritated (E)	1293, 1298
irritating (E)	1297
irritato (I)	1298
irrité (F)	1298
Irrtum (D)	3310
irruente (I)	1585
ispirazione (con) (I)	3096
issue (E)	3005
istampita (I)	2370
istesso (I)	1735
it follows (E)	1796
Jabadao (D, E, F, I)	2548
Jabo (D, E, F, I)	2549
Jacara (D, E, F, I)	2550
jack (E)	64, 438, 440
Jagd (D)	2277
Jagdhorn (D)	132
Jagdmusik (D)	3129
Jahreszeit (D)	3353
jähzornig (D)	1292
Jaleo (D, E, F, I)	2551
jambe (F)	3444
Jambus (D)	1990
jambus (F)	1990
Janitscharenmusik (D)	3172
Jarabe (D, E, F, I)	2552
jauchzend (D)	1238
jaw (E)	3454
jazz guitar (E)	11
jazz trombone (E)	183
jazz trumpet (E)	176
Jazzbesen (D)	322
Jazzgitarre (D)	11
Jazzposaune (D)	183
Jazztrompete (D)	176
je m'excuse (F)	3326
jede (D)	1759
jeder (D)	1759
jedes (D)	1759
jedesmal (D)	1760
jedoch (D)	1732, 1768
jesting (E)	1458

jeté (F)	101	Kammerkantate (D)	2281
jeter (F)	2672	Kammermusik (D)	3130
jetzt (D)	2877	Kammerorchester (D)	3197
jeu (F)	54	Kammersonate (D)	2466
jeu de gongs (F)	288	Kammerton (D)	2980
jeu de timbres (F)	261	Kanal (D)	488
jeu perlé (F)	466	Kanon (D)	2279
jeux d'orgue (F)	439	Kantate (D)	2280
jew's harp (E)	315	Kantilene (D)	2286
jig (E)	2358	Kanzone (D)	2295
joindre (F)	2858	Kanzonette (D)	2300
joint (E)	3429	Kapelle (D)	2930
joke (E)	3317	Kapellmeister (D)	3506
joking (E)	1019	Kapellmeisterin (D)	3506
joli (F)	1589	Kapodaster (D)	39
jolly (E)	1233	kapriziös (D)	917
Jota (D, E, F, I)	2553	Karneval (D)	2932
joue (F)	3448	Karnevalslied (D)	2287
jouer (F)	2840	Kartondämpfer (D)	224
jouer à vue (F)	2843	Kassation (D)	2304
jouer d'oreille (F)	2842	Kassettenrekorder (D)	553
jouer faux (F)	2833	Kastagnetten (D)	269
jouer par cœur (F)	2841	Kasten (D)	35
jovial (D, E, F)	1237	Kastrat (D)	656
joyeusement (F)	1177	Katzenmusik (D)	3138
joyeux (F)	1236, 1311	kaum (D)	1639
joyful (E)	1236	Kavatine (D)	2305
joyous (E)	1311	kazoo (E)	301
jubeln (D)	2716	keck (D)	1522
jubelnd (D)	1238	keep on (E)	1830
jubilant (E, F)	1155, 1238	keep quiet! (E)	3334
judas (F)	3351	Kehle (D)	3446
jugendlich-dramatischer		kehlig (D)	610
Sopran (D)	631	Kehlkopf (D)	3451
jump (E)	3307	Kehlstimme (D)	709
jumped (E)	107	Kehrreim (D)	2105
jusqu'au (F)	1703	kein (D)	1751
jusqu'au signe (F)	1704	keinesfalls (D)	1721
jusque (F)	1809	kennen (D)	2809
just (E)	1812	Kern (D)	408
juste (F)	1146, 1991	Kernspalt (D)	201
justement (F)	1706	Kessel (D)	229, 359
Kadenz (D)	1910	Ketten (D)	274
kadenzierend (D)	1651	kettledrums (E)	336
Kakophonie (D)	2920	keuchend (D)	970
kalt (D)	1200	keusch (D)	1037

key (E)	203, 448, 2169	Klangstäbe (D)	279
key change (E)	1918	Klangsteuerung (D)	492
key signature (E)	1889	Klangsynthese (D)	573
key work (E)	211	Klangumwandlung (D)	587
key-note (E)	2168	klangvoll (D)	1511
keyboard (E)	447	Klappe (D)	203, 420
keyboard instrument (E)	3379	Klappenmechanik (D)	211
keyboard instruments (E)	3377	Klappholz (D)	286
keyboards (E)	577	Klappsitz (D)	3365
keyed glockenspiel (E)	264	klar (D)	1043, 1315
keyed xylophone (E)	345	Klarinette (D)	122
Kiefer (D)	3454	Klarinettist (D)	3495
Kiel (D)	438	Klarinettistin (D)	3495
Kinderchor (D)	663	Klassik (D)	2945
Kinderlied (D)	2297	klassisch (D)	2944
Kinderstimme (D)	714	klassische Musik (D)	3122
kindlich (D)	1272	klatschen (D)	2657
kindly (E)	1231	Klaviatur (D)	447
kinetic (E)	1044	Klaviaturglockenspiel (D)	
Kinn (D)	3455		264, 266
Kinnhalter (D)	62	Klaviaturxylophon (D)	345
Kinnlade (D)	3454	Klavichord (D)	394
Kirche (D)	2940	Klavier (D	400, 404
Kirchenchor (D)	662	Klavierauszug (D)	3288
Kirchenkantate (D)	2282	Klavierkonzert (D)	2314
Kirchenlied (D)	2285	Klaviersonate (D)	2468
Kirchenmusik (D)	3131, 3166	Klavierstuhl (D)	440
Kirchensonate (D)	2467	klein (D)	1773
Kirchentonart (D)	2022	klein (Intervall) (D)	2016
kit (E)	22	kleine Arie (D)	2258
Klage (D)	2372	kleine Flöte (D)	160
klagend (D)	1301	kleine Fuge (D)	2352
kläglich (D)	1186	kleine Klarinette (D)	120
Klammer (D)	1873	kleine Posse (D)	2275
Klang (D)	2142	kleine Trommel (D)	332
Klangänderung (D)	594	kleiner Finger (D)	3456
Klangbild (D)	3069	kleines Scherzo (D)	2456
Klangboden (D)	449	(der) kleinste (D)	1740
Klangeffekt (D)	503	klimpern (D)	2835
Klangerzeugung (D)	546	klingelnd (D)	1557
Klangfarbe (D)	2948	klingen lassen (D)	1700, 1727
Klangfülle (D)	3342	klopfen (D)	2671
Klanggemisch (D)	535	Klöppel (D)	356
Klanghölzer (D)	279	Knabenchor (D)	660
Klangregler (D)	494	knapp (D)	1639, 1669, 1770
Klangspeicherung (D)	526	Knarre (D)	309

knee (E)	3445
Knie (D)	3445
Knochen (D)	3463
Knopf (D)	37, 410
Knopfgriff-Akkordeon (D)	396
kokett (D)	1045
kokettierend (D)	1045
Koleda (D, E, F, I)	2554
Kolo (D, E, F, I)	2555
Kolophonium (D)	43
Koloratur (D)	669
Koloraturarie (D)	2256
Koloratursopran (D)	629
komisch (D)	1049
komische Oper (D)	2407
Komma (D)	1935
Komödie (D)	2950
Komparse (D)	2951
Komparsin (D)	2951
komponieren (D)	2685
Komponist (D)	3497
Komponistin (D)	3497
Komposition (D)	2955
Kompressor (D)	493
Kondensatormikrophon (D)	529
konkrete Musik (D)	3123
Konservatorium (D)	2961
Konsonant (D)	2962
Konsonanz (D)	1940
Kontaktmikrophon (D)	530
Kontinuität (D)	2964
Kontrabass (D)	14
Kontrabassist (D)	3499
Kontrabassistin (D)	3499
Kontrabassklarinette (D)	125
Kontrabassposaune (D)	182
Kontrabasstuba (D)	187
Kontrafagott (D)	127
Kontrapunkt (D)	1941
Kontrast (D)	2966
Kontrasubjekt (D)	1943
Kontratenor (D)	603
Kontretanz (D)	2321
konzentriert (D)	1054
Konzert (D)	2309, 2958
Konzert für Orchester (D)	2312
Konzertagentur (D)	2878
konzertant (D)	1668
konzertante Sinfonie (D)	2460
konzertanter Tanz (D)	2326
Konzertarie (D)	2253
Konzertetüde (D)	2472
konzertieren (D)	2696
konzertierend (D)	1668
Konzertkasse (D)	2920
Konzertmeister (D)	3251
Konzertmeisterin (D)	3251
Konzertouvertüre (D)	2415
Konzertsaal (D)	3306
Konzertsaison (D)	3354
Konzertstück (D)	2426
Kopf (D)	3268, 3480
Kopfhörer (D)	495
Kopfsatz (D)	2079
Kopfstimme (D)	711
Kopfstück mit Schnabel (D)	230
kopieren (D)	2690
Kopist (D)	3500
Kopistin (D)	3500
Koppel (D)	407
Kornett (D)	128
Körpergewicht (D)	468
korrekt (D)	2969
Korrepetition (D)	3261
Korrepetitor (D)	3520
Korrepetitorin (D)	3520
korrigieren (D)	2692
Kostüm (D)	2971
Kotillon (D)	2324
kräftig (D)	849, 1590
kraftvoll (D)	1593
kratzen (D)	2727
krebsgängig (D)	2094
kreischend (D)	1535
kreisend (D)	733
Kreuz (D)	1954
kreuzen (D)	2734
kreuzsaitig (D)	421
kriegerisch (D)	1248, 1328
kristallklar (D)	1062
Kritik (D)	2970
kritisieren (D)	2695

Krummhorn (D)	138
Kuckuckspfeife (D)	282
Kuhglocke (D)	258
kühl (D)	1198
kühn (D)	988, 997
Kujawiak (D, E, F, I)	2556
Kulisse (D)	3270
Kunst (D)	2893
Künstler (D)	3489
Künstlereingang (D)	3012
Künstlerin (D)	3489
künstlerisch (D)	2894
Künstlername (D)	3265
Künstlerzimmer (D)	2927
künstlich (D)	993
Kürbisrassel (D)	290, 296
kurz (D)	1650
kürzer und schneller als Adagio (D)	721
kürzer und schneller als Largo (D)	750
kurzer Vorschlag (D)	1870
Kürzung (D)	1866
l'art du décor (F)	3316
l'avant-scène (F)	3259
l'istesso tempo (I)	756
l'œuvre intégrale (F)	3087
La (F, I)	2214
La bémol (F)	2216
La bemolle (I)	2216
La dièse (F)	2215
La diesis (I)	2215
La doppio bemolle (I)	2218
La doppio diesis (I)	2217
La double bémol (F)	2218
La double dièse (F)	2217
la même chose (F)	1735
labbro (I)	3450
labial pipe (E)	415
Labialpfeife (D)	415
laborieux (F)	1529
lacerated (E)	1299
lacero (I)	1299
lächeln (D)	2824
lächelnd (D)	687
lachen (D)	2791
lachend (D)	682
lächerlich (D)	1433
lacking (E)	822
lacrimando (I)	1389
lacrimoso (I)	1300
Lage (D)	3233
Lagenwechsel (D)	93
lagnoso (I)	1301
lagrimoso (I)	1300
lai (F, I)	2371
Laie (D)	2986
laienhaft (D)	3252
laisser vibrer (F)	1727
laissez vibrer (F)	1700
lame (E)	952
lament (E)	2372
lamentation (F)	2372
lamenting (E)	1301
lamento (I)	2372
lamento funebre (I)	2398
lamentoso (I)	1301
Lampenfieber (D)	3221
Lancers (D)	2373
lancieri (I)	2373
lanciers (E, F)	2373
lancinante (I)	1533
landa (I)	2374
Lande (D)	2374
lande (F)	2374
Ländler (D, E, F, I)	2557
ländlich (D)	943, 1449
lands (E)	2374
lang (D)	1730
längeres Fugenthema (D)	1884
langsam (D)	722, 753, 754
langsamer werdend (D)	826
Langspielplatte (D)	533
langue (F)	3452
languendo (I)	1302
languette (F)	409
languid (E)	1303
languidamente (I)	1302
languide (F)	1303
languidezza (con) (I)	1302
languido (I)	1303
languishing (E)	1302

languissamment (F)	1302	laye (F)	442
languissant (F)	1303	layman (E)	2986
langweilig (D)	3184	lazy (E)	1393
largamente (I)	1304	le même mouvement (F)	756
largando (I)	821	le mieux possible (F)	1624
large (F)	751	le plus... (F)	1711
largement (F)	1304	le plus doucement possible	
largeur (F)	3097	(F)	866
largeur de bande (F)	519	le plus fort possible (F)	865
larghetto (I)	750	le plus possible (F)	1712
larghezza (I)	3097	le rideau s'ouvre (F)	3066
larghezza di banda (I)	519	le rideau se baisse (F)	3064
largo (I)	751	le rideau se ferme (F)	3067
largo assai (I)	752	le rideau se lève (F)	3065
laringe (I)	3451	leader (E)	3251
Lärm (D)	566	leading motif (E)	2031
lärmend (D)	1448	leading note (E)	2118
larmoyant (F)	1390	leading soprano (E)	620
larmoyant (F)	1300	leading tone (E)	2118
larynx (E)	3451	leaned (E)	843
larynx (F)	3451	leaning (E)	842
las (F)	1305	leap (E)	3307
lasciar vibrare (I)	1727	leather stick (E)	349
lasciate vibrare (I)	1700	Lebe wohl! (D)	2876
lassé (F)	1305	lebendig (D)	1602
lässig (D)	1269	lebhaft (D)	728, 782
lasso (I)	1305	lebhafter werdend (D)	789
last (E)	1843	leçon (F)	3102
last movement (E)	2180	Lederschlägel (D)	349
last time (E)	1842	leer (D)	1858
lastra (I)	292	leere Saite (D)	97
lau (D)	1549, 1552	left (E)	3337
Lauf (D)	2185	left pedal (E)	434
laufend (D)	745	leg (E)	3444
laughing (E)	682	legare (I)	2745
launenhaft (D)	917	legato (I)	854
launisch (D)	1033	legatura (I)	2004
laut (D)	849	legatura di fraseggio (I)	2005
Laute (D)	20	legatura di valore (I)	2006
Lautkunde (D)	3046	legen (D)	2749
Lautsprecher (D)	481	legend (E)	2376
Lautsprecherbox (D)	567	Legende (D)	2376
Lautstärke (D)	598	légende (F)	2376
lavolta (I)	2375	léger (F)	1307
lavorare (I)	2744	leger line (E)	2149
lay (E)	2371	légèrement (F)	1306

leggenda (I)	2376
leggere (I)	2746
leggere a prima vista (I)	2843
leggerezza (con) (I)	1306
leggermente (I)	1306
leggero (I)	1307
leggiadro (I)	1036
leggiero (I)	1307
leggio (I)	3098
legnetti da percuotere (I)	279
legni (I)	3099
legno (I)	3100
legno frullante (I)	293
lehren (D)	2736
Lehrer (D)	3510
Lehrerin (D)	3510
Leich (D)	2371
leicht (D)	1307, 3028
leichte Musik (D)	3149
leichter gemacht (D)	3329
leichtfertig (D)	1206
Leichtigkeit (D)	3029
leichtsinnig (D)	1516
leidend (D)	1116
leidenschaftlich (D)	981
leidenschaftslos (D)	1514, 1552
Leier (D)	17
Leierkasten (D)	478
leihen (D)	2772
leise (D)	864
Leitmotiv (D)	2031
Leitton (D)	2118
Leitung (D)	2989
Lektion (D)	3102
lena (con) (I)	989
lenient (E)	1271
lent (F)	722, 754
lentamente (I)	753
lentando (I)	826
lentement (F)	753
lentissimo (I)	723
lento (I)	754
lernen (D)	2731, 2837
les autres (F)	1707
les bois (F)	3373
les cuivres (F)	3374
les mêmes (F)	1708
lesen (D)	2746
Lesginka (D, E, F, I)	2558
less (E)	1736
lessing (E)	897
lesson (E)	3102
leste (F)	1308
lesto (I)	1308
let sound (E)	1727
let vibrate (E)	1727
letizia (con) (I)	1235
letter (E)	3101
lettera (I)	3101
lettre (F)	3101
letzte (D)	1843
letzter (D)	1843
letztes Mal (D)	1842
leuchtend (D)	1317
leutselig (D)	929
levare (I)	2850
levata (I)	1999
levate i sordini (I)	1728
levée (F)	1999
level (E)	522
lever (F)	2850
lever la voix (F)	612
lèvre (F)	3450
lezione (I)	3102
lezione collettiva (I)	3103
leziosamente (I)	1309
liaison (F)	2004
liberamente (I)	1310
libero (I)	755
libre (F)	755
librement (F)	719, 1310
libretto (E, I)	678
libro (I)	3104
licenza (con) (I)	1310
lid (E)	420
lidio (I)	2007
lié (F)	854
liebenswürdig (D)	959
lieber (D)	1772
Liebesfuß (D)	213
Liebesoboe (D)	157
liebevoll (D)	933, 965

Liebhaber (D)	2986	links (D)	3337
liebkosend (D)	918	lip (E)	3450
lieblich (D)	1504	lip (E)	244
Lied (D, E, F, I)	2295, 2559	Lippe (D)	3450
(Kirchen-)Lied (D)	2285	liquid (E)	1312
Lied ohne Worte (D)	2451	liquide (F)	1312
Liedersammlung (D)	3271	liquido (I)	1312
lier (F)	2745	lira (I)	19
lieto (I)	1311	lire (F)	570, 2746
lieu (F)	1731	lirica (I)	679
lieve (I)	1307	liricamente (I)	1313
ligado (I)	854	lirico (I)	1313
ligature (E)	2134	liscio (I)	1314
light (E)	1307	lispeln (D)	649
light music (E)	3149	lisse (F)	1314
lighting (E)	3068	listener (E)	2895
lightly (E)	1306	listening centre (E)	2938
lightly detached (E)	103	Litanei (D)	2377
ligne (F)	2095	litania (I)	2377
ligne supplémentaire (F)	2149	litanie (F)	2377
like (E)	1659	litany (E)	2377
like a cadenza (E)	1664	litofono (I)	294
like a march (E)	947	Litophon (D)	294
like a peasant dance (E)	945	litophone (E, F)	294
limelights (E)	3105	little (E)	1773
limitatore (I)	520	little by little (E)	1774
limiter (E)	520	little finger (E)	3456
limiteur (F)	520	little jest (E)	2275
limpid (E)	1043	little scherzo (E)	2456
limpide (F)	1043	liturgical drama (E)	2392
limpido (I)	1043	liturgisches Drama (D)	2392
limping (E)	952	liutaio (I)	3511
limply (E)	1343	liuto (I)	20
line (E)	2095, 3422	live broadcast (E)	591
linea (I)	2095	live recording (E)	556
linéaire (F)	521	live transmission (E)	591
linear (D, E)	521	Live-Aufnahme (D)	556
linear construction (E)	1937	Live-Sendung (D)	591
lineare (I)	521	livello (I)	522
lingua (I)	3452	lively (E)	728, 784, 1602
linguetta (I)	209	livre (F)	3104
Linie (D)	2095	livret (F)	678
Linienführung (D)	1937	livret d'opéra (F)	678
Liniensystem (D)	2063	lo stesso (I)	1808
linkes Pedal (D)	434	lo stesso tempo (I)	756
linkisch (D)	1239	lobby (E)	3286

loben (D)	2705	lucid (E)	1315
Lobgesang (D)	2363	lucidamente (I)	1315
lockern (D)	2793	lucide (F)	1315
lockernd (D)	813	lucido (I)	1315
loco (L)	1729	luftig (D)	928
lodare (I)	2705	Luftpause (D)	624
Loge (D)	3210	Luftröhre (D)	3482
loge (F)	3210	Luftstoß (D)	3340
loggione (I)	3053	lügen (D)	2748
lointain (F)	855	lugubre (F, I)	1316
lombardischer Rhythmus		luisant (F)	1013
(D)	2104	lukewarm (E)	1549
long (E, F)	1730	lukewarmly (E)	1552
long-playing record (E)	533	lullaby (E)	2399
longing (E)	1356	lumière (F)	196
longuement (F)	1730	lumineux (F)	1317
longueur d'onde (F)	523	luminoso (I)	1317
lontano (I)	855	Lungen (D)	3470
look (E)	3332	lunghezza d'onda (I)	523
loosening (E)	813	lungo (I)	1730
löschen (D)	489	lungs (E)	3470
losco (I)	1561	luogo (I)	1731
losschnellend (D)	1456	lusingando (I)	1318
lostrennen (D)	2831	lusingato (I)	1319
Lotusflöte (D)	149	lustig (D)	1222
louche (F)	1561	lustro (con) (I)	1320
loud (E)	849	lute (E)	20
loudness (E)	598	luth (F)	20
loudspeaker (E)	481	luthier (F)	3511
louer (F)	2705	lutin (F)	3045
lourd (F)	1386	lutrin (F)	3098
Loure (D, E, F, I)	2560	luttuosamente (I)	1321
lourré (F)	1831	luxuriant (E)	1436
lovely (E)	1036	lydian (E)	2007
lovingly (E)	935, 966	lydien (F)	2007
low (E)	864, 2913	lydisch (D)	2007
lower (E)	3085	Lyra (D)	19
lower bout (E)	80	lyre (E, F)	19
lower joint (E)	215	lyric (E)	679
lower part (E)	2055	lyric drama (E)	2337
lowering (E)	891, 898	lyric piece (E)	2427
lowest part (E)	2055	lyric soprano (E)	630
LP (D, E)	533	lyric tragedy (E)	2483
luccicante (I)	1013	lyrical tenor (E)	634
lucente (I)	1013, 1317	Lyrik (D)	679
luci della ribalta (I)	3105	lyrique (F)	679

lyrisch (D)	1313
lyrische Komödie (D)	2308
lyrische Tragödie (D)	2483
lyrischer Sopran (D)	630
lyrischer Tenor (D)	634
lyrisches Drama (D)	2337
lyrisches Stück (D)	2427
ma (I)	1732
ma non tanto (I)	1733
ma non troppo (I)	1733
macchina (I)	210
macchina per il tuono (I)	295
machen (D)	2717
machine à rythme (F)	484
machine à vent (F)	284
machine drum (E)	337
machine pour le tonnerre (F)	295
mâchoire (F)	3454
mächtig (D)	1402
mad (E)	1192
madly (E)	1192, 1379
Madrigal (D)	2378
madrigal (E, F)	2378
madrigale (I)	2378
maecenas (E)	3109
maestoso (I)	1322
maestria (con) (I)	1323
maestro di ballo (I)	3512
maestro sostituto (I)	3520
magazine (E)	3298
Magen (D)	3478
maggiolata (I)	2379
maggiore (I)	2008
magic (E)	1324
magico (I)	1324
magique (F)	1324
magisch (D)	1324
Magnetband (D)	537
Magnetbandgerät (D)	552
magnetic head (E)	585
magnetic tape (E)	537
Magnetkopf (D)	585
magnétophone (F)	552
Mailied (D)	2379
mailloche (F)	362
main (E)	2080

main (F)	3453
main accent (E)	1868
main guidonienne (F)	2009
main part (E)	3302
main theme (E)	2078
mainly (E)	1815
mains croisées (F)	462
maintenant (F)	2877
maintenez (F)	1830
mais (F)	1732
mais pas trop (F)	1733
maison d'édition musicale (F)	2935
maître de ballet (F)	3512
maîtresse de ballet (F)	3512
maîtrise (F)	3323
majestätisch (D)	1322
majestic (E)	1322
majestueux (F)	1322
majeur (F)	2008
major (E)	2008
make vibrate (E)	1700
making fun (E)	1031
...mal (D)	1855
maladroit (F)	1239
Malagueña (D, E, F, I)	2561
maldestro (I)	1239
male voice (E)	715
malerisch (D)	1395
malgrado (I)	3106
malgré (F)	3106
malicieux (F)	1327
malicious (E)	1327
malin (F)	1215
malinconia (con) (I)	1325
malinconico (I)	1326
malizioso (I)	1327
maligno (I)	1327
mallet (E)	362
man nehme weg (D)	1807
management (E)	2989
mancando (I)	822
manche (F)	61
mandolin (E)	21
Mandoline (D)	21
mandoline (F)	21

mandolino (I)   21
manetta (I)   427
Manfredina (D, E, F, I)   2562
Mangel (D)   2982
mani incrociate (I)   462
manico (I)   61
manierato (I)   932
maniéré (F)   932
manly (E)   1329
Männerchor (D)   666
Männerstimme (D)   715
männlich (D)   1329
mano (I)   3453
mano guidoniana (I)   2009
Manseque (D, E, F, I)   2563
mansueto (I)   1396
Manta (D, E, F, I)   2564
mantenete (I)   1830
mantice (I)   428
Manual (D)   429
manual (E)   429
manuale (I)   429
Manubrium (D)   427
manuel (F)   429
many (E)   1827
maracas (E, F, I)   296
marcando (I)   856
marcare (I)   2747
marcato (I)   857
march (E)   2380
marche (F)   2380
marche funèbre (F)   2381
marche nuptiale (F)   2382
marche triomphale (F)   2383
Märchen (D)   3031
marcia (I)   2380
marcia funebre (I)   2381
marcia nuziale (I)   2382
marcia trionfale (I)   2383
marimba (F)   297
marimba (I)   297
marimba(phone) (E)   297
Marimbaphon (D)   297
marinesca (I)   2384
marinière (F)   2384
mark (E)   1795

marked (E)   857
markieren (D)   2747
markierend (D)   856
markiert (D)   857
markig (D)   1132
marking (E)   856
marqué (F)   857
marquer (F)   2747
Marsch (D)   2380
marteau (F)   364, 430
martelé (F)   463
martellando (I)   858
martellato (I)   463
martelletto (I)   430
martello (I)   364, 430
martial (E, F)   1328
marvellous (E)   3110
marziale (I)   1328
mascarade (F)   2385
mascella (I)   3454
maschera (I)   3107, 3108
mascherata (I)   2385
Maschinenpauke (D)   337
maschio (I)   1329
mask (E)   3107
Maske (D)   3107
Maskenspiel (D)   2385
Maskerade (D)   2385
masque (E, F)   2385, 3107
mass (E)   2389
mass for the dead (E)   2390
mäßig (D)   758
mäßig bewegt (D)   729
mäßigen (D)   2753
mäßigend (D)   823, 912
massimo (I)   1734
masterpiece (E)   2929
mastery (E)   1323
Matelote (D)   2384
matelote (F)   2384
Matrosentanz (D)   2384
matt (D)   1361
mattinata (I)   2386
Maultrommel (D)   315
mauresque (F)   2395
maximum (F)   1734

may song (E)	2379	Meisterwerk (D)	2929
Mäzen (D)	3109	melancholic (E)	1326
mazurca (I)	2387	mélancolique (F)	1326
Mazurka (D)	2387	melanconico (I)	1326
mazurka (E, F)	2387	mélangé (F)	1741
mazza (I)	362	mélanger (F)	534
mazza del tambur maggiore		mélangeur de son (F)	527
(I)	363	Mellotron (D)	524
mazzuolo (I)	362	mellotron (E, I)	524
mbira (I)	313	mellow (E)	1375
measure (E)	2018	melodia (I)	2011
measure number (E)	2046	melodic (E)	1332, 2012
measured (E)	1742	melodic instrument (E)	3381
mécanique (F)	431	melodico (I)	1332, 2012
mécaniquement (F)	1330	Melodie (D)	2011
mécanisme des clefs (F)	211	mélodie (F)	2011
mécanisme du piston (F)	210	Melodieinstrument (D)	3381
meccanica (I)	431	Melodiesaite (D)	51
meccanicamente (I)	1330	Melodiestimme (D)	2057
meccanismo delle chiavi (I)	211	mélodieusement (F)	1333
mecenate (I)	3109	mélodieux (F)	1332
mécène (F)	3109	melodiös (D)	1333
mechanical music (E)	3151	melodioso (I)	1333
mechanically (E)	1330	melodious (E)	1333
Mechanik (D)	431	mélodique (F)	2012
Mechanikbogen (D)	56	melodisch (D)	1332, 2012
mechanisch (D)	1330	Melodram (D)	2388
mechanische Musik (D)	3151	Melodrama (D)	2388
medesimo (I)	1735	melodrama (E)	2388
medesimo tempo (I)	756	mélodrame (F)	2388
mediant (E)	2010	melodramma (I)	2388
Mediante (D)	2010	melody (E)	2011
médiante (F)	2010	melody part (E)	2057
mediante (I)	2010	mélomane (F)	2883
meditando (I)	1331	melomane (I)	2883
méditatif (F)	1331	mélotron (F)	524
meditating (E)	1331	melted (E)	1218
meditativo (I)	1331	membrana (I)	365, 368
medley (E)	2433	même (le) (F)	1735
meek (E)	1396	mémorisation (F)	525
mehr (D)	1770	mémorisation du son (F)	526
mehr als (D)	1771	memorizzazione (I)	525
Mehrchörigkeit (D)	2067	memorizzazione del suono (I)	526
Mehrspurverfahren (D)	555	men's choir (E)	666
mehrstimmig (D)	1861	men's chorus (E)	666
Mehrstimmigkeit (D)	2068	menaçant (F)	1336

menacing (E)	1336
meno (I)	1736
Mensur (D)	2018
mensuration (E)	2018
mentir (F)	2748
mentire (I)	2748
mento (I)	3455
menton (F)	3455
mentoniera (I)	62
mentonnière (F)	62
menuet (F)	2391
Menuett (D)	2391
meraviglia (con) (I)	1537
meraviglioso (I)	3110
mercy (E)	681
mercyful (E)	1392
mero (I)	1413
merry (E)	3033
merveilleux (F)	3110
mescolatore di suono (I)	527
messa (I)	2389
messa dei defunti (I)	2390
messa di (da) Requiem (I)	2390
messa di (in) voce (I)	613
messa in scena (I)	3111
messanza (I)	2442
Messe (D)	2389
messe (F)	2389
messe des morts (F)	2390
messen (D)	2752
Messglöckchen (D)	263
Messklingeln (D)	263
mestamente (I)	1334
mestizia (con) (I)	1574
mesto (I)	1335
mesure (F)	2152
mesure (F)	1902, 2018
mesuré (F)	1742
mesure binaire (F)	2154
mesure composée (F)	1903
mesure simple (F)	1904
mesure ternaire (F)	2157
mesurer (F)	2752
metà (I)	1737, 2225
metal block (E, F, I)	298
metal castanets (E)	271
metal mute (E)	225
metal string (E)	48
metalizzare il suono (I)	245
Metallblock (D)	298
Metalldämpfer (D)	225
Metallkastagnetten (D)	271
Metallophon (D)	299
Metallsaite (D)	48
metalofono (I)	299
metalophone (E)	299
métalophone (F)	299
meticoloso (I)	1463
méticuleux (F)	1463
meticulous (E)	1463
metre (E)	2014, 2152
mètre (F)	2014
metric(al) (E)	2013
metrico (I)	2013
métrique (F)	2013
metrisch (D)	2013
metro (I)	2014
Metronom (D)	3112
Metronomangabe (D)	3082
metronome (E)	3112
métronome (F)	3112
metronome mark(ing) (E)	3082
metronomo (I)	3112
Metrum (D)	2014, 2018
mettere (I)	2749
mettere il punto di valore (I)	2015
mettere in scena (I)	2750
mettere la sordina (I)	246
mettre (F)	2749
mettre en scène (F)	2750
mettre en valeur (F)	1724
mettre la sourdine (F)	246
mezza (I)	1738
mezza forza (I)	1739
mezza luna (I)	300
mezza voce (I)	614
mezzo (I)	1738
mezzo soprano (E)	615
mezzo-soprano (F)	615
mezzo-soprano clef (E)	1926
mezzoforte (I)	859
mezzopiano (I)	860

Mezzosopran (D)	615	minacciosamente (I)	1336
mezzosoprano (I)	615	minaccioso (I)	1336
Mezzosopranschlüssel (D)	1926	mince (F)	1147
Mi (F, I)	2199	mineur (F)	2016
Mi bémol (F)	2201	miniature score (E)	3218
Mi bemolle (I)	2201	minim (E)	2225
Mi dièse (F)	2200	minim beat (E)	1622
Mi diesis (I)	2200	minim rest (E)	2232
Mi doppio bemolle (I)	2203	minima (I)	2225
Mi doppio diesis (I)	2202	minimo (I)	1740
Mi double bémol (F)	2203	minimum (E, F)	1740
Mi double dièse (F)	2202	minor (E)	2016
mi-doux (F)	860	minore (I)	2016
mi-fort (F)	859	minuet (E)	2391
microfono (I)	528	minuetto (I)	2391
microfono a condensatore (I)	529	minuziös (D)	1463
microfono a contatto (I)	530	minuzioso (I)	1463
microfono elettrodinamico (I)	531	Mirliton (D)	301
		mirliton (F, I)	301
microfono elettromagnetico (I)	532	miroitant (F)	1013
		mis en relief (F)	870
microphone (E, F)	528	miscelare (I)	534
microphone à condensateur (F)	529	Mischpult (D)	527
		mise en scène (F)	3111
microphone à contact (F)	530	misolidio (I)	2017
microphone électrodynamique (F)	531	Misserfolg (D)	3036
		Missklang (D)	2923
microphone électromagnétique (F)	532	Misston (D)	3186
		mistake (E)	3310
microsolco (I)	533	misteriosamente (I)	1337
middle joint (E)	214	misterioso (I)	1337
middle part (E)	2056	mistero (I)	2392
migliorare (I)	2751	mistico (I)	1338
mignolo (I)	3456	misto (I)	1741
mignon (F)	1036, 1080	mistuned (E)	3361
Mikrophon (D)	528	mistura (I)	535
mild (E)	1396	misty (E)	1348
militairement (F)	948	misura (I)	2018
militarily (E)	948	misurare (I)	2752
militärisch (D)	948	misurato (I)	1742
Militärkapelle (D)	2911	mit (D)	1666
militarmente (I)	948	mit Ausdehnung (D)	967
Militärmusik (D)	3152	mit Abscheu (D)	1428
Militärtrommel (D)	332	mit Adel (D)	1354
military band (E)	2911	mit Anbetung (D)	925
military music (E)	3152	mit Andacht (D)	1417

mit aufgehobener Dämpfung
(D)   472
mit Aufschwung (D)   1501
mit Ausdauer (D)   1385
mit Ausdehnung (D)   1148
mit Ausdruck (D)   1149
mit Bangen (D)   977
mit Beben (D)   1202
mit Bedauern (D)   1440
mit Bedeutung (D)   1582
mit Begeisterung (D)   1136
mit Begierde (D)   1010
mit Behändigkeit (D)   941
mit Beharrlichkeit (D)   1285
mit Beständigkeit (D)   1385
mit Bestimmtheit (D)   1094
mit Betrübnis (D)   919
mit Bitterkeit (D)   962
mit Bravour (D)   1012
mit Bünden versehen (D)   74
mit Charakter (D)   1034
mit Dämpfer (D)   96, 459
mit dem / - der / - den (D)   1666
mit dem Bogen (D)   94
mit der Bogenstange (D)   95
mit der Hand (D)   378
mit der Stimme (D)   1657
mit Deutlichkeit (D)   1042
mit Diskretion (D)   1099
mit Eifer (D)   1609
mit einem Finger (D)   1667
mit Einfachheit (D)   1470
mit einiger Freiheit (D)   740
mit Ekstase (D)   1151
mit Eleganz (D)   1127
mit Empfindsamkeit (D)   1471
mit Empfindung (D)   1475
mit Emphase (D)   1133
mit Energie (D)   1131
mit Entrüstung (D)   1047
mit Entschlossenheit (D)
                                      1072, 1442
mit Ergebung (D)   1424
mit Ergötzen (D)   1084
mit Erhabenheit (D)   1129
mit Ernsthaftigkeit (D) 1244, 1482

mit Erregung (D)   1130
mit Feierlichkeit (D)   1398, 1509
mit Feinheit (D)   1184
mit Fertigkeit (D)   1092
mit Festigkeit (D)   1171
mit Feuer (D)   1214
mit Fleiß (D)   1097
mit Flexibilität (D)   1187
mit Frechheit (D)   1286
mit Freimut (D)   1197
mit Freude (D)   1235
mit Frieden (D)   1370
mit Frische (D)   1204
mit Fröhlichkeit (D)   955
mit Frohlocken (D)   1156
mit Furcht (D)   1555
mit Galanterie (D)   1224
mit gedämpfter Stimme (D)   635
mit Gefälligkeit (D)   1230
mit Gefühl (D)   1475
mit Geläufigkeit (D)   743
mit Gemütsbewegung (D)   1130
mit Genauigkeit (D)   1145
mit Genuss (D)   1226
mit Geringschätzung (D)   1464
mit Geschicklichkeit (D)   1092
mit geschlossenem Mund (D)   636
mit Geschmack (D)   1249
mit Geschwindigkeit (D)   744
mit Gewalt (D)   1595
mit Geziertheit (D)   1429
mit Glanz (D)   1320
mit Gleichgültigkeit (D)   1266
mit Glückseligkeit (D)   1235
mit Groll (D)   1441
mit Größe (D)   1242
mit großer Freiheit (D)   737
mit großer Geschwindigkeit
(D)   763
mit größter Kraft (D)   847
mit halber Stimme (D)   614, 637
mit Haltung (D)   1400
mit Härte (D)   1122
mit Hartnäckigkeit (D)   1366
mit Heftigkeit (D)   1586
mit heiterer Gelassenheit (D) 1480

mit Heiterkeit (D)	1221
mit Herz (D)	1065
mit Hingabe (D)	916
mit Hochachtung (D)	1365
mit Hochgenuss (D)	1226
mit Hochmut (D)	992
mit höchster Virtuosität (D)	1056
mit Höflichkeit (D)	929
mit höherem Tempo (D)	797
mit Hohn (D)	1457
mit Humor (D)	1577
mit Inbrunst (D)	1176
mit Ironie (D)	1294
mit Jubel (D)	1156
mit Kälte (D)	1199
mit Keckheit (D)	1002
mit Klarheit (D)	1042
mit Koketterie (D)	1046
mit Kraft (D)	1193
mit Kühnheit (D)	987, 999
mit Langsamkeit (D)	736
mit Lärm (D)	1534
mit Lauheit (D)	1548
mit Lebenskraft (D)	1592
mit Lebhaftigkeit (D)	1600
mit Leichtigkeit (D)	937, 1306
mit Leidenschaft (D)	1373
mit Leidenschaftslosigkeit (D)	1548
mit leiser Stimme (D)	635, 876
mit Liebe (D)	964
mit Liebenswürdigkeit (D)	958, 1230
mit Liebesglut (D)	1275
mit Lust (D)	1603
mit Mäßigung (D)	1340
mit Meisterschaft (D)	1323
mit Müdigkeit (D)	1528
mit Mühe (D)	1168
mit Mut (D)	975
mit Nachdruck (D)	1131
mit Natürlichkeit (D)	1347
mit Niedergeschlagenheit (D)	1461
mit Phantasie (D)	1162
mit Präzision (D)	1403
mit Prunk (D)	1398, 1487
mit Raffinesse (D)	1421
mit Raserei (D)	1203
mit Rastlosigkeit (D)	1502
mit Reinheit (D)	1411
mit Respekt (D)	1444
mit Ruhe (D)	1023, 1564
mit Sanftheit (D)	1114
mit Sanftmut (D)	1114
mit Schärfe (D)	995
mit Schaudern (D)	1202, 1416
mit Schmelz (D)	1302
mit Schmerz (D)	1111, 1118
mit Schnelligkeit (D)	741
mit Schüchternheit (D)	1554
mit Schwäche (D)	1070
mit Schwermut (D)	1325
mit Schwung (D)	1501
mit Seele (D)	974
mit Seelenfrieden (D)	1370
mit Seelenqual (D)	972
mit Selbstgefälligkeit (D)	1539
mit Sicherheit (D)	1498
mit Sorgfalt (D)	922
mit Sorglosigkeit (D)	1355
mit Spaß (D)	1158
mit Staunen (D)	1537
mit Steifheit (D)	1434
mit Stolz (D)	1181
mit Strenge (D)	742, 1434, 1484
mit Tapferkeit (D)	1582
mit Trägheit (D)	1269
mit Traurigkeit (D)	1574
mit Überschwang (D)	1136
mit Überschwänglichkeit (D)	1143
mit Überzeugung (D)	1058
mit Unbefangenheit (D)	1101
mit Unbeständigkeit (D)	1607
mit Ungeduld (D)	1253
mit Ungestüm (D)	1255
mit Ungezwungenheit (D)	1521
mit Unruhe (D)	1281
mit Unschuld (D)	1279
mit Vehemenz (D)	1586
mit Verachtung (D)	1106
mit Verehrung (D)	1588
mit Vergnügen (D)	1110

mit Vertrauen (D)	1179	moaning (E)	1228
mit Verwegenheit (D)	987	mobile (F, I)	1339
mit Verzückung (D)	1151	mocking (E)	1006, 1031
mit Verzweiflung (D)	1105	mockingly (E)	1020
mit Virtuosität (D)	1596	modal (D, E, F)	2019
mit vollem Ton (D)	1769	modale (I)	2019
mit voller Kraft (D)	847	modalità (I)	2020
mit voller Stimme (D)	647	Modalität (D)	2020
mit Vorsicht (D)	1410	modalité (F)	2020
mit Vorstellungskraft (D)	1251	modality (E)	2020
mit Wärme (D)	1025	mode (E, F)	2021
mit Weite (D)	967	mode ecclésiastique (F)	2022
mit Wildheit (D)	1174	model (E)	3113
mit Willen (D)	1605	modèle (F)	3113
mit Wonne (D)	1084	modello (I)	3113
mit Wucht (D)	1255	moderando (I)	823
mit Würde (D)	1096	moderare (I)	2753
mit Wut (D)	1415	moderatamente (I)	757
mit Zartheit (D)	1079	moderate (E)	758
mit Zärtlichkeit (D)	1546	moderately (E)	757
mit Zauber (D)	1166	moderating (E)	823, 912
mit Zorn (D)	1047	moderato (I)	758
mit Zuneigung (D)	933	moderazione (con) (I)	1340
mit Zurückhaltung (D)	1505	modéré (F)	758
mit zwei Schlägeln (D)	377	modérément (F)	757
mite (I)	1396	modérer (F)	2753
mitigando (I)	906	modern (D, E)	3114
Mitleid (D)	681	moderne (F)	3114
mitleidig (D)	1392	moderno (I)	3114
mitschneiden (D)	2784	modest (E)	1576
Mitschnitt (D)	556	modestamente (I)	1576
mittelleise (D)	860	modestement (F)	1576
mittelstark (D)	859	modificare (I)	2754
Mittelstimme (D)	2056	modification du son (F)	594
Mittelstück (D)	214	modifier (F)	2754
Mitwirkung (D)	2946	modo (I)	2021
mixage (F)	535	modo ecclesiastico (I)	2022
mixed (E)	1741	modulare (I)	2023
mixed chorus (E)	667	Modulation (D)	2024
mixed voices (E)	716	modulation (E, F)	2024
mixer (F)	534	modulation passagère (F)	2025
mixing board (E)	527	modulazione (I)	2024
mixo-lydien (F)	2017	modulazione di transizione
mixolydian (E)	2017	(I)	2025
mixolydisch (D)	2017	moduler (F)	2023
mixte (F)	1741	modulieren (D)	2023

Modus (D)	2021	mordace (I)	1344
modus (E)	2021	mordant (F)	1344, 2027, 2028
moelleux (F)	1375	mordant supérieur (F)	2029
möglich (D)	1780	Mordent (D)	2027, 2028
möglichst (D)	1781	mordent (E)	2027, 2028
moins (F)	1736	mordent with note above (E)	2029
moins rapide que allegro (F)	726	mordente (I)	1344, 2027
moitié (F)	1737	mordente inferiore (I)	2028
Moll (D)	2016	mordente superiore (I)	2029
molle (I)	1341	more (E)	1770
mollezza (con) (I)	1341	more then (E)	1771
moltissimo (I)	1743	morendo (I)	824
molto (I)	1744	moresca (I)	2395
molto accentuato (I)	861	Moreske (D)	2395
Moment musical (D)	2393	Morgenständchen (D)	2386
moment musical (F)	2393	morire (I)	680
momento musicale (I)	2393	Moriskentanz (D)	2395
Monferrina (D, E, F, I)	2565	mormorando (I)	1345
monodia (I)	2026	mormorato (I)	1345
Monodie (D)	2026	morne (F)	1066
monodie (F)	2026	morning music (E)	2386
Monodram (D)	2394	morris dance (E)	2395
monodrama (E)	2394	mosso (I)	759
monodrame (F)	2394	most vivacious (E)	783
monodramma (I)	2394	mostrare (I)	2755
monody (E)	2026	motet (E, F)	2397
monofonia (I)	2026	Motette (D)	2397
monophony (E)	2026	moteur (F)	1044
monoton (D)	1342	motif (E, F)	2030
monotone (F)	1342	motif conducteur (F)	2031
monotono (I)	1342	motion (E)	1745
monotonous (E)	1342	Motiv (D)	2030
monter l'accord (F)	2653	motivo (I)	2030
monter l'intonation (F)	2653	motivo conduttore (I)	2031
monter sur les planches (F)	2924	motivo ricorrente (I)	2031
montrer (F)	2755	moto (I)	1745
mood (E)	3358	moto contrario (I)	2032
mood music (E)	3126	moto obliquo (I)	2033
moog (E)	572	moto perpetuo (I)	2396
moquant (F)	1019	moto retto (I)	2034
moqueusement (F)	1031	motor (E)	1044
morbidezza (con) (I)	1343	motore (I)	1044
morbido (I)	1547	motorisch (D)	1044
morceau (F)	2921	motteggiando (I)	1019
morceau de concert (F)	2426	mottetto (I)	2397
morceau imposé (F)	3226	mou (F)	1341

mourir (F)	680
mournful (E)	1213, 1321
mournfully (E)	1334
mouth (E)	3431
mouth organ (E)	117
mouth-hole (E)	208
mouthpiece (E)	198, 199
mouvant (F)	795
mouvement (F)	1745, 2035
mouvement contraire (F)	2032
mouvement initial (F)	778
mouvement oblique (F)	2033
mouvement parallèle (F)	2034, 2036
mouvement perpétuel (F)	2396
movable (E)	1339
moved (E)	1050
movement (E)	2035
movendo (I)	795
movimento (I)	1745, 2035
movimento parallelo (I)	2036
moving (E)	795, 1051
moving away (E)	895
moving forward (E)	790
mû (F)	759
much (E)	1710, 1744
müde (D)	1528
mue (F)	616
muet (F)	3180
muffle (E)	1816
muffled (E)	379
mühevoll (D)	1529
mühsam (D)	1168
mühselig (D)	1381
multiple (E, F)	1746
multiplo (I)	1746
multitrack recording (E)	555
Mund (D)	3431
Mundharmonika (D)	117
Mundloch (D)	208
Mundspalt (D)	196
Mundstück (D)	199
Muñeira (D, E, F, I)	2566
munter (D)	994
muovendo (I)	795
muoversi (I)	2756
Murciana (D, E, F, I)	2567
murmelnd (D)	1345
murmuring (E)	1345
mürrisch (D)	983
musa (I)	3115
muscle (E, F)	3457
muscolo (I)	3457
Muse (D)	3115
muse (E, F)	3115
Musette (D, E, F, I)	2568
music (E)	3116
music computer (E)	505
music critic (E)	3505
music dictation (E)	1951
music drama (E)	2338
music festival (E)	3035
music for strings (E)	3159
music hall (E)	3416
music lover (E)	2883
music lyre (E)	218
music of the future (E)	3135
music publishing house (E)	2935
music school (E)	2866, 3324
music stand (E)	3098
music therapy (E)	3179
music-paper (E)	2933
musica (I)	3116
musica a programma (I)	3117
musica a quarti di tono (I)	3118
musica aleatoria (I)	3119
musica antica (I)	3120
musica assoluta (I)	3121
musica classica (I)	3122
musica concreta (I)	3123
musica contemporanea (I)	3124
musica corale (I)	3125
musica d'ambiente (I)	3126
musica d'avanguardia (I)	3127
musica d'uso (I)	3132
musica da ballo (I)	3128
musica da caccia (I)	3129
musica da camera (I)	3130
musica da chiesa (I)	3131
musica da consumo (I)	3132
musica da salotto (I)	3133
musica da tavola (I)	3134

musica dell'avvenire (I)	3135
musica della Passione (I)	3140
musica descrittiva (I)	3136
musica di corte (I)	3137
musica di gatti (I)	3138
musica di Natale (I)	3141
musica di scena (I)	3142
musica di sottofondo (I)	3139
musica dodecafonica (I)	3143
musica domestica (I)	3147
musica drammatica (I)	3144
musica elettronica (I)	3145
musica esotica (I)	3146
musica familiare (I)	3147
musica folcloristica (I)	3161
musica funebre (I)	3148
musica informatica (I)	536
musica leggera (I)	3149
musica lirica (I)	3150
musica liturgica (I)	3131
musica meccanica (I)	3151
musica militaire (I)	3152
musica nella (della) strada (I)	3153
musica orchestrale (I)	3154
musica per balletto (I)	3155
musica per banda (I)	3156
musica per coro (I)	3125
musica per film (I)	3157
musica per la scuola (I)	3158
musica per strumenti a corda (I)	3159
musica per strumenti a fiato (I)	3160
musica popolare (I)	3161
musica profana (I)	3162
musica puntillistica (I)	3163
musica pura (I)	3121
musica religiosa (I)	3164
musica rinascimentale (I)	3165
musica sacra (I)	3166
musica scenica (I)	3142
musica seria (I)	3167
musica seriale (I)	3168
musica sinfonica (I)	3169
musica sperimentale (I)	3170
musica strumentale (I)	3171
musica turca (I)	3172
musica tzigana (I)	3173
musica vocale (I)	3174
musical (E)	2307
Musical (D)	2307
musical (E, F)	3175
musical box (E)	475, 479
musical clock (E)	477, 479
musical comedy (E)	2308
musical competition (E)	2960
musical contest (E)	2960
musical electronics (E)	508
musical imagery (E)	3269
"musical moment" (E)	2393
musical press (E)	3357
musical saw (E)	316
musicale (I)	3175
musicalità (I)	3176
musicalité (F)	3176
musicality (E)	3176
musician (E)	3513
musicien (F)	3513
musicien d'orchestre (F)	3518
musicien professionel (F)	3177
musicienne (F)	3513
musicienne d'orchestre (F)	3518
musicista (I)	3513
musicista di professione (I)	3177
musicologia (I)	3178
musicologie (F)	3178
musicologist (E)	3514
musicologo (I)	3514
musicologue (F)	3514
musicology (E)	3178
musicoterapia (I)	3179
musicothérapie (F)	3179
Musik (D)	3116
Musik für Saiteninstrumente (D)	3159
Musik für Streichinstrumente (D)	3159
Musikakademie (D)	2866
musikalisch (D)	3175
„musikalischer Augenblick" (D)	2393
Musikalität (D)	3176

Musikcomputer (D)   505
Musikdiktat (D)   1951
Musikdrama (D)   2338
Musikelektronik (D)   508
Musiker (D)   3513
Musikerin (D)   3513
Musikfest(spiel) (D)   3035
Musikgeschichte (D)   3362
Musikhochschule (D)   2866
Musikinstrumentenkunde
   (D)   3206
Musikkritiker (D)   3505
Musikkritikerin (D)   3505
Musikliebhaber (D)   2883
Musikliebhaberin (D)   2883
Musikschule (D)   3324
Musiktheorie (D)   3400
Musiktherapie (D)   3179
Musikverlag (D)   2935
Musikwettbewerb (D)   2960
Musikwissenschaft (D)   3178
Musikwissenschaftler (D)   3514
Musikwissenschaftlerin (D)   3514
musique (F)   3116
musique à programme (F)   3117
musique aléatoire (F)   3119
musique ancienne (F)   3120
musique chorale (F)   3125
musique classique (F)   3122
musique concrète (E, F)   3123
musique contemporaine (F)   3124
musique d'ambiance
   (F)   3126
musique d'avant-garde (F)   3127
musique d'avenir (F)   3135
musique d'église (F)   3131
musique d'orchestre (F)   3154
musique de ballet (F)   3155
musique de chambre (F)   3130
musique de chasse (F)   3129
musique de cour (F)   3137
musique de danse (F)   3128
musique de film (F)   3157
musique de fond (F)   3139
musique de la Passion (F)   3140

musique de la Renaissance
   (F)   3165
musique de Noël (F)   3141
musique de rue (F)   3153
musique de salon (F)   3133
musique de scène (F)   3142
musique de table (F)   3134
musique descriptive (F)   3136
musique dodécaphonique
   (F)   3143
musique domestique (F)   3147
musique dramatique (F)   3144
musique électronique (F)   3145
musique en quarts de ton (F) 3118
musique exotique (F)   3146
musique expérimentale (F)   3170
musique folklorique (F)   3161
musique fonctionelle (F)   3132
musique funèbre (F)   3148
musique instrumentale (F)   3171
musique légère (F)   3149
musique liturgique (F)   3131
musique lyrique (F)   3150
musique méchanique (F)   3151
musique microtonale (F)   3118
musique militaire (F)   2911, 3152
musique par ordinateur (F)   536
musique populaire (F)   3161
musique pour harmonie (F)   3156
musique pour instruments
   à cordes (F)   3159
musique pour instruments
   à vent (F)   3160
musique profane (F)   3162
musique pure (F)   3121
musique religieuse (F)   3164
musique sacrée (F)   3166
musique scolaire (F)   3158
musique sérielle (F)   3168
musique sérieuse (F)   3167
musique symphonique (F)   3169
musique turque (F)   3172
musique tzigane (F)   3173
musique vocale (F)   3174
Muskel (D)   3457
Muster (D)   3113

muta (I)	616, 1747
mutando (I)	1652
mutare (I)	2676
Mutation (D)	616
mutation (E)	616
mute (E)	1816, 3180
mute off (E)	248
muted (E)	96
mutig (D)	976
muto (I)	3180
mystérieusement (F)	1337
mystérieux (F)	1337
mysterious (E)	1337, 1497
mystic (E)	1338
mystique (F)	1338
mystisch (D)	1338
nacaire (F)	302
Nacara (sarazenische Handpauke) (D)	302
nacchere (I)	269
naccherone (I)	302
nach (D)	1690
nach Art der Hirten (D)	1374
nach Art der Zigeuner (D)	951
nach Art der/des/von (D)	946
nach Belieben (D)	718, 719, 724
nach deutscher Tanzart (D)	949
nach Gehör spielen (D)	2842
nach oben (D)	1726
nach türkischer Art (im Stil der Janitscharen-Musik) (D)	950
nach ungarischer Art (D)	956
nach unten (D)	1717
nachahmen (D)	2730
nachahmend (D)	1713
Nachahmung (D)	1996
nachdenken (D)	2792
nachdenkend (D)	1331
nachdenklich (D)	1384
nachdrücklich (D)	1132
nachgeben (D)	2679
nachgebend (D)	899
nachgelassen (D)	3237
Nachhall (D)	502
Nachklang (D)	563
nachlassen (D)	2679
nachlassend (D)	828
nachlässig (D)	1350
Nachschlag (D)	1930
nachsichtig (D)	1271
Nachspiel (D)	2432
nächste (D)	1785
nächstes Mal (D)	3260
nächstfolgend (D)	1785
Nachtigall (D)	699
Nachtstück (D)	2401
Nacken (D)	3460
Nadel (Grammophon) (D)	547
Nagel (D)	3483
Nagelgeige (D)	31
nahe (D)	3423
nahe am Griffbrett (D)	115
nahe am Korpus anzupfen (D)	105
naïf (F)	1278
nail (E)	3483
nail violin (E)	31
naiv (D)	1278
naïvement (F)	1278
nakers (E)	302
Nänie (D)	2398
nape of the neck (E)	3460
narrando (I)	1346
narrante (I)	1346
narrating (E)	1346, 1419
narrator (E)	3181
narratore (I)	3181
närrisch (D)	1192
nasal (D, E, F)	617
nasale (I)	617
nascosto (I)	1748
Nase (D)	3458
nasello (I)	66
naso (I)	3458
nastro magnetico (I)	537
national anthem (E)	2364
Nationalhymne (D)	2364
natural (E)	1906, 3182
natural notes (E)	2146
natural tones (E)	2146
natural trumpet (E)	177

naturale (I)	3182	nerf (F)	3459
naturalezza (con) (I)	1347	Nerv (D)	3459
naturally (E)	1347	nerve (E)	3459
naturel (F)	3182	nerveusement (F)	1351
naturellement (F)	1347	nervig (D)	1351
Naturklangspeicher (D)	574	nervo (I)	3459
natürlich (D)	3182	nervös (D)	1351
natürliche Position (D)	247	nervosamente (I)	1351
Naturtöne (D)	2146	nervously (E)	1351
Naturtrompete (D)	177	nessuno (I)	1751
ne....pas (F)	1753	net (F)	3267
neapolitan sixth (E)	2121	nettamente (I)	1352
neapolitanische Sexte (D)	2121	nettement (F)	1352
near (E)	3423	netto (I)	3267
near the sounding board (E)	105	neu (D)	3190
nearly (E)	1789	neu belebend (D)	791
neat (E)	3267	neue Musik (D)	3124
nebbioso (I)	1348	neuf (F)	3190
nebelhaft (D)	1349	Neufassung (D)	3189
Nebelhorn (D)	281	neugierig (D)	1067
neben (D)	1613, 2111	neuma (E, I)	2037
Nebenbetonung (D)	1869	neume (E, F)	2037
Nebennote (D)	2039	Neumen (D)	2037
Nebenrolle (D)	2956	new (E)	3190
Nebenton (D)	2172	new version (E)	3189
neblig (D)	1348	next (E)	1785
nébuleux (F)	1349	next time (E)	3260
nebuloso (I)	1349	nez (F)	3458
nebulous (E)	1349	nice (E)	1036
nécessaire (F)	3183	nicht (D)	1753
necessario (I)	3183	nicht gehalten (D)	1756
necessary (E)	3183	nicht genug (D)	1835
neck (E)	56, 61, 3434	nicht mitwirken (D)	1823, 1824
neckisch (D)	1458	nicht schnell (D)	760
needle (E)	547	nicht sehr (D)	1754
négligemment (F)	1350	nicht viel (D)	1754
negligentemente (I)	1350	nicht zu sehr (D)	1755
negligently (E)	1350	nicht zu viel (D)	1757
nehmen (D)	2769	nichtig (D)	1206
neighbour note (E)	2172	nichts (D)	1752
nel (I)	1749	niedergeschlagen (D)	1335
nella (I)	1749	niederlegen (D)	2765
nello (allo) stesso modo (I)	1750	niedrig (D)	2913
nello stesso tempo (I)	1847	niedriger (D)	3085
nenia (E, I)	2398	niemand (D)	1751
nénie (F)	2398	niente (I)	1752

Nietenbecken (D)	304	nostalgic (E)	1356
nightingale (E)	699	nostalgico (I)	1356
nimble (E)	940	nostalgie (F)	3185
ninna nanna (I)	2399	nostalgique (F)	1356
ninth (E)	2246	nostalgisch (D)	1356
nitido (I)	1043	not (E)	1753
niveau (F)	522	not as fast as allegro (E)	726
no one (E)	1751	not at all (E)	1752
nobilmente (I)	1353	not enough (E)	1835
nobiltà (con) (I)	1354	not fast (E)	760
noblement (F)	1353	not held (E)	1756
nobly (E)	1353	not much (E)	1754
nobody (E)	1751	not slurred (E)	874
noch (D)	1636	not so (E)	1755
noch einmal (D)	1637	not too much (E)	1757
noch einmal! (D)	2919	not very (E)	1754, 1755
nochmals (D)	1686	nota (I)	2038
nocturne (E, F)	2401	nota ausiliare (I)	2039
noioso (I)	3184	nota cambiata (I)	2040
noire (F)	2226	nota di passaggio (I)	2041
noise (E)	566	nota falsa (I)	3186
noise reduction (E)	561	nota principale (I)	2042
noise supression (E)	561	nota puntata (I)	2043
noisily (E)	1448	notable (F)	3187
noisy (E)	1448	Notation (D)	2044
nombre de mesures (F)	2046	notation (E, F)	2044
non (I)	1753	notazione (I)	2044
non legato (I)	874	Note (D)	2038
non lié (F)	874	note (E, F)	2038
non molto (I)	1754	note changée (F)	2040
non préparé (F)	3074	note cluster (E)	1994
non presto (I)	760	note de passage (F)	2041
non tanto (I)	1755	note pointée (F)	2043
non tenu (F)	1756	note principale (F)	2042
non tenuto (I)	1756	note secondaire (F)	2039
non troppo (I)	1757	note value (E)	2183
nona (I)	2246	Noten schreiben (D)	2812
noncuranza (con) (I)	1355	Notenbalken (D)	2134, 2176
None (D)	2246	Notendruck (D)	3357
none (F)	2246	Notenfahne (D)	1934
nonet (E, F)	2400	Notenhals (D)	1989
Nonett (D)	2400	Notenhalter (D)	218
nonetto (I)	2400	Notenpapier (D)	2933
nonostante (I)	3106	Notenpult (D)	3098
nose (E)	3458	Notenschrift (D)	2044
nostalgia (I)	3185	Notenständer (D)	3098

Notenwert (D)	2183
noter (F)	2812
notevole (I)	3187
nothing (E)	1752
notice (F)	2885
notieren (D)	2812
nötig (D)	3183
notina (I)	2045
Notiz (D)	2885
Notturno (D)	2401
notturno (I)	2401
nourished (E)	1357
nourri (F)	1357
nouvelle version (F)	3189
novelette (E, F)	2402
novelletta (I)	2402
Novellette (D)	2402
now (E)	2877
nuage (F)	3191
nuance (F)	2948, 3331
nuancer (F)	2726
nuances (F)	2987
nuca (I)	3460
nulla (I)	1752
number (E)	3188
numérique (F)	499
numéro (F)	3188
numero (I)	3188
numero di battute (I)	2046
Nummer (D)	3188
nuova versione (I)	3189
nuovo (I)	3190
nuptial (E, F)	1358
nuque (F)	3460
nur (D)	1812
nursery song (E)	2297
nutrito (I)	1357
nuvola (I)	3191
nuziale (I)	1358
obbligato (E, I)	1758, 2047
obbligatorio (I)	1758
oben (D)	1726, 1814
ober (D)	3388
Oberarm (D)	3432
Oberbügel (D)	79
Oberek (D, E, F, I)	2569

Obersattel (D)	39
Oberstimme (D)	2058
Oberstück (D)	234
Obertas (D, E, F, I)	2570
Obertöne (D)	2145
obligat (D)	1758, 2047
obligatoire (F)	1758
obligatory (E)	1758
obligé (F)	1758, 2047
oblique motion (E)	2033
Oboe (D)	156
oboe (E, I)	156
Oboe d'amore (D)	157
oboe d'amore (E, I)	157
Oboist (D)	3515
oboist (E)	3515
oboista (I)	3515
Oboistin (D)	3515
obscur (F)	1544
obstinate (E)	1367
obstinately (E)	1366
obstiné (F)	1367
ocarina (E, F, I)	158
occhiata (I)	3332
occhio (I)	3461
ochetus (I)	2403
octave (E, F)	2245
octet (E)	2412
octuor (F)	2412
odd (E)	1531
Ode (D, E, F, I)	2571
oder (D)	1763
oder auch (D)	1763
œil (F)	3461
œuvre (F)	3194
œuvre chorale (F)	2408
off-beat (E)	2155
offen (D)	1638
offended (E)	1359
offensé (F)	1359
öffentlich (D)	3266
offertoire (F)	2404
offertorio (I)	2404
Offertorium (D)	2404
offertory (E)	2404
offeso (I)	1359

öffnen (D)	2658	ondoyant (F)	102
oficleide (I)	159	ondulante (I)	1360
oft (D)	1818	onduleux (F)	1360
often (E)	1818	one string (E)	474
oftmals (D)	1818	ongle (F)	3483
ogni (I)	1759	only (E)	1812
ogni volta (I)	1760	onorario (I)	3193
ohne (D)	1800	opaco (I)	1361
ohne Anstrengung (D)	1478	opaque (E, F)	1361
ohne bestimmtes Zeitmaß		open (E)	1638, 2074
(D)	770	open air (E)	3052
ohne Dämpfer (D)	110	open string (E)	97
ohne davonzurennen (D)	1802	opening night (E)	3244
ohne Eile (D)	769	Oper (D)	2405
ohne Instrumente (D)	1612, 1805	opera (E, I)	2405, 3194
ohne Unterbrechung (D)	1803	opéra (F)	2405
ohne Wiederholung (D)	1804	opéra bouffe (F)	2406
ohne zu schleppen (D)	771	opera buffa (I)	2406
ohne zu wechseln (D)	1801	opera chorus (E)	664
Ohr (D)	3462	opera comica (I)	2407
ohrenbetäubend (D)	1644	opéra comique (F)	2407
Okarina (D)	158	opera corale (I)	2408
Oktave (D)	2245	opera orchestra (E)	3199
Oktett (D)	2412	opera seria (I)	2409
omaggio (I)	3192	opéra sérieux (F)	2409
omesso (I)	1761	operatic (E)	2337
omis (F)	1761	operatic aria (E)	2254
omitted (E)	1761	operatic music (E)	3150
omofonia (I)	2048	operatic overture (E)	2414
omogeneo (I)	1218	operetta (E, I)	2410
on (E)	1814, 1821	Operette (D)	2410
on enlève (F)	1807	opérette (F)	2410
on his place (E)	1628	Opernarie (D)	2254
on the (E)	1821	Opernchor (D)	664
on the fingerboard (E)	115	Opernmusik (D)	3150
on the rim (E)	387	Opernorchester (D)	3199
on the stage (E)	3385	Opernouvertüre (D)	2414
on the string (E)	82	Operntextbuch (D)	678
on the tip of the tongue (E)	1618	ophicleide (E)	159
once (E)	1845	ophicléide (F)	159
once again (E)	1637	Ophikleide (D)	159
once more (E)	1686	oppressé (F)	1362
onda (I)	538	oppressed (E)	1362
onde (F)	538	oppresso (I)	1362
ondeggiando (I)	102	opprimé (F)	1362
ondeggiante (I)	1360	oppure (I)	1763

optional (E)	1699	Orchestrion (D)	476
opus (L)	3194	orchestrion (E, F, I)	476
or (E)	1763	order (E)	3203
ora (I)	2877	ordinario (I)	1762
orage (F)	3398	ordinary (E)	1762
orageusement (F)	1541	ordinateur musical (F)	505
orageux (F)	1542	ordine (I)	3203
oratorio (E, F, I)	2411	Ordnung (D)	3203
Oratorium (D)	2411	ordre (F)	3203
Orchester (D)	3195	orecchio (I)	3462
Orchesteranordnung (D)	2995	orecchio assoluto (I)	3204
Orchestereinsatz (D)	3011	oreille (F)	3462
Orchestergraben (D)	3050	oreille absolue (F)	3204
Orchestermusik (D)	3154, 3169	organ (E)	398
Orchestermusiker (D)	3518	organ concerto (E)	2313
Orchestermusikerin (D)	3518	organetto (I)	478
orchestra (E, I)	3195	organetto automatico (I)	477
orchestra box (E)	3050	organico (strumentale) (I)	3205
orchestra d'archi (I)	3198	Organist (D)	3516
orchestra d'opera (I)	3199	organist (E)	3516
orchestra da ballo (I)	3196	organista (I)	3516
orchestra da camera (I)	3197	organiste (F)	3516
orchestra da salotto (I)	3200	Organistin (D)	3516
orchestra dell'opera (I)	3199	organo (I)	398
orchestra della radio (I)	3201	organo di Barberia (I)	478
orchestra sinfonica (I)	3202	organo elettronico (I)	539
orchestral layout (E)	2995	organo Hammond (I)	540
orchestral music (E)	3154	organo pieno (I)	464
orchestral pit (E)	3050	organo portativo (I)	399
orchestralist (E)	3518	organologia (I)	3206
orchestrare (I)	2757	organologie (F)	3206
Orchestration (D)	2049	organology (E)	3206
orchestration (E, F)	2049	Orgel (D)	398
orchestrazione (I)	2049	Orgelkonzert (D)	2313
orchestre (F)	3195	Orgelpunkt (D)	2062
orchestre à cordes (F)	3198	orgoglioso (I)	1363
orchestre d'opéra (F)	3199	orgue (F)	398
orchestre de chambre (F)	3197	orgue de Barbarie (F)	478
orchestre de danse (F)	3196	orgue électronique (F)	539
orchestre de l'opéra (F)	3199	orgue Hammond (F)	540
orchestre de la radio (F)	3201	orgue portatif (F)	399
orchestre de salon (F)	3200	orgueilleux (F)	1363
orchestre symphonique (F)	3202	original (D, E, F)	3207
orchestrer (F)	2757	original speed (E)	778
orchestrieren (D)	2757	original version (E)	3421
Orchestrierung (D)	2049	originale (I)	3207

orizzontale (I)	2050
orlo (I)	366
Ornament (D)	2051
ornament (E)	2051
ornamento (I)	2051
ornando (I)	926
ornato (I)	927
orné (F)	927
ornement (F)	2051
ornementé (F)	1865
orologio a carillon (I)	479
orologio a soneria (I)	477
orrendo (I)	1364
orrido (I)	1364
orrore (con) (I)	1416
Ort (D)	1731
os (F)	3463
oscillateur (F)	541
oscillation (E, F)	542
oscillation triangulaire (F)	592
oscillator (E)	541
oscillatore (I)	541
oscillazione (I)	542
oscuro (I)	1544
osservanza (con) (I)	1365
ossia (I)	1763
osso (I)	3463
ostentativo (I)	1491
ostentatoire (F)	1491
ostinatezza (con) (I)	1366
Ostinato (D)	1901
ostinato (I)	1367
ostinazione (con) (I)	1366
Oszillator (D)	541
ôter (F)	2850
ôter la sourdine (F)	248
other (E)	1634
otherwise (E)	1633, 1763
ottava (I)	2245
ottavino (I)	160
ottavizzare (I)	245
ottavo (I)	2227
ottetto (I)	2412
ottoni (I)	3208
ou bien (F)	1763
oublier (F)	2700
ouïe (F)	57, 3413
out of tune (E)	3361
outer part (E)	2054
output (E)	593
outside (E)	3052
ouvert (F)	1638
Ouvertüre (D)	2413
ouverture (F, I)	196, 2413
ouverture d'opéra (F)	2414
ouverture d'opera (I)	2414
ouverture da concerto (I)	2415
ouverture de concert (F)	2415
ouvreur (F)	3108
ouvreuse (F)	3108
ouvrir (F)	2658
overbearing (E)	1594
overstrung scale (E)	421
overture (E)	2413
ovvero (I)	1763
pacatamente (I)	1368
pacato (I)	1369
pace (con) (E, I)	1370, 2152
pacifico (I)	1369
Pädagogik (D)	3222
padded stick (E)	353
padiglione (I)	212
padiglione piriforme (I)	213
padiglioni in alto (I)	237
padovana (I)	2423
page (E, F)	3209
pagina (I)	3209
painful (E)	1119, 1381
painstaking (E)	1463
paisible (F)	1369
paisiblement (F)	1368
palais (F)	3464
palate (E)	3464
palato (I)	3464
palco (I)	3210
palcoscenico (I)	3314
pallet (E)	454
palm of the hand (E)	3465
palmo della mano (I)	3465
Palotas (D, E, F, I)	2572
palpito (I)	3211
panchina (I)	443

pancia (I)	3466	parodie (F)	2417
Panflöte (D)	151	parody (E)	2417
panpipes (E)	151	parola (I)	3214
panting (E)	970	parole (F)	3214
pantomima (I)	3212	parrucca (I)	3215
Pantomime (D)	3212	part (E)	3301
pantomime (E, F)	3212	part-writing (E)	1938
papier à musique (F)	2933	parte (I)	3301
Papierblatt (D)	3043	parte di ripieno (I)	2187
par cœur (F)	2884	parte estrema (I)	2054
par hasard (F)	3804	parte inferiore (I)	2055
paradiesisch (D)	1371	parte intermedia (I)	2056
paradis (F)	3053	parte melodica (I)	2057
paradisiac (E)	1371	parte superiore (I)	2058
paradisiaco (I)	1371	partecipare (I)	2759
paradisiaque (F)	1371	parterre (F)	3230
parafrasi (I)	2416	partials (E)	2147
paragone (I)	3213	participer (F)	2759
parallel (D, E)	2053	Partie (D)	3301
parallel motion (E)	2034	partie (F)	3301
parallel movement (E)	2036	partie de dessus (F)	2058
Parallelbewegung (D)	2034	partie extrême (F)	2054
parallèle (F)	2053	partie finale (F)	1655
parallele nascoste (I)	2052	partie inférieure (F)	2055
Parallelen (D)	2141	partie mélodique (F)	2057
parallèles cachées (F)	2052	partie principale (F)	2188
Parallelführung (D)	2036	partie supérieure (F)	2058
parallelo (I)	2053	parties de remplissage (F)	2187
Paralleltonart (D)	2167	Partita (D, E, F, I)	2573
Parameter (D)	543	partition (F)	3216
parameter (E)	543	partition de direction (F)	3217
paramètre (F)	543	partition de poche (F)	3218
parametro (I)	543	partition pour piano (F)	3288
parapenne (I)	63	partition vocale (F)	618
Paraphrase (D)	2416	Partitur (D)	3216
paraphrase (E, F)	2416	partitura (I)	3216
pardon (F)	3326	partitura per il direttore (I)	3217
pareil (F)	1808	partitura tascabile (I)	3218
paresseux (F)	1393	partitura vocale (I)	618
parfait (F)	3224	partout (F)	1681
Parkett (D)	3230	party (E)	3034
parlando (I)	1372	pas (F)	3220
parlare (I)	2758	pas beaucoup (F)	1754
parler (F)	2758	pas trop (F)	1755, 1757
parodia (I)	2417	pas vite (F)	760
Parodie (D)	2417	pass auf! (D)	2900

passable (F)	2994	Pauken (D)	336
Passacaglia (D)	2418	Paukenfell (D)	365
passacaglia (E, I)	2418	Paukenschlägel (D)	355
passacaille (F)	2418	Paukenwirbel (D)	383
Passage (D)	2059, 3219	Pauker (D)	3524
passage (E, F)	2059, 3219	Paukerin (D)	3524
passage du pouce (F)	465	paume de la main (F)	3465
passage rapide de notes (F)	2185	paura (con) (I)	1377
passaggio (I)	2059, 3219	paura dinanzi al pubblico (I)	3221
passaggio del pollice (I)	465	pauroso (I)	1378
Passamezzo (D, E, F, I)	2574	pausa (I)	2060, 3090
passare (I)	2760	pausa di biscroma (I)	2236
Passepied (D)	2419	pausa di croma (I)	2234
passepied (E, F, I)	2419	pausa di minima (I)	2232
passer (F)	2760	pausa di semibiscroma (I)	2237
passing chord (E)	1875	pausa di semibreve (I)	2231
passing note (E)	2041	pausa di semicroma (I)	2235
passing the thumb under (E)	465	pausa di semiminima (I)	2233
Passion (D)	2420	pausa generale (I)	2061
passion (E, F)	2420	Pause (D)	2060, 3091
passion music (E)	3140	pause (E, F)	1946, 2060, 2231
passionate (E)	981	pause générale (F)	2061
passionately (E)	981	Pausenwert (D)	2184
passionato (I)	981	Pausenzeichen (D)	3327
passione (I)	1373, 2420	pausiere (D)	1823
passionné (F)	981	pausieren (D)	1824
passionnément (F)	981	pavan (E)	2423
Passionsmusik (D)	3140	pavana (I)	2423
passo (I)	3219, 3220	Pavane (D)	2423
pasticcio (E, I)	2421	pavane (F)	2423
pastiche (E, F)	2421	paventato (I)	1378
pastoral (E, F)	1374, 2422	pavillon (F)	200, 212, 300
Pastorale (D)	2422	pavillon en l'air (F)	237
pastorale (F, I)	1374, 2422	pavillon piriforme (F)	213
pastoso (I)	1375	pazzamente (I)	1379
Pastourelle (D, E, F, I)	2575	pazzescamente (I)	1379
pastourelle (F)	2422	peaceable (E)	1369
pataud (F)	1239	peaceably (E)	1368
patetico (I)	1376	peaceful (E)	1368
pathetic (E)	1376	peak (E)	66
pathétique (F)	1376	pear-shaped bell (E)	213
pathetisch (D)	1376	pearly (E)	466
patimento (con) (I)	1111	peasant dance (E)	2331
patron (E)	3109	peau (F)	365, 368
patte (F)	215	peau de batterie (F)	357
pattern (E)	3113	peau supérieure (F)	357

pedagogia (I)	3222	pendant toute la durée (F)	1767
pédagogie (F)	3222	pendule à carillon (F)	477, 479
pedagogy (E)	3222	pendule à musique (F)	479
Pedal (D)	432	pénétrant (F)	1380
pedal (E)	432	penetrante (I)	1380
pedal drum (E)	339	penetrating (E)	1380
pedal harp (E)	2	pénétré (F)	1058
pedal keyboard (E)	436	pénible (F)	1381
pedal point (E)	2062	péniblement (F)	1529
pédale (F)	432	Penillion (D, E, F, I)	2576
pedale (I)	432	penosamente (I)	1529
pedale d'armonia (I)	2062	penoso (I)	1381
pédale de la grosse caisse (F)	367	pensando (I)	1382
pédale de prolongation (F)	435	pensare (I)	2761
pedale del piano (I)	434	penser (F)	2761
pedale della gran cassa (I)	367	pensieroso (I)	1383
pedale destro (I)	433	pensif (F)	1383
pedale di risonanza (I)	433	pensive (E)	1383
pédale droite (F)	433	pensosamente (I)	1384
pédale forte (F)	433	pensoso (I)	1383
pédale gauche (F)	434	pentagramma (I)	2063
pédale hi-hat (F)	275	pentatonic (E)	2064
pédale inférieure (F)	2062	pèntatonico (I)	2064
pedale sinistro (I)	434	pentatonique (F)	2064
pedale tonale (I)	435	pentatonisch (D)	2064
Pedalharfe (D)	2	per (I)	1764
pédalier (F)	436	per finire (I)	1765
pedaliera (I)	436	per l'ultima volta (I)	1766
Pedalklaviatur (D)	436	per tutta la durata (I)	1767
Pedalpauke (D)	339	perçant (F)	1380, 1536
Pedalwerk (D)	432	perce (F)	425
pedana (I)	3231	percepibile (I)	3223
pedestal (E)	81	perceptible (E, F)	3223
peep-hole (E)	3351	percettibile (I)	3223
peg box (E)	42	percing (E)	1380
Pegel (D)	522	percosso (I)	862
peiné (F)	982	percuotere (I)	380
peinlich genau (D)	1463	percussion instruments (E)	3375
peinture sonore (F)	3269	percuté (F)	862
peinvoll (D)	1117	perdendosi (I)	905
Peitsche (D)	286	perfect (E)	1991, 3224
peitschend (D)	872	perfect cadence (E)	1914
pelle (I)	368	perfect pitch (E)	3204
pen-name (E)	3265	perfection (E, F)	3225
penando (I)	833	perfekt (D)	3224
pendant (F)	1692	perfetto (I)	3224

perfezionarsi (I)	2762
perfezione (I)	3225
perfide (F)	1160
perfido (I)	1160
performance (E) 3015, 3273,	3350
performer (E)	3089
performing practice (E)	3238
performing rights (E)	2991
perigordino (I)	2424
Perigourdine (D)	2424
perigourdine (E)	2424
périgourdine (F)	2424
period (E)	2065
Periode (D)	2065
période (F)	2065
période pré-classique (F)	3239
periodo (I)	2065
perlato (I)	466
perlé (F)	466
perlend (D)	466
perno (I)	437
però (I)	1768
perpetual (E)	3227
perpetual motion (E)	2396
perpétuel (F)	3227
perpetuo (I)	3227
perpetuum mobile (L)	2396
perruque (F)	3215
perseveranza (con) (I)	1385
persistant (F)	1367
persistent (E)	1367
persistente (I)	1367
personne (F)	1751
Perücke (D)	3215
pesant (F)	1386
pesante (I)	1386
pesato (I)	1387
pesé (F)	1387
peso del braccio (I)	467
peso del corpo (I)	468
Petenera (D, E, F, I)	2577
pétillant (F)	1207
petit (F)	1773
petit corps (F)	234
petit doigt (F)	3456
petit scherzo (F)	2456
petite branche (F)	234
petite clarinette (F)	123
petite farce (F)	2275
petite flûte (F)	160
petite note (F)	2045
pettinatura (I)	3228
petto (I)	3467
peu (F)	1773
peu à peu (F)	1774
peureux (F)	1378
pezzo (I)	2921
pezzo caratteristico (I)	2425
pezzo da concerto (I)	2426
pezzo di mezzo (I)	214
pezzo imposto (I)	3226
pezzo inferiore (I)	215
pezzo lirico (I)	2427
Pfeife (D)	142, 413
pfeifen (D)	2722
pfeifend (D)	717
pfiffig (D)	1015
Pflichtstück (D)	3226
phalange (F)	3441
phalanx (E)	3441
phantastisch (D)	1164
pharynx (E, F)	3442
philharmonic (E)	3040
philharmonique (F)	3040
philharmonisch (D)	3040
phonetics (E)	3046
Phonetik (D)	3046
phonétique (F)	3046
phonograph (Am.)	517
Phrase (D)	1984
phrase (E, F)	1984
phrasé (F)	1985
phrase mark (E)	2005
phraser (F)	2724
phrasieren (D)	2724
Phrasierung (D)	1985
Phrasierungsbogen (D)	2005
phrasing (E)	1985
phrygian (E)	1986
phrygien (F)	1986
phrygisch (D)	1986
piacere (con) (I)	1110

piacevole (I)   1388
piacevolezza (con) (I)   1388
piangendo (I)   1389
piangente (I)   1390
piangevole (I)   1390
Pianino (D)   404
pianissimo (I)   863
Pianist (D)   3517
pianist (E)   3517
pianista (I)   3517
pianiste (F)   3517
Pianistin (D)   3517
piano (E, F, I)   400, 864
piano à queue (F)   401
piano accordion (E)   397
piano concerto (E)   2314
piano droit (F)   404
piano mécanique (F)   480
piano préparé (F)   402
piano score (E)   3288
piano sonata (E)   2468
piano stool (E)   443
Pianoakkordeon (D)   397
pianoforte (F, I)   400
pianoforte a coda (I)   401
pianoforte a un quarto di
    coda (I)   403
pianoforte preparato (I)   402
pianoforte verticale (I)   404
Pianola (D)   480
pianola (I)   480
piatti (I)   303
piatti chiodati (I)   304
piatti cinesi (I)   305
piatti turchi (I)   306
piatto (I)   1314
piatto charleston (I)   307
piatto sospeso (I)   308
picardische Terz (D)   2159
picardy third (E)   2159
piccante (I)   1391
piccato (I)   103
picchettato (I)   95
picchiettato (I)   103
piccolo (E, F)   160
piccolo (I)   1773

pick-up (E, F)   564
picking up again speed (E)   767
picking up again volume (E)   767
picturesque (E)   1395
piece (E)   2921
pièce (F)   2921
pièce de charactère (F)   2425
pièce lyrique (F)   2427
pied (F)   67, 3468
piede (I)   3468
pieno (I)   1769
pienone (I)   3014
piercing (E)   1527
pietà (I)   681
pietoso (I)   1392
pieux (F)   1394
piffero (I)   161
pigro (I)   1393
Pikkolo (D)   160
pincé (I)   104, 2028
pincé étouffé (F)   1870
pio (I)   1394
pious (E)   1394
pipe (E)   142, 413
pipeau (F)   121, 190
piquant (F)   1391
piqué (F)   103, 877
pirolo (I)   36
Piston (D)   129
piston (E, F)   216
piston flute (E)   149
pistone (I)   216
pitch (E)   2002
pitch (E)   1881
pitch level (E)   1881
pitch pipe (E)   2979
pitié (F)   681
pittoresco (I)   1395
pittoresque (F)   1395
pity (E)   681
pitying (E)   1392
più (I)   1770
più che (I)   1771
più del (I)   1771
più forte possibile (I)   865
più piano possibile (I)   866

più tosto (I)	796
più veloce (I)	797
piuttosto (I)	1772
piv (I)	162
Piva (D, E, F, I)	2578
pizzicato (F, I)	104
placando (I)	906
place (E, F)	1731, 3234, 3235
place assise (F)	3235
place debout (F)	3236
placid (E)	1396
placide (F)	1396
placido (I)	1396
placing of the voice (E)	613
plagal (D, E, F)	2066
plagal cadence (E)	1915
plagale (I)	2066
plagale Kadenz (D)	1915
plagiare (I)	2763
plagiarism (E)	3229
Plagiat (D)	3229
plagiat (F)	3229
plagier (F)	2763
plagiieren (D)	2763
plagio (I)	3229
plain-chant (F)	2293
plainsong (Gregorian chant) (E)	2293
plaintif (F)	1186, 1301
plaintive (E)	1186
plaisant (F)	1388
plaisanterie (F)	3317
Plakat (D)	2934
plan (E)	3253
planche à laver (F)	252
planche de friction (F)	333
planches (F)	3314
planchette ronflante (F)	293
plaque de protection (F)	63
plat (F)	1314
plate (E)	206
platea (I)	3230
plateau (F)	206
Plattenspieler (D)	516
Platz (D)	3234
Platzanweiser (D)	3108

Platzanweiserin (D)	3108
plaudern (D)	2681
Playback (D)	544
playback (E, F, I)	544
playbill (E)	3254
player piano (E)	480
player roll (E)	418
playful (E)	1233, 1234
pleadingly (E)	1540
pleasant (E)	1388
pleased (E)	1422
pleasing (E)	1388
plectre (F)	64, 438
plectrum (E)	64, 438
plectrum guard (E)	63
plein (F)	1357, 1769
plein d'allant (F)	1015
plein de couleur (F)	1048
plein de dignité (F)	1076
plein de vivacité (F)	1597
plein jeu (F)	464
Plektrum (D)	64, 438
plettro (I)	64, 438
plot (E)	3407
plötzlich (D)	1685, 1715
plucked (E)	104
plucked instruments (E)	3376
plump (D)	1239
pluralité des chœurs (F)	2067
plus (F)	1770
plus court et plus rapide que adagio (F)	721
plus court et plus rapide que largo (F)	750
plus du (F)	1771
plus lent ou plus rapide que andante (F)	730
plus que (F)	1771
plus rapide (F)	797
plus vite (F)	796
plutôt (F)	1772
pochette (F, I)	22
pocket score (E)	3218
poco (I)	1773
poco a poco (I)	1774
poco a poco meno (I)	1775

poco a poco più (I)   1776
poco meno (I)   1777
poco più (I)   1778
poderoso (I)   1402
Podest (D)   3231
podio (I)   3231
Podium (D)   3231
podium (F)   3231
Poem (D)   2428
poem (E)   2428
poema (I)   2428
poema sinfonico (I)   2429
poème (F)   2428
poème symphonique (F)   2429
poetic (E)   1397
poetico (I)   1397
poétique (F)   1397
poggiato (I)   843
poi (I)   1690
poi segue (I)   1779
poids du bras (F)   467
poids du corps (F)   468
poignant (F)   1533
poignet (F)   3473
point (E, F)   66, 2084, 3268
point culminant (F)   2888
point d'arrêt (F)   1946
point d'orgue (F)   1946
pointé (F)   2083
pointe (F)   66, 3268
pointed out (E)   1723
pointer (F)   2015
pointillisme musical (F)   3163
pointillist music (E)   3163
pointu (F)   1391
poitrine (F)   3467
polacca (I)   2430
polca (I)   2431
policoralità (I)   2067
polifonia (I)   2068
polifonia policorale (I)   2067
polimetria (I)   2069
poliritmica (I)   2070
politonalità (I)   2071
Polka (D)   2431
polka (E, F)   2431

pollice (I)   3469
polmoni (I)   3470
Polo (D, E, F, I)   2579
Polonaise (D)   2430
polonaise (E, F)   2430
polpastrello (I)   3471
Polska (D, E, F, I)   2580
polso (I)   3472, 3473
Polster (D)   422
Poltergeist (D)   3045
polternd (D)   1195
polychoral music (E)   2067
polymetre (E)   2069
polymétrie (F)   2069
Polymetrik (D)   2069
Polyphonie (D)   2068
polyphonie (F)   2068
polyphony (E)   2068
polyrhythm (E)   2070
Polyrhythmik (D)   2070
polyrythmie (F)   2070
Polytonalität (D)   2071
polytonalité (F)   2071
polytonality (E)   2071
Pommer (D)   118
pompa (con) (I)   1398
pompa a tiro (I)   217
pompa mobile a coulisse (I)   217
pompeux (F)   1488
pomposo (I)   1488
pompous (E)   1488
ponctué (F)   841
ponderato (I)   1387
pondéré (F)   1399
ponderoso (I)   1399
ponderous (E)   1399
pont (F)   2072
ponte (I)   2072
pontet (F)   371
ponticello (I)   65
pop song (E)   2298
popolare (I)   3232
populaire (F)   3232
populär (D)   3232
popular (E)   3232
popular music (E)   3161

porre (I)	2765
portamento (I)	619
portamento (con) (I)	1400
portamusica (I)	218
portando (I)	867
portare (I)	2764
Portativ (D)	399
portative organ (E)	399
portato (I)	868
porté (F)	868
portée (F)	2063
porter (F)	2764
porter la voix (F)	619
posare (I)	2765
posatamente (I)	1401
posato (I)	1401
Posaune (D)	180
Posaunist (D)	3526
Posaunistin (D)	3526
posé (F)	1401
pose de la voix (F)	613
posément (F)	1401
poser (F)	2749
position (E, F)	3233
position fondamentale (F)	2073
position large (F)	2074
position naturelle (F)	247
position serrée (F)	2075
posizione (I)	3233
posizione fondamentale (I)	2073
posizione lata (I)	2074
posizione normale (I)	247
posizione stretta (I)	2075
Posse (D)	2346
possenhaft (D)	1020, 1165
possente (I)	1402
possibile (I)	1780
possibilmente (I)	1781
(as) possible (E, F)	1780
post horn (E)	135
poster (E)	2934
Posthorn (D)	135
posthume (F)	3237
posthumous (E)	3237
postlude (E, F)	2432
postludio (I)	2432
posto (I)	1731, 3234
posto a sedere (I)	3235
posto in piedi (I)	3236
postponed (E)	3293
postumo (I)	3237
pot-pourri (E, F, I)	2433
potente (I)	1402
Potentiometer (D)	545
potentiometer (E)	545
potentiomètre (F)	545
potenziometro (I)	545
Potpourri (D)	2433
pouce (F)	3469
poulailler (F)	3053
pouls (F)	3472
poumons (F)	3470
pour (F)	1764
pour finir (F)	1765
pour la dernière fois (F)	1766
pour le chant (F)	651
pourtant (F)	1768
poussé (F)	87, 691
pousser (F)	2830
powerful (E)	1402
Präambel (D)	2434
prächtig (D)	1167
prachtvoll (D)	1167
prahlerisch (D)	1491
Praller (D)	2029
Pralltriller (D)	2029
präludieren (D)	2768
Präludium (D)	2435
präpariert (D)	3242
präpariertes Klavier (D)	402
prassi d'esecuzione (I)	3238
pratica d'esecuzione (I)	3238
pratique de l'exécution (F)	3238
prayer (E)	3241
praying (E)	1405
präzis (D)	1404
preamble (E)	2434
préambule (F)	2434
preambulo (I)	2434
précédent (F)	1782
precedente (I)	1782
preceding (E)	1782

preceding tempo (E)   1828
precious (E)   1430
precipitando (I)   798
precipitare (I)   2766
precipitate (E)   761
precipitately (E)   798
precipitato (I)   761
précipité (F)   761
précipiter (F)   2766
precipitoso (I)   761
précis (F)   1404
precise (E)   1404
precisione (con) (I)   1403
preciso (I)   1404
pre-classical period (E)   3239
preclassicismo (I)   3239
preface (E)   3240
préface (F)   3240
prefazione (I)   3240
pregando (I)   1405
pregare (I)   2767
preghiera (I)   3241
prelude (E)   2435
prélude (F)   2435
préluder (F)   2768
preludiare (I)   2768
preludio (I)   2435
premendo (I)   884
premier mouvement (F)   2079
premier violon solo (F)   3251
Premiere (D)   3244
première (F)   3244
première chanteuse (F)   620
première édition (F)   3247
première exécution mondiale
   (F)   3246
première fois (F)   3248
première représentation (F) 3245
prendere (I)   2769
prendre (F)   2769
preparare (I)   2770
preparation (E)   2076
préparation (F)   2076
preparato (I)   3242
preparazione (I)   2076
préparé (F)   3242

prepared (E)   3242
prepared piano (E)   402
préparer (F)   2770
prepotente (I)   1594
près (F)   3423
près de la table (F)   105
près du chevalet (F)   116
presence (E)   3243
presentare (I)   2771
présenter (F)   2771
presenza (I)   3243
presque (F)   1789
presque comme une fantaisie
   (F)   1414
presque rien (F)   869
press (E)   3356
press stud (E)   410
pressando (I)   799
pressante (I)   799
Presse (D)   3356
pressé (F)   747
presse (F)   3356
presse musicale (F)   3357
pressez (F)   799
pressing (E)   799
pressing forward (E)   808
pressing on (E)   749
presso (I)   3423
presso la tavola (I)   105
prestamente (I)   765
prestare (I)   2772
prestissimo (I)   762
presto (I)   763
prêter (F)   2772
pretty (E)   1589
previous tempo (E)   776
prickelnd (D)   1207
prier (F)   2767
prière (F)   3241
prikly (E)   1391
prima (I)   1783, 3244
prima che (I)   1784
prima di (I)   1784
prima donna (I)   620
prima edizione (I)   3247
prima esecuzione (I)   3245

prima esecuzione mondiale (I)	3246
prima frase (I)	2077
prima volta (I)	3248
Primarius (D)	3251
prime (Am.)	2238
Prime (D)	2238
primitif (F)	3249
primitiv (D)	3249
primitive (E)	3249
primitivo (I)	3249
primo leggio (I)	3250
primo tema (I)	2078
primo tempo (I)	2079
primo violino (I)	3251
principal (E, F)	2080, 3250
principal part (E)	2188
principal voice (E)	2188
principale (I)	2080
principiante (I)	3019
principio (I)	3086
private concert (E)	2959
Probe (D)	3261
proben (D)	2798
Probespiel (D)	2902
probieren (D)	2777
procedendo (I)	788
prochain (F)	1785
prochaine fois (F)	3260
producer (E)	3519
production (E)	3111
production du son (F)	546
produzione del suono (I)	546
profan (D)	3252
profane (E, F)	3252
profano (I)	3252
professeur (F)	3510
professional musician (E)	3177
professor (E)	3510
Professor (D)	3510
professore (I)	3510
professore d'orchestra (I)	3518
professoressa (I)	3510
professoressa d'orchestra (I)	3518
Professorin (D)	3510
profond (F)	1406
profondo (I)	1406
profound (E)	1406
progetto (I)	3253
Programm (D)	3254
programma (I)	3254
programme (E, F)	3254
programme music (E)	3117
Programmmusik (D)	3117, 3136
progredire (I)	2773
progrès (F)	3255
progress (E)	3255
progresser (F)	2773
progression (E, F)	2081
progressione (I)	2081
progresso (I)	3255
project (E)	3253
projecteur (F)	3289
Projekt (D)	3253
projet (F)	3253
Prolog (D)	2436
prologo (I)	2436
prologue (E, F)	2436
prolongation (E, F)	3256
prolonger (F)	2774
prolonging (E)	825
prolungamento (I)	3256
prolungando (I)	825
prolungare (I)	2774
prominente (I)	1723
promoter (E)	3257
promoteur (F)	3257
promotore (I)	3257
prompt (D, E, F)	764, 772
promptement (F)	764
prompter (E)	3522
promptly (E)	764, 807
prononcé (F)	1407
prononcer (F)	2775
prononciation (F)	621
pronounced (E)	1407
prontamente (I)	764
pronto (I)	764
pronuncia (I)	621
pronunciare (I)	2775
pronunciation (E)	621
pronunciato (I)	1407

pronunziato (I)	1407
proporre (I)	2776
proportion (E, F)	3258
proporzione (I)	3258
proposer (F)	2776
proposition (F)	2077, 2082
Proposta (D)	2082
proposta (I)	2082
propre (F)	3267
props (E)	2869
proscenio (I)	3259
prossima volta (I)	3260
prossimo (I)	1785
proud (E)	1363
proudly (E)	1180
prova (I)	3261
prova generale (I)	3262
provare (I)	2777
Provenzalische Trommel (D)	325
provisional (E)	3263
provisoire (F)	3263
provisorisch (D)	3263
provocant (F)	1408
provocante (I)	1408
provocative (E)	1408
provvisorio (I)	3263
prudence (E, F)	3264
prudent (E, F)	1409
prudente (I)	1409
prudenza (con) (I)	1410, 3264
prunkvoll (D)	1488
Psalm (D)	2453
psalm (E)	2453
psalmodic (E)	1452
Psalmodie (D)	2108
psalmodie (F)	2108
psalmodierend (D)	1452
psalmody (E)	2108
psaltérion (F)	23
Psalterium (D)	23
psaltery (E)	23
psaume (F)	2453
pseudonimo (I)	3265
Pseudonym (D)	3265
pseudonym (E)	3265
pseudonyme (F)	3265

pubblico (I)	3266
public (E, F)	3266
Publikum (D)	3266
publique (F)	3266
puff (E)	3340
puis poursuit (F)	1779
puissance (F)	3049
puissant (F)	1402
pulito (I)	3267
pulling (E)	838
Puls (D)	3472
pulse (E)	3472
Pumpventil (D)	216
pungente (I)	1391
Punkt (D)	2084
punktieren (D)	2015
punktiert (D)	2083
punktierte Note (D)	2043
punktuelle Musik (D)	3163
punta (I)	66, 3268
puntale (I)	67
puntato (I)	2083
puntina (I)	547
punto culminante (I)	2888
punto di valore (I)	2084
punto doppio (I)	2085
pupil (E)	2879
pupitre (F)	3098
pupitre portatif (F)	218
pur (F)	1413
pure (E)	1413
pure tone (E)	2171
purezza (con) (I)	1411
purfling (E)	59
purità (con) (I)	1411
puritain (F)	1412
puritan (E)	1412
puritanisch (D)	1412
puritano (I)	1412
puro (I)	1413
pushed (E)	691
pushing (E)	808
puzzling (E)	1135
qua (I)	1786
quadrifonia (I)	548
quadriglia (I)	2437

Quadrille (D)	2437	Querpfeife (D)	161
quadrille (E, F)	2437	Querstand (D)	1974
quadrille à la cour (F)	2373	Quersteg (D)	232
quadro di distribuzione (I)	549	Quetschung (D)	1870
quadro musicale (I)	3269	„queue" (F)	1655
Quadrophonie (D)	548	queue de la note (F)	1989
quadrophonie (F)	548	qui (I)	1786
quadrophony (E)	548	quick (E)	774, 781
Quadrupelkonzert (D)	2310	quick passage (E)	2185
quadruple concerto (E, F)	2310	quicker (E)	797
quadruple croche (F)	2230	quickly (E)	781
quadruplet (E)	2086	quiet (E)	1024
qualche (I)	1787	quietly (E)	1565
qualvoll (D)	1560	quieto (I)	1024
quanto (I)	1788	quietschfidel (D)	994
quart de soupir (F)	2235	quil (E)	438
quarta (I)	2241	quinta (I)	2242
quarta corda (I)	45	quintage (F)	245
Quarte (D)	2241	Quinte (D)	2242
quarte (F)	2241	quinte (F, I)	2242, 3270
quarter note (Am.)	2226	quinteggiare (I)	245
quarter note rest (Am.)	2233	Quintenzirkel (D)	1933
quarter-tone music (E)	3118	quintet (E)	2440
quartet (E)	2438	Quintett (D)	2440
Quartett (D)	2438	quintette (F)	2440
quartetto (I)	2438	quintette à vent (F)	2441
quartetto d'archi (I)	2439	quintetto (I)	2440
quartina (I)	2086	quintetto per (di) fiati (I)	2441
quarto (I)	2226	quintina (I)	2088
quarto tempo (I)	2087	quinto tempo (I)	2089
Quartole (D)	2086	Quintole (D)	2088
quartolet (F)	2086	quintolet (F)	2088
quasi (I)	1789	quintuplet (E)	2088
quasi niente (I)	869	quite (E)	1610
quasi una fantasia (I)	1414	quivering (E)	1201
quatrième corde (F)	45	Quodlibet (D)	2442
quatrième mouvement (F)	2087	quodlibet (E, F, I)	2442
quatuor (F)	2438	rabbia (con) (I)	1415
quatuor à cordes (F)	2439	rabbioso (I)	991
quaver (E)	2227	raccapriccio (con) (I)	1416
quaver rest (E)	2234	raccoglimento (con) (I)	1417
que (F)	1653	raccolta (I)	2947
quelque(s) (F)	1787	raccolta di canzoni (I)	3271
quelque peu (F)	1625	raccolto (I)	1418
Querbalken (D)	2176	raccontando (I)	1419
Querflöte (D)	153	raccontare (I)	2778

raccorciare (I)	2779	Rand (D)	366
raccourcir (F)	2779	range (E)	606, 3022
Rache (D)	701	Rankett (D)	163
Rachen (D)	3446	rankett (E, I)	163
Rachenhöhle (D)	3442	râper (F)	381
racket (E, F)	163	râpeur (F)	310
raconter (F)	2778	râpeur en bambou (F)	311
raddolcendo (I)	907	rapid (E)	766
raddolcente (I)	907	rapidamente (I)	765
raddoppiare (I)	2780	rapide (F)	732, 766, 781
raddoppio (I)	2090	rapidement (F)	732, 765, 781
radiant (E)	1420	rapidly (E)	765
radieux (F)	1420	rapido (I)	766
radio choir (E)	661	rappel (F)	3285
radio chorus (E)	661	rappeler (F)	2788
radio orchestra (E)	3201	rappresentazione (I)	3273
radio recording (E)	558	rapsodia (I)	2443
radio transmission (E)	588	rasch (D)	732, 781
radiodiffusion (F)	3272	raschelnd (D)	1208
radiodiffusione (I)	3272	raschiare (I)	381
radioso (I)	1420	rasend (D)	1216, 1276
Radleier (D)	17	raspa (I)	310
(sich) räuspern (D)	684	raspe (E)	310
raffinatezza (con) (I)	1421	Raspel (D)	310
rafforzando (I)	886	rassegnato (I)	1423
raffrenando (I)	819	rassegnazione (con) (I)	1424
raganella (I)	309	Rassel (D)	321
rageur (F)	991	rastlos (D)	1503
raggiante (I)	1420	rather (E)	1625, 1772
raggruppare (I)	2781	Ratsche (D)	309
Rahmen (D)	450	rätselhaft (D)	1135, 1497
Rahmentrommel (D)	323	rattenendo (I)	839
raide (F)	1435	rattle (E)	309, 321
railleur (F)	1006	rau (D)	622, 1450
raise the bell (E)	237	rauco (I)	622
raised (E)	1896	raucous (E)	622
raked (E)	113	Raum (D)	3022
ralenti (F)	827	Raumakustik (D)	2875
ralentir (F)	2782	Raumklang (D)	576
rallegrato (I)	1422	rauque (F)	622
rallentando (I)	826	Rauschen (D)	566
rallentare (I)	2782	rauschend (D)	1345
rallentato (I)	827	Rauschunterdrückung (D)	561
Rampe (D)	3284	raving (E)	1081
rampe (F)	3284	ravivé (F)	801
Rampenlicht (D)	3105	ravvivando (I)	800

ravvivato (I)	801
rayonnement (F)	3243
Ré (F)	2194
Re (I)	2194
Ré bémol (F)	2196
Re bemolle (I)	2196
Ré dièse (F)	2195
Re diesis (I)	2195
Re doppio bemolle (I)	2198
Re doppio diesis (I)	2197
Ré double bémol (F)	2198
Ré double dièse (F)	2197
re-awakening (E)	888
réaction (F)	550
real answer (E)	2100
reale Antwort (D)	2100
réalisation (F)	2091
realism (E)	3419
Realität (D)	3274
réalité (F)	3274
reality (E)	3274
realization (E)	2091
realizzazione (I)	2091
really (E)	3418
realtà (I)	3274
reanimating (E)	802
reazione (I)	550
rebondir (F)	2794
rebounding (E)	106
recapitulation (E)	2097
receding (E)	895
recherché (F)	1430
Rechner (D)	504
Rechteck (D)	560
rechtes Pedal (D)	433
rechts (D)	2976
recita (I)	3273
recital (E)	2958
récital (F)	2958
recitando (I)	1425
récitant (F)	3181
recitare (I)	2783
récitatif (F)	2444
récitatif accompagné (F)	2445
récitatif seulement avec continuo ("sec") (F)	2446
recitative (E)	2444
recitative with continuo accompaniment ("dry") (E)	2446
recitative-like (E)	1287
recitativo (I)	2444
recitativo accompagnato (I)	2445
recitativo secco (I)	2446
réciter (F)	2783
reciting (E)	1425
reco-reco (F, I)	311
recommencer (F)	2789
reconfortant (F)	1055
record (E)	500
record player (E)	516
recorder (E)	152
recording (E)	554
rectangle (E, F)	560
recueil (F)	2947
recueil de chansons (F)	3271
recueilli (F)	1418
redegewandt (D)	3820
redend (D)	1372
redoublement (F)	2090
Redowa (D, E, F, I)	2581
reduction (E)	3287
réduction (F)	3287
réduire (F)	2779
Reduktion (D)	3287
reed (E)	191
reed organ (E)	390
reed pipe (E)	414
Reel (D, E, F, I)	2582
réenregistrement (F)	544
réexposition (F)	2097
réfléchi (F)	1387
réfléchir (F)	2792
Refrain (D)	2105
refrain (E, F)	2105
regard (F)	3332
regarder (F)	2861
Regel (D)	3276
regelmäßig (D)	3277
regia (I)	551, 3275
Regie (D)	3275
régie (F)	3275

Regisseur (D)   3519
régisseur (F)   3519
Regisseurin (D)   3519
regista (I)   3519
Register (D)   439, 623
register (E)   439, 623
Registerzüge (D)   411
registrare (I)   2784
registration (E, F)   469
registratore (I)   552
registratori a cassetta (I)   553
registrazione (I)   469, 554
registrazione a più piste (I)   555
registrazione dal vero (I)   556
registrazione di
   dimostrazione (I)   557
registrazione
   radiofonica (I)   558
registrazione televisiva (I)   559
registre (F)   427, 439, 606, 623
Registrierung (D)   469
registro (I)   439, 623
règle (F)   3276
régleur de tonalité (F)   494
regola (I)   3276
regolare (I)   3277
regolatore del suono (I)   494
regular (E)   3277
régulier (F)   3277
rehearsal (E)   3261
Reibbrett (D)   333
reiben (D)   386
Reibtrommel (D)   273
reich (D)   1431
reichlich (D)   2867
Reigen (D)   2359
Reihe (D)   2120
Reihenfolge (D)   3203
Reim (D)   3290
rein (D)   1413
rein singen (D)   653
reiner Ton (D)   2171
reinlich (D)   3267
reißen (D)   2834
reizend (D)   1036
reizvoll (D)   1589

Rejdovak (D, E, F, I)   2583
rejoicing (E)   1177
rejouer (F)   2802
réjoui (F)   1422
Réjouissance (D, E, F, I)   2584
relâche (F)   3633
related key (E)   2166, 2167
relatif (F)   2092
relation (F)   2093
relationship (E)   2093
relative (E)   2092
relativo (I)   2092
relaxed (E)   1438
relazione (I)   2093
releasing (E)   828
relevé (F)   1723
religieux (F)   1426
religiös (D)   1426
religioso (I)   1426
religious (E)   1426
religious music (E)   3164
remain silent (E)   1823
remarcable (F)   3187
remarkable (E)   3187
reminiscendo (I)   1432
reminiscing (E)   1432
remote control (E)   584
remove the mutes (E)   1728
remplaçant (F)   3345
remplaçante (F)   3345
remplacer (F)   2826
remplacer au pied levé (F)   2808
remuer (F)   2756
Renaissance (D, E, F)   3292
renaissance music (E)   3165
Renaissancemusik (D)   3165
rendere (I)   2785
rendre (F)   2785
renforcé (F)   887
renforcer (F)   2796
rennend (D)   745
renverser (F)   2806
renvoyé (F)   3293
renvoyer (F)   2797
repeat (E)   2096, 2097
repeat performance (E)   3279

repeat sign (E)	2116
repente (I)	1685
Repertoire (D)	3278
répertoire (F)	3278
repertoire playbill (E)	3278
repertorio (I)	3278
repertory (E)	3278
répéter (F)	2798
répétiteur (F)	3520
repetition (E)	2096
répétition (F)	2096, 3261
répétition générale (F)	3262
répétitrice (F)	3520
replica (I)	3279
réplique (F)	3279
répondre (F)	2801
reponse (E)	100
réponse (F)	2099
réponse réelle (F)	2100
réponse tonale (F)	2101
repos (F)	3294
reprendre (F)	2799
représentation (F)	3273
Reprise (D)	2097
reprise (F)	2096, 2097, 3279
reproduction (E, F)	562
Requiem (D, E, F, I)	2390, 2585
requiem mass (E)	2390
Requisiten (D)	2869
resentful (E)	1441
résigné (F)	1423
resigned (E)	1423
resigniert (D)	1423
resin (E)	43
resolute (E)	1073
resolution (E)	2098
résolution (F)	2098
resonance (E)	563
résonance (F)	563
resonant (E)	1443
resonant body (E)	40
Resonanz (D)	563
Resonanzboden (D)	40
Resonanzboden (D)	449
Resonanzkörper (D)	40
Resonanzsaite (D)	52
résonateur (F)	369
Resonator (D)	369
resonator (E)	369
résonnant (F)	1439, 1443
résonner (F)	1727
résoudre (F)	2800
resounding (E)	1443
respect the text (E)	1791
respecter le texte (F)	1791
respectful (E)	1444
respirando (I)	1427
respirare (I)	2786
respiration (F)	624, 3280
respirazione (I)	3280
respirer (F)	2786
respiro (I)	624, 3280
resplendent (E)	1211, 1492
resplendissant (F)	1211
ressenti (F)	1476
ressentir (F)	2815
rest (E)	2060, 3294
rest value (E)	2184
restare (I)	2787
rester (F)	2787, 2832
restless (E)	1281, 1503
restricting (E)	804
result (E)	3008
retard (F)	2102
retardation (E)	2102
retardé (F)	830
retarder (F)	2803
retarding (E)	829
retenir (F)	2804
retentir (F)	2795
retentissant (F)	1195, 1439, 1527
retenu (F)	831
retro (I)	3281
retrograde (E)	2094
rétrograde (F)	2094
retrogrado (I)	2094
retroscena (I)	3282
rettangolo (I)	560
retto (I)	1687
return (E)	2097
returning (E)	1792

returning to the original
  speed (E)   779
rêve (F)   2464
revêche (F)   983
réveillé (F)   888
revenir (F)   2851
rêver (F)   2822
reverb (E)   565
reverberation (E)   3297
révérbération (F)   565, 3297
révérence (F)   3080
révérenciel (F)   1445
reverent (E)   1445
rêverie (F)   2464
rêveur (F)   1507
review (E)   3298
Revision (D)   3283
revision (E)   3283
révision (F)   3283
revisione (I)   3283
revived (E)   801
reviving (E)   800
Revolutionsgesang (D)   2302
Revue (D)   3298
revue (F)   3298
Rezitativ (D)   2444
Rezitativ nur mit Continuo
  („trocken") (D)   2446
rezitativisch (D)   1287
rezitierend (D)   1425
Rhapsodie (D)   2443
rhapsodie (F)   2443
rhapsody (E)   2443
Rheinländer (D, E, F, I)   2586
rhyme (E)   3290
rhythm (E)   2103
rhythm brush (E)   322
rhythm units (E)   484
rhythmer (F)   2805
rhythmic (E)   871
rhythmic instrument (E)   3382
rhythmical (E)   871
rhythmisch (D)   871
rhythmisieren (D)   2805
Rhythmus (D)   2103
Rhythmusinstrument (D)   3382

Rhythmusmaschine (D)   484
rianimando (I)   802
rib (E)   58
ribalta (I)   3284
ribattuta (E, F)   625
ribattuta di gola (I)   625
ribrezzo (con) (I)   1428
riccio (I)   68
ricco (I)   1431
Ricercar (D)   2447
ricercar (E)   2447
ricercare (F, I)   2447
ricercatezza (con) (I)   1429
ricercato (I)   1430
rich (E)   1431
riche (F)   1431
richiamare (I)   2788
richiamo (I)   3285
richiamo per uccelli (I)   312
richtig (D)   1146, 1991
richtiges Zeitmaß (D)   777
ricochet (F)   106
ricominciare (I)   2789
ricordando (I)   1432
ricordarsi (I)   2790
rideau (F)   3339
rideau d'avant-scène (F)   3338
ridente (I)   682
ridere (I)   2791
ridicolo (I)   1433
ridicolosamente (I)   1433
ridicule (F)   1433
ridiculous (E)   1433
ridotto (I)   3286
ridurre (I)   2779
riduttore di rumore (I)   561
riduzione (I)   3287
riduzione per pianoforte (I)   3288
rien (F)   1752
riesenhaft (D)   1232
riesig (D)   1232
riesposizione (I)   2097
rieur (F)   682
rifinire (I)   2704
riflettere (I)   2792
riflettore (I)   3289

rigadoon (E)	2448
Rigaudon (D)	2448
rigaudon (F, I)	2448
righetta (I)	2149
right (on the) (E)	
	1146, 1687, 2976
right pedal (E)	433
rigid (E)	1435
rigide (F)	1435
rigidezza (con) (I)	1434
rigido (I)	1435
rigo (I)	2095
rigoglioso (I)	1436
rigorosamente (I)	1790
rigoroso (I)	1437
rigorous (E)	1437
rigorously (E)	1790
rigoureusement (F)	1790
rigoureusement en mesure	
(F)	1626
rigoureux (F)	1437
rilasciando (I)	828
rilassando (I)	828
rilassarsi (I)	2793
rilassato (I)	1438
rim (E)	366
rima (I)	3290
rimanere (I)	2787
rimbalzando (I)	106
rimbalzare (I)	2794
rimbombante (I)	1439
rimbombare (I)	2795
rimbombo (I)	3291
rime (F)	3290
rimettendo (I)	767
rimpianto (con) (I)	1440
rimpiazzare (I)	2826
Rinascimento (I)	3292
rinforzando (I)	886
rinforzare (I)	2796
rinforzato (I)	887
ring (E)	3352
ring key (E)	194
ringing (E)	1527
rintronante (I)	1439
rinviare (I)	2797
rinviato (I)	3293
rioso (I)	682
ripetere (I)	2798
ripetitore (I)	3520
ripetizione (I)	2096, 3261
Ripienist (D)	3295
ripièniste (F)	3295
ripieno (I)	3295
ripieno violinist (E)	3295
riposo (I)	3294
riprendendo (I)	767
riprendere (I)	2799
ripresa (I)	2096, 2097
riproduzione (I)	562
rire (F)	2791
risaltato (I)	870
riscaldando (I)	803
risentimento (con) (I)	1441
risentito (I)	1441
rising (E)	881
risolutezza (con) (I)	1442
risoluto (I)	1073
risoluzione (con) (I)	1442, 2098
risolvere (I)	2800
risonante (I)	1443
risonanza (I)	563
rispettare il testo (I)	1791
Rispetto (D, E, F, I)	2587
rispetto (con) (I)	1365, 1444
rispondere (I)	2801
risposta (I)	2099
risposta reale (I)	2100
risposta tonale (I)	2101
ristretto (I)	809
ristringendo (I)	804
risuonare (I)	2802
risuonatore (I)	369
risvegliando (I)	888
risvegliato (I)	888
ritardando (I)	829
ritardare (I)	2803
ritardato (I)	830
ritardo (I)	2102
ritenendo (I)	839
ritenere (I)	2804
ritenuto (I)	831

ritmare (I)	2805	romanticism (E)	3299
ritmato (I)	871	romanticismo (I)	3299
ritmico (I)	871	romantico (I)	1446
ritmo (I)	2103	Romantik (D)	3299
ritmo lombardo (I)	2104	romantique (F)	1446
ritornando (I)	1792	romantisch (D)	1446
ritornare (I)	2851	romantisme (F)	3299
Ritornell (D)	2449	romanza (I)	2450
ritornello (E, I)	2105, 2449	romanza senza parole (I)	2451
ritorto (I)	219	Romanze (D)	2450
ritournelle (F)	2449	rond (F)	1447
ritterlich (D)	1038	Ronda (D, E, F, I)	2589
ritual (E)	3296	ronde (F)	2224, 2359
rituale (I)	3296	Rondeau (D, E, F, I)	2590
rituel (F)	3296	rondeau (F)	2452
rituell (D)	3296	Rondeña (D, E, F, I)	2591
rivelatore (I)	564	Rondo (D)	2452
riverbero (I)	3297	rondo (E, F)	2452
riverbo (I)	565	rondò (I)	2452
riverente (I)	1445	rosa (I)	69
riverso (I)	2106	rose (E, F)	69
rivet cymbals (E)	304	Rosette (D)	69
rivista (I)	3298	rosin (E)	43
rivolto (I)	2107	rossignol (F)	699
roaring (E)	1195, 1439	rostrum (E)	3231
"robbed" (E)	768	rotary valve (E)	205
robuste (F)	1593	rotella (I)	220
robusto (I)	1593	rotondo (I)	1447
rocchetta (I)	163	rotto (I)	3300
rocking (E)	1064	roue de frottement (F)	70
roco (I)	622	rough (E)	1450
roh (D)	1018	roulade (F)	609
Rohrblatt (D)	191	rouleau (F)	220, 418, 420
Röhrenglocken (D)	260	roulement de tambour (F)	382
role (E)	3301	roulement de timbales (F)	383
rôle (F)	3301	round (E)	1447
rôle principal (F)	3302	round dance (E)	2359
rôle secondaire (F)	2956	rovente (I)	984
Rolle (D)	3301	rovesciare (I)	2806
roller (E)	420	rovescio (I)	2107
rolling (E)	1360	row (E)	2120
Rolltrommel (D)	268	royalties (E)	2990
romance (E, F)	2450	rozzo (I)	1246
romance sans paroles (F)	2451	rubando (I)	768
Romanesca (D, E, F, I)	2588	rubato (I)	768
romantic (E)	1446	Rücken (D)	3475

Rückkoppelung (D)	550	rythmé (F)	871
Rückstrahlung (D)	3297	rythme (F)	2103
rückwärts (D)	1684, 3281	rythme lombard (F)	2104
rückwärtsgehend (D)	2094	rythmique (F)	871
rude (F, I)	1450	s'éclaircir la voix (F)	626, 684
Rueda (D, E, F, I)	2592	s'éloigner (F)	2648
rufend (D)	1040	sacco (I)	221
Ruggiero (D, E, F, I)	2593	Sackpfeife (D)	162, 189
rugueux (F)	1450	sacred concerto (E)	2316
Ruhe (D)	3294	sacred music (E)	3166
Ruhe! (D)	3334	sad (E)	1572
ruhevoll (D)	1565	saddle (E)	71
ruhig (D)	1024, 1369, 1565	sadly (E)	1573
rühren (D)	2684	Saeta (D, E, F, I)	2594
rührend (D)	1051	sagely (E)	1451
Rührtrommel (D)	268	sagement (F)	1451
rule (E)	3276	sagen (D)	2758
rullo del timpano (I)	383	sagesse (F)	3303
rullo di tamburo (I)	382	Sägezahn (D)	497
rumba (I)	280	saggezza (I)	3303
Rumbakugeln (D)	296	saggiamente (I)	1451
Rumbastäbe (D)	279	saggio (I)	3304
rumore (I)	566	sagoma inferiore (I)	80
rumorosamente (I)	1448	sagoma superiore (I)	79
rumoroso (I)	1448	sailor-like dance (E)	2384
run (E)	2185	Sainete (D, E, F, I)	2595
rund (D)	1447	saint (E, F)	3308
Rundfunk (D)	3272	Saison (D)	3353
Rundfunkaufnahme (D)	558	saison (F)	3353
Rundfunkchor (D)	661	saison de concerts (F)	3354
Rundfunkorchester (D)	3201	saison théâtrale (F)	3355
Rundfunkübertragung (D)	588	Saite (D)	44
running (E)	745	Saitenchor (D)	54
ruolo (I)	3301	Saitenfessel (D)	39
ruolo principale (I)	3302	Saitenhalter (D)	53
ruota a sfregamento (I)	70	Saiteninstrumente (D)	3371
rural (E)	943	Saitenschraube (D)	371
rusé (F)	1215	sala da ballo (I)	3305
rushing (E)	798	sala da concerto (I)	3306
rustic (E)	1449	salary (E)	3193
rusticano (I)	1449	salle de concert (F)	3306
rustico (I)	1449	salle de danse (F)	3305
rustique (F)	1449	salmeggiando (I)	1452
rustling (E)	1208	salmo (I)	2453
Rute (D)	372	salmodia (I)	2108
ruvido (I)	1450	salon music (E)	3133

salon orchestra (E)	3200
Salonmusik (D)	3133
Salonorchester (D)	3200
saltare (I)	2807
saltare al posto di un'altro (I)	2808
Saltarello (D, E, F, I)	2596
saltato (I)	107, 112
saltellando (I)	1453
saltellato (I)	108
salterello (I)	440
salterio (I)	23
salterio tedesco (I)	24
salto (I)	3307
same (E)	1735
Sammelwerk (D)	2887
Sammlung (D)	2947
samtartig (D)	1587
sanctus bells (E)	263
sanft (D)	1112
sanft werdend (D)	893
sanfter werdend (D)	907
sanftmütig (D)	1396
sang (F)	3474
Sänger (D)	3493
Sängerin (D)	3493
sanglich (D)	703
sangloter (F)	2818
Sangsaite (D)	38
sangue (I)	3474
sans (F)	1800
sans changer (F)	1801
sans comprendre (F)	1261
sans couleur (F)	1477
sans courir (F)	1802
sans effort (F)	1478
sans instruments (F)	1612, 1805
sans interruptions (F)	1803
sans mesure (F)	770
sans passion (F)	1514
sans reprise (F)	1804
sans s'arrêter (F)	1803
sans se presser (F)	769
sans soucis (F)	1516
sans sourdine (F)	110
sans traîner (F)	771
Sansa (D)	313
sansa (E, F, I)	313
santo (I)	3308
sapere (I)	2809
Sapo (D)	314
sapo (E, F)	314
sapo cubano (I)	314
sarabanda (I)	2454
Sarabande (D)	2454
sarabande (E, F)	2454
sarcastic (E)	1454
sarcastico (I)	1454
sarcastique (F)	1454
sardana (E, I)	2455
Sardane (D)	2455
sardane (F)	2455
sarkastisch (D)	1454
sarrusofono (I)	164
Sarrusophon (D)	164
sarrusophone (E, F)	164
sassofonista (I)	3521
sassofono (I)	165
sassofono baritono (I)	166
sassofono basso (I)	167
sassofono contralto (I)	168
sassofono soprano (I)	169
sassofono tenore (I)	170
Sattel (D)	71
Satz (D)	2035
sauber (D)	3267
saut (F)	3307
sauté (F)	107
sauter (F)	2807
sautereau (F)	440
sautillé (F)	90, 108
sauvage (F)	1467
savoir (F)	2809
saw tooth (E)	497
saxhorn (E)	154
saxhorn contrebasse (F)	187
Saxophon (D)	165
saxophone (E, F)	165
saxophone alto (F)	168
saxophone baryton (F)	166
saxophone basse (F)	167
saxophone soprano (F)	169

saxophone ténor (F)	170	Schallwandler (D)	580
Saxophonist (D)	3521	Schalmei (D)	121
saxophonist (E)	3521	Schalttafel (D)	549
saxophoniste (F)	3521	scharf (D)	1391, 1615
Saxophonistin (D)	3521	schattiert (D)	1495
saying (E)	1372	Schattierung (D)	2948, 3331
sbadigliare (I)	683	schauen (D)	2861
sbagliare (I)	2810	schaukelnd (D)	1120
sbagliato (I)	3309	schäumend (D)	1207
sbaglio (I)	3310	Schauspiel (D)	3350
scacciapensieri (I)	315	Schauspieler (D)	3490
scala (I)	2109	Schauspielerin (D)	3490
scala esatonale (I)	2110	Scheide (D)	231
scale (E)	2109	Scheinwerfer (D)	3289
scambio (I)	3311	Schelle (D)	321
scappamento (I)	441	Schellenbaum (D)	300
scarcely (E)	1639	Schellengeläute (D)	320
scarno (I)	1468	Schellentrommel (D)	324
scarso (I)	1773	scherno (con) (I)	1457
scatenato (I)	1455	Scherz (D)	3317
scatola (I)	3312	scherzando (I)	1458
scatola dell'altoparlante (I)	567	scherzend (D)	1019, 1458
scatola musicale (I)	475	scherzetto (I)	2456
scattante (I)	1456	scherzhaft (D)	1020
scelta (I)	3313	scherzino (I)	2456
scemando (I)	908	Scherzo (D, E, F, I)	2597
scena (I)	3314	scherzo (I)	3317
scénario (F)	3315	scherzoso (I)	1458
scenario (I)	3315	schiarirsi la gola (I)	684
scene (E)	3314	schiarirsi la voce (I)	626
scène (F)	3314	Schichtung (D)	2132
scenery (E)	3315	Schicksal (D)	677
scenografia (I)	3316	schiena (I)	3475
scénographie (F)	3316	schietto (I)	1413
scenography (E)	3316	Schifferklavier (D)	397
Schachtel (D)	3312	schimmernd (D)	1013
schalkhaft (D)	1215	schizzo (I)	3318
Schall (D)	2142, 3352	Schlacht (D)	2268
Schallbecher (D)	200, 212	schlaff (D)	1341
Schalldose (D)	498	Schlag (D)	374, 1658, 1902
schallend (D)	1443, 1527	Schlagbass (D)	15
Schallkasten (D)	40	Schlagbrett (D)	63
Schallplatte (D)	500	Schlägel (D)	347, 362
Schallstärke (D)	598	schlagen (D)	380, 2667
Schallstück (D)	212	Schlager (D)	2298
Schalltrichter hoch (D)	237	Schlagfell (D)	357

Schlaggitarre (D)	11
Schlaginstrumente (D)	3375
Schlagstäbe (D)	279
Schlagzeug (D)	253
Schlagzeuger (D)	3492
Schlagzeugerin (D)	3492
Schlangenbass (D)	171
schlau (D)	1215
schlechter Taktteil (D)	2155
Schleifer (D)	1871
schleppen (D)	2852
schleppend (D)	836
schleunig (D)	772
schlicht (D)	1314
schließen (D)	2683
Schlitztrommel (D)	330
schluchzen (D)	2818
schluchzend (D)	686
Schluss (D)	1701
Schlüssel (D)	1921
Schlusskadenz (D)	1912
Schlusssatz (D)	1936, 2180
Schlussstück (D)	2347
Schlussteil (D)	1655
schmachtend (D)	1302, 1303
schmächtig (D)	1147, 1240
schmähend (D)	1291
schmeichelnd (D)	1318
schmerzend (D)	1117
schmerzhaft (D)	1119
schmerzlich (D)	1119
schmettern (D)	245
(Theater-)Schminke (D)	658
schmückend (D)	926
Schnabel (D)	198
Schnarre (D)	309
Schnarrsaite (D)	358
schnaubend (D)	1201
Schnecke (D)	68
schneiden (D)	2845
schnell (D)	734, 763, 765, 766
Schneller (D)	2029
schneller oder langsamer als Andante (D)	730
schneller Schlussteil (D)	2135
Schnitt (D)	582
schön (D)	1705, 2916
schöner Gesang (D)	648
Schönheit (D)	2915
school (E)	3321
school music (E)	3158
schöpferisch (D)	2972
schränken (D)	388
schrapen (D)	381
Schraube (D)	235
schrecklich (D)	1550
schreiben (D)	2811
schreien (D)	2728
schreiend (D)	1580
schrill (D)	1536
Schritt (D)	1992, 3220
schrittweise (D)	1939
schrullig (D)	1154
schüchtern (D)	1553
Schuhplattler (D, E, F, I)	2598
Schule (D)	3321
Schüler (D)	2879
Schülerin (D)	2879
Schulmusik (D)	3158
Schulter (D)	3477
Schulterstütze (D)	72
schütteln (D)	385
Schüttelrohr (D)	317
schwach (D)	1069
schwacher Taktteil (D)	2155
schwächer werdend (D)	894
schwächlich (D)	1069
Schwammschlägel (D)	352
schwankend (D)	1004
„Schwanz" (D)	1655
schwärmerisch (D)	163, 1141
Schwebung (D)	487, 542
schweige (D)	1823
Schweigen (D)	3334
schweigen (D)	1824, 2844
Schwellkasten (D)	417
schwer (D)	1386, 2984
schwerer Taktteil (D)	2156
schwerfällig (D)	1386
schwermütig (D)	1326
Schwerpunkt (D)	1867
Schwert (D)	3347

schwierig (D)   2984
Schwierigkeit (D)   2985
schwimmend (D)   1225
schwingen (D)   2862
Schwingung (D)   542, 596
Schwingungserzeuger (D)   541
Schwirrholz (D)   293
schwülstig (D)   969
schwungvoll (D)   1014
scie musicale (F)   316
scintillante (I)   1489
scintilleting (E)   1489
sciolto (I)   1459
sconsolato (I)   1090
scontroso (I)   983
scoperto (I)   384
scoppiante (I)   1460
scoramento (con) (I)   1461
scordato (I)   3361
scordatura (E, F, I)   109
score (E)   3216
scorrendo (I)   1462
scorretto (I)   3319
scorrevole (I)   1462
scotch snap (E)   2104
Scottish dance (E)   2457
scozzese (I)   2457
scraper (E)   290, 310
screaching (E)   1535
screaming (E)   1580
screw (E)   235
scrittura (I)   3320
scrivere (I)   2811
scrivere della musica (I)   2812
scrivere delle note (I)   2812
scroll (E)   68
scrupoloso (I)   1463
scrupuleux (F)   1463
scrupulous (E)   1463
scuola (I)   3321
scuola di balletto (I)   3322
scuola di coro (I)   3323
scuola di musica (I)   3324
scuola viennese (I)   3325
scuotere (I)   385
scurire (I)   568

scuro (I)   1544
scusa (I)   3326
sdegno (con) (I)   1464
sdegnoso (I)   1464
se (I)   1793
se bisogna (I)   1794
se concentrer (F)   2687
se détendre (F)   2793
se mouvoir (F)   2756
se perfectionner (F)   2762
se relaxer (F)   2793
se souvenir (F)   2790
se taire (F)   1824, 2844
se tromper (F)   2810
season (E)   3353, 3355
seat (E)   3234, 3235
sec (F)   1465
secco (I)   1465
Sechzehntel (D)   2228
Sechzehntelpause (D)   2235
second (E)   2239
second corps (F)   214
second movement (E)   2113
second theme (E)   2112
second thème (F)   2112
seconda (I)   2239
secondaire (F)   2111
secondario (I)   2111
secondary (E)   2111
secondary accent (E)   1869
secondary dominant (E)   1961
secondary subject (E)   2112
seconde (F)   2239
secondo tema (I)   2112
secondo tempo (I)   2113
secouer (F)   385
section violinist (E)   3295
secular (E)   3252
secular cantata (E)   2283
secular music (E)   3162
sedate (E)   1401
sedately (E)   1401
sedere (I)   3476
sedicesimo (I)   2228
seducente (I)   1466
seductive (E)   1466

séduisant (F)	1466
see (E)	1854
seelenvoll (D)	1025
sega (I)	316
segnale d'intervallo (I)	3327
segno (I)	1795
segno d'espressione (I)	2114
segno di ripetizione (I)	2116
segno di ritornello (I)	2116
segno dinamico (I)	2115
segreta (I)	442
segue (I)	1796
seguire (I)	2813
seguite (I)	1797
seguito (I)	3328
sehen (D)	2861
sehr (D)	1744
sehr betont (D)	861
sehr genau (D)	1820
sehr gut! (D)	2922
sehr langsam (D)	723, 748, 752
sehr laut (D)	850
sehr lebhaft (D)	727, 783, 1601
sehr leise (D)	863
sehr rhythmisch (D)	846
sehr sanft (D)	1115
sehr schnell (D)	727, 762
sehr viel (D)	1743
Seite (D)	3209
Seitenbewegung (D)	2033
Seitenthema (D)	2112
seizième de soupir (F)	2237
Sekunde (D)	2239
Selbstlaut (D)	3425
selection (E)	3313
sélection (F)	3313
selezione (I)	3313
sella (I)	71
seltsam (D)	1531
selvaggio (I)	1467
semblable (F)	1808
semibiscroma (I)	2230
semibreve (E, I)	2224
semibreve rest (E)	2231
semicroma (I)	2228
semiminima (I)	2226
semiquaver (E)	2228
semiquaver rest (E)	2235
semitone (E)	2117
semitono (I)	2117
semplice (I)	1468
semplicemente (I)	1469
semplicità (con) (I)	1470
semplificare (I)	2814
semplificato (I)	3329
sempre (I)	1798
sempre lo stesso (I)	1799
sempre più animato (I)	805
Sendung (D)	3409
senken (D)	2626
senkrecht (D)	2186
Senkung (D)	2162
sens (F)	3330
sense (E)	3330
sensibile (I)	2118
sensibilità (con) (I)	1471
sensibilmente (I)	1472
sensible (F)	2118
sensiblement (F)	1472
sensitively (E)	1472
senso (I)	3330
sensual (E)	1473
sensuale (I)	1473
sensuel (F)	1473
sentimental (D, E, F)	1474
sentimentale (I)	1474
sentimento (con) (I)	1475
sentire (I)	2815
sentito (I)	1476
senza (I)	1800
senza cambiare (I)	1801
senza colore (I)	1477
senza correre (I)	1802
senza fermarsi (I)	1803
senza fretta (I)	769
senza interruzioni (I)	1803
senza misura (I)	770
senza replica (I)	1804
senza sforzo (I)	1478
senza sordina (I)	110
senza strascicare (I)	771
senza strumenti (I)	1805

senza trascicare (I)	771	serrando (I)		810
separare (I)	2816	serrato (I)		806
separated (E)	1806	serré (F)	806,	809
separato (I)	111, 1806	sessantaquattresimo (I)		2230
séparé (F)	1806	sesta (I)		2243
séparer (F)	2816	sesta napolitana (I)		2121
septet (E)	2460	sestetto (I)		2459
Septett (D)	2460	sestina (I)		2122
septième (F)	2244	set (E)		3315
septième de dominante (F)	2123	settima (I)		2244
Septime (D)	2244	settima di dominante (I)		2123
Septole (D)	2124	settimina (I)		2124
septolet (F)	2124	settimino (I)		2460
septuor (F)	2460	setzen (D)		2749
septuplet (E)	2124	setzen Sie fort (D)		1671
sequence (E, F)	2119	seufzen (D)		2825
Sequencer (D)	569	seufzend (D)		1513
sequencer (E, F, I)	569	Seufzer (D)		688
Sequenz (D)	2119	seul (F)		1811
sequenza (I)	2119	seulement (F)		1812
serafico (I)	1479	seventh (E)		2244
seraphic (E)	1479	severe (E)		1485
séraphique (F)	1479	sévère (F)		1485
serein (F)	1481	severità (con) (I)		1484
serenade (E)	2458	severo (I)		1485
sérénade (F)	2458	Sevillana (D, E, F, I)		2599
serenata (I)	2458	Sexte (D)		2243
serene (E)	1481	sextet (E)		2459
serenità (con) (I)	1480	Sextett (D)		2459
sereno (I)	1481	Sextole (D)		2122
serial music (E)	3168	sextolet (F)		2122
série (F)	2120	sextuor (F)		2459
serie (I)	2120	sextuplet (E)		2122
série de trilles (F)	657	sfacciato (I)		1486
serielle Musik (D)	3168	sfarzo (con) (I)		1487
series (E)	2120	sfarzoso (I)		1488
serietà (con) (I)	1482	sfavillante (I)		1489
sérieux (F)	1483	sferzando (I)		872
serio (I)	1483	sfidando (I)		1490
serioso (I)	1483	sfiorare (I)	570,	2817
serious (E)	1483	sfogato (I)		1638
serious music (E)	3167	sfoggiando (I)		1491
serious opera (E)	2409	sfolgorante (I)		1492
Serpent (D)	171	sforzando (I)		873
serpent (E, F)	171	sforzato (I)		873
serpentone (I)	171	sfregare (I)		386

sfrenato (I)	1493
sfrontato (I)	1494
sfuggevole (I)	1210
sfumando (I)	1495
sfumato (I)	1495
sfumatura (I)	3331
sgabello (I)	443
sgargiante (I)	1598
sgomento (con) (I)	1496
sguardo (I)	3332
shaded (E)	1495
shading (E)	3331
shake (E)	2027, 2178
shaken (E)	1832
shaker (E, I)	317
shank (E)	220
Shanty (D, E, F, I)	2600
sharp (E)	1391, 1954
shawm (E)	121
sheet (E)	3043
shell (E)	359, 361
shift (E)	93, 1819
shifty (E)	1561
shimmering (E)	1013
shining (E)	1013
shivaree (E)	3138
short (E)	1650
short appoggiatura (E)	1870
short aria (E)	2258
shoulder (E)	3477
shoulder rest (E)	72
shouting (E)	1580
show (E)	3350
showing off (E)	1491
showy (E)	1598
shrill (E)	1536, 1615
Si (F, I)	2219
si (F)	1793
Si bémol (F)	2221
Si bemolle (I)	2221
si cela est possible (F)	1781
Si dièse (F)	2220
Si diesis (I)	2220
Si doppio bemolle (I)	2223
Si doppio diesis (I)	2222
Si double bémol (F)	2223
Si double dièse (F)	2222
si leva (I)	1807
si nécessaire (F)	1794
si toglie (I)	1807
sibillino (I)	1497
sich beruhigend (D)	892
sich besänftigend (D)	816
sich bewegen (D)	2756
sich entfernen (D)	2648
sich entfernend (D)	895
sich erinnern (D)	2790
sich erinnernd (D)	1432
sich erschöpfend (D)	818
sich hingebend (D)	915
sich konzentrieren (D)	2687
sich räuspern (D)	626
sich täuschen (D)	2810
sich überstürzend (D)	798
sich verlierend (D)	905
sich vervollkommnen (D)	2762
sich weiterbilden (D)	2762
sich wohl fühlend (D)	1053
sicher (D)	2939
Sicht (D)	3424
siciliana (E, I)	2461
Siciliano (D)	2461
sicilienne (F)	2461
sicurezza (con) (I)	1498
sicuro (I)	2939
side (E)	58
sidedrum (E)	332
siegen (D)	702
siegreich (D)	1599
siehe (D)	1854
siffler (F)	2722
sifflet (F)	142
sigh (E)	688
sighing (E)	1513
sight (E)	3424
sign (E)	1795
signal d'entracte (F)	3327
Signalhorn (D)	132
signe (F)	1795
signe d'expression (F)	2114
signe d'interprétation (F)	2114

signe de liaison du phrasé
    (F)   2005
signe de répétition (F)   2116
signe de tenue (F)   2006
signe dynamique (F)   2115
Silbe (D)   3333
silence (E, F)   2060, 3334
silencieux (F)   1499
silent (E)   1499, 1824
silenzio (I)   2060, 3334
silenzio! (I)   3334
silenzioso (I)   1499
silky (E)   1547
sillaba (I)   3333
sillet (F)   71, 76
simbolo (I)   3335
similar (E)   1808
simile (I)   1808
simple (E, F)   1468
simple time (E)   1904
simplement (F)   1469
simplifié (F)   3329
simplified (E)   3329
simplifier (F)   2814
simply (E)   1469
simulare (I)   685
simulé (F)   3042
simuler (F)   685
simultané (F)   3336
simultaneo (I)   3336
simultaneous (E)   3336
sin (I)   1809
sincere (E)   1500
sincère (F)   1500
sincero (I)   1500
sincope (I)   2125
sincronizzazione (I)   571
sine tone (E)   579
sine-wave generator (E)   515
sinfonia (I)   2413, 2462
sinfonia concertante (E)   2463
sinfonia concertante (I)   2463
Sinfonie (D)   2462
Sinfoniekonzert (D)   2317
Sinfonieorchester (D)   3202
Sinfonietta (D, E, F, I)   2601

sinfonische Dichtung (D)   2429
singen (D)   2677
singend (D)   1030
singende Säge (D)   316
singer (E)   3493
singhiozzando (I)   686
singhiozzare (I)   2818
singing (E)   1030
single manual (E)   458
single tonguing (E)   240
Singsaite (D)   38
Singspiel (D, E, F, I)   2602
sinister (E)   1316
sinistra (a) (I)   3337
sinistre (F)   1316
sinistro (I)   1316
sinken (D)   2674
Sinn (D)   3330
sinnend (D)   1331
sinnlich (D)   1473
sino (I)   1809
sino al (I)   1703
sintesi del suono (I)   573
sintetizzatore (I)   572
sinusoidali (I)   515
Sinuston (D)   579
Sinustongenerator (D)   515
siparietto (I)   3338
sipario (I)   3339
siren (E)   318
sirena (I)   318
Sirene (D)   318
sirène (F)   318
sirène de brume (F)   281
siringa (I)   151
sistema tonale (I)   2126
sistre (F)   319
sistro (I)   319
Sistrum (D)   319
sistrum (E)   319
Sitar (D)   25
sitar (E, F, I)   25
Sitz (D)   3234
Sitzplatz (D)   3235
sixte (F)   2243
sixte napolitaine (F)   2121

sixteenth note (Am.)	2228	snuff box (E)	475
sixteenth note rest (Am.)	2235	so (E)	1827
sixth (E)	2243	so gut es geht (D)	1624
sixty-fourth note (Am.)	2230	so laut wie möglich (D)	865
sixty-fourth note rest (Am.)	2237	so leise wie möglich (D)	866
sizzle cymbals (E)	304	so much (E)	1827
sketch (E)	3318	so sehr (D)	1827
skin (E)	357, 368	so viel (D)	1827
skip (E)	3307	so viel wie (D)	1788
Skizze (D)	3318	so viel wie möglich (D)	1712
Skordatur (D)	109	soave (I)	1504
sky (E)	2943	sobbing (E)	686
slancio (con) (I)	1501	sober (E)	1506
slap bass (E)	15	sobre (F)	1506
slargando (I)	812	sobrietà (con) (I)	1505
Slavic dance (E)	2332	sobrio (I)	1506
slawischer Tanz (D)	2332	società di canto (I)	642
slegato (I)	874	société chorale (F)	642
sleigh bells (E)	320	socle (F)	81
slender (E)	1147	sodann folgt (D)	1779
slentando (I)	813	sofern (D)	1793
slide (E)	217, 1871	soffiare (I)	2821
slide casing (E)	231	soffio (I)	3340
slide trombone (E)	184	soffrendo (I)	1116
slide trumpet (E)	179	sofort (D)	1822
sliding (E)	853	sofort umblättern (D)	1856
slit drum (E)	330	soft (E)	864, 1112
slow (E)	722, 754	soft attack (E)	644
slower (E)	827	soft pedal (E)	434
slowing down (E)	826	softening (E)	893
slowly (E)	753	soggetto (I)	2127
slur (E)	2004	sogleich (D)	1822
small (E)	1773	sognante (I)	1507
smania (con) (I)	1502	sognare (I)	2822
smanioso (I)	1503	sogno (I)	2464
smettere (I)	2819	soigné (F)	921
smiling (E)	687	soigneusement (F)	921
sminuendo (I)	902	Sol (F, I)	2209
smooth (E)	1314, 1518	Sol bémol (F)	2211
smorzando (I)	909	Sol bemolle (I)	2211
smorzare (I)	2820	Sol dièse (F)	2210
smorzato (I)	875	Sol diesis (I)	2210
smorzo (I)	444	Sol doppio bemolle (I)	2213
snappy (E)	1015	Sol doppio diesis (I)	2212
snare (E)	358	Sol double bémol (F)	2213
snare drum (E)	332	Sol double dièse (F)	2212

solch (D)	1825
sold out (E)	3014
sole (E)	1846
Soleà (D, E, F, I)	2603
solemn (E)	1508
solenne (I)	1508
solennel (F)	1508
solennità (con) (I)	1509
solerte (I)	1308
solfège (F)	2128
Solfeggetto (D, E, F, I)	2604
Solfeggio (D)	2128
solfeggio (I)	2128
soli (I)	1811
solid voice (E)	713
Solist (D)	3341
solista (I)	3341
soliste (F)	3341
Solistin (D)	3341
solito (I)	1810
sollecitando (I)	785
sollecito (I)	772
Solmisation (D)	2129
solmisation (F)	2129
solmisazione (I)	2129
solmization (E)	2129
solo (I)	1811
solo instrument (E)	3383
Soloinstrument (D)	3383
soloist (E)	3341
soltanto (I)	1812
sombre (F)	1066
some (E)	1625, 1787
somewhat (E)	1849
somewhat faster and lighter than adagio (E)	721
somewhat freely (E)	740
somewhat quicker and lighter than largo (E)	750
somewhat quicker or slower than andante (E)	730
somiere (I)	445
sommesso (I)	635, 1510
sommier (F)	445
sommo (I)	1813
somptueux (F)	1167
son (F)	2142
son fondamental (F)	2143
son sinussoidale (F)	579
sonagliera (I)	320
sonaglio (I)	321
sonata (E, I)	2465
sonata da camera (I)	2466
sonata da chiesa (I)	2467
sonata per pianoforte (I)	2468
Sonate (D)	2465
sonate (F)	2465
sonate d'église (F)	2467
sonate de chambre (F)	2466
sonate pour piano (F)	2468
sonatina (E, I)	2469
Sonatine (D)	2469
sonatine (F)	2469
sonderbar (D)	1009
song (E)	2295, 2298
song without words (E)	2451
songbook (E)	3271
sonnailles (F)	320
sonnerie (F)	3352
sonore (F)	1511
sonorità (I)	3342
sonorité (F)	3342
sonority (E)	3342
sonoro (I)	1511
sonorous (E)	1511
sons harmoniques (F)	2145
sons naturels (F)	2146
sons ouverts (F)	2146
sons partiels (F)	2147
sonst (D)	1633
sopprimere (I)	2823
sopra (I)	1814
Sopran (D)	627, 631
Sopranblockflöte (D)	147
sopranino recorder (E)	146
Sopraninoblockflöte (D)	146
Sopranistin (D)	627
soprano (E, F, I)	627
soprano clarinet (E)	123
soprano clef (E)	1927
soprano dramatique (F)	628

soprano dramatique lyrique
  d'agilité (F)   631
soprano drammatico (I)   628
soprano léger (F)   629
soprano leggero (I)   629
soprano lirico (I)   630
soprano lirico spinto (I)   631
soprano lyrique (F)   630
soprano recorder (Am.)   147
soprano saxophone (E)   169
Sopransaxophon (D)   169
Sopranschlüssel (D)   1927
soprattutto (I)   1815
sordina (I)   1816
sordina a cappello (I)   222
sordina a doppio cono (I)   223
sordina di cartone (I)   224
sordina di metallo (I)   225
sordina diritta (I)   226
sordina hush-hush (I)   227
sordina wawa (I)   228
sordino (I)   1816
sordo (I)   3343
sordone (I)   172
Sordun (D)   172
sordun (E, F)   172
sorgfältig (D)   921
sorglos (D)   1350
sorpresa (I)   3344
sorridendo (I)   687
sorridere (I)   2824
sorrowful (E)   920
sorry (E)   3326
sort (F)   677
sortie (F)   593, 3414
sorvolando (I)   1512
sospirando (I)   1513
sospirare (I)   2825
sospiro (I)   688
sostenere (I)   689
sostenuto (I)   773
sostenuto pedal (E)   435
sostituire (I)   2826
sostituta (I)   3345
sostituto (I)   3345
sostituzione delle dita (I)   470

sostituzione enarmonica (I)   2130
sottile (I)   1147
sotto (I)   1817
sotto la direzione di ... (I)   3346
sottodominante (I)   2131
sottomesso (I)   1510
sottovoce (I)   876
Soubrette (D)   690
soubrette (E, F, I)   690
soudain (F)   1715
souffle (F)   3038, 3340
souffler (F)   2821, 2839
soufflet (F)   428
Souffleur (D)   3522
souffleur (F)   3522
Souffleuse (D)   3522
souffleuse (F)   3522
soufflieren (D)   2839
soumis (F)   1510
sound (E)   2142
sound board (E)   449
sound control (E)   492
sound duration (E)   1967
sound effect (E)   503
sound engineer (E)   3523
sound mixer (E)   527
sound mixture (E)   535
sound moderation (E)   594
sound modulation (E)   587
sound picture (E)   3069
sound post (E)   33
sound production (E)   546
Sound Sampler (D)   574
sound sampler (E)   574
sound sampler (memorizza-
  zione del suono) (I)   574
sound shaping (E)   587
sound storage (E)   526
sound transducer (E)   580
sound wave (E)   596
sound-board (E)   445
sound-box (E)   40
sound-hole (E)   57
sounding as written (E)   1729
soundsampler (F)   574
soundtrack (E)   491

soupape (F)	454
soupir (F)	624, 688, 2233
soupirer (F)	2825
sourd (F)	379, 3343
sourdine (F)	434, 444, 1816
sourdine à calotte (F)	222, 227
sourdine à double cône (F)	223
sourdine droite (F)	226
sourdine en carton (F)	224
sourdine en métal (F)	225
sourdine wa-wa (F)	228
sourir (F)	2824
sournois (F)	1284
sous (F)	1817
sous la direction de ... (F)	3346
sous-dominante (F)	2131
sousafono (I)	173
Sousaphon (D)	173
sousaphone (E, F)	173
soutenir (F)	689
soutenu (F)	773
souvent (F)	1818
sovente (I)	1818
sovrapposizione (I)	2132
soyeux (F)	1547
space (E)	2133
spacieux (F)	1515
spacious (E)	1515
spada (I)	3347
spalla (I)	3251, 3477
spalliera (I)	72
spanischer Tanz (D)	2333
Spanish dance (E)	2333
spannen (D)	388
spannend (D)	1125
Spannung (D)	597, 3399
sparire (I)	2827
sparkling (E)	1207, 1489
spartito (I)	3216
spaßhaft (D)	1019
spassionato (I)	1514
spaventoso (I)	1364
spazio (I)	2133
spazioso (I)	1515
spazzole (I)	370
spazzolino metallico (I)	322
speaker cabinet (E)	567
speaking (E)	1372
special (E)	3348
spécial (F)	3348
special effects equipment (E)	578
speciale (I)	3348
specification (E)	460
spectacle (F)	3350
spectral (F)	1517
spectre (F)	575
spectrum (E)	575
spedendo (I)	807
spedito (I)	774
speech (E)	100
speech song (E)	655
speed (E)	2152
speedy (E)	775
spegnendo (I)	910
spegnere (I)	2828
Speicherung (D)	525
Spektrum (D)	575
spensierato (I)	1516
spento (I)	848, 911
speranza (I)	3349
spesso (I)	1818
spettacolo (I)	3350
spettrale (I)	1517
spettro (I)	575, 3030
spezial (D)	3348
spezzato (I)	3300
spia (I)	3351
spianato (I)	1518
spiccatamente (I)	1519
spiccato (I)	112
spiegando (I)	889
spiegare (I)	2829
spiegata (I)	647
spiegato (I)	1520
Spielblättchen (D)	64
Spieldauer (D)	3001
Spieldose (D)	475
spielen (D)	2840
spielerisch (D)	1234
Spielleiter (D)	3519
Spielleiterin (D)	3519
Spielleitung (D)	3275

Spielplan (D)   2934, 3278
Spieltisch (D)   419
Spieluhr (D)   479
Spielzeit (D)   3355
spigliatezza (con) (I)   1521
spigliato (I)   1522
spike (E)   67
spiky (E)   1391
spinet (E)   405
Spinett (D)   405
spinetta (I)   405
spingendo (I)   808
spingere (I)   2830
spinnend (D)   1182
spinning (E)   1182
spinto (I)   691
spirando (I)   832
spirited (E)   1524
spirito (con) (I)   1523
spiritoso (I)   1524
spiritual (E)   1525
spirituale (I)   1525
spirituel (F)   1524, 1525
spirituoso (I)   1524
Spitzdämpfer (D)   226
Spitze (D)   66, 3268
spitzig (D)   1344
splendente (I)   1492
splendid (E)   1211
splendide (F)   1211
splendido (I)   1211
sponge-headed stick (E)   352
spontan (D)   1526
spontané (F)   1526
spontaneo (I)   1526
spontaneous (E)   1526
spostamento (I)   1819
spostare (I)   2853
spotlight (E)   3289
spottend (D)   1031
spöttisch (D)   1006
spread out (E)   1520
spreading (E)   968
Sprechchor (D)   668
sprechen (D)   2758
sprechend (D)   1372

Sprecher (D)   3181
Sprechgesang (D)   655
Sprechkasten (E-Gitarre) (D)   4079
Springbogen (D)   89
springen (D)   2807
springend (D)   3854
Springer (D)   440
springing (E)   90, 108
springing (bowing) (E)   89
Springtanz (D, E, F, I)   2605
spritzig (D)   1015
Sprung (D)   3307
spumeggiante (I)   1207
squarciato (I)   1299
squillante (I)   1527
squillo (I)   3352
Stabglockenspiel (D)   261
stabile (I)   1061
stable (E, F)   1061
staccare (I)   2831
staccato (I)   111, 877
staccato volant (F)   89
Stachel (D)   67
stage (E)   3314
stage direction (E)   3275
stage fright (E)   3221
staggering (E)   1004
staging (E)   3111
stagione (I)   3353
stagione concertistica (I)   3354
stagione teatrale (I)   3355
Stahlplatte (D)   292
Stahlsaite (D)   47
stalls (E)   3230
stammelnd (D)   1001
stammering (E)   1001
stampa (I)   3356
stampa musicale (I)   3357
stance (F)   2470
stanchezza (con) (I)   1528
stanco (I)   1528
stand in (E)   3345
Ständchen (D)   2458
standhaft (D)   1172
ständig (D)   1798
standing out (E)   1519

standing-room (E)	3236	step (E)	3220
stanghetta (I)	2134	step dance (E)	3404
Stanza (D)	2470	Stepptanz (D)	3404
stanza (E, I)	2470	sterben (D)	680
staple (E)	233	sterbend (D)	824
star (E)	3359	stereo (E)	576
stare (I)	2832	stereofonia (I)	576
stark (D)	849	Stereophonie (D)	576
stark betonend (D)	851	stéréophonie (F)	576
stark betont (D)	852	stereophony (E)	576
stark hervorgehoben (D)	873	Stern (D)	3359
starker Taktteil (D)	2156	steso (I)	1530
starr (D)	1435	stesso (I)	1735
Statist (D)	2951	stetig (D)	1061
Statistin (D)	2951	stets (D)	1798
stato d'animo (I)	3358	stets das Gleiche (D)	1799
staves (E)	2063	Stichnote (D)	2045
steady (E)	1061	stick (E)	347, 2905
stealthily (E)	1284	Stiefel (D)	221
stecca (I)	3186	Stielkastagnetten (D)	270
steccare (I)	2833	Stierhorn (D)	137
stechend (D)	1391	Stift (D)	233
Stecher (D)	3509	Stil (D)	3360
Stecherin (D)	3509	stile (I)	3360
steel brushes (E)	370	still (D, E)	1499, 1636
steel drum (E)	331	Stimmbalken (D)	41
steel plate (E)	292	Stimmbänder (D)	670
steel string (E)	47	Stimmbildung (D)	604
Steel-Drum (D)	331	Stimmbogen (D)	219
steel-drum (F)	331	Stimmbruch (D)	616
Steg (D)	65	Stimme (D)	705
Stehplatz (D)	3236	stimmen (D)	2643
steif (D)	1435	Stimmer (D)	3486
steigern (D)	2664	Stimmerin (D)	3486
steigernd (D)	883	Stimmfall (D)	611
Steinspiel (D)	294	Stimmführer (D)	3250
stella (I)	3359	Stimmführerin (D)	3250
Stelle (D)	1731, 3219	Stimmführung (D)	1938
stellen (D)	2749	Stimmgabel (D)	2978
Stellung (D)	3233	Stimmgattung (D)	659
Stellvertreter (D)	3345, 3390	Stimmlage (D)	623
Stellvertreterin (D)	3345	stimmlos (D)	638
stem (E)	1989	Stimmpfeife (D)	2979
Stempelflöte (D)	149	Stimmstock (D)	33
stentando (I)	833	Stimmtechnik (D)	694
stentato (I)	1529	Stimmumfang (D)	606

Stimmung (D)   2002, 3358
Stimmung
  (eines Instrumentes) (D)   2873
Stimmungsmusik (D)   3126
stinto (I)   911, 1477
stiracchiando (I)   834
stirando (I)   835
Stirn (D)   3443
stizzito (I)   924
stockend (D)   746
Stockfagott (D)   163
stöhnend (D)   1228
stolz (D)   1363
stomach (E)   3478
stomaco (I)   3478
stonare (I)   692, 2833
stonato (I)   3361
stone discs (E)   294
stop (E)   439
stopgap (E)   3390
stopped (E)   238
storage (E)   525
storia della musica (I)   3362
storico (I)   3363
stormy (E)   1542
Stornello (D, E, F, I)   2606
störrisch (D)   1032
Stoß (D)   1658
stoßen (D)   2830
stoßend (D)   808
stottern (D)   2665
straff (D)   1551
strahlend (D)   1420
straight (E)   1687
straight mute (E)   226
strainer (E)   371
strambo (I)   1531
Strambotto (D, E, F, I)   2607
stramm (D)   1219
strange (E)   1531
strano (I)   1531
straordinario (I)   3364
strapontin (F)   3365
strappare (I)   2834
strappato (I)   113
strapuntino (I)   3365

strascinando (I)   836
Straßenmusik (D)   3153
Strathspey (D, E, F, I)   2608
stravagante (I)   1532
straziante (I)   1533
street music (E)   3153
street organ (E)   478
Streicher (D)   2891
Streichinstrumente (D)   3370
Streichorchester (D)   3198
Streichquartett (D)   2439
Streichrad (D)   70
streifen (D)   2817
streifend (D)   114
streng (D)   1437, 1485
streng im Takt (D)   742, 1626
strength of tone (E)   3049
strengthened (E)   887
strengthening (E)   886
strepito (con) (I)   1534
strepitoso (I)   1195
stress (E)   1867
stretched (E)   1530
stretching (E)   835
stretching out (E)   814
stretta (I)   2135
strettamente (I)   1820
strette (F)   2135, 2136
stretto (E, I)   809, 2135, 2136
Strichart (D)   85
strictement (F)   1820
strictly (E)   1820
strictly in time (E)   1626
strident (F)   1535
stridente (I)   1535
stridulo (I)   1536
striker (E)   347
striking reed (E)   192
strimpellare (I)   2835
string (E)   44
string drum (E)   273
string holder (E)   53
string orchestra (E)   3198
string quartet (E)   2439
string section (E)   2891
stringato (I)   1669

stringed instruments (E)   3371
stringendo (I)   810
strisciando (I)   114
strofa (I)   2137
stroke (E)   1658
stroke of the bow (E)   85
stroked in the middle (E)   373
strong (E)   849
strong beat (E)   2156
Strophe (D)   2137
strophe (F)   2137
struck (E)   862
structure (E, F)   2139
struggling (E)   833
Struktur (D)   2139
strumentale (I)   3366
strumentare (I)   2836
strumentazione (I)   2138
strumentazione variabile (I)   3367
strumenti a corda (I)   3371
strumenti a fiato (I)   3372
strumenti a fiato di legno (I)   3373
strumenti a fiato di ottone (I)   3374
strumenti a percussione (I)   3375
strumenti a pizzico (I)   3376
strumenti a tastiera strumenti
    a tastiera (I)   3377
strumenti ad arco (I)   3370
strumenti generatori di
    effetti (I)   578
strumenti traspositori (I)   3378
strumentini (I)   3099
strumento (I)   3368
strumento a tastiera (I)   3379
strumento accompagnatore
    (I)   3369
strumento di basso continuo
    (I)   3380
strumento di fondamento (I)   3380
strumento elettrofono (I)   507
strumento melodico (I)   3381
strumento ritmico (I)   3382
strumento solistico (I)   3383
struttura (I)   2139
stubborn (E)   1032
Stück (D)   2921

student song (E)   2292
Studentenlied (D)   2292
studiare (I)   2837
studieren (D)   2837
studio (F, I)   551, 2471
studio (transmitting station)
    (E)   551
studio da concerto (I)   2472
studio di virtuosità (I)   2473
studio trascendentale (I)   2474
study (E)   2471
Stufe (D)   1992
stufenweise (D)   1709, 1939
stumm (D)   3180
stupendo (I)   3110
stupore (con) (I)   1537
stürmisch (D)   1541
Stürze (D)   200
Stürze hoch (D)   237
stürzen (D)   2673
stützen (D)   639, 689
stützend (D)   842
Stutzflügel (D)   403
style (E, F)   3360
style de chapelle (F)   1612
Styrienne (D, E, F, I)   2609
su (I)   1821
suave (E, F)   1504
subdiviser (F)   2838
subdolo (I)   1284
subdominant (E)   2131
Subdominante (D)   2131
subdued (E)   875
subduing (E)   909
subito (I)   1822
subject (E)   2127
Subjekt (D)   2127
sublime (E, F, I)   1538
submissive (E)   1510
subscription (E)   2865
substituer (F)   2826
substitute (E)   3390
substitution des doigts (F)   470
substitution enharmonique
    (F)   2130
succès (F)   3384

success (E)	3384
succession (E, F)	2140
successione (I)	2140
successioni parallele (I)	2141
successions parallèles (F)	2141
successo (I)	3384
such (E)	1825
suchen (D)	2680
sudden (E)	1685
suddenly (E)	1715
suddividere (I)	2838
suffering (E)	1116
sufficient (E)	1647
sufficiente (I)	1647
sufficienza (con) (I)	1539
suffisamment (F)	1610
suffisant (F)	1647
suggerire (I)	2839
suggeritore (I)	3522
suggeritrice (I)	3522
suitably (E)	1706
Suite (D, E, F, I)	2610
suite (F)	3328
suite anglaise (F)	2476
suite française (F)	2475
suite francese (I)	2475
suite inglese (I)	2476
suivez (F)	1797
suivre (F)	2813
sujet (F)	2127
sul (I)	1821
sul bordo (I)	387
sul ponticello (I)	116
sull'orlo (I)	387
sulla (I)	1821
sulla scena (I)	3385
sulla tastiera (I)	115
sullo sfondo (I)	3386
summen (D)	636
sumptuous (E)	1167
suonare (I)	2840
suonare a memoria (I)	2841
suonare a orecchio (I)	2842
suonare a prima vista (I)	2843
suoni armonici (I)	2145
suoni naturali (I)	2146
suoni parziali (I)	2147
suono (I)	2142
suono fondamentale (I)	2143
suono simpatico (I)	2144
suono sinusoidale (I)	579
suono trasduttore (I)	580
superbia (con) (I)	991
superbo (I)	957
superflu (F)	3387
superfluo (I)	3387
superfluous (E)	3387
supérieur (F)	3388
superimposition (E)	2132
superior (E)	3388
superiore (I)	3388
superposition (F)	2132
suppléant (F)	3390
supplement (E)	3389
supplément (F)	3389
supplémentaire (F)	3390
supplemento (I)	3389
supplente (I)	3390
suppliant (F)	1540
supplicando (I)	1540
supporti a lettura ottica (I)	581
supporting role (E)	2956
suppression du bruit (F	561
supprimer (F)	2823
suprême (F)	1813
sûr (F)	2939
sur (F)	1821
sur la (F)	1821
sur la levée (F)	1999
sur la scène (F)	3385
sur la touche (F)	115
sur le (F)	1821
sur le bord (F)	387
sur le fond (F)	3386
sure (E)	2939
surly (E)	983
surprise (E, F)	3344
surtout (F)	1815
suspended cymbal (E)	308
suspension (E)	2102
sussiego (con) (I)	1539
sussurrare (I)	649

sustained (E)	773	synthétiseur (F)	572
sustaining pedal (E)	433	syrinx (F)	151
susurrer (F)	649	system (E)	2063
svanendo (I)	837	système tonal (F)	2126
svegliando (I)	890	Szene (D)	3314
sveglio (I)	1091	tabatière à musique (F)	475
svelte (F)	775	tablature (E, F)	2000
svelto (I)	775	table (E)	77
svenevole (I)	1309	table d'harmonie (F)	77, 449
sviluppo (I)	2148	table music (E)	3134
sviscerato (I)	981	tableau de distribution (F)	549
svolgimento (I)	2148	tablette (F)	334
swanee whistle (E)	149	tabor (E)	325
sweet (E)	1112	tabouret de piano (F)	443
sweetening (E)	907	Tabulatur (D)	2000
swell-box (E)	417	tace (I)	1823
swift (E)	732, 1308	tacere (I)	2844
swifter (E)	796	tacesi (I)	1823
swiftly (E)	732	tacet (L)	1824
swinging (E)	1120	taci (I)	1823
switchboard (E)	549	tadeln (D)	2695
sword (E)	3347	Tafelmusik (D)	3134
sybillin (F)	1497	Tagelied (D)	2248
syllabe (F)	3333	tagliare (I)	2845
syllable (E)	3333	taglio (I)	582
Symbol (D)	3335	taglio addizionale (I)	2149
symbol (E)	3335	"tail" (E)	1655
symbole (F)	3335	tail (E)	1934
sympathetic string (E)	52	tailpiece (E)	53
sympathetic tone (E)	2144	tailpin (E)	67
symphonic music (E)	3169	tais-toi (F)	1823
symphonic poem (E)	2429	taisez-vous! (F)	3334
symphonie (F)	2462	take away (E)	1807
symphonie concertante (F)	2463	take care! (E)	2900
symphony (E)	2462	take the damper away (E)	472
symphony concert (E)	2317	taking away (E)	913
symphony orchestra (E)	3202	Takt (D)	1902, 2018
Synchronisation (D)	571	Takt halten (D)	2847
synchronisation (F)	571	Takt schlagen (D)	2668
synchronization (E)	571	Taktart (D)	2153
syncopation (E)	1944, 2125	Taktschlag (D)	1902
syncope (F)	2125	Taktstock (D	2905
Synkope (D)	2125	Taktstrich (D)	2134
synthèse électronique (F)	573	Taktwechsel (D)	1917
Synthesizer (D)	572	Taktzahl (D)	2046
synthesizer (E)	572	tale (I)	1825

talent (E, F)	3391
talento (I)	3391
tallone (I)	73, 3479
talon (F)	73, 3479
talonnant (F)	749
Tam-tam (D)	335
tam-tam (E, F, I)	335
tambour (F)	327, 328
tambour à friction (F)	273
tambour bongo (F)	255
tambour de basque (F)	324
tambour de bois (F)	330
tambour de cadre (F)	323
tambour de provence (F)	325
tambour en bois (F)	329
tambour militaire (F)	332
Tambourin (D, E, F, I)	2611
tambourin (F)	326
tambourin à main (F)	323
tambourin basque (F)	324
tambourin provençal (F)	325
tambourine (E)	324, 326
Tambourstab (D)	363
tamburello (I)	323
tamburello basco (I)	324
Tamburin (D)	324, 325, 326
tamburino (I)	326
tamburino provenzale (I)	325
tamburo (I)	327
tamburo a cornice (I)	323
tamburo a frizione (I)	273
tamburo a mano (I)	328
tamburo basso (I)	324
tamburo di ferro (I)	331
tamburo di latta (I)	331
tamburo di legno (I)	329
tamburo di legno a fessura (I)	330
tamburo militare (I)	332
tamburo muto (I)	340
tangent (E)	446
Tangente (D)	446
tangente (F, I)	446
Tann (D)	3047
tant (F)	1827
Tantiemen (D)	2990
tantièmes (F)	2990
tantino (I)	1826
tanto (I)	1827
Tanz (D)	2906
tanzen (D)	2666
tanzend (D)	1068
Tänzer (D)	3491
Tänzerin (D)	3491
tänzerisch (D)	1068
Tanzkastagnetten (D)	272
Tanzmusik (D)	3128
Tanzorchester (D)	3196
tap dance (E)	3404
tape speed (E)	595
tape-recorder (E)	552
tapfer (D)	1583
tapoter (F)	2835
tappato (I)	238
Tarantella (D)	2477
tarantella (E, I)	2477
tardando (I)	829
tardo (I)	754
tarentelle (F)	2477
tartagliando (I)	1001
Taschengeige (D)	22
Taschenpartitur (D)	3218
tastato (I)	74
Taste (D)	448
Tasteninstrument (D)	3379
Tasteninstrumente (D)	3377
tastiera (I)	75, 447
tasto (I)	76, 448
taub (D)	3343
Tausch (D)	3311
tavola armonica (I)	77, 449
tavola da frizione (I)	333
tavoletta (I)	334
tavoletta sibilante (I)	293
tavolo di missaggio (I)	527
tazza (I)	229
teacher (E)	3510
tearful (E)	1300
teatrale (I)	3392
teatro (I)	3393
Technik (D)	3394
technique (E, F)	3394
technique des doigts (F)	3395

technique numérique (F)	583
technique vocale (F)	694
tecnica (I)	3394
tecnica della respirazione (I)	693
tecnica delle dita (I)	3395
tecnica digitale (I)	583
tecnica vocale (I)	694
tecnico del suono (I)	3523
tedioso (I)	1342
teeth (E)	3436
teilen (D)	2703
teilnehmen (D)	2759
Teiltöne (D)	2147
tel (F)	1825
tel quel (F)	1663
telaio (I)	450
telecast (E)	3409
telecomando (I)	584
télécommande (F)	584
television (E)	3396
télévision (F)	3396
television recording (E)	559
television transmission (E)	589
televisione (I)	3396
telone (I)	3339
tema (I)	2150
tema con variazioni (I)	2478
tema principale (I)	2078
tema secondario (I)	2112
téméraire (F)	988
temerario (I)	988
Tempelblock (D)	254
Temperament (D)	3397
temperament (E)	3397
tempérament (F)	2151, 3397
temperamento (I)	2151, 3397
temperando (I)	912
Temperatur (D)	2151, 3397
temperierte Stimmung (D)	2151
tempestosamente (I)	1541
tempestoso (I)	1541
tempestuous (E)	1541
tempétueux (F)	1542
temple block (E)	254
templeblock (F)	254
tempo (I)	2035, 2152, 2153
tempo anteriore (I)	776
tempo binario (I)	2154
tempo debole (I)	2155
tempo dispari (I)	2157
tempo forte (I)	2156
tempo giusto (I)	777
tempo ordinario (I)	778
tempo pari (I)	2154
tempo précédent (F)	1828
tempo precedente (I)	1828
tempo primo (I)	778
tempo ternario (I)	2157
temporale (I)	3398
temporalesco (I)	1542
temporary (E)	3263
temporary modulation (E)	2025
temps (F)	2152
temps faible (F)	2155
temps fort (F)	2156
temps juste (F)	777
temps premier (F)	778
tenace (F, I)	1543
tenacious (E)	1543
tender (E)	1547
tendere (I)	388
tenderly (E)	965, 1545
tendre (F)	388, 965, 1547
tendrement (F)	966, 1545
tendu (F)	1551
ténébreux (F)	1544
tenebroso (I)	1544
tenendo (I)	1829
teneramente (I)	1545
tenere (I)	2846
tenere il tempo (I)	2847
tenerezza (con) (I)	1546
tenero (I)	1547
tenete (I)	1830
tenez (F)	1830
tenir (F)	2846
Tenor (D)	632
tenor (E)	632
ténor (F)	632
tenor clef (E)	1928
ténor dramatique (F)	633
tenor drum (E)	268

ténor héroïque (F)   633
tenor joint (E)   234
ténor lyrique (F)   634
tenor recorder (E)   148
tenor saxophone (E)   170
Tenorblockflöte (D)   148
tenore (I)   632
tenore di forza (I)   633
tenore drammatico (I)   633
tenore eroico (I)   633
tenore lirico (I)   634
Tenorsaxophon (D)   170
Tenorschlüssel (D)   1928
Tenortrommel (D)   268
tense (E)   1551
tension (E, F)   3399
tensione (I)   3399
tenson (E, F)   2479
tenth (E)   2247
tenu (F)   1831
tenue (I)   1147
tenuto (I)   1831
Tenzone (D)   2479
tenzone (I)   2479
teoria degli affetti (I)   3401
teoria musicale (I)   3400
tepid (E)   1549
tepidly (E)   , 1552
tepido (I)   1549
terminaison (F)   1930
terminare (I)   2848
termination of trill (E)   1930
terminé (F)   1702
terminer (F)   2848
ternaire (F)   2158
ternario (I)   2158
ternary (E)   2158
ternary form (E)   1983
terribile (I)   1550
terrible E, F)   1550
Terz (D)   2240
terza (I)   2240
terza picarda (I)   2159
Terzett (D)   2480
terzetto (I)   2480
terzina (I)   2160

terzo tempo (I)   2161
tesi (I)   2162
teso (I)   1551
tessitura (I)   606
tessiture (F)   606
testa (I)   3480
testa di morto (I)   254
testardo (I)   1032
testata con becco (I)   230
testina magnetica (I)   585
testo (I)   3402
tête (F)   3480
tête avec bec (F)   230
tête magnétique (F)   585
Tetrachord (D)   2163
tetrachord (E)   2163
tétracorde (F)   2163
tetracordo (I)   2163
tetralogia (I)   3403
Tetralogie (D)   3403
tétralogie (F)   3403
tetralogy (E)   3403
tetro (I)   1316
têtu (F)   1032
teuflisch (D)   1273
Text (D)   3402
text (E)   3402
Textbuch (D)   678
texte (F)   3402
that (E)   1653
that's enough! (E)   2914
the curtain closes (E)   3067
the curtain goes down (E)   3064
the curtain goes up (E)   3065
the curtain opens (E)   3066
the curtain rises (E)   3065
the most… (E)   1711
the others (E)   1707
the same (E)   1708, 1735
the same pace (E)   756
the same speed (E)   756
the stage door (E)   3012
theater (Am.)   3393
Theater (D)   3393
Theaterkasse (D)   2920
Theaterschminke (D)   658

Theatervorhang (D)   3339
théâtral (F)   3392
theatralisch (D)   3392
theatre (E)   3393
théâtre (F)   3393
theatrical (E)   3392
Thema (D)   2150
Thema mit Variationen (D)   2478
theme (E)   2150
thème (F)   2150
thème avec variations (F)   2478
thème principal (F)   2078
thème secondaire (F)   2112
theme with variations (E)   2478
then follows (E)   1779
Theorbe (D)   26
théorbe (F)   26
theorbo (E)   26
théorie de l'expression des
    émotions (F)   3401
théorie musicale (F)   3400
theory of emotional
    expression (E)   3401
theory of harmony (E)   2175
theory of music (E)   3400
Thesis (D)   2162
thesis (E)   2162
thésis (F)   2162
thing (E)   2970
thinking (E)   1382
thinning out (E)   901
third (E)   2240
third movement (E)   2161
thirty-second note (Am.)   2229
thirty-second note rest (Am.) 2236
thorax (E, F)   3481
thoughtful (E)   1384, 1418
thread (E)   3041
threatening (E)   1336
three strings (E)   473
three voices (E)   1863
throat (E)   3446
throat voice (E)   709
through composed (E)   1860
through-bass (E)   1900
throughout (E)   1678

thrown (E)   101
thumb (E)   3469
thumb-hold (E)   195
thunder (E)   3412
thunder machine (E)   295
thunder stick (E)   293
thundering (E)   1558
thunderstorm (E)   3398
thundery (E)   1542
ticket (E)   2917
tidy (E)   3267
tie (E)   2006
tied (E)   854
tiède (F)   1549
tièdement (F)   1552
tief (D)   1406, 2913
tief empfunden (D)   1476
tiefer stimmen (D)   2637
tiefgründig (D)   1406
Tiento (D, E, F, I)   2612
tiepidamente (I)   1552
tiepidezza (con) (I)   1548
tiepido (I)   1549
tierce (F)   2240
tierce picarde (F)   2159
Tierstimmeneffekte (D)   2889
tight (E)   809
tightening (E)   810
tightly (E)   806
timbale chromatique (F)   338
timbale chromatique
    mécanique (F)   339
timbale mécanique (F)   337
timbales (F)   336
timbalier (F)   3524
timbre (E, F)   358, 2948
timbrel (E)   324
timbres à clavier (F)   264
timbro (I)   2948
time (E)   2152
time signature (E)   2153
…times (E)   1855
timidamente (I)   1553
timidement (F)   1553
timidezza (con) (I)   1554
timidly (E)   1553

timore (con) (I)	1555
timorosamente (I)	1556
timorous (E)	1378
timorously (E)	1556
timpani (E, I)	336
timpani stick (E)	355
timpanist (E)	3524
timpanista (I)	3524
timpano a macchina (I)	337
timpano cromatico (I)	338
timpano pedale (I)	339
tin whistle (E)	190
tinkling (E)	1557
tintinnando (I)	1557
tiorba (I)	26
tip (E)	66
tip of the bow (E)	83
tip-tap (I)	3404
tiracorda (I)	371
tirage (F)	3005
Tirana (D, E, F, I)	2613
tirando (I)	838
tirant (F)	453
tirante (I)	453
tirare (I)	2849
tiré (F)	86
tired (E)	1305, 1528
tirer (F)	2849
tiring (E)	1168
tiro (I)	231
Tiroler Ländler (D)	2481
Tiroler Lied (D)	2481
tirolese (I)	2481
titubante (I)	1296
to (E)	1764
to accelerate (E)	2640
to accompany (E)	2642
to adapt (E)	2644
to add (E)	2646
to adjourn (E)	2797
to alter (E)	2650
to alternate (E)	2651
to animate (E)	2655
to announce (E)	2656
to answer (E)	2801
to appear (E)	2706
to appear on stage (E)	2707
to applaud (E)	2657
to articulate (E)	2661
to ask (E)	2682
to augment (E)	2664
to be late (E)	2715
to be out of tempo (E)	2714
to be out of tune (E)	2833
to be silent (E)	2844
to beat (E)	2667
to beat the time (E)	2668
to beg (E)	2767
to begin (E)	2733
to blow (E)	2821
to bounce (E)	2794
to brake (E)	2725
to breathe (E)	2786
to breathe out (E)	2712
to calm (E)	2675
to carry (E)	2764
to celebrate (E)	2720
to change (E)	2676
to chat (E)	2681
to choke (E)	389
to clear one's throat (E)	684
to clear one's voice (E)	626
to close (E)	2683
to compose (E)	2685
to concentrate (E)	2687
to conduct (E)	2702
to congratulate (E)	2718
to connect (E)	2858
to continue (E)	2689
to copy (E)	2690
to correct (E)	2692
to cough (E)	695
to count (E)	2688
to cover (E)	568, 2691
to create (E)	2693
to criticize (E)	2695
to cross (E)	2734
to cut (E)	2845
to damp (E)	389
to dance (E)	2666
to declaim (E)	2697
to dedicate (E)	2698

to delay (E)	2803	to hear (E)	2815, 2857
to describe (E)	2699	to hold (E)	2846
to die (E)	680	to hold back (E)	2725, 2804
to die out (E)	98	to howl (E)	2859
to diminish (E)	2701	to hum (E)	654
to disappear (E)	2827	to hurry (E)	2766
to divide (E)	2703	to imitate (E)	2730
to do (E)	2717	to improve (E)	2751, 2762
to dot (E)	2015	to improvise (E)	2732
to double (E)	2780	to indicate (E)	2735
to drag (E)	2852	to inhale (E)	2740
to dream (E)	2822	to insist (E)	2737
to elaborate (E)	2704	to interpret (E)	2738
to embellish (E)	2638	to interrupt (E)	2739
to emphasize (E)	1724	to intone (E)	2741
to emphasize the rhythm (E)	2805	to introduce (E)	2742
to end (E)	1765, 2848	to invert (E)	2743
to enlarge (E)	2654	to join (E)	2858
to enter (E)	2706	to jump (E)	2807
to erase (E)	489	to keep (E)	2846
to exagerate (E)	2708	to keep time (E)	2847
to explain (E)	2829	to knock (E)	2671
to express (E)	2713	to know (E)	2809
to extinguish (E)	2828	to laugh (E)	2791
to exult (E)	2716	to lay down (E)	2765
to fall down (E)	2673	to lead (E)	2729
to feel (E)	2815	to learn (E)	2731
to feign (E)	685	to lend (E)	2772
to fetch (E)	2764	to lengthen (E)	2649
to figure (E)	1931	to let down (E)	2674
to find (E)	2856	to lie (E)	2748
to finish (E)	2721	to link together (E)	2686
to follow (E)	2813	to listen (E)	2662
to force (E)	2723	to look (E)	2861
to forget (E)	2700	to look for (E)	2680
to give back (E)	2785	to lower (E)	2636
to give concerts (E)	2696	to make (E)	2717
to give in (E)	2679	to make a mistake (E)	2810
to go away (E)	2648	to make one's début (E)	2711
to graduate (E)	2726	to mark (E)	2747
to group (E)	2781	to measure (E)	2752
to grow (E)	2694	to mistake (E)	2810
to grumble (E)	2670	to mix (E)	534
to guide (E)	2729	to moderate (E)	2753
to harmonize (E)	2659	to modify (E)	2754
to hasten (E)	2645	to modulate (E)	2023

to move (E)	2684, 2756	to remain (E)	2787
to muffle (E)	389	to remember (E)	2790
to mumble (E)	2669	to remove (E)	2850
to mute (E)	246	to repeat (E)	2798
to notate (E)	2812	to replay (E)	2802
to open (E)	2658	to resolve (E)	2800
to orchestrate (E)	2757	to resound (E)	2795
to overturn (E)	2806	to retake (E)	2799
to pass (E)	2760	to return (E)	2851
to perform (E)	2709, 2738	to rub (E)	386
to phrase (E)	2724	to say (E)	2758
to plagiarize (E)	2763	to scan (E)	570
to play (E)	2840	to score (E)	2836
to play arpeggios (E)	2660	to scrape (E)	381
to play at sight (E)	2843	to scratch (E)	2727
to play by ear (E)	2842	to scream (E)	2728
to play by heart (E)	2841	to see (E)	2861
to play together (E)	3752	to seek (E)	2680
to practise (E)	2710	to separate (E)	2816
to praise (E)	2705	to shade (E)	2726
to pray (E)	2767	to shake (E)	385
to precipitate (E)	2766	to sham (E)	685
to prelude (E)	2768	to shorten (E)	2639, 2779
to prepare (E)	2770	to shout (E)	2728
to present (E)	2771	to show (E)	2755
to proceed (E)	788	to shut (E)	2683
to progress (E)	2773	to sigh (E)	2825
to prolong (E)	2774	to sight-read (E)	2843
to prompt (E)	2839	to sight-sing (E)	652
to pronounce (E)	2775	to simplify (E)	2814
to propose (E)	2776	to sing (E)	2677
to pull (E)	2849	to sing flat (E)	650
to push (E)	2830	to sing in tune (E)	653
to put (E)	2749	to sing out of tune (E)	692
to put off (E)	2797	to sing sharp (E)	671
to raise (E)	2652	to slow down (E)	2782
to raise the voice (E)	612	to slur (E)	2745
to read (E)	2746	to smile (E)	2824
to recall (E)	2788	to sob (E)	2818
to recite (E)	2783	to speak (E)	2758
to recommence (E)	2789	to speak in a low voice (E)	635
to record (E)	2784	to spin the voice (E)	607
to reduce (E)	2779	to stage (E)	2750
to rehearse (E)	2798	to stammer (E)	2665
to reinforce (E)	2796	to start again (E)	2789
to relax (E)	2793	to stay (E)	2787, 2832

to stop (E)	2719, 2819
to stress (E)	2641
to strike (E)	380
to strike a false note (E)	2833
to strike up (E)	2733
to strum (E)	2835
to study (E)	2837
to subdivide (E)	2838
to subdue (E)	2820
to substitute (E)	2826
to support (E)	639, 689
to suppress (E)	2823
to take (E)	2769
to take away (E)	2850
to take off the mute (E)	248
to take over a part (E)	2808
to take part (E)	2759
to talk (E)	2758
to tape (E)	2784
to teach (E)	2736
to tear (E)	2834
to tell (E)	2778
to the (E)	1703
to the coda (E)	1623
to the end (E)	1619
to the final part (E)	1623
to the sign (E)	1627
to think (E)	2761
to think over (E)	2792
to throw (E)	2672
to tie (E)	2745
to tighten (E)	388
to touch (E)	2840
to touch lightly (E)	2817
to transpose (E)	2853
to tread the stage (E)	2924
to treat (E)	2854
to tremble (E)	2855
to try (E)	2777
to tune (E)	2643
to tune down (E)	2637
to tune up (E)	2653
to turn (E)	2864
to understand (E)	2678
to understudy (E)	2808
to undo (E)	2831
to upset (E)	2806
to vary (E)	2860
to vibrate (E)	2862
to wait (E)	2663
to waver in pitch (E)	2833
to whisper (E)	649
to whistle (E)	2722
to widen (E)	2647
to win (E)	702
to wobble (E)	697
to work (E)	2744
to write (E)	2811
to yawn (E)	683
to yell (E)	2863
tobend (D)	1203
tobsüchtig (D)	1217
toccante (I)	1392
toccare (I)	2840
Toccata (D)	2614
toccata (E, F, I)	2614
tocco (I)	471
together (E)	1725, 1847
togliendo (I)	913
togliere (I)	2850
togliere il pedale sinistro (I)	472
togliere la sordina (I)	248
toi, toi, toi (D)	3077
toiling (E)	833
tollkühn (D)	988
tölpelhaft (D)	1239
Tom-tom (D)	340
tom-tom (E, F, I)	340
Tombeau (D, E, F, I)	2615
tomber (F)	2673
Ton (D)	2169
ton (F)	2169
ton concomittant (F)	2172
ton entier (F)	2170
ton naturel (F)	2171
Tonabnehmer (D)	564
Tonadilla (D, E, F, I)	2616
tonal (D, E, F)	2164
tonal answer (E)	2101
tonal effect (E)	503
tonal system (E)	2126
tonale (I)	2164

tonale Antwort (D)	2101
tonalità (I)	2165
tonalità affine (I)	2166
tonalità relativa (I)	2167
Tonalität (D)	2165
tonalité (F)	2165, 2169
tonalité relative (F)	2167
tonalité voisine (F)	2166
tonality (E)	2165
tonando (I)	1558
tonante (I)	1558
Tonart (D)	2165, 2169
Tonartvorzeichnung (D)	1889
Tonartwechsel (D)	1918
Tonballung (D)	1994
Tonband (D)	537
Tonbandgerät (D)	552
Tondauer (D)	1967
Tondichter (D)	3497
Tondichterin (D)	3497
tondo (I)	1447
tone (E)	2169
tone cluster (E)	1994
tone control (E)	494
tone hole (E)	207
tone mixture (E)	535
tone painting (E)	3269
tone synthesis (E)	573
tone system (E)	2126
tone-colour (E)	2948
toneless (E)	643
Tonfall (D)	611
Tonfarbe (D)	2948
Tonfolge (D)	3219
Tongebung (D)	2002
Tongemisch (D)	535
Tongeschlecht (D)	2021
tongue (E)	209, 409, 3452
Tonhaltepedal (D)	435
Tonhöhe (D)	1881
tonic (E)	2143, 2168
tonic sol-fa (E)	2128
tonica (I)	2168
Tonika (D)	2143, 2168
tonique (F)	2168
Tonkopf (D)	585
Tonlänge (D)	1967
Tonleiter (D)	2109
tonlos (D)	643
Tonmalerei (D)	3269
Tonmeister (D)	3523
Tonmeisterin (D)	3523
Tonmischpult (D)	527
tonnant (F)	1558
tonnerre (F)	3412
tono (I)	2169
tono intero (I)	2170
tono naturale (I)	2171
tono secondario (I)	2172
Tonreihe (D)	2120
Tonspur (D)	491
Tonsystem (D)	2126
Tontraube (D)	1994
too (E)	1635
too much (E)	1834
top nut (E)	39
top part (E)	2058
torace (I)	3481
tordion (F)	2482
tormentato (I)	1559
tormented (E)	1559
tormenting (E)	1560
tormentoso (I)	1560
torn (E)	113, 1299
tornando (I)	1792
tornando al tempo (I)	779
tornare (I)	2851
tortiglione (I)	2482
torturant (F)	1560
torve (F)	1561
torvo (I)	1561
tosend (D)	1195
tossire (I)	695
tostamente (I)	780
tosto (I)	780
totalmente (I)	2953
Totenklage (D)	2398
Totenmesse (D)	2390
Totentanz (D)	2328
tottering (E)	1004
touch (E)	471
touchant (F)	1051

touche (F)	75, 448	Tragödie (D)	3406
toucher (F)	471, 2840	trainando (I)	836
touching (E)	1051	traîné (F)	840
touching slightly (E)	114	traîner (F)	2852
toujours (F)	1798	trait (F)	3219
toujours le (la) même (F)	1799	traité d'harmonie (F)	2175
Tourbillon (D, E, F, I)	2617	traiter (F)	2854
Tourdion (D)	2482	traître (F)	1160
tourdion (E)	2482	Traktur (D)	451
tourmenté (F)	931, 1559	trällern (D)	654
tourne-disques (F)	516	trama (I)	3407
tourner (F)	2864	tramando (I)	1568
tournez (F)	1857	tränenvoll (D)	1300
tournez aussitôt (F)	1856	tranquillamente (I)	1565
tous (F)	1838	tranquille (F)	1565
tousser (F)	695	tranquillement (F)	1565
tout (F)	1839	tranquillità (con) (I)	1564
tout à coup (F)	1685	tranquillo (I)	1565
tout de suite (F)	1822	transcendental study (E)	2474
toute (F)	1836	transcription (E, F)	3408
toutes (F)	1838	transducteur acoustique (F)	580
trac (F)	3221	transducteur de son (F)	580
trachea (I)	3482	transfiguré (F)	1566
trachée (F)	3482	transfigured (E)	1566
tracker (E)	453	transformateur (F)	586
traction (F)	451	transformation du son (F)	587
traditore (I)	1160	transformer (E)	586
traduction (F)	3405	Transistor (D)	590
traduzione (I)	3405	transistor (E, F, I)	590
träge (D)	1393	transition (E, F) 2059, 2072, 2173	
tragedia (I)	3406	transizione (I)	2173
tragedia lirica (I)	2483	Transkription (D)	3408
tragédie (F)	3406	translation (E)	3405
tragédie lyrique (F)	2483	transparent (E, F)	1567
tragedy (E)	3406	transponieren (D)	2853
tragen (D)	2764	transponierende Instrumente	
Tragen der Stimme (D)	619	(D)	3378
tragend (D)	867	Transponierung (D)	2174
tragi-comic (E)	1563	transposer (F)	2853
tragi-comique (F)	1563	transposing instruments (E)	3378
tragic (E)	1562	Transposition (D)	2174
tragico (I)	1562	transposition (E, F)	2174
tragicomico (I)	1563	transverse flute (E)	153
tragikomisch (D)	1563	Transzendentaletüde (D)	2474
tragique (F)	1562	trascicando (I)	836
tragisch (D)	1562	trascicare (I)	2852

trascinando (I)	836
trascinare (I)	2852
trascrizione (I)	3408
trasfigurato (I)	1566
trasformatore (I)	586
trasformazione del suono (I)	587
trasmissione (I)	451, 3409
trasmissione dal vivo (I)	591
trasmissione radiofonica (I)	588
trasmissione televisiva (I)	589
trasmutato (I)	1566
trasognato (I)	1507
trasparente (I)	1567
trasportare (I)	2853
trasporto (con) (I)	1136, 2174
tratschen (D)	2681
trattare (I)	2854
trattato d'armonia (I)	2175
trattenendo (I)	839
trattenuto (I)	831
tratto (I)	840
tratto d'unione (I)	2176
Trauermarsch (D)	2381
Trauermusik (D)	3148
trauernd (D)	1321
trauervoll (D)	1213
Traum (D)	2464
träumen (D)	2822
träumend (D)	1507
Träumerei (D)	2464
träumerisch (D)	1507
traurig (D)	1572
travailler (F)	2744
traversino (I)	232
travestimento (I)	3410
tre corde (I)	473
treacherous (E)	1160
treble (E)	38
treble clef (E)	1929
treble recorder (E)	145
treblestring (E)	51
treiben (D)	2830
treibend (D)	808
tremando (I)	1569
tremare (I)	2855
tremblant (F)	452, 1569
tremblement (F)	2178
trembler (F)	2855
trembling (E)	878, 1569
trembloté (F)	878
tremendo (I)	1570
tremendous (E)	1570
tremolando (E, I)	696, 878
tremolare (I)	697
tremolieren (D)	697
tremolierend (D)	696, 878
Tremolo (D)	698
tremolo (E, I)	452, 698, 878
trémolo (F)	698, 878
Tremolo (Harfe) (D)	92
tremolo (harp) (E)	92
trémolo (harpe) (F)	92
trémolo dental (F)	243
Tremulant (D)	452
tremulant (E)	452
trennen (D)	2816
trentaduesimo (I)	2229
Trepak (D, E, F, I)	2618
trepidante (I)	979
très (F)	1744
très accentué (F)	861
très bien! (F)	2922
très détaché (F)	112
très doucement (F)	863
très doux (F)	1115
très en mesure (F)	938
très fort (F)	850
très lent (F)	723, 748
très net (F)	112
très rapide (F)	727
très vif (F)	727, 783
très vite (F)	762
Tresca (D, E, F, I)	2619
Trescone (D, E, F, I)	2620
treuherzig (D)	1027
Trezza (D, E, F, I)	2621
triad (E)	2177
triade (F, I)	2177
Triangel (D)	341
triangle (E, F)	341, 592
triangle-wave (oscillation) (E)	592

triangolo (I)	341, 592
trifling (E)	1206
trill (E)	2178
trillato (I)	1832
trille (F)	2178
trillé (F)	1832
Triller (D)	2178
Trillerkette (D)	657
trillo (I)	2178
trilogia (I)	3411
Trilogie (D)	3411
trilogie (F)	3411
trilogy (E)	3411
Trinklied (D)	2272
Trio (D)	2480, 2622
trio (E, F, I)	2480, 2622
Triole (D)	2160
triolet (F)	2160
triomphal (F)	1571
trionfante (I)	1571
Tripelkonzert (D)	2318
Tripelzunge (D)	249
triple (E, F)	1833
triple articulation (F)	249
triple concerto (E, F)	2318
triple coup de langue (F)	249
triple croche (F)	2229
triple time (E)	2157
triple-tonguing (E)	249
triplet (E)	2160
triplo (I)	1833
triplo colpo di lingua (I)	249
triptych (E)	3411
Triptychon (D)	3411
triptyque (F)	3411
triste (F, I)	1335, 1572
tristement (F)	1334, 1573
tristemente (I)	1573
tristezza (con) (I)	1574
triton (F)	2179
tritone (E)	2179
tritono (I)	2179
Tritonus (D)	2179
trittico (I)	3411
triumphal march (E)	2383
triumphant (E)	1571
triumphierend (D)	1571
Triumphmarsch (D)	2383
trocken (D)	1465
trois cordes (F)	473
trois fois merde (F)	3077
troisième corps (F)	215
troisième mouvement (F)	2161
Troll (D)	3045
tromba (I)	174, 3525
tromba a pistoni (I)	178
tromba a tirarsi (I)	179
tromba a tiro (I)	179
tromba bassa (I)	175
tromba da jazz (I)	176
tromba naturale (I)	177
trombone (E, F, I)	180, 3526
trombone a cilindri (I)	181
trombone à coulisse (F)	184
trombone à pistons (F)	181
trombone a tiro (I)	184
trombone contrabbasso (I)	182
trombone contrebasse (F)	182
trombone da jazz (I)	183
trombone de jazz (F)	183
trombonist (E)	3526
tromboniste (F)	3526
Trommel (D)	267, 327
Trommelfell (D)	365
Trommelreifen (D)	360
Trommelsaite (D)	358
Trommelschlag (D)	376
Trommelschlägel (D)	348
Trommelwirbel (D)	382
Trompete (D)	174
Trompeter (D)	3525
Trompeterin (D)	3525
trompette (F)	174, 3525
trompette à coulisse (F)	179
trompette à pistons (F)	178
trompette basse (F)	175
trompette de jazz (F)	176
trompette naturelle (F)	177
trop (F)	1834
trop peu (F)	1835
troppo (I)	1834
troppo poco (I)	1835

tröstend (D)	1055	tuning fork (E)	2978
trostlos (D)	1090	tuning peg (E)	36
Tröstung (D)	2320	tuning pin (E)	36
Trotto (D, E, F, I)	2623	tuonando (I)	1558
trotzdem (D)	3106	tuono (I)	3412
trotzig (D)	1032	turbato (I)	1575
trou (F)	207	türkische Becken (D)	306
troublé (F)	1575	Turkish cymbals (E)	306
trouver (F)	2856	Turkish music (E)	3172
trovare (I)	2856	Turmglockenspiel (D)	265
trüb (D)	1361	turn (E)	1857, 1993
trübselig (D)	919	turn the page immediately	
Trugschluss (D)	1911	(E)	1856
trumpet (E)	174	Tusch (D)	2343
trumpeter (E)	3525	tutta (I)	1836
trumpetist (E)	3525	tutta la forza (I)	1837
Tuba (D)	185	tutte (I)	1838
tuba (E, F, I)	185	tutti (I)	1838
tuba bassa (I)	186	Tuttigeiger (D)	3295
tuba basse (F)	186	tutto (I)	1839
tuba contrabbasso (I)	187	tuyau (F)	413
tuba ténor (F)	188	tuyau à anche (F)	414
tuba Wagner (F)	188	tuyau à bouche (F)	415
tuba wagneriana (I)	188	twelve-tone music (E)	1959, 3143
tube (E, F)	233, 2928	twice (E)	1617
tubetto (I)	233	twig brush (E)	372
Tubo (D)	276	two strings (E)	461
tubo piccolo (I)	234	two voices (E)	1859
tubo sonoro (I)	276	tympanon (F)	24
tubo sonoro di bambù (I)	342	typographie musicale (F)	3357
tubular bells (E)	260	tyrolienne (E, F)	2481
tugendhaft (D)	1037	tzigane (F)	2491, 3427
tugging (E)	834	U-Musik (D)	3149
Tumba (D, E, F, I)	2624	üben (D)	2710
tumbling (E)	761	über (D)	1814, 3388
tummy (E)	3466	überall (D)	1681
tumultueux (F)	1256	überblasen (D)	245
tumultuoso (I)	1256	überdenken (D)	2792
tumultuous (E)	1256	übereilt (D)	725
tun (D)	2717	Übereinstimmung (D)	3092
tune (E)	2011	überfliegend (D)	1512
tuned (E)	2872	überflüssig (D)	3387
tuned gong-carillon (E)	288	Übergang (D)	2173
tuner (E)	3486	übergehen (D)	2760
tuning (E)	2873	übergreifen (D)	462
tuning bar (E)	41	überhaupt (D)	1815

überhetzt (D) 761
überladen (D) 1035
überleiten (D) 2760
Überleitung (D) 2059, 2072
übermäßig (D) 1693, 1896
Überraschung (D) 3344
überschwänglich (D) 1142, 1601
Übersetzung (D) 3405
überspannt (D) 1142
überspringen (D) 2807
überstürzen (D) 2766
überstürzt (D) 739, 761
Übertragung (D) 3287, 3408
übertreiben (D) 2708
übertrieben (D) 1140
üblich (D) 1762
Übung (D) 3017
udibile (I) 1840
udire (I) 2857
udito (I) 3413
uguale (I) 1841
ulkig (D) 1049
ultima (I) 1843
ultima volta (I) 1842
ultimo (I) 1843
ultimo movimento (I) 2180
ultimo tempo (I) 2180
Umbau (D) 2926
umblättern (D) 2864
Umfang (D) 3022
umile (I) 1576
umkehren (D) 2743, 2806
Umkehrung (D) 2107
umore (con) (I) 1577
umoresca (I) 2484
umoristico (I) 1578
Umspielung (D) 2416
umstimmen (D) 3771
un petit peu (F) 1848
un peu (F) 1849
un peu moins (F) 1777
un peu plus (F) 1778, 1850
un pochettino (I) 1848
un pochino (I) 1848
un poco (I) 1849
un poco più (I) 1850

un tantinet (F) 1826
un'altra volta (I) 1844
una corda (I) 474
una volta (I) 1845
Unabhängigkeit (D) 3083
unaccompanied vocal
  music (E) 1612
unausführbar (D) 3084
unbändig (D) 1493
unbedeckt (D) 384
unbedingt (D) 1642
unbefangen (D) 1100
unbekümmert (D) 1516
unbeständig (D) 1339, 1606
unbestimmt (D) 1581
unbridled (E) 1493
uncertain (E) 3079
unchanged (E) 1714
uncino (I) 78
unconstrained (E) 1100
uncovered (E) 384
und so weiter (D) 3003
undecided (E) 1265
under (E) 1817
under the direction of ... (E) 3346
"under the voice" (E) 876
understudy (E) 3345
undeutlich (D) 1268
undulating (E) 102, 1360
undurchsichtig (D) 1361
une autre fois (F) 1844
une corde (F) 474
une fois (F) 1845
unentgeltlich (D) 3060
unentschieden (D) 1265
unentschlossen (D) 1265, 1296
unerbittlich (D) 1257
unerwartet (D) 3078
unexpected (E) 3078
unfassbar (D) 1261
unfolding (E) 889
ungarischer Tanz (D) 2334
ungeachtet (D) 3106
ungebändigt (D) 1270
ungebunden (D) 874, 1459
ungeduldig (D) 1252

ungefähr (D)	1654	Unterhaltungsmusik (D)		3149
ungekünstelt (D)	1518	unterlassen (D)		1761
ungenau (D)	3073	Unterricht (D)		3102
ungerader Takt (D)	2157	unterrichten (D)		2736
ungestüm (D)	1256	Unterschied (D)		2983
ungezwungen (D)	1522	Unterstimme (D)		2055
unghia (I)	3483	Unterstück (D)		215
unheimlich (D)	1316	unterteilen (D)		2838
uni (F)	1847	unterwürfig (D)		1510
unico (I)	1846	untidy (E)		1102
uniform (E)	1579	until (E)	1703,	1809
uniforme (F, I)	1579	ununterbrochen (D)		1672
unique (E, F)	1846	unveränderlich (D)		3094
unir (F)	2858	unverändert (D)		1714
unire (I)	2858	unvernehmlich (D)		3070
unison (E)	2238	unverschämt (D)		1486
unisono (I)	, 2238	unverständlich (D)		1261
unisono (all') (I)	2181	unvollkommen (D)		1997
unisson (F)	2238	unvollkommene Kadenz (D)		1916
unitamente (I)	1847	unvollständig (D)		3081
unito (I)	1847	unvorbereitet (D)	1620,	3074
unklar (D)	1349	up beat (E)		1999
unkorrekt (D)	3319	up to (E)		1703
unmerklich (D)	3070	up to the sign (E)		1704
unmittelbar (D)	1822	up-bow (E)		87
unmittelbar anschließen (D)	1646	upon (E)		1814
unmöglich (D)	3072	upper (E)		3388
unordentlich (D)	1102	upper bout (E)		79
unplayable (E)	3084	upper part (E)		2058
unprepared (E)	3074	üppig (D)		1436
unregelmäßig (D)	3095	upright piano (E)		404
unrestrained (E)	1455	Uraufführung (D)		3245
unruhig (D)	942	urgent (E, F)		811
unsicher (D)	3079	urgente (I)		811
unspielbar (D)	3084	urging (E)		785
unten (D)	1717	Urheberrecht (D)		2992
unter (D)	1817, 3085	urlando (I)		1580
unter der Leitung von ... (D)	3346	urlare (I)		2859
„unter der Stimme" (D)	876	Urtext (D)		3421
Unterarm (D)	3430	urtümlich (D)		3249
unterbrechen (D)	2739	uscita (I)	593,	3414
Unterbrechung (D)	3090	usher (E)		3108
Unterbügel (D)	80	usherette (E)		3108
unterdrückt (D)	1362	usignolo (I)		699
unterhaltend (D)	2999	usual (E)		1810
„Unterhaltung" (D)	2336	usuale (I)		1762

usw. (D)		3003
Ut (F)		2189
vacillando (I)		1004
vagamente (I)		1581
vagheggiando (I)		1089
vaghezza (con) (I)		1245
vago (I)		1581
vague (E, F)		1581
vaguement (F)		1581
vaillant (F)		1583
vaincre (F)		702
valente (I)		1583
valeur (F)		2182
valeur de la note (F)		2183
valeur de la pause (F)		2184
valeureux (F)		1583
valore (con) (I)		1582, 2182
valore della nota (I)		2183
valore della pausa (I)		2184
valoroso (I)		1583
valorous (E)		1583
valse (F)		2485
valse viennoise (F)		2486
value (E)		2182
valve (E)		216, 454
valve cornet (E)		129
valve trombone (E)		181
valve trumpet (E)		178
valve unit (E)		210
valvola (I)		454
valzer (I)		2485
valzer viennese (I)		2486
vaneggiando (I)		1081
vanishing (E)		837
vaporeux (F)		1584
vaporoso (I)		1584
vaporous (E)		1584
variabile (I)		1851
variable (E, F)		1851
variable Besetzung (D)		3367
variante (I)		1851
variare (I)		2860
Variation (D)		2487
variation (E, F)		2487
variato (I)		1852
variazione (I)		2487

variazione del suono (I)		594
varié (F)		1852
varied (E)		1852
varier (F)		2860
varietà (I)		3415, 3416
Varieté (D)		3416
variété (F)		3415, 3416
variety (E)		3415
variiert (D)		1852
Varsovienne (D, E, F, I)		2625
varying (E)		1851
vast (E)		968
vaste (F)		968
vasto (I)		968
Vaudeville (D, E, F, I)		2626
vaudeville (theatre) (E)		3416
vedere (I)		2861
veemente (I)		1585
veemenza (con) (I)		1586
vehement (E)		1585
véhément (F)		1585
vehemently (E)		1255
veiled (E)		700
vein (E)		3484
veine (F)		3484
velare (I)		389
velato (I)		379, 700
vellum (E)		365, 368
vellutato (I)		1587
veloce (I)		781
veloce passaggio di note (I)		2185
velocemente (I)		781
velocità del nastro (I)		595
velouté (F)		1587
velvety (E)		1587
vena (I)		3484
vendetta (I)		701
venerazione (con) (I)		1588
Veneziana (D, E, F, I)		2627
vengeance (E, F)		701
vent (F)		3417
Ventil (D)		216, 454
Ventilkornett (D)		129
Ventilmaschine (D)		210
Ventilposaune (D)		181
Ventiltrompete (D)		178

vento (I) 3417
ventre (F) 3466
vents (F) 3037
venusto (I) 1589
vêpres (F) 2489
verächtlich (D) 1464
veramente (I) 3418
verändere (D) 1747
veränderlich (D) 1851
verändern (D) 2860
verändert (D) 1566, 1852, 1880
Veränderung (D) 2487
Veranstalter (D) 3257
verbessern (D) 2751
Verbeugung (D) 3080
verbinden (D) 2858
verbittert (D) 961
verborgen (D) 1748
verbreiternd (D) 821
verbreitert (D) 1630
verdächtig (D) 1561
verdeckte Parallelen (D) 2052
verdoppeln (D) 2780
Verdopplung (D) 2090
verdünnend (D) 901
verdunstend (D) 904
verebbend (D) 905
vereinfachen (D) 2814
vereinfacht (D) 3329
verführerisch (D) 1466
verga (I) 372
verge (F) 372
vergessen (D) 2700
vergette (F) 453
Vergleich (D) 3213
vergnüglich (D) 2999
vergnügt (D) 1311
vergriffen (D) 3014
vergrößern (D) 2664
Vergrößerung (der Zeitwerte)
    (D) 1897
verhalten (D) 773
Verhältnis (D) 3258
verhaucht (D) 1495
vérisme (F) 3419
Verismo (D) 3419

verismo (E, I) 3419
Verismus (D) 3419
verklärt (D) 1566
Verkleidung (D) 3410
Verkleinerung (der
    Notenwerte) (D) 1956
verkürzen (D) 2779
Verkürzung (D) 1866
verlängern (D) 2649, 2774
verlängernd (D) 814, 825
Verlängerung (D) 3256
verlangsamen (D) 2782
verlangsamt (D) 827
verlockend (D) 1318
verlöschend (D) 903
vermehrend (D) 880, 883
vermindern (D) 2701
vermindernd (D) 902
vermindert (D) 1955
vernebelt (D) 1348
Verneigung (D) 3080
verpflichtend (D) 1758
verräterisch (D) 1160
verringernd (D) 896
verrückt (D) 1379
Vers (D) 3422
vers (F) 3422
verschieben (D) 2797
Verschiebung (D) 1819
Verschiebungspedal (D) 434
verschieden (D) 1688
verschleiert (D) 700
verschleppend (D) 836
verschmitzt (D) 1327
verschmolzen (D) 1218
verschoben (D) 3293
verschönern (D) 2638
verschwinden (D) 2827
verschwommen (D) 1268
verschwörerisch (D) 1568
verse (E) 2137, 3422
verset (E, F) 2488
Versett (D) 2488
versetto (I) 2488
Versetzungszeichen (D) 1872
Version (D) 3420

version (E, F)	3420	Verzögerung (D)	2102
version originale (F)	3421	verzweifelt (D)	1104
versione (I)	3420	verzweiflungsvoll (D)	1103
versione originale (I)	3421	Vesper (D)	2489
verso (I)	3422	vespers (E)	2489
verstärken (D)	2796	vespri (I)	2489
verstärkend (D)	886	vezzeggiando (I)	1590
Verstärker (D)	483	vezzoso (I)	1589
verstärkt (D)	887	vibrafono (I)	343
versteckt (D)	1748	vibrando (I)	1591
verstehen (D)	2678	vibrant (E, F)	1591
verstimmt (D)	3361	vibrante (I)	1591
verstört (D)	1575	Vibraphon (D)	343
versuchen (D)	2777	vibraphone (E, F)	343
vertagen (D)	2797	vibrare (I)	2862
vertical (E, F)	2186	"vibrated" (E)	879
verticale (I)	2186	vibration (E, F)	596
vertikal (D)	2186	vibration sympathique (F)	2144
Vertonung (D)	2955	vibrato (E, I)	879
Vertrag (D)	3320	vibrazione (I)	596
verträumt (D)	1507	vibré (F)	879
verwandt (D)	2092	vibrer (F)	2862
verwandte Tonart (D)	2166	vibrieren (D)	2862
Verwandtschaft (D)	2093	vibrieren lassen (D)	1700
verwegen (D)	997	vibrierend (D)	1591
verweilen (D)	2787	vibriert (D)	879
verwickelt in etwas (D)	1656	vicendevole (I)	1853
verwirrt (D)	1575	vicino (I)	3423
very (E)	1744	victorieux (F)	1599
very accentuated (E)	861	victorious (E)	1599
very fast (E)	727	vide (F, L)	1854, 1858
very good! (E)	2922	viel (D)	1710, 1744
very lively (E)	727	vièle (F)	27
very loud (E)	850	vielfach (D)	1746
very measured (E)	938	Vielfältigkeit (D)	3415
very much (E)	1743	viella (I)	27
very slow (E)	748, 752	vielle (F)	27
very soft (E)	1115	vielle à roue (F)	17
Verzeichnis (D)	2936	Viennese school (E)	3325
Verzerrung (D)	501	Viennese waltz (E)	2486
verzierend (D)	1185	vierhändig (D)	456
verziert (D)	927, 1865	vierstimmig (D)	1862
Verzierung (D)	608, 1864, 2051	Viertel (D)	2226
verzögern (D)	2803	Viertelpause (D)	2233
verzögernd (D)	829	Vierteltonmusik (D)	3118
verzögert (D)	830	vierter Satz (D)	2087

Vierundsechzigstel (D)   2230
Vierundsechzigstelpause
  (D)   2237
vif (F)   1602
vigore (con) (I)   1592
vigoroso (I)   1593
vigorous (E)   1219, 1593
vigoureux (F)   1593
villageoise (F)   2331
Villancico (D, E, F, I)   2628
Villanella (D)   2490
villanella (E, I)   2490
villanesca (I)   2490
villanesco (I)   1449
villanesque (F)   2490
Villotta (D, E, F, I)   2629
vincere (I)   702
vincitore (I)   1599
Viola (D)   28
viola (E, I)   28
viola da gamba (E, I)   29
viole de gambe (F)   29
violent (E, F)   1594
violento (I)   1594
violenza (con) (I)   1595
violin (E)   30
violin concerto (E)   2315
violin maker (E)   3511
Violine (D)   30
violinist (E)   3527
violinista (I)   3527
violiniste (F)   3527
Violinkonzert (D)   2315
violino (I)   30
violino di ferro (I)   31
violino di fila (I)   3295
Violinschlüssel (D)   1929
violist (E)   3528
violista (I)   3528
violon (F)   30
violon rustique (F)   27
violon de fer (F)   31
violon de file (F)   3295
violon de Hardanger (F)   18
violoncelle (F)   32
violoncellista (I)   3529

violoncelliste (F)   3529
Violoncello (D)   32
violoncello (E, I)   32
Virelai (D, E, F, I)   2630
Virginal (D)   406
virginal (E, F)   406
virginale (I)   406
viril (F)   1329
virile (E, I)   1329
virtuos (D)   1596
virtuose (F)   1596
virtuose Etüde (D)   2473
virtuosità (con) (I)   1596
virtuosity (E)   2473
virtuoso (E, I)   1596
virtuoso study (E)   2473
vis (F)   235
visage (F)   3440
vispo (I)   1597
vista (I)   3424
vistosov (I)   1598
vite (F, I)   235, 763, 780
vitesse de la bande (F)   595
vittorioso (I)   1599
vivace (F, I)   782
vivacious (E)   782
vivacissimo (I)   783
vivacità (con) (I)   1600
vivamente (I)   784
vivant (F)   1602
vivement (F)   784
vivente (I)   1602
vivezza (con) (I)   1600
vivid (E)   1601
vivido (I)   1601
vivo (I)   1602
vocal (E, F)   703, 3425
vocal art (E)   641
vocal concert (E)   2319
vocal cords (E)   670
vocal exercise (E)   605
vocal music (E)   3174
vocal score (E)   618
vocal techniques (E)   694
vocal training (E)   604
vocale (I)   703, 3425

vocalise (E, F)	704	voix inférieure (F)	2055, 2056
vocalist (E)	3493	voix intermédiaire (F)	2056
vocalizzo (I)	704	voix masculine (F)	715
voce (I)	705	voix mixtes (F)	716
voce aspra (I)	706	voix pleine (F)	713
voce chiara (I)	707	voix principale (F)	2188
voce cupa (I)	708	voix supérieure (F)	2058
voce di gola (I)	709	Vokal (D)	3425
voce di petto (I)	710	vokal (D)	703
voce di ripieno (I)	2187	Vokalise (D)	704
voce di testa (I)	711	Vokalmusik (D)	3174
voce estrema (I)	2054	volage (F)	1606
voce femminile (I)	712	volando (I)	1604
voce granita (I)	713	volant (F)	1604
voce infantile (I)	714	volante (I)	1604
voce inferiore (I)	2055	volé (F)	768
voce intermedia (I)	2056	volenteroso (I)	1605
voce maschile (I)	715	Volkslied (D)	2299
voce principale (I)	2188	Volksmusik (D)	3161
voce superiore (I)	2058	Volkstanz (D)	2330
voci miste (I)	716	volkstümlich (D)	3232
vociare (I)	2863	volkstümliche Musik (D)	3161
vociférer (F)	2863	voll (D)	1357, 1447, 1769
Vogelpfeife (D)	312	voll Leben (D)	1015
voglia (con) (I)	1603	voll Lebendigkeit (D)	1597
voice (E)	640, 705	voll Lebhaftigkeit (D)	1014
voice training (E)	604	volle, kräftige Stimme (D)	713
voice type (E)	659	Vollendung (D)	3225
voice-leading (E)	1938	voller Glut (D)	989
voiceless (E)	638	volles Werk (D)	464
voici (F)	3004	vollkommen (D)	3063, 3224
voilà (F)	3004	vollkommene Kadenz (D)	1914
voilé (F)	700	vollständig (D)	2954
voir (F)	2861	volontà (con) (I)	1605, 3426
vois (F)	1854	volonté (F)	3426
voix (F)	705	…volta (I)	1855
voix âpre (F)	706	Volta (D)	2375
voix claire (F)	707	volta (E, I)	2375
voix de gorge (F)	709	volta inferiore (I)	80
voix de poitrine (F)	710	volta subito (I)	1856
voix de remplissage (F)	2187	volta superiore (I)	79
voix de tête (F)	711	voltage (E, F)	597
voix enfantine (F)	714	voltaggio (I)	597
voix extrême (F)	2054	voltare (I)	2864
voix féminine (F)	712	volte (F)	2375
voix grave (F)	708	volteggiando (I)	462, 1604

volti (I)   1857
volubile (I)   1606
volubilità (con) (I)   1607
volume (E, I)   3104
volume (F)   598, 3104
volume sonoro (I)   598
Voluntary (D, E, F, I)   2631
voluptueux (F)   1608
voluptuous (E)   1608
voluta (I)   36
volute (F)   68
voluttuoso (I)   1608
vom Blatt singen (D)   652
vom Blatt spielen (D)   2843
vom Zeichen (D)   1679
vom Zeichen bis zum Schluss
  (D)   1680
von (D)   1674
von Anfang an (D)   1611, 1675
von hier ab (D)   1682
von neuem (D)   1686
von rückwärts (D)   2106
von vorne (D)   1675
vor allem (D)   1815
vorangehend (D)   792
vorantreibend (D)   790
Vorausnahme (D)   1886
vorbereiten (D)   2770
vorbereitet (D)   3242
Vorbereitung (D)   2076
Vorbild (D)   3113
Vorbühne (D)   3259
Vordersatz (D)   2077
vorgeben (D)   685
vorgetäuscht (D)   3042
Vorhalt (D)   2102
vorher (D)   1783
vorhergehend (D)   1782
voriges Zeitmaß (D)   776, 1828
Vorklassik (D)   3239
vorläufig (D)   3263
vorlaut (D)   1494
vorne (D)   1683
vorsagen (D)   2839
Vorschlag (D)   1887
vorschlagen (D)   2776

Vorsicht (D)   3264
vorsichtig (D)   1409
Vorspiel (D)   2435, 3304
vorstellen (D)   2771
Vorstellung (D)   3273, 3350
Vortrag (D)   675, 3015
vortragen (D)   2709, 2783
vortragend (D)   1425
Vortragsbezeichnung (D)   2114
vorwärts (D)   790
vorwärts gehend (D)   788, 792
Vorwort (D)   3240
Vorzeichen (D)   1872, 1889
vorzutragen (D)   2783
vowel (E)   3425
voyant (F)   1598
voyelle (F)   3425
vraiment (F)   3418
vue (F)   3424
vuoto (I)   1858, 2061
waagrecht (D)   2050
wach (D)   1091
wachsen (D)   2694
wackeln (D)   697
Wagner tuba (E)   188
Wagner-Tuba (D)   188
Wahl (D)   3313
wahlfrei (D)   1699
wahnsinnig (D)   1192, 1379
während (D)   1692
wahrnehmbar (D)   3223
wakening (E)   890
Wald (D)   3047
Waldhorn (D)   131
Waldhorn-Tuba (D)   188
walking (E)   792
walking pace (E)   729
wallend (D)   1360
waltz (E)   2485
Walze (D)   220, 418
Walzer (D)   2485
wandering (E)   1109
Wandler (D)   586
Wange (D)   3448
waning (E)   898
wankelmütig (D)   1339

wankend (D)	1004	welcher (D)	1653
wantonly (E)	1379, 1493	welches (D)	1653
warble (E)	609	well (E)	1648
warlike (E)	1248	well balanced (E)	1008
warm (D, E)	1022	well rhythmed (E)	846
warmherzig (D)	1026	Welle (D)	420, 538
warming up (E)	803	Wellenlänge (D)	523
warmly (E)	1021	Welterstaufführung (D)	3246
warten (D)	2663	weltlich (D)	3252
Waschbrett (D)	252	weltliche Kantate (D)	2283
washboard (E, F)	252	weltliche Musik (D)	3162
Wasserklappe (D)	204	wenden (D)	2864
water key (E)	204	wenig (D)	1773
wattierter Schlägel (D)	353	weniger (D)	1736
Wau-wau-Dämpfer (D)	228	weniger bewegt als Allegro	
wave (E)	538, 3058	(D)	726
wave-length (E)	523	wenigstens (D)	2880
weak (E)	1069	wenn (D)	1793
weak beat (E)	2155	wenn nötig (D)	1794
weakening (E)	894, 901	werfen (D)	2672
weakly (E)	1071	Werk (D)	3194
wealthy (E)	1431	werkgetreu (D)	3032
weary (E)	1305	Wert (D)	2182
wechseln (D)	2676	wesentlich (D)	1979
wechselnd (D)	1652	what (E)	1653
Wechselnote (D)	2040	which (E)	1653
Wechselton (D)	2040	whimsical (E)	1154
wedding march (E)	2382	whimsically (E)	1033
weeping (E)	1390	whip (E)	286
weepy (E)	1390	whipped (E)	88, 1209
wegnehmen (D)	2850	whipping (E)	872
wegnehmend (D)	913	whistle (E)	142, 190
wehklagend (D)	1301	whistling (E)	717
wehmütig (D)	1186	who (E)	1653
weich (D)	1112	whole note (Am.)	2224
weicher Einsatz (D)	644	whole note rest (Am.)	2231
weichlich (D)	1343	whole tone (E)	2170
weighted (E)	1387	whole-tone scale (E)	2110
Weihnachtslied (D)	2289	wichtig (D)	3071
Weihnachtsmusik (D)	3141	widening (E)	821
weinend (D)	1389	widerhallen (D)	2795
weinerlich (D)	1390	widerhallend (D)	1443
Weisheit (D)	3303	widmen (D)	2698
weit (D)	855, 968	Widmung (D)	2975
weite Lage (D)	2074	width (E)	3097
welche (D)	1653	wie (D)	1659, 1789

wie anfangs (D)   1660
wie bei (D)   1659
wie beim Eingang (D)   1660
wie ein Bauerntanz (D)   945
wie ein Marsch (D)   947
wie eine Arie (D)   2259
wie eine Ballade (D)   914
wie eine Kadenz (D)   1664
wie es dasteht (D)   1663
wie früher (D)   1661
wie im Rausch (D)   1124
wie oben (D)   1662
wie vorher (D)   1661
wieder (D)   1636
wieder anfangen (D)   2799
wieder aufnehmen (D)   2799
wieder aufnehmend (D)   767
wieder beginnen (D)   2789
wieder belebt (D)   801
wieder erweckend (D)   888
wieder lebhafter (D)   802
wieder von Anfang an bis zum
    Schluss (D)   1676
wieder von Anfang an bis
    zum Zeichen (D)   1677
wiederbelebend (D)   800
Wiedergabe (D)   562
wiederholen (D)   2798
Wiederholung (D)   2096, 3279
Wiederholungszeichen (D)   2116
Wiederkehr (D)   2097
wiegend (D)   1064
Wiegenlied (D)   2399
Wiener Schule (D)   3325
Wienerwalzer (D)   2486
wig (E)   3215
wild (D, E)   1173, 1467
will (E)   3426
Wille (D)   3426
willig (D)   1605
willing (E)   1605
Wind (D)   3417
wind (E)   3417
wind band (E)   2909
wind chest (E)   442
wind instruments (E)   3372

wind machine (E)   284
wind music (E)   3156, 3160
wind quintet (E)   2441
wind section (E)   3037
windcap (E)   202
windchest (E)   445
Windkapsel (D)   202
Windkasten (D)   442
Windlade (D)   445
Windladenraum (D)   412
Windmaschine (D)   284
windpipe (E)   3482
windway (E)   200
wing (E)   234
wings (E)   3270
Wirbel (D)   36
Wirbelkasten (D)   42
Wirbeltrommel (D)   268
wire (E)   322, 3041
wire brushes (E)   370
wirklich (D)   3418
Wirkung (D)   3008
wirkungsvoll (D)   3009
wisdom (E)   3303
wisely (E)   1451
wishful (E)   1603
wissen (D)   2809
witches' dance (E)   2327
with (E)   1666
with a damped voice (E)   635
with abandonment (E)   916
with affection (E)   933
with agility (E)   941
with agitation (E)   942
with amazement (E)   1537
with amiability (E)   958
with amusement (E)   1110
with anger (E)   1047
with anguish (E)   972
with animation (E)   1600
with anxiety (E)   931, 977
with ardour (E)   989
with arrogance (E)   992
with audacity (E)   999
with bitterness (E)   962
with boldness (E)   987, 1002

with breadth (E)	967	with exultation (E)	1156
with brightness (E)	1153	with fantasy (E)	1162
with calmness (E)	1564	with fear (E)	1377
with candour (E)	1028	with feeling (E)	1475
with care (E)	922	with feeling (E)	974
with celerity (E)	734	with ferocity (E)	1174
with character (E)	1034	with fervour (E)	1176
with charm (E)	1166	with fickleness (E)	1607
with clarity (E)	1042	with fineness (E)	1184
with coldness (E)	1199	with fire (E)	1214
with conceit (E)	1539	with firmness (E)	1171
with confidence (E)	1179	with flabbiness (E)	1341
with conviction (E)	1058	with flexibility (E)	1187
with courage (E)	975	with fluency (E)	1188
with damper (E)	459	with force (E)	1193
with dash (E)	1501	with frankness (E)	1197
with delicacy (E)	1079	with frenzy (E)	1083
with delight (E)	1084	with freshness (E)	1204
with desire (E)	1089, 1603	with full force (E)	847
with despair (E)	1105	with full voice (E)	647
with detachment (E)	1548	with fury (E)	1217
with determination (E)	1094	with gaiety (E)	1221
with devotion (E)	1417	with gallantry (E)	1224
with dexterity (E)	1092	with grace (E)	1245
with dignity (E)	1096, 1400	with grandeur (E)	1242
with diligence (E)	1097	with gravity (E)	1244
with din (E)	1534	with grief (E)	919
with discouragement (E)	1461	with half voice (E)	614, 637
with discretion (E)	1099	with hankering (E)	1010
with disdain (E)	1464	with happiness (E)	1226
with disgust (E)	1428	with hardness (E)	1122
with dismay (E)	1496	with harshness (E)	995
with dread (E)	1555	with haste (E)	735
with ease (E)	937, 1521	with heart (E)	1065
with ecstasy (E)	1151	with horror (E)	1416
with effort (E)	1168	with humour (E)	1577
with elegance (E)	1127	with imagination (E)	1251
with emotion (E)	1130	with impatience (E)	1253
with emphasis (E)	1133	with impulsion (E)	1255
with enchantment (E)	1263	with indifference (E)	1266
with energy (E)	1131	with indolence (E)	1269
with enthusiasm (E)	1136	with innocence (E)	1279
with exactitude (E)	1145	with insistence (E)	1285
with exaltation (E)	1143	with insolence (E)	1286
with expansion (E)	1148	with irony (E)	1294
with expression (E)	1149	with jest (E)	1158

with joy (E)   1235
with jubilation (E)   1238
with kindness (E)   1230
with lightness (E)   1306
with liveliness (E)   1600
with loftiness (E)   1129
with love (E)   964
with lustre (E)   1320
with melancholy (E)   1325
with mockery (E)   1457
with moderation (E)   1340
with mouth closed (E)   636
with movement (E)   738, 759
with much freedom (E)   737
with nobility (E)   1354
with noise (E)   1534
with one finger (E)   1667
with pain (E)   1111, 1118
with passion (E)   1373
with peace (E)   1370
with perseverance (E)   1385
with pleasure (E)   1110
with pomp (E)   1398
with precipitation (E)   739
with precision (E)   1403
with pride (E)   1181
with prudence (E)   1410
with purity (E)   1411
with quickness (E)   743
with rage (E)   1415
with rapidity (E)   741
with rapture (E)   1124
with refinement (E)   1421, 1429
with regret (E)   1440
with resentment (E)   1441
with resignation (E)   1424
with resolution (E)   1442
with respect (E)   1365, 1444
with restlessness (E)   1502
with rigidity (E)   1434
with rigour (E)   742
with sadness (E)   1574
with scorn (E)   1106
with selfconfidence (E)   1498
with sensitivity (E)   1471
with serenity (E)   1480

with seriousness (E)   1482
with severity (E)   1484
with simplicity (E)   1470
with skill (E)   1012, 1323
with slowness (E)   736
with sobriety (E)   1505
with softness (E)   1114
with solemnity (E)   1509
with some freedom   (E)   768
with soul (E)   974
with speed (E)   741
with spirit (E)   1523
with splendor (E)   1487
with steadfastness (E)   1385
with taste (E)   1249
with tenderness (E)   1546
with tepidness (E)   1548
with the (E)   1666
with the bow (E)   94
with the hand (E)   378
with the highest virtuosity
  (E)   1056
with the voice (E)   1657
with the wood (E)   95
with thrill (E)   1202
with timidity (E)   1554
with trust (E)   1179
with two sticks (E)   377
with unconstraint (E)   1101
with valour (E)   1582
with vehemence (E)   1586
with velocity (E)   744
with veneration (E)   1588
with verve (E)   1501
with vigour (E)   1592
with violence (E)   1595
with virtuosity (E)   1596
with warmth (E)   1025
with weakness (E)   1070
with weariness (E)   1528
with will (E)   1605
with wrath (E)   1047, 1415
with zeal (E)   1609
without (E)   1800
without changing (E)   1801
without colour (E)   1477

without dragging (E)	771
without haste (E)	769
without hurrying (E)	1802
without instruments (E)	1805
without interruptions (E)	1803
without measure (E)	770
without mute (E)	110
without repetition (E)	1804
without sorrow (E)	1516
witty (E)	1524
witzig (D)	1524
wogend (D)	102, 1360
wohl erwogen (D)	1387
Wohlklang (D)	3026
wohlklingend (D)	990
Wolke (D)	3191
wollüstig (D)	1608
women's choir (E)	665
women's chorus (E)	665
wonderful (E)	3110
wood (E)	3100
wood bloc (F)	254
wood block (E, I)	254
wood drum (E)	329
Woodblock (D)	254
wooden stick (E)	351
woodwind (E)	3099
woodwind instruments (E)	3373
word (E)	3214
work (E)	3194
work for ten players (E)	2335
work song (E)	2288
world première (E)	3246
Wort (D)	3214
worthy (E)	1076
wow-wow mute (E)	228
wrathful (E)	923
wrist (E)	3473
wrong (E)	3309
wrong note (E)	3186
wuchtig (D)	1256
Wulst (D)	197
wunderbar (D)	3110
Wunderkind (D)	2908
wunderlich (D)	1009, 1154
wünschend (D)	1603
würdevoll (D)	1076, 1483
würdig (D)	1076
Wurstfagott (D)	163
wütend (D)	991
xilofono (I)	344
xilofono a tastiera (I)	345
xilomarimba (I)	346
Xylomarimba (D)	346
xylomarimba (E, F)	346
Xylophon (D)	344
xylophone (E, F)	344
xylophone à clavier (F)	345
yielding (E)	899
young dramatic soprano (E)	631
zäh (D)	1543
Zahl (D)	3188
zählen (D)	2688
zählen Sie (bei Pausen) (D)	1670
Zählzeit (D)	2152
Zähne (D)	3436
Zamacueco (D, E, F, I)	2632
zampogna (I)	189
Zanza (D)	313
Zapateado (D, E, F, I)	2633
Zarge (D)	58, 361
zart (D)	1547
zartfühlend (D)	1080
zärtlich (D)	1545
Zarzuela (D, E, F, I)	2634
Zäsur (D)	1920
zauberhaft (D)	1263
zaudernd (D)	1296
zealous (E)	1609
Zeichen (D)	1795
Zeigefinger (D)	3449
zeigen (D)	2735, 2755
Zeitabschnitt (D)	3013
zeitgenössische Musik (D)	3124
Zeitmaß (D)	2152
Zeitschrift (D)	3298
zelante (I)	1609
zélé (F)	1609
zelo (con) (I)	1609
zerbrechlich (D)	1194
zerbrochen (D)	3300
zerrend (D)	834

zerrissen (D) 1299
ziehen (D) 2849
ziehend (D) 838
ziemlich (D) 1610, 1625
ziemlich gut (D) 2994
ziemlich langsam (D) 721
zierend (D) 926
Zigeuner (D) 3427
Zigeunerin (D) 3427
Zigeunerlied (D) 2291, 2491
Zigeunermusik (D) 3173
Zigeunertanz (D) 2329, 2491
Zimbal (D) 9
zingara (I) 3427
zingaresca (I) 2491
zingaro (I) 3427
Zink (D) 130
Zither (D) 8
zither (E) 8
zittern (D) 2855
zitternd (D) 1569
zoccolo (I) 81
zögernd (D) 746, 820
zoppo (I) 952
zornig (D) 923, 1293

Zortzico (D, E, F, I) 2635
zu (D) 1809
zu hoch singen (D) 671
zu spät kommen (D) 2715
zu tief singen (D) 650
zu viel (D) 1834
zu zweit (D) 1616
zuckend (D) 1059
zufolando (I) 717
zufolo (I) 190
zufolo a pistone (I) 149
Zug (D) 217, 453
Zugabe! (D) 2919
Züge (D 411
zügellos (D) 1270, 1493
zügig (D) 766
Zugposaune (D) 184
Zugtrompete (D) 179
zuhören (D) 2662
Zukunftsmusik (D) 3135
zum Anhang (D) 1623
zum letzten Mal (D) 1766
zum Schluss (D) 1765
zum Zeitmaß zurückkehrend
   (D) 779

zunehmen (D)   2694
zunehmend (D)   880, 883
Zunge (D)   209, 409, 3452
Zungenpfeife (D)   414
Zungenschlag (D)   239
Zungenstoß (D)   239
Zupfinstrumente (D)   3376
zurück (D)   1684
zurückgeben (D)   2785
zurückgehalten (D)   831
zurückhalten (D)   2804
zurückhaltend (D)   839
zurückkehren (D)   2851
zurückkehrend (D)   1792
zurückkommen (D)   2851
zurückkommend (D)   1792
zurückprallen (D)   2794
zurückrufen (D)   2788
Zurückschlag (Verzierung)
    (D)   625
zurücksetzend (D)   767
zurücktreten (D)   3785
zusammen (D)   1725, 1847
zusammendrängend (D)   810

zusammengesetzter Takt (D) 1903
zusammenstellen (D)   2781
zuvor (D)   1783
zwei Saiten (D)   461
zweimal (D)   1617
zweimanualig (D)   455
zweistimmig (D)   1859
zweiteilig (D)   1907
zweiteilige Form (D)   1981
zweiter Satz (D)   2113
Zweiunddreißigstel (D)   2229
Zweiunddreißigstelpause
    (D)   2236
Zwerchfell (D)   3437
Zwiebelflöte (D)   301
Zwischendominante (D)   1961
Zwischenraum (D)   2133
Zwischensatz (D)   1971
Zwischenspiel (D)   2365, 2366
Zwölftonmusik (D)   3143
Zwölftontechnik (D)   1959
zyklische Form (D)   1982
Zyklus (D)   2942
Zylinderventil (D)   205